W9-CCN-144

Bloom's Modern Critical Interpretations

Geoffrey Chaucer's
The Canterbury Tales
New Edition

Edited and with an introduction by
Harold Bloom
Sterling Professor of the Humanities
Yale University

BLOOM'S
LITERARY CRITICISM
An imprint of Infobase Publishing

Editorial Consultant, Holly A. Crocker

Bloom's Modern Critical Interpretations:
Geoffrey Chaucer's _The Canterbury Tales_—New Edition
Copyright ©2008 by Infobase Publishing

Introduction ©2008 by Harold Bloom

Bloom's Literary Criticism
An imprint of Infobase Publishing
132 West 31st Street
New York NY 10001

Library of Congress Cataloging-in-Publication Data

Geoffrey Chaucer's The Canterbury Tales / edited with an introduction by
Harold Bloom—New ed.
        p. cm. — (Bloom's modern criticial interpretations)
    Includes bibliographical references and index.
    ISBN 978-0-7910-9618-5 (hardcover : alk. paper)
    1. Chaucer, Geoffrey, d. 1400. Canterbury Tales. 2. Tales, Medieval—History and criticism. 3. Christian pilgrims and pilgrimages in literature. I. Bloom, Harold. II. Title: Canterbury tales.
    PR1874.G456 2008
    821'.1—dc22   2007049158

Cover design by Ben Peterson

Printed in the United States of America
YPI BCL 10 9 8 7 6 5 4 3

This book is printed on acid-free paper.

All links and Web addresses were checked and verified to be correct at the time of publication. Because of the dynamic nature of the Web, some addresses and links may have changed since publication and may no longer be valid.

Contents

Editor's Note

My brief, but pungent, Introduction brings together Chaucer and Shakespeare, partly by the prompting of that great master of paradox, Gilbert Keith Chesterton.

Famous for its opening, the *General Prologue* is investigated for its numerology by Colin Wilcockson, while Katherine Little discovers in Chaucer's Parson a shadow of Wycliff's Lollard Heresy.

The learned Lee Patterson discourses ably in Chaucer's anti-Semitic *Prioress Tale*, which is held to be a masterpiece of authorial self-restraint, while Elizabeth Robertson enables herself to analyze "Christian Feminism" in the *Man of Law's Tale*.

Fiona Somerset praises Chaucer's slyness in employing lewdness to expose hypocrisy, while Louise M. Bishop charmingly explores the delightful confusion between female orifices in the *Miller's Tale*.

In Richard Firth Green's witty reading, the *Canon Yeoman's Tale* demonstrates Chaucer's dismissal of alchemy, after which Lianna Farber fashionably finds in the voice of the virtuous Virginia, in the *Physician's Tale*, a political as well as a personal aspect.

The *Summoner's Tale*'s version of the Dantesque "making a trumpet of the breech" is ingeniously expounded by Peter W. Travis, after which William F. Woods studies psychic emptiness in the *Reeve's Tale*.

HAROLD BLOOM

Introduction

Except for Shakespeare, whom he profoundly influenced, Chaucer is the major literary artist in the English language. My favorite Chaucer critic still remains G. K. Chesterton, who wrote many years before the critics included in this volume. Chesterton—poet, storyteller, ironist—was himself a Chaucerian pilgrim. His wonderful book *Chaucer* (1932) is popular and simple, as he intended, and seems to me to embody the spirit of Chaucer. I like it that there are more than fifty references to Shakespeare in the book, because only Shakespeare (in English) deserves to set the measure for Chaucer. Chesterton, a fierce Catholic polemicist, had a tendency to baptize Chaucer's imagination but I think (contra Chesterton) that Shakespeare learned from Chaucer how to achieve a purely secular kind of transcendence. Chesterton liked to think of Chaucer as a continuator of Dante, but Chaucer's true original was Boccaccio. Chaucer the Pilgrim is a sly parody of Dante the Pilgrim, an irony that Chesterton did not want to see. Yet Chesterton wonderfully observed that "the Chaucerian irony is sometimes so large that it is too large to be seen."

Chaucer's mastery of psychological realism was grounded upon his ironic sense that the chivalric ideal was a lost illusion, to be affirmed only in the mode of nostalgia. Everything that existed represented a falling away from a more generous vision, though Chaucer, profoundly comic in his genius, declined to become a master of regret. Chesterton's own fictions and poems move me because he had learned from Chaucer to long for this abandoned field of romance. Acutely paradoxical as he always was, Chesterton may have missed Chaucer's irony when it is directed against precisely such longing. The

1

late Donald Howard, a distinguished biographer of Chaucer, found the "idea" of the *Canterbury Tales* to be their representation of "a disordered Christian society in a state of obsolescence, decline, and uncertainty."

Chaucer, estranged enough to cultivate a very original kind of detachment, helped suggest to Shakespeare that beautiful disinterestedness that happily makes us forever baffled as to where the creator of Falstaff and Hamlet, Rosalind and Cleopatra, Iago and Macbeth stands in regard to his greatest creations. Shakespearean irony is not always distinguishable from the Chaucerian irony that was its original. Where precisely does Chaucer the Poet, as opposed to Chaucer the Pilgrim, abide in relation to the Pardoner and the Wife of Bath? Does the Knight speak for Chaucer when he tells us that we should always be equable, because constantly we must keep appointments that we have not made?

Chesterton thought that the ultimate difference between Chaucer and Shakespeare was that Shakespeare's tragic protagonists were "great spirits in chains." That seems marvelously true of Hamlet's greatness, and of Lear's. Yet Shakespeare, as Chesterton well knew, was also a major comic ironist, like his precursor, Chaucer. Sir John Falstaff's spirit is not enchained, whatever his final betrayal by Prince Hal, and Falstaff has much in him of the nature and vitalistic excess of the Wife of Bath. When you juxtapose Falstaff and the Wife, you find their common exuberance in her great outcry: "That I have had my world as in my tyme" and in his: "Give me life!" Chaucer's poetic sense of the Blessing became Shakespeare's: "More life."

FIONA SOMERSET

"As just as is a squyre": The Politics of "Lewed Translacion" in Chaucer's Summoner's Tale

In solving the problem posed by Thomas's vernacular utterance, *The Summoner's Tale* makes use of information and techniques of argument drawn from what Middle English writers often call "clergie"; that is, the academic discourse employed chiefly by clerics with some university education.[1] That much has long been recognized: Pearcy's 1967 article on the tale explained quite thoroughly how calling the problem an "inpossible" and submitting it to demonstrative proof using natural science evokes the scholastic tradition of ingenious response to *insolubilia*—or what appear to be impossible or paradoxical statements—and especially the late-fourteenth-century fashion at Oxford, and at Merton in particular, for employing concepts from natural science in logical solutions.[2] But what nobody has yet explained is why and how it matters that in this tale the conventions of clerical argument are not just translated into English, but expertly deployed by lay persons rather than clerics—especially when that "translation" in status from clerical to lay appears in conjunction with the Friar's failure, and the Squire's contrasting success, at gaining lay patronage.[3] While the methods by which the problem is posed and solved are thoroughly clerical, they are transferred to a lay setting, to lay speakers, and to lay adjudication. What needs to be examined is how the kinds of vernacular translation the tale enacts—of learned Latin material to English, of clerical capabilities to the laity, of money and power

Studies in the Age of Chaucer Volume 21 (1999): pp. 187–207. © 1999 New Chaucer Society.

formerly given to the clergy to the laity—reflect contemporary controversy over just these sorts of loss of clerical prerogative.

Why is it feared that translation from Latin to English might entail loss of clerical prerogative, and even of church revenues? Scholars interested in investigating late-medieval English attitudes toward translation have commonly consulted the early fifteenth century's sweeping attempt to prohibit translations of every kind through legislation, Arundel's *Constitutions* implemented in 1409.[4] What sort of impact the *Constitutions* had upon vernacular translation and publication through the fifteenth century is very much open to debate. Regardless of their effects, however, one way to read the *Constitutions* is as a set of aspirations toward the preservation of clerical prerogative by means of the control of information, written into law by clerics for clerics: they are a repository of received opinion, and between their lines we can read what goes without saying when the clergy speak to each other about the laity. Thus, article 7 of the *Constitutions* speaks for concerns much broader and longer abiding than those of a small group of politically influential anti-Wycliffite clergy when, in justifying a prohibition against the production or distribution of any unsanctioned biblical translations or works containing portions of such translation, it asserts that such translation is dangerous. The reason given—on Jerome's authority—is that it is difficult to retain the same sense.[5] Yet why should the possibility of human error be so self-evidently dangerous that no further explanation need be provided for why new translations should be forbidden, all the more so when the source cited is the best-known medieval translator of the bible? Some answer can be found elsewhere among the *Constitutions*, where a wider-ranging set of prohibitions against any sort of "translation" of clerical learning to the laity is set out.

Three other articles of the *Constitutions* focus on "translation" more broadly defined. Article 3 requires that no one preach about the faults of the clergy to the laity, or vice versa.[6] Article 5 prohibits those teaching boys engaged in the study of grammar or arts, or others at an elementary level of learning, from presenting theological material contrary to the church's determination, and particularly from allowing disputations about such material either publicly or privately.[7] And article 8 requires that no one state conclusions that sound as if they are contrary to Catholic truth or good morals, even if those conclusions can be defended by means of sophisticated argument using philosophical terminology.[8] The primary concern of article 3 is to prevent clerical matters' being presented to lay judgment, particularly perhaps where both clerics and laymen are present—since otherwise the presentation of lay affairs to clerics would scarcely seem a concern. Most obviously, the article would prohibit anticlerical polemic before a lay audience; but it would also rule out political sermons addressing the three estates or the body politic as well as any address to a mixed audience. Articles 5 and 8, on the other hand,

focus on lay argumentation: they aim to prevent the laity from being instructed in or allowed to engage in argument, most especially about matters that are
within the exclusive province of clerical pronouncement. The eighth article
seems especially concerned that laymen should not encounter (let alone learn
to use) sophisticated clerical conventions of proof such as those used on *insolubilia,* by means of which apparently impossible statements may be shown
to be logically sound.[9]

The uneasiness about potential lay judgment and argumentation that
we find in the *Constitutions* also appears frequently in the work of polemicists writing squarely within the "Age of Chaucer" in the 1380s and 1390s,
and perhaps especially in the conservative posturings of anti-Wycliffites. For
example, in his *Determinacio,* written probably in the late 1380s, Richard
Maidstone accuses Ashwardby, who apparently has preached about theologically controversial matters to the laity of a self-promoting offense against
propriety:

> These three assertions are errors, as it seems to me. Nor should my
> opponent be surprised that I say "errors." For he himself, while he
> was preaching before the people, where above all an example of
> charity ought to have been given, said that he did not care who,
> how many of, or how much such an honourable audience might be
> offended or made angry by his words. Who therefore should take
> account of the anger of the one who cared nothing for offending
> such an honourable audience, while nonetheless doing more than
> he himself did? I ask how far he should be offended or surprised,
> while he strives so much to aggrandize himself before the laity in
> the mother tongue, that I on the contrary labour to defend myself
> in the schools before clerics in the Latin tongue.
>
> [Isti 3 asserciones sunt tres errores vt michi videtur. Nec miretur
> doctor meus quod dicam errores. Ipse enim dum predicaret ad
> populum, vbi potissimum exemplum caritatis debuit ostendisse,
> dixit se non curare qui, quot, vel quanti de tam venerabili auditorio
> ex suis verbis offenderentur aut essent irati. quis igitur ponderaret
> iram suam, qui tam venerabilis auditorii pro nichilo quasi reputauit
> offensam tamen plus faciendo quam fecit ipse? rogo quatinus non
> offendatur nec miretur, ex quo conatur se tantum magnificare
> coram laicis in lingua materna, quod ego e contrario nitar me
> defendere in scolis et coram clericis in lingua latina.][10]

Ashwardby has preached to the people in a way that fails to show an example
of charity; even saying that he does not care who, how many, or how much

the members of his so-respectable audience are offended or made angry by his words. By this means he has sought to aggrandize himself before the laity in the maternal tongue. In contrast, Maidstone promises that he will defend himself with all proper decorum; that is, in Latin in the schools before clerics.

A similar ostentatious commitment to the normal conventions of clerical audience, and the corresponding implication that any violation of them is a self-promoting offense against charity, appears in William Rymington's *Dialogus inter catholica veritas et heretica depravitas.* Writing a reply to Wyclif's rebuttal of his *XLIV Conclusiones* in the mid-1380s, Rymington claims Wyclif had spread his pernicious doctrine in an inflammatory manner, such that it persists among his disciples even now, after his death. Rymington's more temperately disseminated dialogue will allow the holy mother church to judge the truth:

> Nonetheless because this doctor is dead, yet his pestiferous teaching persists in various writings and in certain of his disciples unknown to me, I have decided that it is better for now, as concerns the business of censuring him and defending myself, to write a dialogue staged between the interlocutors Catholic Truth and Heretical Depravity. In this way holy mother church, or the congregation of catholic clerics, to whose judgement I always humbly submit myself, for my part unswervingly defending catholic truth, will be able to judge between us and put an end to the dispute. For then the christian faithful will be able to inspect [the truth] here, so that they will not be infected by erroneous or heretical teachings.
>
> [Quia tamen doctor iste mortuus est, et eius doctrina pestifera in variis scriptis et in quibusdam ignotis mihi suis discipulis perseuerat, melius pro nunc in hac materia iudicaui super sua reprehencione et mea defensione inter veritatem catholicam et prauitatem hereticam velud inter colloquentes aliquos dialogare, vt iudicare possit inter nos et contentionem dirimere sancta mater ecclesia, seu congregacio cleri catholici, cuius iudicio semper humiliter me submitto, indubitanter vendicans veritatem catholicam pro parte mea quia hic inspicere poterunt christiani fideles ne per doctrinas erroneas seu hereticas inficiantur.]

Rymington submits himself to the "congregation of catholic clerics," but directs the Christian faithful not to assess his Latin dialogue for themselves (though they would probably not be capable of reading it unaided even if they were granted access to it) but to study the arguments of Catholic Truth so as not to become infected with heresy.[11]

All these writers implicitly appeal to a common model of what "proper" lay/clerical interaction would consist in: it posits 1) that the clergy and laity are entirely distinct and have their own separate spheres, 2) that each can be viewed as a seamless, consistent, unified whole, 3) that clerical governance, administration, judgment, and so on should be reserved to the clergy alone, and, crucially, 4) that the Latin literacy, competence in argumentation, and information the clergy have as a consequence of the kind of education they receive are equally their own particular reserved province. Needless to say, in reality relations between clergy and nobility are a lot more tangled and complicated than this model might lead us to believe, but the model does ideological work, for polemicists of many stripes; it can be exploited, and disrupted, to different ends.

From the examples given so far, the reader will already have noticed that one of the most important arenas in which this model does its work is the polemic dialogue involving the laity. There are several extant examples of this sort of dialogue in English or another vernacular, and an extensive Latin tradition lies behind them as well; they are instances of a distinctive and usually highly self-conscious genre that has not been much discussed—largely because it is mainly historians interested in political theory (and not much interested in the format of the works in which they find it) who have read polemical Latin prose dialogues.

Polemic dialogues involving the laity function as a testing ground wherein normal expectations of lay/clerical interaction can be questioned and renegotiated; this kind of "unconventional" questioning had itself become a literary convention. In some such dialogues a lay audience witnesses and is invited to judge an argument staged before them between educated clerics. Many dialogues of this type are embedded within chronicles, where typically the type of lay audience in question would be explained, the dialogue reported in direct discourse, and the audience's reaction recounted.[12] Other dialogues of this type include the poetic twelfth-century dialogue *De presbytero et logico,* which includes within the fictional setting of the dialogue a lay audience that threatens the loser with violence; and dialogues written on behalf of the policies of, dedicated to, and submitted to the judgment of a member of the nobility, as for example Ockham's mid-fourteenth-century *Dialogus,* or the early-fifteenth-century Wycliffite *Dialogue between a Secular and a Friar.*[13] In other polemic dialogues involving the laity, the participants themselves are of contrasting status: one is a lay person, usually a member of the gentry or nobility, and the other an ecclesiastic, generally a clerk. As well as Trevisa's preface to the *Polychronicon,* the *Dialogue between a Lord and a Clerk,* examples include the late-thirteenth-century *Dialogus inter militem et clericem* that Trevisa would translate, and the Wycliffite *Dialogue between a Clerk and a Knight*.[14]

I have written at length elsewhere about Trevisa's *Dialogue between a Lord and a Clerk,* which he wrote ca. 1387 as a preface to his translation of the *Polychronicon,* and his translation and updating, probably in the 1380s to 1390s, of the *Dialogus inter militem et clericem* written by an anonymous supporter of Philip the Fair in around 1297.[15] Here I will concentrate mainly on the Wycliffite dialogues the *Dialogue between a Secular and a Friar* and *Dialogue between a Clerk and a Knight,* which I am in the process of editing.[16] But because the Trevisan dialogues are important nonheretical precursors to the sort of debate mounted in the Wycliffite dialogues and elsewhere, and because they are so closely bound up with issues of late-medieval English translation, I will first allow these two dialogues co introduce the genre.

Trevisa's *Dialogue between a Lord and a Clerk* will serve to show the sort of ideological work that disrupting the "proper" model of lay/clerical interaction can do. Trevisa's justification of "Englysch translacion" in this dialogue is spoken in the person of a Lord who demonstrates clerical capacity by showing a high level of ability in argument of a specifically clerical sort; but also allies his own interests and concerns with those of the lowest level of the laity. It is the Lord in Trevisa's *Dialogue* rather than the Clerk who makes extensive use of the terminology and techniques characteristic of academic argumentation: He introduces what looks as though it will be a confession of limited literacy with the technical term "Y denye" (290/56); he skillfully uses a scholastic distinction on the senses of "need" to explain in what sense it is true that all men "need" to know the chronicles (291/65–81); and he uses a syllogistic argument to show that because preaching in English is good and needful, so is translation into English (292/146–293/153). However, the Lord also asserts common cause with the laity as a whole, including even the poorest and least educated. In contrast to the Clerk's stodgy, conventional objections against his proposal that he should translate the *Polychronicon,* the Lord exhibits a detailed practical knowledge about the wider audience English translation might reach and the various constraints that prevent the ready spread of information to that audience. In the course of his sensitive explanation of the various impediments those who might want or need to read may face ("oþer maner bysynes ... elde ... defaute of wyt ... defauce of katel oþer of frendes to vynde harn to scole ..." (291/65–68)) and of hitches in the mediation process whereby the clerically educated should inform the uneducated ("þe lewed man wot noȝt what a scholde axe ... noþer wot comunlych of whom a scholde axe. Also noȝt al men þat vnderstondeþ Latyn habbeþ such bokes ... also sum konneþ noȝt and some wol noȝt and som mowe noȝt a whyle" (291/84–87)), it becomes apparent that the poor, the stupid, the old, and those without leisure—the whole of the lay population, it seems—all belong to the potential audience he projects for an English translation. In a sense, then, the Lord seems to espouse the clerical model by placing himself amidst an undifferentiated lay audience. But at the same time, his manner of doing so disrupts the model: he usurps clerical capacities in argument to make his point; and indeed, the role he takes up with respect to the lower laity is a quasi-pastoral one of the sort that would normally belong to a cleric. The Lord exploits the kind of solidarity the conventional model of clerical/lay interaction would advocate, but in a way that usurps clerical prerogative: his solidarity consists in pastoral activity rather than lumpen passivity.

The dialogue Trevisa translated, the *Dialogus inter militem et clericem,* illustrates affiliations between the Latin tradition of polemic dialogue and its English and other vernacular adaptations. The *Dialogus* became the focus of a great deal of interest in the late fourteenth and early fifteenth centuries, in France as well as England. The French *Somnium viridarii,* produced in the 1370s, is a massive extension and expansion of it; and a translation into French of the *Somnium viridarii, Le songe du vergier,* was produced in the same decade. Along with Trevisa's translation, several fifteenth-century English manuscripts testify to continuing interest in the Latin version in England—while not ruling out, of course, that the Latin version may have been popular in England earlier as well.

How did Trevisa alter this dialogue to provide a closer fit to the political concerns of late-fourteenth-century England? Briefly, Trevisa finds his material most unpalatable at the point where the Latin dialogue distinguishes between Christ's earthly and heavenly powers—largely, as I explain elsewhere, because he is unable to massage the distinction into a hard and fast separation between secular temporal and sacred ecclesiastical powers.[17] At that point, Trevisa interpolates a long note which, when it finally abandons its attempt to interpret the distinction, issues the most explicit directive of the reader's attention that Trevisa provides anywhere in his works: "But how hit euer be of þe distinccioun þat is made bitwene þe clerk & þe knyȝt, of þe tyme of Cristes manhed & of þe tyme of his myȝt, power, and maieste," Trevisa recommends, "take hede how þei spekiþ eiþer to oþer." If we do just that—pay heed to the style of speech and kind of argumentation that the Clerk and Knight each use on each other—we can see that their respective styles contrast with their conventional roles, and that Trevisa has even heightened the contrast.

The kind of reversal effected in the *Dialogus*—where the layman argues using clerical information, and the cleric is unable to oppose him effectively—had become intensely controversial in the milieu into which Trevisa was translating the dialogue. Especially interesting to late-medieval vernacular readers, as we saw in Trevisa's own dialogue, was the conferral of *pastoral* characteristics on the laity. In this dialogue, yet greater claims are made for a lay pastoral role, and that role is extended to cover questions of legal jurisdiction and rule. Trevisa's alterations add to the effect, as I explain in detail elsewhere—for example, by extending the transferred use of "sauacion" to the point where it covers even defense of the realm.[18]

Two Wycliffite dialogues written close to when Chaucer wrote *The Summoner's Tale,* when as a consequence of the Wycliffite controversy the issue of translation of capacities from "clergie" to "lewed" was at its most heated, provide an especially useful comparison with the dynamics of lay/clerical interaction in *The Summoner's Tale.*[19]

The *Dialogue between a Secular and a Friar* presents itself as the written record of a disputation held before the Duke of Gloucester. The written account is addressed to the duke and submitted to his judgment (fols. 212v–213):

> Moost worschipfulleste and gentilleste lord duke of Glowcestre, ʒoure seruaunt sendiþ ʒou disputusun writen þat was bifore ʒow bytwixe a frere and a seculer ʒoure clerk, preiynge of boþe sidis to chese and apreue þe trewþe. For as seyeþ oure bileue, "ouere alle þing vencuscheþ þe truþe." And as seiþ Aristotle acordynge wiþ oure bileue, "tweyn beynge frendis it is holy to be for honour þe / f. 213/ trewþe." þerfore to ʒou lord þat herde þe disputusun be ʒeue þe fyle, to rubbe aweye þe rust in eiþir partye.

And the dialogue's envoy indicates obliquely what that judgment is meant to be: it asks the duke to "fulfillen in dede þe trewpe;" or bring about a fulfillment of truth through action. After the Secular's repeated comments that it is "untruthful" for members of religious orders to have possessions, it is clear enough what the writer is recommending.

This dialogue consists of a series of propositions by the Friar, each thoroughly refuted in turn by the Secular. Seven exchanges deal with sin and the commandments, one (inserted after the first on the commandments) with temporal possessions of friars, and six (beginning after the seventh question on sin) with voluntary mendicancy. The topics involve arcane scholastic material even where the Secular is not inveighing against the friars, and several of the exchanges are stated and solved in the form of an insoluble proposition. Involving as it does extensive biblical translation, criticism of the clergy to a lay audience, disputation on matters of faith, and use of sophisticated terminology and methods, we might imagine that this dialogue is just the sort of publication that the *Constitutions* would aim to prevent. This "translation" of scholastic material found nowhere else in English into the domain of lay judgment carries along with it the threat of clerical disendowment, even if some of the material translated seems quite innocuous.

The *Dialogue between a Clerk and a Knight* takes this threat a step further. Through a lengthy negotiation of the Clerk and Knight's contract of interaction, and a sustained contestation of their proper respective "lewed" and "clergial" roles—on one level as arguers, and on another, in their argument over jurisdiction and ownership—this dialogue pursues the consequences of the focus on interchange we found in Trevisa's translation. More than that, it enacts the possibilities of intellectual (and, consequently, juridical and monetary) disendowment that the Secular/Friar dialogue, in submitting itself to lay judgment, hopefully holds out.

As usual in dialogues between laymen and clerics, both the Knight and the Clerk begin by approving a definite separation of clerical and lay capacities and roles. In keeping with the conventional model of lay/clerical interaction, the Clerk at the outset attempts to assert that he holds the same pastoral relation to all laymen, whatever their status. Despite the fact that he implicitly tailors his address (as indeed all clerical writers surreptitiously do) to the precise status among the laity of his interlocutor—calling him "ser kniȝt" and worrying about being overcome by his "maistrie"—the Clerk's initial speech still places all members of the laity together in one class, and subordinates that class to all of "holi chirche," from the pope through bishops to ordinary parish clergy. The Clerk starchily disapproves of any "lewed" attempt to "mell" with the clergy (fol. 6):

> I haue grete wonder, he said, þat þe kinge and som of his counseil
> and of his kniȝtes and oþer men of þe temperalte þat schuld be
> gouerned bi holi chirche, as bi þe pope and bi bihsschopes and
> bi þe clergy, melleþ þaim of men of holi chirch and of þair godes
> in mani maners aȝaynes goddes lawe and aȝaines holi chirch. For
> þer ne schuld no man melle o þe pope ne o þe clergi. For þai bene
> abouen alle men bi power ȝeuen to þaim bi Godd himself, als holi
> writt bereþ wittnes and þe law canone also.

"Melling," of course, can mean "speaking" as well as "mixing" or "meddling"; and for the Clerk they come to the same thing: for the Knight to speak about the clergy, even worse to argue like a cleric, is in itself to meddle with matters reserved to the clergy.

Although the Knight too pronounces his disapproval of "melling" so as to condemn clerical "melling" in secular governance, he spends most of his time doing it: he repeatedly evokes, exploits, and then breaks with conventional patterns of lay/clerical interaction. He conjoins himself to the rest of the laity, but on each occasion in a way that also lets him stand apart from them. He acknowledges his position among the lay persons of whose "melling" the Clerk disapproves by—ostensibly humbly—asking the Clerk to instruct him about the doubts lay people share (fol. 6):

> þou spekes of a mater þat clerkes han oft moued amonge þe comone pupel, and þe pepel haþ oft bene and es in a were and in dout þerof. And I myself haue oft wondrid þat þe pope and þe clergi haþe taken vpon hem to supplant þe kinge þat es lorde of his land, and all daie bene about more and more to abrege and lessen his power and his lordschip, which as me þink schuld no man o þis half God haue to done wiþ ne mell him þerof. Naiþeles, bicause þat I am a litil lettrid and understonde somdele holi writt, I drede me þat I miȝt trist to mich to myne own witt in þis matere and so offend and gilt to God. And þou ert a man of holi chirch, a preste, and semes a clerk connynge of clergi: I wold gladlich lerne of þe.

But at the same time, the instruction he is requesting is not available to the general run of the laity who, as Trevisa's Lord pointed out, do not know what they should ask, nor of whom. Similarly, the Knight validates lay criticism of the clergy on the model of the advice given to Balaam by his ass. But this example implies not universal lay authorization, but special authority conferred by grace on those singled out by God's special favor. Again, the Knight labels himself a lay questioner when asking the Clerk to respond patiently, as clerics normally do not when confronted by lay questioners; but once more, his request asserts his special privilege. And when the Knight criticizes the Clerk for engaging in the usual clerical attempt to preserve lay ignorance, he does so in a way that shows that this general ignorance is one he does not share.

In addition to announcing his solidarity with the "lewed" while also stressing his superiority to them, this Knight distances himself yet further from the negative connotations of lewedness by transferring them to clerics. When deciding whether the Clerk is a fit instructor for him at the beginning of their exchange, he counteracts the Clerk's attempt to endow all clerics alike with superior authority by separating learned from unlearned clerics and pronouncing himself willing to be advised only by the learned (fol. 6):

> Bot it es oft sene þat moni prestes and clerkes þat beth gretelich auaunsid gone wele araied and wele fororrid, as þou dos, þat bene no connynge men of clergie ne of resoune. And þerfor, ser, I prai þe tell me what degree of scole þou has, þat I mow knowe wheþer þou be abil of connynge to teche me in þis matere þat I am in dout.

The Knight grudgingly allows the Clerk's membership among the "abil of connynge" (fols. 6r–v):

> I am wele paied, for I hope to be wele taȝt bi þe of þat matere þat we haue /f. 6v/ spoken of. Neuerþeles, I had hopid þat þou haddest bene a maistere of diuinite connynge of Goddes lawe, for þan þou woldist haue said þe soþe and bene noȝt so fauorabil to þe pope as I suppose þou wolt be now, for þou art a doctor of his lawe. Naþeles, tell me and teche me als wele als þou canst. . . .

But if the Clerk is not unlearned, then as far as the Knight is concerned he can only hold the view he has and make the arguments he makes out of hypocritical duplicity. He is even worse than a "lewed" unlearned cleric who is merely ignorant. He is a hypocrite, and even "lewed" in the sense that he gives a bad argument: he asserts a kind of trust in God that (as the Knight notes) is normally used by unlearned laymen or priests, but that in the Clerk's mouth can only be hypocritical (fol. 19):

> Ow, ser clerk, now I se wele þat þou art a þi wittes end. For be þin own wordes in semeþ þat þou ne canst no resourne ne skill for to defend þi cause. Bot riȝt als Iak Roker or a lewd preste answereþ, riȝt so dostow. For it es þe maner of all sich lewde iauels when þai ne conne no forþer, þan þai concluden all þair mater wiþ "God leue it wele be and God ȝeue grace to make a gode ende." And all sich wordes semen holinesse when ȝe mene moste venyme in ȝoure hert.

Of course the Knight also repeatedly places his trust in God. But he is not subject to the same criticism (according to the dialogue's own logic, at any rate) because his trust is simple and genuine—the quality he does whole-heartedly share with even the most uneducated among the laity.

In *The Summoner's Tale*, where clerical capacities are transferred to a lay arena by means of vernacular translation, we see Maidstone's, Rymington's, and Arundel's worst nightmare enacted, as a series of responses voiced by lay persons of differing statuses frustrate, then finally overturn, the friar's attempt to treat all members of the laity as if they were in the same subordinate pastoral position with respect to him. Normally in clerical discourse, as we have seen, a cleric who uses the convenient fiction of lay uniformity needs covertly to accompany it with a quite carefully modulated address to the particular status of his lay interlocutor. Friar John, however, seems blind to the status of the layman he aims to instruct. When he first asserts the universal superiority in understanding of clerics to laymen regardless of status, he backs up his claim with an argument based on clerical poverty (*SumT* 1871–75):

> ... moore we seen of Cristes secree thynges,
> Than burel folk, although they weren kynges.
> We lyve in poverte and in abstinence,
> And burell folk in richesse and despence
> Of mete and drynke, and in hir foul delit.

The argument might be effective if it were voiced by a less obviously prosperous friar, especially if he were addressing nobles, lords, or at minimum prosperous gentry. But here the friar is speaking to the village smallholder Thomas. For someone of Thomas' status—and probably for any other reasonably skeptical lay listener—it is clear that the way of life the friar criticizes is not that of his interlocutor, but his own.

Indeed, Friar John's pastoral advice seems uneasily to gravitate toward addressing a layman of much the same status and position that he himself occupies; the ideal he holds up mirrors the one he claims (yet conspicuously fails) to achieve. When advising Thomas about anger—the very vice he himself is about to succumb to—Friar John makes use of exempla from the advice-to-princes tradition. It might seem incongruous enough already that a friar should be advising a churl using examples about the anger of kings. Yet, advice-to-princes was commonly read by those aspiring to virtuous gentility: the king's rule of self, household, and realm were all thought to work on analogous principles, so that any layman could model whatever governance is expected of him on the same temperate ideal that advice manuals recommend to kings.[20] However, the friar's exemplum-based advice in the end turns out not to be directed to kings or princes even on the overt level.

The morals of the friar's two exempla apply not to the angry kings upon whom they would more typically focus, but—jarringly—to chose in the service of those kings who are subject to their wrath. Already Friar John's opening precept has turned in a surprising direction: ". . . Thomas, yet eft-soones I charge thee, / Be war from Ire that in thy bosom slepeth" (lines 1992–93) sounds like the beginning of advice to Thomas about curbing his own anger, but instead, bizarrely, leads to the warning that Thomas should beware of his wife's anger in case she might murder him (lines 1996–2009). Similarly, when he moves from the household to what Scanlon has labeled the "public exemplum," that is, the exemplum focusing on matters of state,[21] Friar John's first exemplum seems initially to focus on an angry ruler: "It is greet harm and certes greet pitee / To sette an irous man in heigh degree" (lines 2015–16). But the story quickly turns to the three knights deputed to carry out their lord's commands, who are summarily executed for their efforts to exercise their own judgment in response to changed circumstance (lines 2017–2042). Friar John's second story (lines 2043–2073) incorporates the would-be advisor to the prince into the story as well: although the drunken ruler "Irous Cambises" is again the starting point, it is the virtuous "lord of his meynee" who attempts to counsel him to temperance whose son Cambises kills, and who is the subject of the story's moral (lines 2074–2078):

Beth war, therefore, with lordes how ye pleye.
Singeth *Placebo* and "I shal if I kan,"
But if it be unto a povre man.
To a povre man men sholde his vices telle,
But nat to a lord, thogh he sholde go to helle.

Friar John repeatedly slips our of advising Thomas about: how to manage his own ire, and into showing him how to be a loyal servant and word-mincing court flatterer mindful of the power and potentially erratic temperament of his lord. This advice has scant usefulness for a small-holder intent on managing his own farm, unconcerned with household politics and lacking any ambitions for court patronage; it applies much more directly to the friar himself, or else to a layman of similar status aiming to attain the same sort of relationship with his lord.

In uncomfortably direct proximity to these explanations of how advisors to princes should judiciously bend the truth, Friar John next assures Thomas that he himself is an advisor of objectively perfect rectitude: "Thou shalt me fynde as just as is a squyre," or measuring square, he assures him.[22] The advice-giving role Friar John claims to fulfill here places him in uneasy tension with the mode of behavior he himself has suggested. Already, on its face, Friar John's claim to rectitude conflicts with the word-mincing, flattering advisory mode he has recommended to Thomas. But the blatant pun makes it even worse: the friar is also comparing himself to a *squire*, a lay person of just the status that his advice on court conduct covertly addresses—and just the status in the lord or king's household that the friar himself aspires to.

The vernacular eruption with which Thomas responds to this speech rudely shatters the friar's model of clerical superiority, and precipitates his request for justice from his lay lord—during which despite the lord's pretense of deference to his confessor, the friar nonetheless finds himself in just the same sort of subservient position as any lay petitioner. The friar puts himself forward as a generic representative, unproblematically equivalent to any other, of a unified and harmonious ecclesiastical hierarchy.[23] The injury done to him is a wrong done to his order as a whole, and more than that, to the whole church (lines 2190–2193):

"Sire;" quod this frere, "an odious meschief
This day bityd is to myn ordre and me,
And so, *per consequens,* to ech degre
Of hooly chirche—God amende it soone!"

Yet once he has presented his case, the friar finds himself subject to a series of lay determinations thac progressively accomplish a vernacular translation in the fullest possible sense: stage by stage they define his response as "lewed" while endowing the "lewed" churl's utterance with clerical authority.

My reading of the mechanics of this layward progression, and my interpretation of its end result, are my main point of difference with Scanlon's reading of this tale. In my view it is not enough to view the lower-status lay persons in the lord's service as straightforward exponents or instruments of his power.[24] Instead, it is important to see how the stable, harmonious lay hierarchy that in the end dismisses the friar is something the tale has to *achieve.* It must do so in opposition to a powerful clerical ideology (however ineptly it has been expressed by the friar) of universal lay subservience to the whole of the clerical hierarchy; and by means of a usurpation of clerical authority that supersedes class division. A succession of lay speakers each contributes to forging what becomes a lay unanimity, voiced in clerical terms, that drowns out the friar.

First to respond, the lady and lord begin by dismissing the churl Thomas. But whereas the lady does so quite summarily, in a way that puts the friar in the wrong only to the extent of highlighting the excessiveness of his anger (lines 2202–9), the lord's response has the effect of translating Thomas's insult into a scholastic problem (lines 2218–2237):

"How hadde this cherl ymaginacioun
To shewe swich a probleme to the frere?
Nevere erst er now herde I of swich mateere.
I trowe the devel putte it in his mynde.
In ars-metrike shal ther no man fynde,
Biforn this day, of swich a question.
Who sholde make a demonstracion
That every man sholde have yliche his part
As of the soun or savour of a fart?
O nyce, proude cherl, I shrewe his face!
Lo sires," quod the lord, "with harde grace!
Who evere herde of swich a thing er now?
To every man ylike? Tel me how.
It is an inpossible; it may nat be.
Ey, nyce cherl, God lete him nevere thee!
The rumblynge of a fart, and every soun,

Nis but of eir reverberacioun,
And evere it wasteth litel and litel awey.
Ther is no man kan deemen, by my fey,
If that it were departed equally."

The lord has no greater respect for Thomas than the lady, but he is fascinated by the apparent insolubility of the problem itself. Even more so, tellingly, he is fascinated that it was a *churl*—a person of nonclerical status and, even more surprisingly, among the laity a person of low social status—who was able to pose the intriguing problem of how Friar John can fulfill his promise to distribute Thomas's donation equally among his convent. His response affirms both his own distance from Thomas in the lay hierarchy, and the conventional attitude that only clerics have the necessary knowledge to pose, solve, or adjudicate problems: he accentuates class distinctions rather than forging new alliances.[25]

This lay judgment of the tale's central lay/clerical interchange has half-accomplished a vernacular translation (in the extended sense): the lord's curiosity about Thomas's answer has at least turned it into a problem posed in terms of the lord's knowledge of natural science, even if it has not yet brought any respect for the "cherl" Thomas. The tale's next interjection, the squire's clerical but at the same time courtly solution, carries the translation further. By subjecting Thomas's utterance in the form of the problem posed by the lord to a scientifically informed solution couched in the sort of witty, courteous form best judged to please his lord, the squire validates the scholastic interest the lord has found in it (lines 2246–2250, 2253–2286). But he also reclaims it, and its utterer, as worthy of favorable judgment in the lay court; he transforms its insult into elegantly amusing vulgarity, and the churl who has posed it into a thinker deserving of the respect due to anyone who can pose a question worthy of close attention.

Finally, the harmonious secular unanimity forged by the squire's jocular anticlericalism accomplishes a further lay judgment that has the effect of transferring clerical authority entirely to its lay challengers (lines 2287–2292):

The lord, the lady, and ech man, save the frere,
Seyde that Jankyn spak, in this matere,
As wel as Euclide dide or Ptholomee.
Touchynge the cherl, they seyde, subtiltee
And heigh wit made hym speken as he spak;
He nys no fool, ne no demonyak.

The lord's household—lord, lady, and everyone else present with the exception of the friar—draws on the scholastic mathematical authorities Euclid and Ptolemy to validate the squire as a *clerical* speaker, and even goes so far as to transform the churl Thomas into a subtly *clerical* thinker.

Of course, an element of farce has crept in by this point. But it has the effect, I think, nor so much of doing any damage to the lay unanimity that the progressive translation and appropriation of clerical prerogative have accomplished here, as of lampooning, in company with the terminology and techniques in which it is normally couched, the position of clerical authority. However radical they may be, Wycliffites always take "clergie" very seriously: in this one sense, it can be said that Chaucer has "translated" clerical authority even further than they—right off the edge.

Notes

1. All quotations from Chaucer are taken from the paperback edition of Larry D. Benson, gen. ed., *The Riverside Chaucer*, 3rd ed. (Oxford: Oxford University Press, 1988); subsequent quotations from *The Summoner's Tale* will be identified by line number only. The title quotation comes from line 2090. Since most of the contemporary clerical material I will cite has never been published in any form or, if it has, is not widely available, I will give all quotations in the original Latin as well as in English. All translations are my own.

For a more extended discussion of attitudes to 'clergie', see my *Clerical Discourse and Lay Audience in Late Medieval England* (Cambridge University Press, 1998), especially the introduction, pp. 3–5, 10–16. I am grateful to Robert Hanning for his comments, and to Glending Olson for his continuing generous willingness to exchange writings and ideas on *The Summoner's Tale*. Thanks also to the Bodleian Library, to the library of Trinity College Dublin, and to the Durham University Library, for permission to quote from unpublished manuscripts in their possession.

2. Roy J. Pearcy, "Chaucer's "An Inpossible" ("Summoner's Tale" III, 2231)" *N&Q*, n.s., 14 (1967): 322–325. On late-fourteenth-century argumentation, see further John E. Murdoch, *"Subtiliates Anglicanae* in Fourteenth-Century Paris: John of Mirecourt and Peter Ceffons" in Madeleine Pelner Cosman and Bruce Chandler, eds., *Machaut's World: Science and Art in the Fourteenth Century*, Annals of the New York Academy of Sciences, vol. 314 (New York: New York Academy of Sciences, 1978), pp. 51–86; and Edith Dudley Sylla, "The Oxford Calculators," in Norman Kretzmann, Anthony Kenny, and Jan Pinborg, eds., *The Cambridge History of Later Medieval Philosophy* (Cambridge: Cambridge University Press, 1982; rpt. 1988), pp. 540–563.

3. Larry Scanlon has explained that the tale stages a conflict between clerical and lay power, trenchantly dismissing the stale argument about whether the tale is theological or anticlerical: of course it is both; *Narrative, Authority and Power: The Medieval Exemplum and the Chaucerian Tradition* (Cambridge: Cambridge University Press, 1994), pp. 160–175. However, as I show here, the politics of lay/clerical division in the tale can be further explained by reference to contemporary polemical writings and in the light of late-fourteenth-century topics of controversy.

4. Recent discussions of the *Constitutions* sensitive to the ways they reflect contemporary attitudes to translation include Nicholas Watson, "Censorship and Cultural Change in Late-Medieval England: Vernacular Theology, the Oxford

Translation Debate, and Arundel's Constitutions of 1409," *Speculum*, 70 (1995): 822–864; Ralph Hanna III, "The Difficulty of Ricardian Prose Translation: The Case of the Lollards," *MLQ*, 51 (1990): 319–40; and Anne Hudson, "Lollardy: The English Heresy?," *Studies in Church History*, 18 (1982): 261–283, reprinted in Anne Hudson, *Lollards and Their Books* (London: Hambledon Press, 1985), pp. 141–163, The *Constitutions* are printed in David Wilkins, ed., *Concilia Magnae Britanniae et Hiberniae*, 3 vols. (Oxford: Clarendon Press, 1964), 3:314–19, hereafter *Constitutiones*.

5. "Also, it is a dangerous matter, as Jerome attests, to translate the text of sacred scripture from one language to another. For in such translation the same precise sense is not easily retained; so much so that blessed Jerome, divinely inspired though he was, confessed that he often erred. Therefore we establish and ordain that no one henceforth should translate the text of sacred scripture into the English language, or any other language, on his own authority, whether in the form of a book, shorter written work, or treatise. Nor should anyone read any such book, writing, or treatise produced recently since the time of the said John Wyclif, or to be produced later, either in whole or in part, publicly or covertly, on pain of greater excommunication" ["Periculosa quoque res est, testante beato Jeronymo, textum sacrae scripturae de uno in aliud idioma transferre, eo quod in ipsis translationibus non de facili idem in omnibus sensus retinetur, prout idem beatus Jeronymus, etsi inspiratus fuisset, se in hoc saepius fatetur erase; statuimus igitur et ordinamus, ut nemo deinceps aliquem textum sacrae scripturae auctoritate sua in linguam Anglicanam, vel aliam transferat, per viam libri, libelli, aut tractatus, nec legatur aliquis huiusmodi liber, libellus, aut tractatus jam noviter tempore dicti Johannis Wycliff, sive citra, compositus, aut inposterum componedus, in parte vel in toto, publice, vel occulte, sub maioris excommunicationis poena . . ."]; Wilkins, ed., *Constitutiones*, 3:317.

6. "Furthermore, just as a good father sows wheat in land suited to it, so that it may bear more fruit, we wish and we order, that a preacher of the word of God coming in the manner written above, to preach to the clergy or people, should properly relate his subject to his audience, sowing his seed as is fitting for the audience. He should preach to the clergy about the vices that sprout amongst them, and to the laity about the sins generally practiced among them, and not the other way around" ["Insuper, sicut bonus paterfamilias triticum spargit in terram ad hoc dispositam, ut fructum plus afferat; volumus et mandamus, ut praedicator verbi Dei veniens juxta formam superius annotatam, in praedicando clero sive populo, secundum materiam subjectam se honeste habeat, spargendo semen secundum convenientiam subjecti auditorii; clero praesertim praedicans de vitiis pullulantibus inter eos, et laicis de peccatis inter eos communiter usitatis, et non e contra"]; Wilkins, ed., *Constitutiones*, 3:316.

7. "Likewise, because what a new vessel takes in seems well-tried, we establish and ordain that masters, or anyone teaching arts or grammar, instructing boys or others in primary subjects, should not include while instructing them any discussion about catholic faith, the sacrament of the altar, or the other sacraments, or any theological matter, that contradicts what the church has determined. Nor should there be anything about the exposition of sacred scripture, except the giving of a customary, established exposition of a text. Nor should they permit their students or disciples to dispute publicly or privately about catholic faith or the sacraments" ["Similiter, quia id quod capit nova testa inveterate sapit, statuimus et ordinamus, quod magistri sive quicunque docentes in artibus, aut grammatica, pueros, seu alios quoscunque in primitivis scientiis instruentes, de fide catholica, sacramento altaris,

seu aliis sacramentis ecclesiae, aut material aliqua theologica, contra determinata per ecclesiam, se nullatenus intromittant instruendo eosdem; nec de expositione sacrae scripturae, nisi in exponendo textum, prout antiquitus fieri consuevit; nec permittant scholares suos sive discipulos de fide catholica, seu sacramentis ecclesiae publice disputare etiam vel occulte"]; Wilkins, ed., *Constitutiones*, 3:317.

8. "Furthermore, since the determiner of all things [i.e., God] cannot be determinately described by terms of human invention, either philosophical or otherwise, and blessed Augustine rather often recanted true conclusions, because they were offensive to the ears of the religious, we establish, and under the most particular witness of divine judgement we prohibit any person or persons of whatever degree, status, or condition, from asserting or proposing conclusions or propositions that sound adverse to catholic faith or good behaviour, beyond what is necessary for teaching in his own faculty, within the schools or outside them, in disputation or communication, with a prefatory protestation or without, even if they may be defended by some curiousity of words or terms. For as blessed Hugh says in his book *On the Sacraments*, "Too often what is well said, is not well understood" ["Praeterea, cum terminis philosophicis sive alias humanitus adinventis concludi non poterit omnium terminator, beatusque Augustinus veras conclusiones, quia religiosorum aurium fuerant offensivae, saepius revocavit; statuimus, et sub obtestatione divini judicii specialissime inhibemus, ne quis, vel qui, cuiuscunque gradus, status, aut conditionis existat, conclusiones aut propositiones in fide catholica seu bonis moribus adverse sonantes, praeter necessariam doctrinam facultatis suae, in scholis, aut extra, disputando aut communicando, protestatione praemissa vel non praemissa, asserat vel proponat, etiamsi quadam verborum aut terminorum curiositate defendi possint: nam teste beato Hugone, de sacramentis, "Saepius quod bene dicitur, non bene intelligitur:]; Wilkins, ed., *Constitutiones*, 3:317.

9. On *insolubilia*, see n. 2.

10. Valerie Edden, "The Debate Between Richard Maidstone and the Lollard Ashwardby (ca. 1390)," *Carmelus*, 34 (1987): 113–134, 122–123; on the dating, see 114–115.

11. William Rymington, *Dialogus inter catholica veritas et heretica depravitas* (Oxford, Bodleian Library MS Bodl. 158 fols. 188–197, fol. 188).

12. Although many other examples might be mentioned, see for example the several dialogues embedded in the *Continuatio Eulogii*, in F. S. Haydon, ed., *Eulogium Historiarum*, 3 vols., Rolls Series, vols. 10–12 (London, 1858–1863), 3:333–421 and 389–394; and my discussion focusing on one dialogue in particular in *Clerical Discourse*, ch. 5, pp. 148–153.

13. See "De Presbytero et Logico," in Thomas Wright, ed., *The Latin Poems Commonly Attributed to Walter Mapes*, Camden Society, vol. 16 (London: J. B. Nichols & Son, 1841), pp. 251–257; William of Ockham, *Opera Politica*, ed. Jürgen Miethke (Darmstadt, 1992); Trinity College Dublin 244 fols. 212v–219.

14. Trevisa's *Dialogue between a Lord and a Clerk* is published in Ronald Waldron, "Trevisa's Original Prefaces on Translation: A Critical Edition," in Edward Donald Kennedy, Ronald Waldron, and Joseph S. Wittig, eds., *Medieval English Studies Presented to George Kane* (Woodbridge, Suffolk: D. S. Brewer, 1988), pp. 285–299. Trevisa's translation of the *Dialogus inter militem et clericem* appears in Aaron J. Perry, ed., *Dialogus inter Militem et Clericem, Richard fitzRalph's Sermon: 'Defensio Curatorum' and Methodius: þe Bygynnyng of þe World and þe Ende of Worldes' by John Trevisa, vicar of Berkeley*, Early English Text Society [EETS], o.s., 167

(London, 1925). The Wycliffite *Dialogue between a Clerk and a Knight* appears in Durham University Library Cosin v. iii. 6. Subsequent references will be made parenthetically in the text by page and line number.

15. See my *Clerical Discourse*, ch. 3, pp. 62–100. My discussion here will include many of the same examples used in the book.

16. The two dialogues will appear in the volume *Four Wycliffite Dialogues*, to be published by EETS.

17. See my *Clerical Discourse*, ch. 3, pp. 82–87.

18. See my *Imaginary Publics*, ch. 3, pp. 91–93.

19. Chaucer is thought to have written *The Summoner's Tale* between approximately 1392 and 1395. (See Larry D. Benson's guide to the dating of Chaucer's works, *The Riverside Chaucer*, p. xxv.) The *Dialogue between a Secular and a Friar* may probably be dated before 1397 on the basis of its dedication and envoy, which state that it is the written record of a dialogue staged before "Lord Glowcestre," probably referring to Thomas of Woodstock (d. 1397). The *Dialogue between a Clerk and a Knight* contains no such precise indications, although Anne Hudson has noted that the Clerk shows no surprise at the Knight's knowledge of Scripture, so that a date of composition before the implementation of Arundel's *Constitutiones* in 1409 may seem more likely; see Anne Hudson, "A Lollard Quaternion," *RES*, n.s., 22 (1971): 451–465, reprinted in Hudson, *Lollards and Their Books*, 193–200; quote from p. 195. Further details will appear in my introduction to *Four Wycliffite Dialogues*, and descriptions appear in Hudson, "A Lollard Quaternion."

20. For a summary of the debate and a balanced bibliography, see the recent assessment of scholarly views on the late-medieval English audience for advice-to-princes literature in Judith Ferster, *Fictions of Advice: The Literature and Politics of Counsel in Late Medieval England* (Philadelphia: University of Pennsylvania Press, 1996), pp. 178–185. On the rhetoric of linked realms of governance in advice-to-princes literature, and more particularly in attempts to advise Richard II during his reign, see *Clerical Discourse*, ch. 3 p. 75 and n. 23. For a different interpretation of the relationship during Richard's reign (and more broadly) between advice-to-princes literature, contemporary political writing, and political activity, see Ferster, *Fictions of Advice*, pp. 176–178 (in summary), as well as pp. 67–88 (for a political survey), pp. 89–107 (on Chaucer's *Melibee* and the reign of Richard II), pp. 108–159 (on Gower, Hoccleve, Richard's deposition, Henry IV, and Henry V).

21. Scanlon describes the characteristics of the public exemplum much more fully, distinguishing it from the sermon exemplum in the process, in *Narrative, Authority, and Power*, pp. 81–87.

22. See line 2090 and note.

23. Valuable work has been done on the antifraternal material employed in the squire's reply: see Penn R. Szittya, *The Antifraternal Tradition in Medieval Literature* (Princeton, N.J.: Princeton University Press, 1986), pp. 232–246, for a thorough treatment and summary of previous scholarship. I focus here on the logic of the friar's claims, which rather than being narrowly profraternal mount a defense based on his status as a member (and therefore representative) of the church. On the broadening of the debate in the later fourteenth century such that arguments previously applied for or against some particular religious group were directed instead at corrupt church members with little regard to their precise status, see Wendy Scase, *"Piers Plowman" and the New Anti-clericalism* (Cambridge: Cambridge University Press, 1989), especially the introduction, pp. 1–14.

24. While Scanlon does note that the Squire's comic advantage in presenting a solution to the problem Thomas has posed "results as much from his own social position as his superior wit" (*Narrative, Authority, and Power,* p. 173), for Scanlon all there is to say about the quire's social position is that he is a layman: the lord's household speaks through different mouths, but with one voice.

25. Many critics have noted that the lady and lord distance themselves socially from Thomas. Lee Patterson intriguingly points out that the Lord's ideological difficulties with Thomas's problem begin before its apparent insolubility, in bafflement at the mere notion of equal division: twice the Lord's expostulation begins at the notion that "every man yliche" should have a part; Lee Patterson, *Chaucer and the Subject of History* (London: Routledge, 1991), pp. 320–321. If this is indeed one focus of the Lord's objection, his bewilderment at a theory of social organization that could be either an alternative secular arrangement, or the terms of a cloistered institutional religious rule, seems appropriate. I pursue the Lord's concern with division in a different direction in my forthcoming paper on Eucharistic blasphemy in the *Summoner's Tale* and elsewhere. Glending Olson is as far as I know the only other scholar to have noticed the Eucharistic implications of the Lord's version of this problem of division.

COLIN WILCOCKSON

The Opening of Chaucer's General Prologue *to* The Canterbury Tales: *A Diptych*

The opening thirty-four lines of the General Prologue set the scene, and divide into two equal halves. The first sixteen lines, commencing 'Whan that . . .', are concerned with matters general: the renewal of nature in April with the simultaneous desire of men and women to set out on pilgrimages. The central two lines (17–18) are a *rime riche* (perfect rhymes on words that are different parts of speech). They state the object of the pilgrimage the journey to the shrine of Thomas Becket:

> The hooly blisful martir for to seke,
> That hem hath holpen whan that they were seeke.

The remaining sixteen lines, commencing 'Bifil that . . .', home in on a specific group of pilgrims: their reception at the Tabard Inn and their plans for the next day. Then follows a paragraph (ll. 35–42) which is clearly separated from the foregoing by 'But nathelees'. In it Chaucer explains that he will present the reader with character sketches of the individual pilgrims, including their social rank and their dress.

The divisions I have indicated are reinforced by the scribe of the Ellesmere MS. He reserves illuminated capital letters for particular indication. Thus, each new pilgrim's description commences with a decorated initial

The Review of English Studies, New Series, Volume 50, Number 199 (August 1999): pp. 345–350. © 1999 Oxford University Press.

letter: ℌ knyght ther was . . . 𝔚ith hym ther was his sone a yong squier . . . 𝔗her was also a nonne . . .', and so on. When the descriptions are complete and Chaucer moves on to the more general narrative (ll. 715–858), only the first capital of that entire 143-line passage is illuminated: '𝔑ow have I toold you soothly . . .'. Yet at the beginning of the General Prologue we find the decorated capital at the first line: 𝔚han that Aprill . . .'; so, too, directly after the *rime riche*, at line 19: '𝔅ifil that in that seson . . .'; and at line 35: '𝔅ut nathelees . . .'. Thus the second sixteen-line section I have mentioned is separated, and the scribe draws our attention to a new beginning after line 34.

This drawing of attention to structural configuration by coloured capitals is of a piece with the two successive uses of the device in sections XVI (last stanza) and XVII (first stanza) of *Pearl*, evidently to emphasize that section XV contains a cryptic six (rather than the usual five) stanzas. Apart from this 'extra' decorated capital in section XVI only the first capital letter of each section of *Pearl* is coloured. As each stanza has twelve lines, the 'five stanza per section' form totals sixty lines per section. Section XV contains, however, seventy-two lines (i.e. six stanzas), unbroken by a new capital letter. But in section XVI an 'intrusive' capital letter introduces the fifth stanza, drawing attention to the fact that *there would have been* a coloured capital there if the previous section had contained the regular five stanzas of the other nineteen sections of the poem. The next stanza again has a coloured capital, because that introduces section XVII. It has often been pointed out that the resulting number of stanzas—101—is also (and surely more than coincidentally) the number of verse-paragraphs in another work by the same poet, *Sir Gawain and the Green Knight*. Some editors have, however, assumed that there was a non-authorial addition of a stanza in section XV of *Pearl*; but, as the last word of the elongated section XV is 'neuerþelese' (nevertheless), a word taken up as the first word of section XVI, there would appear to be an allusion to the numerology. Furthermore, 'neuer þe les' is the final phrase of every one of the six stanzas of section XV.[1] Had the 'intrusive' capital occurred at stanza 6 of section XV, one might argue that the scribe, accustomed to a five-stanza section, anticipated a new section and painted a decorated capital. But its removal till later reinforces its cryptic significance. 'But nathelees' (But nevertheless) is the phrase Chaucer also uses in line 35 of the General Prologue, perhaps, like the *Pearl*-poet, to alert his readers to the preceding number of lines.

The Chaucerian thirty-four-line passage is tightly structured. The thematic link between the natural description and the pilgrimage is that of death and rebirth. On the earthly level, the rebirth of springtime follows the death of winter and the drought of March. On the spiritual level, men's thoughts turn to the martyr who suffered physical death, but who is now alive in spirit and active in restoring life-forces to the sick. Early in the passage, Chaucer integrates these earthly-spiritual themes of death and resurrection by means of semantic confusion followed by fusion:

> And bathed every veyne in swich licour
> Of which *vertu* engendred is the flour;
> Whan Zephirus eek with his sweete breeth
> *Inspired* hath in every holt and heeth The tendre croppes . . .
>
> (11. 3–7; emphasis added)

The confusion occurs in the semantic fields of 'vertu' and 'inspired'. Both words, depending on context, could in the fourteenth century have theological or, as in the present instance, literally etymological senses (Latin *virtus*, strength; Latin *inspirare*, breathe into). The most common use of 'inspire' in the fourteenth century carries the implication 'infusion of a divine presence'.[2]

It was thought in the Middle Ages that God created the world in March.[3] The Nun's Priest remarks upon it:

> Whan that the month in which the world began
> That highte March, whan God first maked man . . .
>
> (vii. 3187–3188)

In line 2 of the General Prologue Chaucer specifically mentions the 'droghte of March' which is broken by April rain. In the Creation story the dry Earth is brought to life by water; God then breathes into the clay (*inspiravit*) to make man.[4] Though the March drought has been 'attributed to literary convention, but is a fact',[5] the rather unusual 'inspired' triggers off this whole series of connotations which connect the nature description with the Creation story.

These are not the only words Chaucer uses in the passage with the intention of indicating that there is a spiritual *significatio* in the physical world around us. Because their thoughts are on love, the birds do not sleep in April. Chaucer comically says that nature 'priketh hem . . . in hir corages' (1. 11). The word 'corage' (Latin *cor;* French *coeur*) in the context means erotic love—and there may well be a sexual word-play on 'priketh'.[6] When 'corage' is next used in the passage, however, it is qualified by the adjective 'devout': 'To Caunterbury with ful devout corage' (1. 22). Its meaning has moved from the natural to the spiritual, from *eros* to agape.

Given this tendency, it may well be that the language used about the sun is intended to indicate a shift from the astronomical to the spiritual, through word-play. The sun is described anthropomorphically: it is young, it runs, it goes to rest. In the second half of the passage the pilgrims retire to sleep and agree 'erly for to rise'. The birth-death-resurrection permeating the passage may well contain the *adnominatio* sun/son (Son of God). The connection between sunrise and the resurrection of Christ the martyr archetype is present in the biblical accounts. In Mark 16:2 we read that it was on a Sunday that the two Marys met the risen Christ: 'Et valde mane [very early in the morning] .. . orto iam sole [at sunrise]'. In verse 9, we are told that Christ himself rose early: 'Surgens autem mane'. In English there exists the potential for word-play on sun/son not available in Latin. Use seems to be made of this potential (in precisely the same context) in *Piers Plowman*.[7] Dead men arise from their graves at the death of Christ and prophesy:

> Life and Deeth in this derknesse, hir oon fordooth hit oother
> Shal no wight wite witterly who shal have the maistrie
> Er *Son*day about *sonne risyng*.
>
> (xviii. 65–67)

Alastair Fowler discusses the importance of 'centrality' of position in medieval and Renaissance thinking. He gives as an example the placing of the throne at the centre of one side of a table, and remarks: 'In the linear form, elaborate symmetries often surround the significant middle point.'[8] He goes on to illustrate this pattern in many works of Renaissance literature. We have seen how the mirroring of semantic possibilities is a recurrent theme in the two halves of the Chaucerian passage. 'Elaborate symmetries' are indeed present in repeated words. The only rhyme-words which are repeated are centrally pivoted:

A corages (1. 11)
B pilgrymages (1. 12)
C seke (1. 17)
C seeke (1. 18)
B pilgrimage (1. 21)
A corage (1. 22)

If we look at all repeated nouns in the passage, we find the same pattern confirmed:

sonne
nyght
corages
pilgrymages
pilgrimage
corage
nyght
sonne

This kind of patterning in medieval literature has been observed by a number of scholars. For example, in his article 'Central and Displaced Sovereignty in Three Medieval Poems' (namely, The *Awntrys of Arthure,* Henryson's *Morall Fabillis,* and *Sir Gawain and the Green Knight*), A. C. Spearing analyses the importance of the central line of some medieval poems with the elaborate patterning reflected by each half, and aptly states: 'I suggest that its structure is comparable to that of a pictorial diptych.'[9] Spearing observes that diptych structures are common in medieval poetry, even when a numerological structure is absent (the Ceyx and Alcyone story and the Man in Black in the *Book of the Duchess,* for example). John Scattergood notes a self-enclosing, fold-over pattern in Chaucer's *ABC, Anelida and Arcite, The Complaint unto Pity,* and *Womanly Noblesse.*[10] P. M. Kean, writing on *Pearl,* states: 'The climax . . . is the great stanza on God's plenitude of grace which comes at the exact centre of the poem.'[11] Ian Bishop, also writing about *Pearl,* similarly remarks: 'the author of *Pearl,* instead of enunciating his text explicitly at the beginning of his composition, places it at the centre—which is the most important position in a poem whose external structure is nearly circular and whose internal structure is more or less symmetrical'.[12] Both Kean and Bishop also analyse that poem's use of numerology.

St Erkenwald is a classic diptych poem. It consists of 352 lines. Line 1 begins with a large capital letter, 'At London . . .'. The only other large capital occurs directly after line 176, the half-way point in the poem. Line 177 reads, 'Then he turnes to the toumbe and talkes to the corce . . .', where the word 'turnes' draws attention to the leaving of one set of considerations to 'turn' to another.[13] Clifford Peterson, in his edition of *St Erkenwald,* remarks: 'The presence of this capital . . . is almost certainly not accident. It divides the poem precisely into two halves of 176 lines and coincides with the beginning of a major portion of the poem, the dialogue between the bishop and the corpse, a dialogue which brings out the poem's main concerns, heavenly and worldly justice and the salvation of the righteous heathen.'[14]

Numerology is almost certainly at work in the Chaucerian passage. It contains thirty-four lines, and the half-way division at line 17 requires the two halves to 'share' the hinging *rime riche* couplet. Augustine, in a discussion of the number of fish in the story of the miraculous draught of fishes (John 21: 11), explains that 153 is the Pythagorean triangular figure of 17, and that 17 is significant because 10 can denote the Decalogue, and 7 the gifts of the Holy Ghost which make it possible for man to fulfil the 10 laws and thus become a saint.[15] 'In this number [17] there is found, as in other numbers representing a combination of symbols, a wonderful mystery', Augustine writes. He then goes on to adduce the evidence of Psalm 17, where David praises God for delivering him from the hand of Saul: 'He in His Church, that is, His body, still endures the malice of enemies.' If Chaucer had in mind this particular passage from Augustine, the Beckett parallel would have been seen as particularly apt. Fowler notes that the dominant interpretation by the Church Fathers was that 153 represented symbolically the number of the Elect.[16] In *The City of God*, Augustine again remarks on the connotation of 10 with the Decalogue, and on the saintly connotation of the number 7: 'The theory of number is not to be lightly regarded, since it is made quite clear in many passages of the holy Scriptures, how highly it is to be valued . . . The number seven is also perfect . . . it was on the seventh day . . . that the rest of God is emphasised, and in this rest we hear the first mention of "sanctification".'[17] It is perhaps significant that line 17 of the Chaucerian passage contains the first mention of 'the holy, blisful [blessed] martyr', the saint whose shrine at Canterbury is the object of the pilgrims' quest.

The pivotal balance at the *rime riche* forms a hinge for the cunningly integrated diptych pattern of the passage, whose very form reinforces, is indeed part of, its spiritual significance.

NOTES

1. Many commentators accept that the additional stanza is authorial. The resulting 101 stanzas and 1212 lines may be numerologically significant: the poem makes constant reference to the book of Revelation, and mentions the 144,000 souls who will be saved according to that book. The 1212 lines in *Pearl* may be intended to imply 12 x 12 = 144. Gollanz, however, in the EETS facsimile edition, remarks in reference to the coloured capital on fo. 52a, 'By an error, this verse begins a new section in the MS'.

2. The earliest occurrence recorded in *MED* of 'inspired' meaning 'to breathe into' is this General Prologue instance. In Vulgate Genesis 2:5–7 (the Creation story) we are told that, though God had made the plants of the earth, they did not grow because He had not caused rain to fall on the ground. He therefore caused the earth to yield a mist to water the earth. He then created a man from the dust and breathed ('inspiravit') the spirit into him: 'sed fons ascendebat e terra, irrigans universam superficiem terrae. Formavit igitur Dominus Deus hominem de limo terrae, et inspiravit in faciem eius spiraculum vitae, et factus est homo in animam viventem.' The first example in *MED* of 'inspire' meaning to breathe or put life into a human body is in the Wyclif Bible (*c.*1382), Wisdom 15: 11. For the sense 'fill with religious ardour' *MED* cites a 1390 passage, and gives many 15th-cent. examples. Chaucer uses *inspire/enspire* on three further occasions the Canon's Yeoman's Tale, G, l.1470 (meaning 'enlighten'), and in two cases to imply that a supernatural being takes over the mind of a human: *Troilus and Criseyde*, III.712 ('Venus, this nyght thow me enspire'), and IV.187 ('What goost may yow enspire?')

3. See *Bede: Opera de Temporibus*, ed. C. W. Jones (Cambridge, Mass., 1943): *De ratione temporum*, VI. 6–7, 190–195.

4. See n. 2 above.

5. See L. D. Benson's note on General Prologue, 1.2, in *The Riverside Chaucer* (Boston, Mass., 1987), 799, where he also refers to critical suggestions about the 'convention'. Quotations from Chaucer in this article from that edition.

6. See T. W. Ross, *Chaucer's Bawdy* (New York, 1972), 167–169.

7. For Langland's use of this sort of word-play, see A. V. C. Schmidt, *The Clerkly Maker: Langland's Poetic Art* (Woodbridge, Suffolk, 1987), 125–128.

8. A. Fowler, *Triumphal Forms* (Cambridge, 1970), 23.

9. RES ns 33/131 (1982), 247–261.

10. A. J. Minnis with V. J. Scattergood and J. J. Smith (eds.), *The Shorter Poems*, Oxford Guides to Chaucer (Oxford, 1995). For discussion of the self-enclosing structure of *ABC* see p. 464; of *Anelida and Arcite*, p. 471; of *Complaint unto Pity*, pp. 471–472; and of *Womanly Noblesse*, p. 479.

11. P. M. Kean, *The Pearl* (London, 1967), 178.

12. I. Bishop, *Pearl in its Setting* (Oxford, 1968), 35 and 28.

13. There is a unique copy of the work, BL MS Harley 2250, fos. 72^v-75^v.

14. *St Erkenwald*, ed. C. Peterson (Berkeley, Cal., 1977), 26.

15. See C. Butler, *Number Symbolism* (London, 1970), 27; see also V. F. Hopper, *Medieval Number Symbolism* (New York, 1938), 80–82. *The Works of Aurelius Augustine*, trans. M. Dodds, 15 vols. (Edinburgh, 1871–1876), i. 229–230: letter LV. 17.31. Dodds supplies an illustration of the Pythagorean triangle with base 17 on p. 230. See also Fowler, *Triumphal Forms*, 184–185, and M.S. Restvig, 'Structure as Prophecy: The Influence of Biblical Exegesis upon Theories of Literary Structure', in A. Fowler (ed.), *Silent Poetry* (London, 1970), 32–72, esp. pp. 41–55.

16. Fowler, *Triumphal Forms*, 184–185, where there is also a drawing of the Pythagorean triangle with base 17.

17. Trans. H. Bettenson (Harmondsworth, 1972), 46i–6.

KATHERINE LITTLE

Chaucer's Parson and the Specter of Wycliffism

In the prologue to *The Man of Law's Tale*, both the Host and the Shipman accuse the Parson of heresy. The Host calls the Parson a "Lollere" twice: once in response to the rebuke about swearing and the second time in anticipation of a "predicacioun" (*MLE* 1173, 1177).[1] The Shipman builds on this association between the term "Lollere" and preaching (lines 1179–1183):

> ... "Heer schal he nat preche;
> He schal no gospel glosen here ne teche.
> We leven alle in the grete God," quod he;
> "He wolde sowen som difficulte,
> Or springen cokkel in our clene corn."

Here the Shipman defines "Lollere" preaching as teaching and interpreting the gospel, and he wants to forestall this activity because he deems it potentially heretical. In this exchange between the Host and the Shipman, the term "Lollere" is so clearly defined in relation to preaching that we can be sure that Chaucer knew what he was about in using it. While this use certainly does not establish the Parson as a Lollard, it should suggest that Chaucer wanted his readers to think of the Parson in relation to Lollardy.[2] Indeed, earlier critics took the Parson's Lollardy quite seriously

Studies in the Age of Chaucer, Volume 23 (2001): pp. 225–253. © 2001 New Chaucer Society.

in their attempts to prove "Chaucer . . . a Wicliffite," in the words of Hugo Simon.[3] But, of course, attempts to discuss the Parson's possible Lollardy run up against what seems to be a split in his characterization—between his appearance in *The General Prologue* and in his *Tale*. On the one hand, the accusation of Lollardy cited above seems to be confirmed by the portrait in *The General Prologue*. This Parson "Cristes gospel trewely wolde preche" (*GP* 481), and his single-minded adherence to interpreting and teaching the gospel (apparently the Shipman's definition of heresy) supports the term "Lollere."[4] On the other hand, *The Parson's Tale* does not confirm the heretical tendencies suggested by his earlier appearances. Rather, as a penitential manual that reinforces the necessity of auricular confession, it concerns itself with one of the practices vehemently opposed by the Wycliffites.[5] Scholars have come up with a number of ways for resolving this apparent contradiction between the Parson's religious beliefs, mainly by privileging the tale as more definitive, perhaps because it has come to be seen as closely allied with Chaucer's own voice.[6] The end result is to confirm the Parson's orthodoxy. The note in *The Riverside Chaucer* asserts that while "Chaucer had friends who were Lollards, and he may have been sympathetic to some aspects of the movement," *The Parson's Tale* "is perfectly orthodox."[7] As this note makes clear, the argument for the Parson's orthodoxy depends upon eliding or resolving the questions raised by his earlier appearances and appeals to the tale as the final proof of what Chaucer wanted his readers to think of the Parson. Some scholars have drawn attention to the Parson's inconsistencies, viewing the *Tale* as an oblique criticism of the Parson, whose words do not fit the ideal portrait given in *The General Prologue*.[8] Others read the *Tale* as a mistake, following Charles A. Owen Jr., who claims that *The Parson's Tale* was "perhaps not an ending ever intended by Chaucer" but was an independent work that was appended at the time of Chaucer's death.[9] However, few scholars have discussed these inconsistencies in terms of what they might say about the Parson's religiosity.[10] Indeed, the variety of solutions offered by recent scholarship for the Parson's inconsistencies (and the textual problems associated with the *Tale*) are remarkably unified in that they all ultimately maintain Chaucer's orthodoxy, and, in this way, Chaucer's orthodoxy seems to have become a kind of Chaucerian orthodoxy.

Nevertheless, as scholars of religious practices have shown us, the orthodoxy of late medieval England was a fluid and changing set of practices and not a static set of propositions.[11] To say, therefore, that someone was orthodox in the 1380s and 1390s means relatively little, since orthodoxy was in the process of defining itself in relation to a heterodoxy that had only recently appeared.[12] Opening the question of Chaucer's orthodoxy once again allows us to pay renewed attention to the shape of Chaucer's religious belief, particularly the ways in which he might be less concerned with timeless and static ideals and more specifically interested in contemporary religious conflict.[13] I would like to emphasize that I'm not asking whether or not Chaucer was a Wycliffite (a relatively fruitless exercise); rather, I would like to reinvestigate the contours of an orthodoxy that was at times sympathetic to Wycliffite beliefs. The Parson is the focus of this study because the evidence puts him on both sides of this late-medieval religious conflict (orthodox and heterodox). In this essay, I shall argue that the split between the Parson of *The General Prologue* and that of *The Parson's Tale* allows Chaucer to explore a debate over lay instruction that was brought into sharp focus by Wycliffite calls for reform. In this way, the two versions of the Parson reflect an uneasy and unresolved dialectic within lay instruction between, on one side, the demands for reform and, on the other, the limits of clerical language to enact that reform. The incompatibility of the two Parsons reflects the larger incompatibility of two objectives found in lay instruction at this particular historical moment: to reform its language and to provide a language for reform (of both the self and the larger community of the church).

Wycliffism and the Instruction of the Laity

If we approach Wycliffism as a series of doctrinal differences that set Wycliffites apart from the established church—views on the Eucharist, confession and absolution, and the power of the pope (to name only a few of the most well known)—Chaucer's affiliation with Wycliffism seems tenuous.[14] Part of the problem with earlier claims for or against Chaucer's Wycliffism is that they have described the heresy as too programmatic, a list of beliefs that can or cannot be correlated with Chaucer's poetry.[15] Moreover, finding any kind of systematic belief structure in Chaucer's poetry has been notoriously difficult. Because they are more flexible, newer critical approaches to Wycliffism seem more promising. These approaches understand Wycliffism not only as a set of doctrines that distinguish Wycliffites from the established church but also as the specific expression of a more general concern with religious language—a concern of particular urgency to Wycliffites and non-Wycliffites alike in late-fourteenth- and early-fifteenth-century England.[16] We have come to understand Wycliffites as part of a broader movement to articulate theology in the vernacular, as Nicholas Watson has shown in a number of recent articles. Thus, they shared with Chaucer an interest in appropriating "clergie" for a larger, lay public.[17]

The Wycliffite interest in translating clerical language from Latin into the vernacular was only one aspect of their desire to reform clerical language. I would like to concentrate here on another: their attempt to redefine the language of lay instruction.[18] This redefinition was based, of course, in the most foundational belief of the Wycliffites—that Scripture is the primary authority for the church.[19] As Anne Hudson writes, "[T]he primary cause that underpins all the variety of Wycliffite beliefs is their stress on the bible and their insistence that it formed the only valid source of doctrine and the only pertinent measure of legitimacy."[20] As scholars have noted, this belief has a dramatic effect on the Wycliffite view of church authority and church doctrine.[21] Its effect on Wycliffite language and on the relationship between Wycliffite language and the traditional language of lay instruction has been less studied.[22] It is this aspect of Wycliffism that is of importance in understanding Chaucer's Parson, a figure in whom the concerns of lay instruction are made clearly apparent.

The traditional language of lay instruction must be understood in relation to the two practices most responsible for its development and dissemination: preaching and confession. The history of these two practices in England and Europe more generally has been the subject of numerous studies.[23] Here I would merely like to point out two related aspects of lay instruction that are particularly relevant to the Wycliffites. First, the two practices are closely linked, as is made clear both in theory, such as the Constitutions of the Fourth Lateran Council, and in practice, the vernacular sermon literature that circulated in late medieval England in which the listeners are exhorted to confess their sins.[24] Second, the languages of preaching and confession are very similar; both practices instruct listeners/readers in the *pastoralia* (the essential requirements of the faith usually include the Pater, Ave, Creed, Ten Commandments, seven sins and seven virtues, seven works of mercy, and the sacraments).[25] In addition, both practices often use illustrative stories (exempla) to explain belief and to inform the laity of these requirements. It is, therefore, often difficult to classify devotional writings (as handbooks or sermon collections), since many were put to both public and private use.[26]

The Wycliffites challenge traditional lay instruction by condemning (and offering reformed versions of) both the preaching and the confessional practices of the established church. For the Wycliffites, preaching becomes the sole means of lay instruction, and the energies devoted to preaching are apparent in that massive sermon cycle, the *English Wycliffite Sermons,* which was quite clearly an attempt to provide what the Wycliffites saw as so severely lacking: biblical exposition in English. Indeed, the entire sermon cycle is a response to the claim that contemporary priests have prevented the laity from learning about the Bible: priests "seyn hit fallyþ not to hem to knowe Godes lawe, for þey seyn hit ys so hyȝ, so sotyl and so holy þat al only scribes and pharises schulden speke of þis lawe."[27] In some respects, the Wycliffite attention to preaching fits with the laity's growing interest in access to devotional material in the vernacular (mentioned above). Yet it is important to remember that the Wycliffite reform goes beyond a concern to provide more preaching in the vernacular, a view that also crops up in satires of lazy priests.[28] For the Wycliffite view of preaching consistently reveals an interest in reforming the language of preaching: only the Bible was to be preached to the laity.[29] This concern with the language of preaching appears throughout the *English Wycliffite Sermons* (and much Lollard polemic in general). For example, a sermon writer states, "Crist prechede not fablis *but þe gospel of God, þat was goode typingus of the kyngdom of heuene.*"[30] This opposition between biblical language and all other language is central to the sermon writers' understanding of lay instruction and is developed throughout the sermons. In another sermon, the writer states that "Crist telluþ in þis gospel þe maneris of a good herde, so þat herby we may wyten how owre herdis faylen now." A good "herde" [pastor] feeds his flock on Scripture, because "þe pasture is Godes lawe þat euermore is greene in trewþe, and roton pasture ben oþere lawys and oþre fables wiþowte grownd."[31] In this passage, the writer distinguishes between the "true" language of lay instruction, the Bible (particularly the gospel), and the "false" language of sermon exempla and other laws. This polemic against other laws and other fables has a striking effect on the sermons, which omit the *pastoralia* and the exempla that appear regularly in orthodox preaching.[32]

The same focus on reforming the language of lay instruction is also apparent in Wycliffite discussions of confession. Undergirding the Wycliffite rejection of confession is a critique of confessional language.[33] Wycliffites systematically point out that confession has been corrupted by the improper use of language: the penitent's confessional language is forced or seduced from him or her or silenced altogether.[34] For example, both the writer(s) of *The Twelve Conclusions* and that of the Wycliffite tract *Nota de confessione* imagine that confession generates sinful narratives of desire. The author of the *Nota* writes that "prestis & wymmen shulde turne her faces to-gider, & speke of lustful þoutes & dedis, which myʒt do harme to hem boþe, but þis lawe ʒyuep occasioun to do synne as it falliþ oft."[35] In addition, the insistence on the word "rownyng" in both the *Nota* and the *English Wycliffite Sermons* suggests the same kind of sinful privacy that accompanies the "lustful" thoughts and deeds. Here the wrong kind of language, "rownyng" and sinful talk, is consistently contrasted with the right kind of language—open (public confessions) and confessions to God: "Confessioun þat man makiþ of synne is made of man in two maners. Summe is mad oonly to god truly by herte or mouþe. And sum confessioun is made to man, and þat may be on many maneres; ouþer opynly & generaly, as men confesseden in þe oolde lawe; Or priuely & rownyngly, as men confessen nowe-adaies."[36] The author goes on to extol the first two forms and condemn the third.[37]

Moreover, in rejecting auricular confession the Wycliffites challenge the role of contrition in confessional language.[38] As the writer of *The Sixteen Points* (a list of Lollard errors) claims, ". . . schrift of mouþe is not nedeful to hclþe of soule, but only sorowe of hert doþ awey euery synne."[39] The emphasis on contrition underlines their attachment to a certain kind of wordlessness or voicelessness during confession (the confessions to God). This view is implicit even in *The Sixteen Points,* since shrift of "mouth" (the words of confession) is contrasted with sorrow of "hert" as if these two were mutually exclusive. In addition, this view finds even greater expression in other Wycliffite writings, both the *English Wycliffite Sermons,* which I have discussed at length elsewhere, and the *Nota.*[40] The author of the latter writes, ". . . for as many synnen greuously wiþ—inne in herte as did þe fend, so many men maken aseeþ bi sorow of herte, þat may not speke or wante oportunytee to shryue hym to man bi voice."[41] Here the author insists that interior sins and amends may not be voiced and do not, therefore, require the language of the penitential (language that has already been condemned as encouraging sin). More generally, the Wycliffites' polemic against the traditional forms of lay instruction establishes a strong dichotomy between true language—their biblical preaching and wordless confessions to God—and the false language of the others with their "fables" and "rownyngs." The relentlessness with which Wycliffites repeat these convictions about preaching and confession across the sermon cycle (and in other polemical writings) is testament to a perceived crisis in the language of lay instruction and a desire to reform that language by restricting its scope and ensuring its authority.[42]

Wycliffism and *The General Prologue*

In order to argue that the Parson is a response to Wycliffism and to the crisis in the language of lay instruction that it revealed, I want first to establish that the Parson is not merely a traditional ideal. To be sure, the elements of the Parson's ideal nature have their roots in older traditions of estates satire, as Jill Mann has made clear in her important study *Chaucer and Medieval Estates Satire.*[43] And Larry Scanlon has shown how the Parson grows out of an anticlericalism Chaucer shares with Gower, whose orthodoxy remains unquestioned.[44] But to understand Chaucer's Parson only in terms of this older model (to which both estates satire and Wycliffite polemic are indebted) is to pass up the opportunity to see how Chaucer's anticlericalism might fit with the "new" anticlericalism that Wendy Scase has discussed in relationship to *Piers Plowman.*[45] Moreover, linking Gower and Chaucer to the same version of orthodoxy disguises the important differences between their representations of the clergy. A comparison with Gower's ideal priesthood will indicate how close to Wycliffism Chaucer's Parson stands in the portrait of *The General Prologue.* Yet it is worth noting that even Gower's view of the clergy suggests that it was next to impossible for any writer in the 1380s and 1390s to invoke a traditional anticlericalism without thinking of and responding to the Lollards. In the Prologue to the *Confessio amantis,* Gower splits his discussion of the clergy into two parts: what clergy used to be like and what they are like now. He begins:

To thenke upon the daies olde,
The life of clerkes to beholde,
 Men sein how that thei weren tho
Ensample and reule of alle tho
Whiche of wisdom the vertu soughten.[46]

Gower repeats the importance of the priest's example and links it to the preaching material,

Wherof the people ensample tok;
Her lust was al upon the book,
Or forto preche or forto preie,
To wisse men the ryhte weie

And thus cam ferst to mannes Ere
The feith of Crist and alle goode."[47]

Although Gower does not explicitly name "the book," one must assume that he refers to the gospel, since he emphasizes with "and thus" that people come to hear of the "feith of Crist" through the preaching of priests. Here, love of the book, preaching, and praying all contribute equally to guiding men in "the ryhte weie." After describing this original state, Gower signals a shift to the state of the church nowadays with "Bot now men sein is otherwise" (line 240) and discusses the failure of the church for almost two hundred lines. It is in this section that Gower attacks Lollardy:

Which proud Envie hath mad to springe,
Of Scisme, causeth forto bringe
This new Secte of Lollardie,
And also many an heresie
Among the clerkes in hemselve.
It were betre dike and delve
And stonde upon the ryhte feith,
Than knowe al that the bible seith
And erre as somme clerkes do.[48]

This attack on Lollardy comes after Gower has articulated an ideal that shares quite a bit with the Lollard ideal—back in the old days, priests were not covetous, studied "the book," provided good examples, and taught people the "feith of Crist" (line 237). And the attack makes perfect sense for a writer who is indulging in anticlericalism in the late fourteenth century, because Gower must distinguish his supposedly timeless ideal from that offered by the Lollards in order to defend his own orthodoxy. It is Gower himself who sees the relationship between his views and the Lollards, because there is nothing in the content of this ideal (as he has stated it) that would mark him as unquestionably orthodox. In other words, he has not talked about the sacraments as he does in the *Vox clamantis,* where an attack on Lollardy is not necessary to reinforce his orthodoxy.[49] In this way, Gower himself shows his reader that his ideal is no longer timeless, but reflects the specific debates over priests' duties in late-fourteenth-century England.

After denouncing the Lollards, he finds that he cannot return to the ideal he first suggested; after all, it has led him to worry about its connection to Lollardy. As a result, he modifies his ideal priest for a present in which competing ideals have become more and more polemically charged. In the passage cited above, he separates "ryhte feith" from "al that the bible seith" so that these are no longer coterminous as they were in the first part of his discussion. Here Gower describes a faith that exists independently of Scripture; clergy should no longer have their "lust al upon the book," because that would make them Lollards. Therefore, the Bible is reduced in importance: there are "betre" ways of following belief.[50]

Gower finds his way out of this dilemma, how to be anticlerical but not Lollard, by coming up with a new ideal priest that is not based on Christ, or even Christ's apostles, both of which can be found in both traditional and Wycliffite writing about priests. Instead, Gower chooses Aaron (line 437). The point is that Gower *knows* that any ideal for the clergy has already been infected with the reforming zeal of the Lollards, that it is not possible to draw priestly examples from the Gospels without invoking or echoing Lollard calls for reform. Hence his interest in distancing himself from "this new Secte" (line 349), an interest also apparent in his use of "men sein" to introduce his criticisms: those "men" who attack priests could, after all, include Lollards. Once Lollards have laid claim to the traditional anticlerical ideal, the established church must come up with a different ideal for lay members to follow. Gower manufactures a new ideal by invoking Aaron; and the trajectory he begins leads eventually to Nicholas Love, twenty-odd years later, who revises Christ's life for lay instruction so that it is not about preaching and teaching but about suffering.[51]

In sum, Gower's view of the clergy reveals a struggle between his desire for reform and his desire to distance himself from the Lollards, a struggle that he resolves, relatively uneasily, by attacking them. In addition, he sets aside the biblical aspect of this reform in order to invoke nonbiblical traditions, the "matiere / Essampled of these olde wyse" that he holds quite dear. Gower is well aware that any insistence on the Bible coupled with calls for reform looks suspiciously like Lollardy.[52]

In contrast to Gower, Chaucer does not seem to be at all concerned about whether or not his ideal is viewed as Wycliffite; instead he simply gives us a portrait of a reformed priest. Most important in this portrait of reform is its scriptural basis: "This noble ensample to his sheep he yaf, / That first he wroghte, and afterward he taughte. / Out of the gospel he tho wordes caughte" (*GP* 496–498). Chaucer not only connects the Parson's teaching specifically to the Gospel three times in the course of the description, he suggests that the Parson's use of the Bible is directly related to his education:[53] "He was also a lerned man, a clerk, / That Cristes gospel trewely wolde preche" (*GP* 480–481). There is here none of the anti-intellectualism that informs Gower's portrait and that of other estates satires, in which learning is not always necessary for a good priest.[54] In addition, Scripture provides the past ideal and therefore the authority over priestly duties; the Parson is specifically imitating both Christ and the apostles and not Gower's "life of clerkes" in some undefined "daies olde."[55] In thus emphasizing the biblical authority and origin for the Parson's preaching, Chaucer draws attention to the absence of the church. In addition, as both David Lawton and Larry Scanlon have noted, there are no references to the institution of the Church and to the pastoral language associated with it, such as the sins, which figure so largely in the *Tale*.[56] Chaucer also emphasizes the Wycliffite undertones of this portrait by making it quite clear that the Parson's duties are focused on lay instruction, a focus that the Host and Shipman respond to quite vigorously in the Epilogue to *The Man of Law's Tale*. As David Aers has noted, there is no mention of any of the sacraments in this description, especially not the Eucharist, but not even the sacrament of penance, surprisingly enough, the matter for his tale.[57] Finally, unlike Gower, Chaucer does not include anything in his description to distance the Parson's portrait from Lollardy, nor does he include any indications that this ideal is in danger from the Lollards.

If one accepts the Parson's Wycliffite nature, one can see what is particularly Chaucerian about this portrait: Chaucer was a very good reader of Wycliffite discourse, in much the same way that he was a good reader of antifeminist satire or fabliaux. In this brief description, Chaucer not only demonstrates the Wycliffites' reformed priesthood but also draws our attention to the consequences of this reform for the language of lay instruction. For it is not this version of the Parson who tells *The Parson's Tale*, although his commitment to lay instruction through preaching has been made quite apparent not only here in *The General Prologue* but also in his second appearance in the Epilogue to *The Man of Law's Tale*. In other words, this version of the Parson remains voiceless, not, as I shall argue, because Chaucer changed his mind by the time he got to the *Tale* but because this Parson's reformed language is troubled by an incapacity to point beyond itself. Both the Parson and his language belong to an ideal world in which words and deeds have an unproblematic relationship. This relationship is evident both in the description of his "noble ensample" (*GP* 496) and in the last line of the portrait, in which doing and saying become the same thing: ". . . Cristes loore and his apostles twelve / He taughte; but first he folwed it hymselve" (lines 527-528). For the Parson, words have no separate status from actions because both point back to the foundational text of the Gospels." In this way, the relationship between language and what it denotes is absolute; language has been pared down to an unproblematic representation of the truth contained in the Gospels.[59] There are no questions here about the potentialities and problems of biblical exposition, of making sense out of God's word for the laity. Chaucer has associated his Parson with an understanding of language that is particularly Wycliffite.

As I have already noted, Wycliffites responded to the crisis in lay instruction by limiting lay instruction to biblical language, and the writers of the *English Wycliffite Sermons* demonstrate this desire throughout the sermon cycle.[60] Indeed, the very presence of this massive sermon cycle with its biblical exposition in English underlines their belief that "all cristene men han nede to knowe byleue of þe gospel, and so to knowe þe lif of Crist, and þe wisdam of hise wordis."[61] In expounding and disseminating the gospel, the Wycliffites consistently claim a unity of words and deeds: ". . . for alle werkys of Crist ben good lore to cristen men to techen hem how þey schal lyue for to gete þe blisse of heuene."[62] Here the author equates "werkys" with "lore" so that the deeds and the words are the same. In itself, this claim is unsurprising and echoes both Gower's and Chaucer's understanding of exemplarity: that Christ or the Parson, respectively, illustrated his words with his deeds. But when the Wycliffite author approaches the biblical texts of the sermons, he must interpret the "werkys" and "lore." He is then faced with an interpretive problem: a circularity of reference.[63] For example, in the sermons on the Sunday Gospels, Jesus is invoked as the model for the preacher, yet his preaching lacks literal content: it is always interpreted figuratively to refer to preaching. The sermon for the Fifth Sunday after Trinity contains the story of Simon (Peter) fishing.[64] In this story, the nets are read figurally as the matter of preaching: "þese nettys þat fyscherus fysche wiþ bytoknen Godys lawe in whyche vertuwes and trewþus ben knytted," and the action of the fishers is read as the action of preachers: "Þese fyscherys of God schulden waschen þer nettys in þis ryuer, for Cristys prechowres schulden clenely tellen Godys lawe and not medle wiþ mannys lawe þat is trobly watur."[65] But the river's figuration is ambiguous: it is opposed to "mannys lawe" in that it is clean, and it is also said to represent "a wondurly ful burthe."[66] This figuration does not make any sense because it opens up the possibility that both the water and the nets have the same function—to convert believers; in this way, the story "fishermen catch fish in the water with nets" could mean either that preachers catch believers with God's law or that preachers should wash God's law in God's law, In short, the interpretation has collapsed under the weight that the writer wishes to give God's law, and this collapse makes it impossible for the listener to see the relationships of the elements clearly. Even if we can make sense of the figuration, we still have not been told what God's law actually contains, nor have we been told what this interpretation means for the laity or for the priests (besides further preaching of God's law).[67] Despite the repeated calls for the necessity of preaching God's law, the sermon leads the listener away from its content. Such interpretations of Jesus' action, and there are many in the Wycliffite sermon cycle, prevent the listener from actually getting at the interpretations of what he said.[68]

I have tried to show here that the Wycliffite emphasis on the Gospels produces an interpretive cul-de-sac, the circularity evident in preaching about preaching.[69] Despite the constancy of God's law across these sermons, God's law tends to remain an empty vessel, its meaning evacuated. If the words that Jesus speaks only stand for "holy writ" always and in every circumstance, they lose the specificity with which they were first spoken. To be sure, this loss of specificity can be attributed to the polemical nature of Wycliffite writing, the necessity of reading the contemporary circumstances into all biblical passages. In this way, Jesus seems always to be preaching about the Wycliffites rather than the other way around. While this version of Jesus is certainly empowering, it is also hermetic and, in a certain way, voiceless, since it eternally repeats and reproduces a model whose only language is received from the Bible. It is this heremeticism that Chaucer dramatizes in the Parson of *The General Prologue*. The Parson invokes a particular ideal, but it is one that seems unable to extend reform beyond itself. Even his isolation from the other pilgrims suggests a certain hopelessness about the possibility of his re-forming influence.[70]

The *Tale* and the Limits of Orthodox Language

In the *Tale,* Chaucer's concern with clerical language shifts to the other side of the debate: language authorized by the church, particularly that provided by the penitential tradition. Here Chaucer has the Parson establish his commitment to orthodoxy only to explore its limits to describe reform. First, the Parson separates himself from his earlier appearances by reasserting the authority he derives from the institutional church. In his *Prologue,* he takes pains to defend the orthodoxy of his language. He insists that he will sow wheat: "Why sholde I sowen draf out of my fest, / When I may sowen whete, if that me lest?" (lines 35–36), a statement that appears to be a direct response to the Shipman's earlier accusation: "He wolde sowen som difficulte, / Or springen cokkel in our clene corn" (*MLT* 1182–1183). Moreover, the Parson asserts that he will accept others' authority over

his language: ". . . this meditacioun / I putte it ay under correccioun / Of
clerkes, for I am nat textueel" (*ParsP* 55-57). This last claim is quite at odds
with the portrait of the gospel preacher we get in *The General Prologue*. If
he follows Scripture, then he is "textueel" and to that degree is not susceptible to correction. Second, by accepting another clerk's authority over his
language, he might be invoking the institutional authority of the church,
which is altogether absent in *The General Prologue*. At the very least, he is
asserting his place within a larger estate (the clergy) from which his earlier
portrait seemed to separate him. Even his disavowal of fables does not seem
consistent with his earlier appearance, because he does not oppose fables
with the Gospels or Christ's lore (*ParsP* 31-34):

> "Thou getest fable noon ytoold for me,
> For Paul, that writeth unto Thymothee,
> Repreveth hem that weyven soothfastnesse
> And tellen fables and swich wrecchednesse."

At first glance, this sentiment may remind the reader of Wycliffite polemic
against the wrong kind of language: "Cryst ȝyueþ auctorite furst to hise
disciples . . . 'he þat heruþ ȝow, in þat he heruþ me'" and "by þis cause schulde
men worshipe prechowrus, and dispuyson hem þat prechen fables or lesyn-
ges."[71] Yet there is an important change between the Parson of *The General
Prologue* and the Parson here. To be sure, he does not tell an exemplum,
one of the "fables" he excoriates, but he does not tell a biblical story either.
In fact, during the tale he sets aside both the Ten Commandments and the
Pater Noster, both of which regularly appear in vernacular sermons and
penitential manuals as part of the *pastoralia*, and he does so for the same reason—that they are above his ability. For the first, he claims that "so heigh a
doctrine I lete to divines" (*ParsT* 956) and for the second, "The exposicioun
of this hooly preyere, that is so excellent and digne, I bitake to thise maistres
of theologie" (line 1042). With these statements, the Parson seems to have
left the world of reformed lay instruction entirely behind.

   Although the *Tale* maintains the orthodoxy established in the Parson's
Prologue and avoids taking any directly controversial positions, its reassertion of
orthodoxy is haunted by the Parson's earlier incarnation and his association with
Wycliffism.[72] In the *Tale*, Chaucer shifts the focus from a reformed language
and reformed priest to the language through which self-reform is traditionally
intended to take place—penance. Here Chaucer's Parson does find a voice to
speak to the pilgrims, but it is a voice that is interestingly fragmented, not only
between the two main sources, Raymond of Pennaforte's *Summa de poenitentia*
and William Peraldus's *Summa vitiorum*, but also within the translation of those
sources.[73] Although an earlier scholar considered the *Tale* a "clumsy combination

of two religious treatises," this view seems to have fallen out of favor, replaced by Lee Patterson's claim for "theoretical cohesion" of the parts."[74] Yet neither of these approaches has explored the possibility that Chaucer's work of lay instruction might be (might have to be) disunified because of the particular pressure on the language through which that instruction would be articulated. To be sure, it is almost certain that Chaucer did make revisions to his sources and, in doing so, made his work more cohesive, but he did not quite succeed (or finish) in unifying the Parson's voice. The *Tale's* disunity can be read as responding to Wycliffism in two ways, each of which matches one of the two main sources. In the first section, the Parson explores the language of contrition through translating Pennaforte's *Summa*. As I have already mentioned, the Wycliffites were very much concerned with the role of contrition in confession. Yet, in translating this tract, Chaucer does not continue to promote the Parson's association with Wycliffism. Rather, he has shifted to considering what it means to talk about contrition—to discover a language for it in English.[75] This section seems to be a positive move, an endorsement of the church's thinking about the capacity of language to describe individual and interior experience. Indeed, in this section the Parson is particularly concerned with providing a language of interiority, as is apparent in his six steps to contrition. All of these require thought and remembrance: "shame and sorwe for his gilt" (*ParsT* 134); realization of "thraldom" (line 142); "drede of the day of doom and of the horrible peynes of helle" (line 158); "sorweful remembraunce of the good that he hath left to doon here in erthe, and eek the good that he hath lorn" (line 231); "remembrance of the passioun that oure Lord Jhesu Crist suffred for oure synnes" (255); a "hope of three thynges; that is to seyn, foryifnesse of synne, and the yifte of grace wel for to do, and the glorie of hevene" (line 283). Patterson has discussed the changes from Raymond of Pennaforte's *Summa,* the source for the section on contrition, which Chaucer has greatly expanded and varied.[76] It would seem that Chaucer is here answering the Wycliffite charges: "sorowe of hert" does find a voice and a language that can be translated and disseminated.

Moreover, in doing so, Chaucer far surpasses the language of contrition circulating in the vernacular. For example, in *The Boke of Penance*, included in the *Cursor mundi*, the author devotes only 126 lines to contrition, whereas he devotes the majority of the pamphlet to his discussion of the other two stages of penitence (confession and satisfaction)." First he discusses the three degrees of contrition (shame, thought, and dread):

> þarfor agh sinful man and wiif
> On þis maner þair hert to riif
> And stand it if it nede to be
> Wit thorn, glaiue, nail wit al thre
> Wit quilk þat crist for us was stongen.[78]

One can see from this small section, that this author's discussion is far less nuanced than Chaucer's. Perhaps this different approach to contrition would be best described as informational and pragmatic: Here's what you need to know about contrition (rather than Chaucer's approach, which also responds to the question "What does it mean to feel contrite?"). Moreover, the author reinforces the separation between his reader (assumed to be a layperson) and the priest when he ends the discussion of contrition with a warning to the "lewd" readers not to question the necessity of "shrift of mouth":

> Bot þou sal not þe queþer vnder-tak
> þat reuth allan forgiues þe sak,
> Bot crist him-self thoru reuth allan,
> þat inwardli in hert es tan."

Here the author emphasizes that the penitent should not be the one to judge the level of his contrition and reminds the reader that he/she should not assume that contrition (here "reuth") can achieve forgiveness. In other words, the reader is not supposed to think deeply about the role of contrition in his/her own penitential process, the trajectory through different inward states, but to simply understand that it is necessary.

Unlike the author of the *Boke,* the Parson constructs a detailed portrait of self-examination out of the authoritative language he has received from Pennaforte. The Parson rejects the familiarity of the *Boke* (the "thou" and "us") in order to retain the sophistication of the original. For example, the Parson describes what should be done using the third person: "The causes that oghte moeve a man to Contricioun been sixe. First a man shal remembre hym of his synnes" (*ParsT* 133). In rejecting the "realistic and hortatory" language of the penitential tradition, Chaucer distances himself from both vernacular forms of lay instruction with which he would have been familiar: Wycliffite polemic and orthodox penitentials.[80] This apparent distance does not mean, however, that there's no space for a personal voice, and, in fact, the Parson's own voice intrudes upon his subject. There are the Parson's comments on his own work, such as "And now, sith I have declared yow what thyng is Penitence, now shul ye understonde [etc.]" (line 95).[81] This first kind of "I" is generalized, with no interest in revealing the Parson's interior. But there is a second kind of "I" that is penitential and formed of all the various "I's" in his authorities to construct a voice that we assume to be the Parson himself. For example, in the first cause of contrition he quotes Ezekiel: "I wol remembre me alle the yeres of my lyf in bitternesse of myn herte" (line 135). Although this interiotity is patched together out of a variety of authorities— Ezekiel, St. Bernard, Seneca, and Job—the Parson seems to be building up a sense of what happens inside the sinner: "I shal have remembrance" (line 256); "I wol remembre" in "myn herte" (line 135); and "I may a while biwaille and wepe" (line 176).

This second kind of "I" suggests the possibilities for the penitential voice most strongly when the Parson reaches the end of this section on contrition; an "I" appears that is radically different from the other "I's" in the tale.[82] Here the Parson cites a passage from Augustine, one quite similar to those from Ezekiel—"I wot certeynly that God is enemy to everich synnere" (line 303)—and then explicates it:

> And how thanne? He that observeth o synne, shal he have foryif-nesse of the remenaunt of his othere synnes? Nay. / And forther over, contricioun sholde be wonder sorweful and angwissous; and therfore yeveth hym God pleynly his mercy; and therfore, when my soule was angwissous withinne me, *I* hadde remembrance of God that my preyere myghte come to hym. (lines 303–304; emphasis mine)[83]

This "I" is not Augustine speaking. Moreover, this "I" does not appear in the source for this section, the *Summa* of Pennaforte.[84] Despite its similarity to Jonah's complaint, the Parson does not indicate that he is quoting an authority, as he does with his other authorities' first-person voices. We can only assume, therefore, that this is the Parson's own voice and that he refers to his own sins. This slippage suggests that in the space between the dutifully translating and commenting "I" and the "I" of biblical authority the Parson (and perhaps his readers/penitents) can build his own interiority.

In addition to its focus on the interior, the view of contrition in this section is completely uninterested in the relationship between priest and penitent. The Parson does not reject the priest, nor does he indicate that self-examination should lead toward the priest (in contrast to the *Boke*, which imagines that the self-examination generated by this poem is channeled into the proper institutional forms). Perhaps, more importantly, this self-examination is one that precedes and is not explicitly linked to the detailed exposition of the sins. Although the tract imagines an interiority created around sin, as the penitent feels shame and sorrow for it, sin retains its broadest possible meaning; it is not categorized and defined. It would seem, then, that the discussion of contrition is not only unaffected by this crisis in lay instruction but asserts the promising possibilities of translating clerical language into the vernacular.

Yet when the Parson reaches his discussion of confession (and leaves the *Summa* behind), his tone shifts. In this section, he relics on two different (even contrary) approaches to sin, which correspond to the parts of his discussion: ". . . it is necessarie to understonde whennes that synnes spryngen, and how they encreesen, and whiche they been" (line 321).[85]

The first approach informs all three parts and provides the same kind of theoretical (and sophisticated) language that he used in the section on contrition. The second approach, which informs the catalogue of sins from the *Summa vitiorum* and their remedies from the *Postquam*, focuses even more thoroughly on "whiche they been" and introduces an extensive taxonomizing of sin.[86] While the first approach to sin explains its relevance to the individual sinner, the second approach, the catalogue of sins, raises questions about the limits of personal reform through penitential language. In the first part, the Parson maps out the progress of sin just as he has mapped out the progress of contrition: "The firste thyng is thilke norissynge of synne of which I spak biforn, thilke fleshhly concupiscence. / And after that comth the subjeccioun of the devel . . . / And after that, a man bithynketh hym wheither he wol doon or no thilke thing to which he is tempted" (lines 350–352). Here the Parson continues his focus on the inner life of the penitent, as indicated in the words "norissynge," "subjeccioun," "bithynketh." But when he comes to cataloguing the sins, he abruptly changes his tone. Indeed, he seems so caught up in taxonomizing that there is no space for relating the sins as a theoretical concept to the person sinning. For example—and almost any example will do—in the section on Pride, he writes, "For certes, swiche lordes sellen thanne hir lordshipe to the devel of helle, whanne they sustenen the wikkednesse of hir meynee. / Or elles, whan this folk of lowe degree, as thilke that holden hostelries, sustenen the thefte of hire hostilers" (lines 439–440). In this passage, "man" has changed to "swiche lordes" and "this folk," and the interest has shifted from making the listener aware of how he might understand his sin to the overwhelming presence of his sin.

We are back to the question about the lack of unity in the treatise, but perhaps now we can see it from a different perspective. The catalogue of sins suggests the difficulty of finding a language for confession, the second step of the penitential process, not incidentally the part that the Wycliffites rejected almost absolutely. In other words, Chaucer fails to connect the language of contrition with the language of confession. This failure is important, because it is not typical for penitential manuals.[87] Here we might look at *The Boke of Penance*, which Patterson cites as having a similar structure. Like *The Parson's Tale*, this tract is made up of a discussion of the three parts of shrift: "reuþ," "shrift," and "buxum beting of misdide."[88] Like *The Parson's Tale*, the author inserts a discussion of the seven sins into the discussion of shrift. However, there is an important difference: after itemizing the sins, the author includes a guide on how to confess them: "Bot nu sal I tell þe her nest / Hu þu sal sceu þi scrift to preist."[89] For example, the formula for confessing pride is as follows:

Qua þat o sin o pride wil rise,
He sal him scriue on þiskin-wise,

'Til our lauerd crist and þe,
Mi gastli fader, yeild I me
Plighti for my syn o pride
In pointes þat sal vn-hyde.[90]

The author then closes this discussion by giving the reader a prayer to recite "Apon þi scrift."[91] Clearly, this author is very much concerned with how to put sin into language and, therefore, how to establish the language of confessional practice.[92]

The Parson's discussion of sin also reasserts the necessity of putting the language of contrition into the received language of sin; after all, the section on the sins follows the discussion of confession. But there is something lost in his version, since the discussion of sin is never explicitly linked to speaking—either that of the priest or of the penitent. Instead, the catalogue of sins resembles a diatribe with no other stated object than "Now is it bihovely thyng to telle whiche been the sevene deedly synnes, this is to seyn, chieftaynes of synnes" (*ParsT* 387). One might well ask, Why is this list "bihovely"? To what use is the list going to be put? Moreover, its distance from the speaking "I" is made clear in the absence of the "I" that characterizes the section on contrition. Here we only have the commenting "I"—"yet wol I shewe a partie of hem" (line 390)—not the interior "I" of Ezekiel and of the other authorities. The failure of language is also made clear at the end of the treatise on sin (lines 956–957):

> Now after that I have declared yow, as I kan, the sevene deedly synnes, and somme of hire braunches and hire remedies, soothly, if I koude, I wolde telle yow the ten commandementz. / But so heigh a doctrine I lete to divines. Nathelees, I hope to God, they been touched in this tretice, everich of hem alle.

It was quite common for penitents to confess according to the Ten Commandments, as a glance at *Handlyng Synne*, Thomas of Chobham, and Jean Gerson reveals. One must ask, then, why Chaucer has his Parson abandon one form of confessional speech when he maintains the language of the sins. Perhaps the attempt to describe every conceivable sin has exhausted the Parson or thrown him into a kind of aporia in the face of the *pasrtoralia* he is required to transmit.

In Chaucer's section on the seven sins, sin does not enable a discussion of the self, the "I," as has the section on contrition.[93] This aspect of the tale only becomes clear when the reader sees how easy it is to set aside the rest of *The Parson's Tale* and to use the catalogue of sins to order the pilgrims in *The Canterbury Tales*, to reduce them to "lust" or "sloth" without regard for the nuances with which they were created. The exegetical critics who happily matched up the sins of *The Parson's Tale* with the pilgrims of *The Canterbury Tales* indicate the ways in which a language intended to reveal the workings of the self may actually end up concealing from us who we are. This concern over the limits of late-medieval pastoral language appears in both orthodox and Wycliffite writers alike—in Julian of Norwich, who does not see the sins as they are most commonly categorized, and in the writers of the *English Wycliffite Sermons,* who struggle to articulate a new, reformed language for describing the self.[94]

NOTES

I would like to thank David Aers for his helpful comments on a draft of this essay.

1. All citations come from Larry D. Benson, gen. ed., *The Riverside Chaucer,* 3d ed. (Boston: Houghton Mifflin, 1987). Hereafter, references shall appear parenthetically in the text. For the etymology of the word *Lollard,* see n. 1173 (*Riverside Chaucer,* p. 863) and, more fully, Wendy Scase's discussion in Piers Plowman *and the New Anticlericalism* (Cambridge: Cambridge University Press 1989), pp. 149–160. The association between Lollards and tares *(cokkel)* comes from the Latin *lollium.* See n. 1173 and n. 1183. I should note here that I will use the terms *Lollard* and *Wycliffite* interchangeably.

2. There are, of course, textual problems with this passage: it does not appear in Ellesmere or Hengwrt, and, therefore, some scholars conclude that it "bears witness to an early stage of composition" (*Riverside Chaucer,* p. 862). Although the passage may not reflect Chaucer's final order for the tales (ibid.), its relevance to the Parson's characterization should not be dismissed.

3. Hugo Simon, "Chaucer a Wicliffite: An Essay on Chaucer's Parson and Parson's Tale," *Essays on Chaucer,* pt. 3, Chaucer Society, 2d ser., 16 (London, 1876), pp. 227–292. Simon makes his argument about interpolations rather haphazardly and impressionistically. Nevertheless, his question "What was Chaucer's relation to the Church?" is still worth asking even if this particular answer is guided by farfetched speculations (p. 229). R. S. Loomis was similarly convinced: "[I]t is safe to say that when Chaucer spoke of the Parson as teaching Christ's lore and that of the apostles, he left no doubt in the minds of contemporary readers that here was the ideal priest conceived according to the Lollard view"; see Loomis, "Was Chaucer a Laodicean?" Richard J. Schoeck and Jerome Taylor, eds., *Chaucer Criticism:* The Canterbury Tales (Notre Dame, Ind.: Notre Dame University Press, 1960), p. 303. See also Douglas J. Wurtele, who takes Simon's charge seriously (although he argues against it), in "The Anti-Lollardry of Chaucer s Parson," *Mediaevalia* 11 (1985): 151–168.

4. Repeated again in *GP* 489, 527–528: "Out of the gospel he tho wordes caughte" and "Cristes loore and his apostles twelve / He taughte; but first he folwed it hymselve."

5. I will discuss Wycliffism in greater detail below.

6. As Chaucer's voice, the tale can then demonstrate Chaucer's appropriation of clerical authority, his removal from the world of fiction, a personal penitential

mauual, or a comment on the rest of the tales (although this last interpretation seems to have long since fallen by the wayside). These views belong to Larry Scanlon, *Narrative, Authority, and Power* (Cambridge: Cambridge University Press, 1994), ch. 1; Lee Patterson, "*The Parson's Tale* and the Quitting of the *Canterbury Tales*," *Traditio* 34 (1978): 331–381; Albert Hartung, "The *Parson's Tale* and Chaucer's Penance," in R. G. Newhauser and John A. Alford, eds., *Literature and Religion in the Later Middle Ages* (Binghamton, N.Y.: Center for Medieval and Early Renaissance Studies, 1995), pp. 61–80; and Bernard Huppé, *A Reading of the* Canterbury Tales (Albany: SUNY Press, 1964), respectively. There are, of course, critics who insist that the Parson's voice is as ironically distanced from Chaucer as the other pilgrim's voices: John Finlayson, "The Satiric Mode and the Parson's Tale" *ChauR* 6 (1971): 94–116, and Judson Boyce Allen, "The Old Way and the Parson's Way: An Ironic Reading of the Parson's Tale," *JMRS* 3 (1973): 255–271.

7. *Riverside Chaucer,* p. 363 n. 1173.

8. Both David Aers and Donald Howard also note the discrepancy between the "benygne" man of *The General Prologue* and the "tendency to chide and reprimand" in his later appearances. See Aers, *Chaucer, Langland and the Creative Imagination* (London: Routledgc, 1980), p. 110, and Howard, *The Idea of the* Canterbury Tales (Berkeley: University of California Press, 1976), pp. 376–378.

9. Charles A. Owens Jr., "What the Manuscripts Tell Us about the Parson's Tale," *MAE* 63 (1994): 245. See also Miceal P. Vaughan, "The Invention of the *Parson's Tale*," in Thomas A. Prendergast and Barbara Kline, eds. *Rewriting Chaucer* (Columbus: The Ohio State University Press, 1999), pp. 45–90.

10. For exceptions, see R. S. Loomis and David Lawton. Loomis attributes the shift between *The General Prologue* and the *Tale* to the very different religious and political atmospheres at the times of composition: It was safe to use Wycliffite terms to describe the Parson while Chaucer was writing *The General Prologue* in the 1380s, but by the time Chaucer composed a tale for the Parson (at the end of his life), putative Wycliffite beliefs had become far more dangerous ("Was Chaucer a Laodicean." pp. 304–305). Lawton also notices this disjuncture between the *Tale* and "the Parson's portrait in the *General Prologue*, with its recurrent focus not on the Parson's place in the church hierarchy but rather on his personal grounding in 'Cristes gospel'" and states that "we run the risk of underreading them if we overlook their historical context" (David Lawton, "Chaucer's Two Ways: The Pilgrimage Frame of the *Canterbury Tales*," *SAC* 9 [1987]: 36), a sentiment with which I agree. Perhaps the most recent account of the Parson's religiosity has been offered by Scanlon, who maintains that the portrait in *The General Prologue* is evidence of Chaucer's anticlericalism, but it is an anticlericalism general to late medieval England (and therefore does not make the Parson unorthodox). See his *Narrative, Authority, and Power*, ch.1.

11. See, for example, Sarah Beckwith, *Christ's Body* (London: Routledge, 1993); Miri Rubin, *Corpus Christi: The Eucharist in Late Medieval Culture* (Cambridge: Cambridge University Press, 1991); and Nicholas Watson, "Conceptions of the Word: The Mother Tongue and the Incarnation of God," *New Medieval Literatures* 1 (1997): 85–124. This is, of course, by no means an exhaustive list of this kind of work.

12. See Paul Strohm's *England's Empty Throne* (New Haven, Conn.: Yale University Press, 1998), ch. 2, in which he argues for new approach to the study of heresy in England. Rather than see the Lollard as preexisting the category of heretic,

we should see that "the Lollard was from the beginning less a real threat to orthodox control than orthodoxy's rhetorical plaything" (p. 34). In their important work on Wycliffism, both Anne Hudson and Margaret Aston emphasize the ways in which "'Wycliffite' concerns coincided with the intellectual interests of the time"; Hudson, *The Premature Reformation: Wycliffite Texts and Lollard History* (Oxford: Clarendon Press, 1988), p. 393. My work is greatly indebted to both Hudson's study and Aston's work in *Lollards and Reformers: Images and Literacy in Late Medieval Religion* (London: The Hambledon Press, 1984), particularly ch. 1, 4, 5, 6.

13. For recent studies that have put Chaucer's poetry in conversation with contemporary religious debates, see Paul Strohm, "Chaucer's Lollard Joke: History and the Textual Unconscious," *SAC* 17 (1995): 23–42; David Aers and Lynn Staley, *The Powers of the Holy: Religion, Politics, and Gender in Late Medieval English Culture* (University Park: Pennsylvania State University Press, 1996); Fiona Somerset, "As Just as is a 'Squyre': The Politics of 'Lewed Translacion' in Chaucer's *Summoner's Tale*," *SAC* 21 (1999): 187–207; and Glending Olson, "The End of the *Summoner's Tale* and the Uses of Pentecost," *SAC* 21 (1999): 209–245.

14. For an account of Wycliffite "Reformation Ideology," see Hudson's *Premature Reformation*, ch. 6–8.

15. Scholars who have argued for or against the Parson's Wycliffism, such as Loomis, Wurtele, and Simon, to whom he's responding, seem to be most concerned with what I would call "circumstantial evidence": the "external evidence" of Chaucer's friends and the "internal evidence" of the Parson's morality (these terms come from Wurtele, "Anti-Lollardry," p. 152), rather than with systematic study of Wycliffite writings and possible rhetorical or theoretical similarities between those writings and Chaucer's.

16. The increasing lay interest in devotional works in late-fourteenth- and fifteenth-century England is something of a scholarly commonplace. For an overview, see W. A. Pantin, *The English Church in the Fourteenth Century* (Toronto: University of Toronto Press, 1980), ch. 9 and 10. See also Vincent Gillespie, "Vernacular Books of Religion," in Jeremy Griffiths and Derek Pearsall, eds., *Book Production and Publishing in Britain, 1375–1475* (Cambridge: Cambridge University Press, 1989), pp. 317–344; Michael G. Sargent, "Minor Devotional Writings," and Thomas J. Heffernan, "Sermon Literature," in A. S. G. Edwards, ed., *Middle English Prose* (New Brunswick, N.J.: Rutgers University Press, 1986), ch. 9 and 10, respectively. For an analysis of how Wycliffites fit into this growing "devotional literacy," see Aston, *Lollards and Reformers*, ch. 4 and 6; the citation is the title of ch. 4.

17. These new approaches to Wycliffism are primarily concerned with translation. See Rica Copeland, "William Thorpe and His Lollard Community," in Barbara Hanawalt and David Wallace, eds., *Bodies and Disciplines: Intersections of Literature and History* (Minneapolis: University of Minnesota Press, 1996), pp. 199–221, and her "Childhood, Pedagogy, and the Literal Sense: From Late Antiquity to the Lollard Heretical Classroom," *New Medieval Literatures* 1 (1997): 125–156; Ralph Hanna, "The Difficulty of Ricardian Prose Translation, The Case of the Lollards," *MLQ* 51 (1990): 319–340; Fiona Somerset, *Clerical Discourse and Lay Audience in Late Medieval England* (Cambridge: Cambridge University Press, 1998); and Nicholas Watson, "Censorship and Cultural Change in Lace-Medieval England: Vernacular Theology, the Oxford Translation Debate, and Arundel's Constitutions of 1409," *Speculum* 70 (1995): 821–864.

18. See works by Copeland, Hanna, and Somerset cited in n. 17.

19. Hudson writes that Wycliffites insisted on Scripture as the sole authority for the Church: *sola scriptura* "is probably a reasonable summary of many of his followers' attitudes" (*Premature Reformation*, p. 228). John Wyclif's view is rather more complicated; see Paul de Vooght, *Les sources de la doctrine chrétienne* (Bruges, 1954), pp. 168–200; and Michael Hurley, "'Scriptura sola': Wyclif and His Critics," *Traditio* 16 (1960): 275–352.

20. Hudson, *Premature Reformation*, p. 280. See also ch. 5, "Lollard Biblical Scholarship."

21. See, for example, Hudson's *Premature Reformation*.

22. However, see Christina von Nolcken, "A 'Certain Sameness' and Our Response to It in English Wycliffite Texts," in Richard Newhauser and John Alford, eds., *Literature and Religion in the Later Middle Ages* (Binghamton, N.Y.: Center for Medieval and Early Renaissance Studies, 1995), pp. 191–208; Anne Hudson, "A Lollard Sect Vocabulary?" *Lollards and Their Books* (London, 1985), pp. 165–180; and Katherine Little, "Catechesis and Castigation: Sin in the Wycliffite Sermon Cycle," *Traditio* 54 (1999): 213–244 (on which much of the following account of Wycliffite language is based).

23. Scholars generally locate the origin of standardized pastoral instruction as the Fourth Lateran Council of 1215. For a discussion of the impact of this council on pastoral instruction in England, see Leonard E. Boyle, "The Fourth Lateran Council and Manuals of Popular Theology," in Thomas J. Heffernan, ed., *The Popular Literature of Medieval England* (Knoxville: University of Tennessee Press, 1985), pp. 30–43; Pantin, *English Church*, ch. 9–10; and R. N. Swanson, *Religion and Devotion in Europe, c. 1215–c. 1515* (Cambridge: Cambridge University Press, 1995), pp. 25–30 and ch. 3. For preaching, see H. Leith Spencer's *English Preaching in the Late Middle Ages* (Oxford: Clarendon Press, 1993). For confession, the literature is far more extensive, and the findings more in dispute. But see John Bossy, "The Social History of Confession in the Age of Reformation," *TRHS*, 5th ser., 25 (1975): 21–38, and Thomas N. Tentler, *Sin and Confession on the Eve of the Reformation* (Princeton, N.J.: Princeton University Press, 1977).

24. Decree 10 makes clear that both preaching and confession are central to lay instruction: "We therefore order that there be appointed in both cathedral and other conventual churches suitable men whom the bishops can have as coadjutors and cooperators not only in the office of preaching but also in hearing confessions and enjoining penances and in other matters which are conducive to the salvation of souls"; *Decrees of the Ecumenical Councils*, ed. Norman P. Tanner (London: Sheed and Ward; Washington, D.C.: Georgetown University Press, 1990), 1:240. For vernacular sermons, almost any sermon in Mirk's *Festial*, ed. Theodor Erbe, Early English Text Society [hereafter EETS], e.s., vol. 96 (London: Trubner, 1905) or *Middle English Sermons*, ed. Woodburn O. Ross, EETS, vol. 209, (London: Oxford University Press, 1940) will do.

25. The interrelationships between *pastoralia* and *exempla* (and/or biblical narratives) is made clear in such texts as Robert Mannyng of Brunne's *Handlyng Synne*, ed. Idelle Sullens (Binghamton, N.Y.: Medieval and Renaissance Texts and Studies, 1983); *Jacob's Well*, ed. Arthur Brandeis, EETS, vol. 115 (London: Kegan Paul, Trench, Trübner, 1900); Mirk's *Festial*; and the *Middle English Sermons*. In England, the elements of pastoral instruction were drawn up and circulated by John Pecham, archbishop of Canterbury, in 1281 and by John Thoresby, archbishop of York, in 1357. For a discussion of this history, see Spencer, ch. 5 and Pantin, ch. 9.

26. On this, see Spencer, *English Preaching,* chap. 2.

27. Anne Hudson and Pamela Gradon, eds., *English Wycliffite Sermons,* 5 vols. (Oxford: Clarendon Press, 1983–1996), v. 1, 232 [hereafter *EWS*].

28. Jill Mann, *Chaucer and Medieval Estates Satire* (Cambridge: Cambridge University Press, 1973), pp. 65–66 on the importance of the ideal priest's teaching, especially by example.

29. Spencer finds that "there seems to be some substance to the view that the patristic type of homily [preaching the gospel] had fallen out of fashion in the late thirteenth century and the fourteenth . . . Controversialists writing before Arundel's Constitutions also reported the opinion that only *pastoralia* should be preached to the laity" (*English Preaching,* p. 158). See, further, her ch. 4 in full.

30. The italics refer to the scriptural text that this writer is translating. See *EWS* 2:49.

31. *EWS* 1:48.

32. See Little, "Catechesis and Castigation," in which this effect is discussed at length.

33. In rejecting confession, the Wycliffites are also rejecting the priest's authority over the penitent. For examples of this position, see *The Twelve Conclusions and The Sixteen Points on which Bishops accuse Lollards,* both printed in Anne Hudson, ed., *Selections from English Wycliffite Writings* (hereafter *SEWW*) (Toronto: University of Toronto Press, 1997), pp. 19–29. Although the latter is not as vehement as some later Wycliffite writings, it does assert the importance of contrition over confession (pp. 20-21). See also Hudson, *Premature Reformation,* pp. 294–299.

34. For anrifraternal satire see Penn Szittya, *The Antifraternal Tradition in Medieval Literature* (Princeton, N.J.: Princeton University Press, 1986).

35. See *Nota de conffessione,* in *English Works of Wyclif hitherto unprinted,* ed. F. D. Matthew, EETS, vol. 74 (London: Trübner, 1880, 1902), p. 330. In *The Twelve Conclusions,* the author writes, "þe ix conclusiun þat holdith þe þuple lowe is þat þe articlis of confessioun þac is sayd necessari to saluaciun of man, with a feynid power of absolicion enhaunsith prestis pride, and geuith hem opertunite of priui calling othir þan we wele now say. For lordis and ladys ben arestid for fere of here confessouris þat þei dur nout seyn a treuth, and in time of confessiun is þe beste time of wowing and of priue continuance of dedli synne" (*SEWW,* 27). Here the author is also concerned with the erotic potential of the traditional language of confession (for "wowing") and also ofthe priests' ability to scare their penitents into silence.

36. *Nota,* pp. 327–328.

37. See Little, "Catechesis and Castigation," pp. 240–241.

38. In doing so, they reopened a controversy over contrition that had preoccupied earlier theologians. See Tentler, *Sin and Confession,* pp. 22–27 and 250–301.

39. *SEWW,* p. 19.

40. See Little, "Catechesis and Castigation," pp. 241–244.

41. *Nota,* 338.

42. It is worth noting that the established church reacted to this dichotomy by championing the other side—*pastoralia* and *exempla* to the exclusion of Scripture. As Spencer writes, "[T]he principle was traditionally understood that both gospel preaching and pastoral teaching were of equal importance. . . . Yet, in the fourteenth and fifteenth centuries, the effect of the Church authorities' hostility to unsupervised gospel preaching was to set up an opposition between the two" (*English Preaching,* p. 199).

43. Jill Mann points out that "this is no abstract, timeless figure; Chaucer envisages him in a realistic spatial and temporal existence," but she does not link this existence to historical events outside the Prologue itself (*Estates Satire*, p. 66).

44. Scanlon, *Narrative, Authority, and Power*, ch. 1.

45. See Piers Plowman *and the New Anticlericalism*. For Scase, the newness of this anticlericalism is its emphasis on clerical dominion (p. 7).

46. *Confessio amantis*, in G. C. Macaulay, ed., *John Gower's English Works*, 2 vols., EETS, e.s., vols. 81 and 82 (London: Kegan Paul, 1900–1901), Prol. 193–97.

47. Ibid., ProL 229–237.

48. Ibid., Prol. 347–255.

49. See n. 15.

50. In the excursus on world religion in book 5, Gower's anticlericalism becomes even more confused. He attacks Lollardy as "newe lore," shifts abruptly to Christ's example, and then returns to attacking "Prelatz." It is important to note that Gower's anticlericalism in the *Confessio* is markedly different than in the *Vox;* one can assume that his choice of English forced him to change his tack.

51. In the early fifteenth century, the established church authorized and circulated a particular model for imitation—the suffering Jesus who appears in Nicholas Love's *Mirror of the Blessed Life of Jesus Christ*, ed. Michael Sargent (New York: Garland Press, 1992). This ideal is about as far as one can get from the Parson.

52. *Confessio amantis*, Prol. 6–7.

53. Loomis writes, ". . . now three times Chaucer hammers home the point that the Parson took his doctrine from the gospel" ("Was Chaucer a Laodicean?" p. 302).

54. Mann, *Estates Satire*, p. 65. See, however, Spencer's caveat that "verbal instruction in 'God's word' need not always mean merely instruction in bible texts, but might signify the formulations of the Church, founded in some sense upon scripture" (*English Preaching*, p. 145). Nevertheless, Chaucer's use of the word "gospel," which Gower avoids, suggests that he is opposing gospel to other kinds of preaching the Parson might have indulged in (and still be considered moral): saints' lives, exempla, and *pastoralia*.

55. It is important to note that Chaucer uses the phrase to describe his Parson that Gower attributes to Christ. Gower does not apply this ideal directly to priests (only indirectly in his second attack on Lollardy in book 5). Gower writes (in the voice of Genius) (5.1825–1830):

> Crist wroghte ferst and after tawhte,
> So that the dede his word arawhte;
> He yaf ensample in his persone,
> And we the wordes have al one,
> Lich to the Tree with leves grene
> Upon the which no fruit is sene.

Although this passage is strikingly similar to the portrait of Chaucer's Parson, as noted by Scanlon (*Narrative, Authority, and Power*, p. 9). Gower goes out of his way to avoid relating Christ here to either the Lollards (whom he has just finished discussing) or priests, whom he goes on to attack after an exemplum about Priest Thoas.

56. Lawton, "Chaucer's Two Ways," p. 36, and Scanlon, ibid., p.10.

57. See David Aers, *Faith, Ethics, and Church: Writing in England,* 1360–1409 (Rochester, N.Y.: Boydell and Brewer, 1999), pp. 46–47. Hudson also notes that "what is omitted is, for the date, as significant as what is included: there is no mention of the Parson's administration of the mass, no allusion to his role as confessor" (*Premature Reformation,* p. 391).

58. But see Scanlon, who writes that the Parson's exemplarity "distances clerical authority from the textual" (*Narrative, Authority, and Power,* p. 10). Nevertheless, almost every sentence in the description points to a biblical reference, and the Parson's authority comes from enacting and speaking the words of the gospel.

59. Patterson also finds this understanding of language in the *Tale:* "for the Parson homiletic language remains essentially denotative" *(Parson's Tale,* p. 361). But in *The General Prologue,* the denotative nature of language is explicitly linked to the Gospels.

60. See Kantik Ghosh, "'Authority' and 'Interpretation' in Wycliffite, Anti-Wycliffite, and Related Texts, c. 1375–1430" (Ph.D. diss., Cambridge University, 1995), ch. 4. Ghosh writes of "the important hermeneutic assumption underlying the vernacular Wycliffite sermons, an assumption inherited from Wyclif: an extreme categorical disjunction between God's law and man's" and states that the Wycliffites "attempt to fix and define meaning theoretically while in practice retaining the creative prerogatives of traditional exegesis" (p. 122).

61. Here the author is praising Paul's writings "for þei ben pure, sutel, and plenteuous to preche þe puple" (*EWS* 1:479).

62. *EWS* 1:248. This is, of course, a sentiment repeated across Wycliffite writing. In itself, the sentiment is not heterodox, but the insistence that the "werkys" are only found in holy writ (and not the other teachings of the church) does separate the Wycliffites from less radical contemporaries.

63. There are, of course, interpretive problems endemic to biblical exegesis, particularly allegorizing. As David Aers writes, "[A]nalysis of exegetical practice has shown the tendency of medieval figuralists to dissolve events and actions, and with these both the text's images and existential dimensions"; *Piers Plowman and Christian Allegory* (London: Edward Arnold, 1975), p. 32. Nevertheless, Wycliffite biblical exegesis closes down the relationship between literal and spiritual meaning in quite notable ways because Wycliffites reject what they see as excessive allegorizing by the established church. Consider, for the purposes of comparison, John Wyclif's exposition of this same passage, in which he is quite interested in figuration, particularly of the nets: "Supposito hoc sensu allegorico accedendo ad sensum tropologicum, notandum quod triplex est rete [Christ, the devil, and the world]" (p. 47). Finally, he states that Christ's net works by way of the seven works of mercy ("recipit autem hoc rete dum laxatur in mare seculi per foramina aquas tribulacionis mundane sed irretitus in septem operibus spiritualismisericordie trahitur ad litus terre vivencium" [p. 248]), which Wyclif goes on to list and discuss (*Sermones,* 3 vols., ed. Johann Loserth [London: Wyclif Society, 1887], 1:246–248). The discussion of what preachers/fishermen are supposed to do (catch the faithful) is accompanied by how they are supposed to do it (with the seven works of mercy). Hudson also notes that "very little" of the English sermon can be traced to Wyclif's sermon (*EWS* 4:198).

64. Spencer also notes the problematic nature of this sermon, specifically the definition of "God's law" (*English Preaching,* pp. 147 and 194). Interestingly enough, G. R. Owst cites a derivative of this sermon (from MS Royal 18) as evidence for the

views of "a simple vernacular homilist" without noting its affiliation with Wycliffism; *Preaching in Midieval England* (Cambridge: Cambridge University press, 1926), p. 2. The sermon appears as no. 44 in the collection *Middle English Sermons.* According to Spencer, it is one of three sermons in this collection that also appear in MS Rylands 109, Sidney Sussex 74, and Bodley 95, which all contain derivatives from the *EWS* (*English Preaching,* p. 308).

65. *EWS* 1:242.

66. In both Wyclif's sermon and the *Glossa ordinaria,* the water Genesareth figures the world. Moreover, neither of these interpretations contains any reference to washing the nets in the water. Wyclif writes "stagnum Genezareth est turbata fragilitas huius conversacionis lapse, cum mundi confidencia sit labilis et inconstans" (*Sermones* 1:246), and the *Glossa* cites Bede: "stagnum praesens saeculum designat"; *Glossa ordinaria,* in *Patrologiae cursus completus series Latina,* ed. J-P. Migne (Paris: Garnier Freres, 1844–), 114:256. Hudson writes in the note to the sermon that "the interpretation of the washing of the nets has probably been developed independently by the English writer" (*EWS* 4:200).

67. Wyclif's exposition differs markedly, because he uses the allegorical meanings to emphasize not only that priests should preach but *what* priests should preach—the seven works of mercy.

68. The polemic against the preachers of the established church for indulging in the wrong kind of preaching also leads the Wycliffite sermon writers away from detailing what the right kind of preaching would be. See, for example, sermon 48, *EWS* 1:438–442.

69. Ghosh comes to similar conclusions (for different reasons) about Wyclif's writing in his article "Eliding the Interpreter: John Wyclif and Scriptural Truth": "*De Veritate* thus points the way towards a hermeneutic cul-de-sac"; "The baffled idealism of Wyclif's tract and its profound unease with inherited hermeneutics which can neither be accepted nor rejected out of hand, given the nature of Christianity as the evolving religion of a (ceaselessly interpreted) text, arise from an increasingly threatened perception of the extent to which the theoretical source of all transcendent certitude, the Bible, is implicated in rhetoric through institutionalized and variable interpretive practices (*New Medieval Literatures* 2 [1998]: 224).

70. Jill Mann also notes the Parson's isolation (along with that of the Ploughman): "The Parson and the Ploughman indeed correspond to the ideal of the estates writer, but Chaucer seems to be showing us that this ideal is inadequate to account for the workings of society. This is the basis on which society *should* be organised; but the isolation of these two figures in the *Prologue* shows us that the actuality is something different. The Parson does not seem to impinge on the other pilgrims, nor does the Ploughman. They exist in a separate sphere which is as exclusive and specialised as those inhabited by the other pilgrims" (*Estates Satire,* p.73).

71. *EWS* 2:30.

72. Patterson calls the theology "bland" (*Parson's Tale,* p. 353 n. 61). While the tale is purposely nonconfrontational on such matters as justification of auricular confession, it seems quite troubled about such matters as contrition; see below.

73. For a discussion of the sources, see Kate O. Petersen, *The Sources of the Parson's Tale* (Boston: Ginn, 1901); and Siegfried Wenzel, "The Sources for the 'Remedia' of the Parson's Tale," *Traditio* 27 (1971): 433–454. Beryl Rowland also notes the different voices: "[T]he essential difference between the penitential treatises and *The Parson's Tale* is that the latter contains more than one voice"; "Sermon

and Penitential in the *Parson's Tale* and their Effect on Style," *Florilegium* 9 (1987): 132. She identifies these two voices as "that of the instructor addressing the parish priest and that of the latter his parishioners" (p. 134).

74. The first is the view of Mark H. Liddell, "A New Source of the Parson's Tale," in *An English Miscellany Presented to Dr. Furnivall* (Oxford: Clarendon Press, 1901), p. 256. Liddell writes that "none of the Latin, English, or French treatises on this subject that I have seen (and I have examined a great number in the hope of finding the source of Chaucer's work) are so confused and disproportioned as Chaucer's is" (p. 257). Similarly, Rowland states that "the homogeneity of style that they [critics] imply does not exist" ("Sermon and Penitential," p. 131). Lee Patterson, who studied the same treatises as Liddell, came to quite different conclusions: "Chaucer has elected to use just those elements from the paradigms of religious writing that will enforce a sense of theoretical cohesion" (*Parson's Tale*, p. 340); see further, pp. 344–351 As will become clear below, I am greatly indebted to Patterson's article, particularly to his view that "Chaucer is introducing an intellectual and theoretical concern into material that is far more commonly treated in a realistic and hortatory fashion" (p. 345).

75. Although this translation would constitute the lay appropriation of "clergie" that Chaucer shares with the Wycliffites (see n. 17), Wycliffites were, of course, uninterested in translating penitential manuals, since they opposed confession (and therefore would find confessional manuals unnecessary). Nevertheless, Chaucer's translation of Pennaforte retains the sophistication of Pennaforte's manual, and therefore shares with Wycliffism a rejection of the simplicity (at times insulting simplicity) with which vernacular devotional aids addressed their lay readers. In fact, Rita Copeland's statement about Lollard teaching, which "refuses pastoral formulas that equate laity with puerility; and it does so by rejecting the historical baggage of pastoral condescension," can be nicely appropriated to describe what Chaucer is doing in the section on contrition ("Childhood, Pedagogy," p. 156).

76. Patterson, *"Parson's Tale,"* pp. 353–356. Patterson notes that two of Pennaforte's degrees are combined, and "a new more generous feeling is added (number five), 'remembrance of the passion that oure Lord Jhesu Crist suffred for youre synnes'" (p. 355).

77. The *Boke's* view of contrition seems to be representative of vernacular handbooks. *Jacob's Well* does not spend much time on the "watyr of contricyoun," focusing rather on the "scoope of penauns," and the writer provides exempla that illustrate only the second two stages of penance: confession and satisfaction (pp. 64–68). *Handlyng Synne* does discuss "sorowe of hert" as the sixth point of shrift, but seems to be interested in externalizing the sins rather than an inner mapping of sorrow: "Þy self berest þan on þy bak / Þy vyle synne þat makþ þe blak" (lines 11561–11562).

78. *The Boke of Penance*, in R. K. Morris, ed., *Cursor mundi*, 7 vols., EETS, o.s., 57 (London: Trübner, 1874–1893), vol. 5, lines 26014–26018.

79. Ibid., lines 26080–26083.

80. The phrase is Patterson's *(Parson's Tale*, p. 344).

81. See similarly, "Now soothly, whoso wel remembreth hym of thise thynges, I gesse that his synne shal nat turne hym into delit" (line 175); "Now shal a man understonde in which manere shal been his contricioun. I seye that it shal been universal and total" (line 292); and "Wherfore I seye that many men ne repenten hem nevere of swiche thoghtes and delites" (line 298).

82. Rowland also notes the interjection of this different voice: "the passage [on contrition] concludes with an intrusive 'I' (298, 304, 308) that has more force than the single rhetorical 'I gesse' (175), and it appears, in these instances, to be the writer of the tract, addressing the priest" ("Sermon and Penitential," p. 134).

83. Wenzcl's notes in *The Riverside Chaucer* attribute this citation to Jonah 2:8 (p. 958 n. 303).

84. *Summa sancti Raymundi de Peniafort* (Farnsborough, Hants.: Gregg Press, 1967), bk. 3, section 10, pp. 649–650. See also Petersen, *Sources*, pp. 15–16.

85. Chaucer seems to be following different sources here. He uses a tract that is similar to Pennaforte for the discussion of confession (lines 316–386) and Peraldus for "a large part of lines 390–955" (*Riverside Chaucer*, p. 956; see also p. 958 n. 318–979). Petersen describes the first section as "sin in general" (lines 321–386) and writes, "Raymund's tract has important correspondences with the *P.T.*, although they are not brought together as in the *P.T.*" (ibid., p. 34).

86. It is worth noting chat at this stage in the *Summa*, sin does not receive the same kind of attention it does in Chaucer's tract. See *Summa*, bk. 3, section 13, p. 653. Petersen notes the following: "At section 17, v. 321, where the Parson fails to expound his second topic of Confession, and in connection with this second topic of Confession in Raymund, the subject of Sin is introduced. The treatment of this topic in Raymund is brief, and hardly interrupts the transition to the third topic of Confession. In the *P.T.*, on the contrary, the exposition of Sin is so full as almost to assume the proportions of a separate treatise. Moreover, from its length and elaboration, the digression interrupts the regular course of the argument, and becomes, as it were, an interpolation between the beginning and the main part of Confession" (*Sources*, p. 34).

87. Patterson writes that "the inclusion of these elements into one work not only is not unusual in penitential manuals but is virtually mandatory" and that "it would be hard to conceive of a more orderly development" ("*Parson's Tale*," p. 350).

88. *Boke*, lines 25934, 25935.

89. Ibid., lines 28068–28069.

90. Ibid., lines 28077–28079.

91. Ibid., line 28591.

92. In *Handlyng Synne*, the author informs the reader that the purpose of the book is "Synne to shewe, vs to frame, / God to wrshepe, þe fende to shame" (lines 5–6) and puts the Ten Commandments within the context of confession: "þe comuandementys of þe olde lawe / þyse ten were fyrst vs ȝeuyn And fyrst we welyn of hem be shreuyn" (lines 14–16). After detailing the Ten Commandments, the seven sins, the sin of sacrilege, and the sacraments, the author ends with the twelve points and twelve graces of confession.

93. Patterson, *Parson's Tale*, p. 350.

94. For Julian, see, for example, ch. 27 of the long text: *The Shewings of Julian of Norwich*, ed. Georgia Ronan Crampton (Kalamazoo, Mich.: Medieval Institute Publications, 1994).

LEE PATTERSON

"The Living Witnesses of Our Redemption": Martyrdom and Imitation in Chaucer's Prioress's Tale

The Jews are for us the living words of Scripture. They are dispersed all over the world so that by expiating their crime they may be everywhere the living witnesses of our redemption. . . . It is an act of Christian piety both to "vanquish the proud" and also "to spare the subjected," especially those from whom we have a law and a promise, and whose flesh was shared by Christ Whose name be forever blessed.

—St. Bernard of Clairvaux[1]

In late-fourteenth-century England, a Christian writer allows to be retold an antisemitic tale, one that first appeared in the twelfth century but whose immediate historical origins lie in events at the end of the eleventh century, and whose deep origins go back almost to the beginning of historical time, to the story of Abraham and Isaac. The reteller whom Chaucer chooses for this performance is a superior member of contemporary English female monasticism, but one who is unable to distinguish between present events and those, like the murder of little Hugh of Lincoln, which she thinks occurred only "a litel while ago" (686). The story of Hugh's "martyrdom," in fact, emerged almost 150 years earlier, in a mid-thirteenth-century England that still had a Jewish community.[2] Far from irrelevant, this historical layering is central to the meaning of the tale that is now retold. For the dynamic that controls the *Prioress's Tale* is created by a tension between two extremes.

Journal of Medieval and Early Modern Studies, Volume 31, Number 3 (2001): pp. 507–560.
© 2001 Duke University Press.

On the one hand is an absolutist desire for purity, on the other the obstinate historicity to which these temporal strata witness.

The terms in which this tension is expressed are complex, and the operation that controls their deployment is mimesis. I wish to expand this term beyond its formal Platonic and Aristotelian meanings to include a full range of imitative practices, including (but not limited to) ventriloquism, impersonation, reproduction, duplication, parody, and mimicry. While I shall begin by focusing on the *Prioress's Tale* and its fictive setting, my argument will expand to incorporate the relationship between the two great religious formations on which the tale is founded, Christianity and Judaism—a relationship, I shall argue, that Chaucer explores with his usual sophistication. How one might define sophistication in this context will be my final objective.

The *Prioress's Tale* and history

The *Prioress's Tale* is organized by a parallel between teller and protagonist. As the little clergeon learns the antiphon in honor of the Virgin "by rote" and uncomprehendingly reproduces it, so does the Prioress, adopting the persona of "a child of twelf month oold, or lesse" (484) rehearse the widely told story of the clergeon murdered by Jews for his devotion to the Virgin.[3] Indeed, the tale establishes the clergeon's song as a model of linguistic innocence, a privileged speech that the *Prioress* seeks to imitate. We can understand the dynamics of this imitation by examining a paradigmatic moment in the narrative, when Chaucer reminds us precisely who is telling this tale and what is her frame of reference. As the Prioress relates the murder of the boy and the casting of his body into the cloacal pit, she interrupts her tale with two *exclamationes*, one addressed to the Jews—"O cursed folk of Herodes al newe" (574)—and the other addressed to the clergeon himelf:

> O martir sowded to virginitee,
> Now maystow syngen, folwynge evere in oon
> The white Lamb celestial—quod she—
> Of which the grete evaungelist, Seint John,
> In Pathmos wroot, which seith that they that goon
> Biforn this Lamb, and synge a song al newe,
> That nevere flesshly wommen they ne knewe. (579–585)

The biblical passage to which the Prioress refers is Apocalypse 14:1–5, verses which served (and still serve) as the epistle reading for the Feast of the Holy Innocents:

> And I beheld, and lo a Lamb stood upon mount Sion, and with
> him an hundred forty-four thousand, having his name and the

name of his Father, written on their foreheads. . . . And they sung as it were a new canticle, before the throne, and before the four living creatures, and the ancients; and no man could say the canticle, but those hundred forty-four thousand, who were purchased from the earth. These are they who were not defiled with women: for they are virgins. These follow the Lamb whithersoever he goeth. These were purchased from among men, the firstfruits to God and to the Lamb. And in their mouth there was found no lie; for they are without spot before the throne of God.[4]

At the moment of violation and defilement, as the mutilated martyr lies in the pit "where as thise Jewes purgen hire entraille" (573), the Prioress breaks into her narrative—a break imitated by Chaucer with his own intrusive "quod she"—in order to imagine his transcendence. This is a transcendence constituted not merely by the clergeon's enrollment in the company of the Holy Innocents but by his song: no lie having been found in his mouth—a verbal purity coextensive with his sexual innocence—he is empowered to sing the *canticus novus* offered up to God. The next chapter of Apocalypse records the words of this *canticus Agni:*

> Great and wonderful are thy works, O Lord God Almighty; just and true are thy ways, O King of ages. Who shall not fear thee, O Lord, and magnify thy name *[magnificabit nomen tuum]*? For thou only art holy: for all nations shall come, and shall adore in thy sight, because thy judgments are manifest. (15:3–4)

As the Prioress makes clear by opening her prologue with a citation of these lines—"O Lord, oure Lord, thy name *[nomen tuum]* how merveillous / Is in this large world ysprad *[magnificabit]*" (453–454)—her tale is itself an effort at such a *canticus Agni*. It is a song both to and about the Lamb and—insofar as the Innocents are assimilated to their divine exemplar—by the lamb as well. Driven by this scriptural ideal, the entire tale adopts stylistic features that are evidently part of an effort to imitate a wholly innocent language. For one thing, the tale is ostentatiously exclamatory, including no less than twelve separate outbursts, (454–455, 467–468, 481, 554, 560, 574, 579, 607, 641, 645, 655, and 684). Rather than understand this apostrophic style as simply an effect of the teller's emotionalism, we should see it as being her attempt to imitate the original *exclamatio* that the tale celebrates, *O alma redemptoris!* Indeed, *exclamatio* is itself a stylistic feature characteristic of Marian poetry generally.[5] Second, as others have shown, the tale is filled with echoes of the liturgy, both the Little Office of the Virgin and the Mass of the Holy Innocents, citations by means of which the Prioress seeks to accommodate

her language to the hieratic norms of a liturgical discourse that is purged
of historical impurities and endowed instead with an institutional solidity
and transpersonal validity.[6] Indeed, the final action of the tale—the bearing of the clergeon into the abbey and his speech (649–669)—invokes the
liturgical processions and sermons associated with the Boy Bishop rituals
enacted by choristers. In these processions the choristers sang an antiphon
drawn from Apocalypse 14:3 and one of the four great Marian antiphons, a
group that included *O alma redemptoris.*[7] Especially popular in England, and
enacted with regularity in monastic houses and nunneries, the boy bishop
would recite the lesson "as if reading" *(quasi legendo)* and then deliver a sermon written for him by a literate member of the abbey.[8] The theme of innocent ventriloquism—of mimicking a cultural form without understanding
it—is thus present in one of the primary contexts from which the *Prioress's
Tale* arises. And in keeping with the parallelism that the Prioress establishes
between herself and her protagonist, like the *canticus Agni* the tale is itself
a celebration of both the "great and wonderful . . . works" accomplished by
God (through the Virgin) and an account of how the making "manifest" of
his "judgments" also redounds to his glory: "Mordre wol out, certeyn it wol
nat faille, / And namely"—in another allusion to the *canticus Agni*—"ther
th'onour of God shal *sprede*" (576–577).

Consistent with this purpose, then, the tale is directed toward an apoca-
lyptic ahistoricism by soliciting a typological or exegetical reading that would
appropriate the historical event it records into a timeless pattern of divine action.[9] In the Middle Ages, the Holy Innocents were traditionally understood
as types of Christ, who was himself in turn often represented in late medieval
religious writing and drama as a sacrificial child.[10] Thus the analogy implicit
throughout the tale between the widow and her son and the Virgin and Christ
becomes virtually explicit as he lies in the abbey "biforn the chief auter, whil
the masse laste" (636). The clergeon figures forth that other Child present
but not visible in the eucharistic wafer—a wafer that is then itself figured in
the "greyn" that lies upon his tongue.[11] In thus calling upon a Christological
pattern of sacrifice, the action of the Prioress's narrative seeks to abolish the
temporality that conditions and constrains the historical life—the life from
which, as a conventual, she has in fact sworn to absent herself.

It is because of such an abolition that the Prioress is able to refer to the
murder of Hugh of Lincoln in 1255 as having taken place "but a litel while
ago"(686)—a historical reference that has, as we shall see, depths of significance
to which she seems blind. At virtually every level the *Prioress's Tale* witnesses
to a drive toward the pure, the immaculate, and the unalloyed—toward, that is,
the ahistorical. The Marian chastity that it celebrates witnesses to this concern most explicitly, as does the radical polarization it establishes between
the redeemed and the unregenerate. In most of the analogues to this tale

found elsewhere, the miracle of the postmortem singing acts as an agency of conversion; and in the other tales of Christian sacrifice in the *Canterbury Tales*—those of the Man of Law, the Clerk, and the Second Nun—the conversion of unbelievers is the central purpose to which the protagonists' sufferings are put. But not here: with the Jews already exterminated, the clergeon rehearses his story not before those in need of conversion but before the Christian congregation gathered in the abbey to celebrate the Mass.[12] Moreover, the goal toward which his own life and death are directed is beyond the historical world. The grain in his mouth both enables the clergeon's singing and keeps him in the world, and in removing it the abbot both fulfills what is clearly the clergeon's wish and reveals the assumptions that underwrite the *Prioress's Tale* as a whole: the clergeon's earthly hymning—and his life—are quickly foregone in favor of the immortality he will be granted in heaven and the divine *canticus* that he will sing in the company of the Lamb. Moreover, the gesture with which the abbot responds to this final miracle reveals the goal toward which it urges its witnesses:

> And whan this abbot hadde this wonder seyn,
> His salte teeris trikled doun as reyn,
> And gruf he fil al plat upon the grounde,
> And stille he lay as he had ben ybounde. (673–676)

Pathos, to be sure, but also immobility, a deathlike trance that prefigures the death that will ultimately reunite him with the clergeon. As the Prioress herself then says, "Ther he is now, God leve us for to meete!" (683).

In triumphing over the cloacal filth into which he is plunged, the clergeon triumphs over a hyperbolic image not just of "foule usure and lucre of vileynye"(491) but of a world in which boys are beaten for learning an antiphon in honor of the Virgin and in which monks are not as holy as they "oghte be" (642)—over, in short, a historical world stubbornly resistant to redemption. Ironically, however, the very articulation of this transcendence is embedded (as the glancing allusion to the *Shipman's Tale* in this concern about misbehaving monks reminds us) within the very tale-telling game in which the Prioress is engaged.

Despite her efforts to escape into the absolutism of the eternal, the thematic links that Chaucer establishes between her tale and others in the Canterbury collection are a part of *his* effort to enforce a sense of historical contingency. With her glancing allusion to the *Shipman's Tale*, we can see that she means her tale to counter the amoral commercialism that he so unabashedly celebrates, just as her adoption of the socially and emotionally elevated rhyme royal form is an implicit reproach to his bourgeois values and vulgar punning.[13] More substantive intertextual commentaries on her tale are

offered by the Nun's Priest and the Second Nun. The critique offered by the
Nun's Priest is twofold.[14] First, in having Chauntecleer both tell and then
ignore the legend of St. Kenelm (3110–3121), whose history closely parallels
that of the clergeon, the Nun's Priest implies that the Prioress no more grasps
the effective lesson of her tale than does Chauntecleer his many proofs of the
reliability of dreams.[15] And second, the "greyn" that contains the pure spirit of
the *Prioress's Tale* is mocked both by the "corn" that Chauntecleer "chukketh
whan he hath . . . yfounde" (3182) and the Nun's Priest's disingenuous claim
that the reader of his wonderfully multivalent tale should simply "Taketh the
fruyt and lat the chaf be stille" (3443). There is, the Nun's Priest implies, no
simple transcendental significance, no absolute meaning, that can be recovered from any merely human narrative. Nor should we overlook the commentary offered by the Second Nun, who as the Prioress's chaplain is responsible
for seeing that her mistress upholds the dignity of her office.[16] Both the clergeon and St. Cecilia have their throats cut, but whereas the little boy sings
a song he cannot understand, Cecilia continues her work of instruction and
conversion; and whereas the Prioress declines to specify the historical setting
of her tale and presents a martyr's tale modelled on rumors of ritual murder
discredited by both ecclesiastical and civil authorities, the Second Nun tells a
historically localized tale of early Christian martyrdom whose authenticity is,
within Chaucerian culture, beyond question.[17] And most important, whereas
the Prioress aims at a pathos that many have found sentimental, the Second
Nun effaces the affective and the psychological in favor of an impassive tri-
umphalism and doctrinal pedagogy that transcends human suffering.[18]

The effect of Chaucer's contextualization of the *Prioress's Tale* within
the *Canterbury Tales* as a whole through these allusions is to draw our attention to aspects of the tale that are specific to the Prioress, both to her character and to her historical moment. The tale is suited with special aptness
to the historically specific teller described in the *General Prologue*. This is a
tale expressive through many of its details—its sentimental diminutives, its
concern with (and interest in) the suffering of the small and the helpless, its
simultaneous invocation of and disgust with uncleanness, and its display of
an affectivism incompletely subordinate to the discipline of Christian love—
of the personality of the woman who tells it. This is also true of the tale's
maternalism. The Prioress tells a story about the special closeness between a
boy and his mother, whether that mother be figured as the earthly "wydwe"
(509) or the heavenly "mayde Mooder" (467) who is the Virgin. Taught by
his mother to honor her heavenly exemplar, the clergeon is thus impelled by a
doubly motivated filial love. But it is a love that arouses the rage of the Jews,
for whom it violates their "lawes reverence"(564), and the boy is not just murdered but mutilated: as he himself says after his miraculous resurrection, "My
throte is kut unto my nekke boon" (649). This narrative has a shape that to the

post-Freudian reader is almost self-evidently Oedipal, with the Jews forced to play the role of the father who punishes with mutilation any transgression of the paternal law that forbids the reunification of mother and child in order to impel the boy into the world of singular identity and social difference that constitutes history.[19] In asserting the triumph of the maternal, the tale turns the harsh paternal law against itself: the Jews are executed according to their own "lawe" (hence the provost cites the Old Testament injunction, "Yvele shal have that yvele wol deserve" [632]), the provost and abbot join in the Marian celebration, and the clergeon is reunited with his heavenly Mother.

> My litel child, now wol I fecche thee,
> Whan that the greyn is fro thy tonge ytake.
> Be nat agast, I wol thee nat forsake. (667–669)

Indeed, so deeply controlling is this subtext that the reunification is accomplished by a physical act that once again invokes a paternally inflicted mutilation. The abbot "[the clergeon's] tonge out caughte and took awey the greyn" (671), a gesture whose oddly violent quality witnesses to the underlying psychological dynamic. Even more striking is the effect of this presumably beneficial act upon the abbot: "And still he lay *as he had ben ybounde*" (676), a phrase that recalls the provost's treatment of the Jews—"the Jewes leet he *bynde*" (620). In this world the father who invokes the punishment for maternal reunification is not only himself punished, but his act of vengeance echoes in the behavior of other paternal figures whose agency is supposed to be salvific.[20] This uneasy recapitulation undermines the Prioress's certainty that good and evil are absolutely separate and opposed, and it will acquire more significance when we turn to the tale's notorious antisemitism and explore its historical roots.

The Prioress's wished-for innocence, or unintentional naiveté, are further highlighted by the theme of childhood that runs throughout Fragment VII.[21] The "mayde child . . . yet under the yerde" (95–97) of the *Shipman's Tale* reappears in the *Prioress's Tale* as the "yong and tendre"(524) clergeon who fears he will be "beten thries in an houre" (542) for learning the antiphon. The *Tale of Sir Thopas* not only parodies what for Chaucer was a childishly unsophisticated genre—the tail-rhyme romance—but is itself about a child frightened by a bully with a slingshot. *Sir Thopas* is followed by the *Tale of Melibee*—itself a book of instruction for the young—with its wounded Sophie. The *Monk's Tale,* one of those tragedies that Boethius's Lady Philosophy locates among the "softe and delitable thynges" with which she nourishes her "nory" (*Boece* 1, pr. 3.13) until he is ready for stronger medicines, ends (in the Ellesmere order) with the tale of Ugolino and "his litel children thre" (2411). And the *Nun's Priest's Tale,* a story about a son who attempts to surpass his father, is an Aesopic fable like those often used in medieval schoolroom exercises. Of all these tales, however, the only one in which childishness is central conceptually and ideologically is the *Prioress's Tale*. By making the clergeon seven years old, the Prioress places him on the border between innocence and experience, on the way to maturation. But by then having him turn away from the "prymer" (517) he is learning at the reading school to the "antiphoner" (519) of the song school, she makes him deliberately regress. John Burrow argues that "the specification of the boy's age (not found in [all but one of] the analogues) puts him just on the borderline between *infantia*, the age of innocence, and its successor, *pueritia*" and that his interest in the antiphon sung by his "felawe"(525) signals "one of those critical moments of transition from one age to another, delicately rendered by Chaucer." But far from being a sign of maturation, the turn away from the primer to the antiphoner, from reading to song, is a turn from a reading school that leads to full participation in the adult world to a song school in which children were kept in a state of suspended animation, practicing a mindless ventriloquism until their voices broke and they were thrust out into a world for which they were wholly unprepared.[22] The Prioress has him choose, in short, a form of infant speechlessness in preference to the complex uncertainty of the world of maturation on the other side of language.

The childishness of the Prioress's way of telling her tale has often been remarked upon. In 1925 Sister Madeleva defined the tale, disturbingly if probably accurately, as the kind that "Sisters are telling to the smaller and even the grown children in Catholic boarding schools the world over today; they are the stories that the children clamor for again and again and never tire of hearing. . . . No child ever ventured in wide-eyed awe into a convent corridor but some motherly old Nun broke through the barrier of his shyness with a battery of just such stories."[23] Some fifty years later Alfred David cited Sister Madeleva's testimony in the course of his own persuasive description of the tale as "basically a fairy story that has been turned into hagiography, . . . a children's story told with a childlike fantasy."[24] Unlike Sister Madeleva, however, David also described the limitations of this childishness: "The piety is sincere but naive; the tenderness verges on sentimentality; and the morality of the tale is not religious but is a disguised form of the poetic justice of fairy tales."[25] And although he was too polite to say so, he would probably have agreed with the opinions of other, more judgmentally minded critics that the *Prioress's Tale* is "a case of arrested development" and that the Prioress herself is a woman who "has not put away childish things: her pets, her locket, her Stratford French."[26]

Childish innocence in the *Prioress's Tale* is imagined as absence, a void or blank unmarked by the historical life. Since the seven-year-old clergeon is still marginally within the category of infancy, he is theologically identical to the Holy Innocents, children two years old and less. And since for the Middle Ages infancy was by definition a condition of speechlessness, the clergeon shares with the Innocents the very inarticulateness that, paradoxically, enables them to express the glory of God's works.[27] As exegetes argued, and as was inscribed in the liturgy of the Feast of the Holy Innocents, the Innocents bore witness to God not by speaking but by dying—"non loquendo, sed moriendo confessi sunt."[28] The *canticus Agni* they sing before the Lamb is thus speech that proceeds not *from* but *through* them: they are vehicles for the transmission of a song that has a divine origin. And just as the martyred Innocents convey a message that is not their own, so the little clergeon chants an *Alma redemptoris* incomprehensible to him and, after his death, delivers a speech that is possible only because of the miraculous "greyn" placed upon his tongue by the Virgin.[29] The clergeon's glory, like that of the Virgin herself, proceeds from the fact that his purity makes him a fit receptacle for divinity: as she "ravyshedest doun fro the Deitee, / Thurgh [her] humblesse, the Ghost that in [her] alighte" (469–470), so does his innocence render him sufficiently void of earthly being to serve as a medium of transmission for a transcendent message. Hence the clergeon did not really sing the song but "it passed thurgh his throte" (548), just as he himself passed "thurgh the strete" of a Jewry that "was free and open at eyther ende" (493–494)—and just as Jesus passed through his Virgin Mother.

While the Prioress seeks to imitate this theologically conceived innocence, what she in fact expresses is merely the nostalgic *desire* for innocence with which the historical consciousness is burdened, a desire frustrated in the moment of its conception. On the one hand is the *tabula rasa* that constitutes innocence as instantiated in the idea of the child; on the other is the complexity of feeling that the no longer innocent woman brings to that idea. Chaucer articulates this opposition largely at the level of language: given the ideal form of speech implied by the clergeon's perfect (because uncomprehending) rehearsal of the *Alma redemptoris,* the Prioress's breathless sequence of exclamations is unintentionally parodic. And Chaucer's intrusive "quod she" (581)—the second of these intrusions, the other occuring in the second line of the prologue (454)—reminds us not only that it is the Prioress who speaks but, more tellingly, that it is Chaucer who speaks through the Prioress: the divine ventriloquism the clergeon effortlessly "parfourn[s]" is enacted here in a densely mediated form.[30]

But although the *Prioress's Tale* expresses the imagined needs of a specific—if imagined—teller, it nonetheless offers itself as self-evident, a narrative so simple and straightforward that it requires no interpretation. This self-evidence is symbolized in the tale by the "greyn" on the clergeon's tongue. The privileged member of the cortex/nucleus dialectic in terms of which the medieval hermeneutic was typically defined, the "greyn" repre-

processions, lending it a visibly dramatic character, and dramas on this theme were a persistent feature of the Christmas celebrations in both monasteries and, especially, nunneries. Among the accounts of St. Swithun's monastery at Winchester for 1441 there is a payment "for the boys of the Almonry together with the boys of the chapel of St. Elizabeth, . . . dancing, singing and performing plays before the Abbess and nuns of St. Mary's Abbey in their hall on the Feast of the Innocents"—a practice that continued in nunneries until the dissolution.[43] This element of the tale makes relevant the detail in the *General Prologue* that the Prioress is admired for the "seemliness" of her singing of the Divine Office. In a larger sense the Prioress is what we might call a "liturgical personality."[44] Just as she takes pains "to countrefete cheere / Of court" (139–140), so she expresses herself through the elaborate forms of her tale. Both *General Prologue* and *Prioress's Tale* display a dialectic between emotion and expression, between desire and its forms of enactment. Just as the portrait of the Prioress in the *General Prologue* shows two models of social identity—pious nun and aristocratic lady—that seek to express the appetitive self, so in the tale we see two models of generic control—liturgical performance and miracle story—that seek to restrain narrative desire within conventional (and conventual) bounds.[45]

If it is an error to think of the Marianism expressed by the miracle stories as deeply pious, it is an even larger mistake to read it as by definition antisemitic. Contrary to a widespread assumption, antisemitism is not in fact central either to the genre of the Marian miracle nor to Marianism generally.[46] It is certainly true that the status of the Virgin was one of the points of dispute in the polemic between Jews and Christians throughout the Middle Ages.[47] It is also probably true that, at some level, some Christians drew a contrast between the purity of the Virgin (especially as a symbol of the Church) and a totalized Christendom that was tainted by the mere presence of Jews in its midst.[48] But the vast majority of Marian miracles were not antisemitic.[49] Of Adgar's 49 miracles, 3 are antisemitic. Of Gautier's 59 miracles, 6 feature Jews and of these only 4 could be described as antisemitic.[50] Although a number of the exempla collected by Caesarius of Heisterbach are antisemitic, none of the 58 Marian miracles in Book VII of the *Dialogus miraculorum* are. The Marian *cántigueiros* ascribed to Alfonso X of Spain touch on the typical antisemitic themes, yet of the 427 songs only 30 (or about 7 percent) fall into this classification.[51] Of the 187 Middle English miracles, only 7 are antisemitic: Peter Whiteford is thus right to point out that antisemitic miracles are even less common in England than on the Continent.[52]

Yet the antisemitism of the *Prioress's Tale* is both blatant and surprisingly extensive. The tale contains virtually every slander against the Jews circulated by medieval Christians. "Hateful to Christ and to his compaignye" (492), the Jews are repeatedly described as "cursed" (574, 578, 599, 631, 685), an allusion to Matthew 27:24 where they tell Pilate that they accept responsibility for killing Jesus: "His blood be on us, and on our children." Their slaughter of the little clergeon is presented as a reenactment of this initial crime, and thus invokes the blood libel—a specifically English contribution to the bill of indictment—that the Prioress alludes to in her final invocation of "yonge Hugh of Lyncoln, slayn also / With cursed Jewes" (684–685). When the Prioress says that "Mordre wol out, . . . The blood out crieth on youre cursed dede" (576–578), she alludes to the murder of Abel (a type of Christ) by Cain (the Wandering Jew) as described in Genesis 4:10–14. Jews are inspired by a Satan who "hath in Jues herte his waspes nest" (558), one of the most prominent elements of late medieval antisemitic propaganda.[53] And they are economic criminals, practicing "foul usure and lucre of vileynye" (491), a phrase that incorporates both moneylending and price-gouging.[54] The Prioress even includes in her defamation the unbiblical assertion that the Jews are "cursed folk of Herodes" (574), aligning herself with the popular belief that the Holy Innocents were the Christian victims of a Jewish tyrant, whereas—as is made clear in both learned treatises and vernacular works like the mystery plays—they were actually the Jewish victims of a Gentile ruler.[55] Given this accumulation of insult, Philip Alexander has reason to designate the *Prioress's Tale* "an antisemitic tract . . . , [perhaps] the best antisemitic tract ever written."[56]

Was Chaucer, then, an antisemite? The governing protocol of the *Canterbury Tales*—the invention of fictional tellers for every tale—makes such a hypothesis seem as improbable as saying that Chaucer is the Reeve, or the Clerk, or the Pardoner. Rather, by giving the Prioress one of the two most popular antisemitic Marian miracle tales,[57] and adding to it gratuitous anti-Jewish calumny, Chaucer forces the reader to accommodate the Prioress's antisemitism to the tale's total meaning. The central dynamic of the Prioress's performance is mimesis—whether understood as a spiritually superficial liturgical formalism or as a verbal ventriloquism that subsumes guilty teller within innocent protagonist—and it serves, as I have argued, to protect the Prioress from painful historical knowledge and even more painful self-knowledge. Yet the tale's antisemitism raises a more profound issue. Any act of mimesis, of imitation or reproduction, asks the question of priority: which is the copy, which the original? Does the Prioress imitate the clergeon (as a preexisting reality), or is the clergeon simply an imitation of the (preexisting) Prioress's idea of childhood? Is the *Prioress's Tale* an imitation of authentic liturgical acts, or is not all ritual by definition an act of mimicry of older, unsanctioned behaviors? However familiar to contemporary criticism, these questions are not foreign to Chaucer, whose explorations of written culture as an echo chamber in the *House of Fame* and *Troilus and Criseyde* are well known.[58] But when placed in the context of religious difference they stand at the very heart of medieval culture, raising a series of profound questions—precisely the questions the Prioress wants to avoid. To what extent is the "new" religion of Christianity an imitation of its rejected "old" form, Judaism? Has Christianity in fact superseded, even annulled its predecessor, or has it become simply another version of a Judaically defined monotheism? And has Judaism retained its original identity, or has it not undergone a process of "inward acculturation" to Christianity through the absorption of elements derived from its now dominant offspring?[59] From its first appearance in the twelfth century until her retelling or reproduction of it in the fourteenth, the *Prioress's Tale* of the little clergeon is deeply implicated in these questions. It is thus to the origins and history of this story that we now turn.

Jewish martyrdom: Its sources and effects

The origins of the *Prioress's Tale*, and of many of the topoi of antisemitism, emerge from the events surrounding the First Crusade of 1096. As some of the crusaders moved down the Rhine toward the east, they redirected their fervor toward the nearest non-Christians, the recently settled communities of Ashkenazic Jews.[60] The massacres that resulted are described in vivid detail in Hebrew chronicles compiled in the twelfth century. The precise degree of historical accuracy of these chronicles is still a matter of debate, but the central facts—recorded also in Christian sources—are not in dispute.[61] In the face of these attacks, the Jews of the Rhineland reacted not passively but with armed resistance and—most important—with an activist martyrdom. Over and over the Hebrew chronicles tell of Jews who committed ritual suicide rather than accept forced conversion. Here is one of the most vivid and symbolically important instances, from the anonymous *Chronicle* inaccurately attributed to Solomon bar Simson:[62]

> Who has seen or heard of an act like the deed of the righteous and pious young Mistress Rachel, daughter of Isaac, son of Asher, and wife of Judah? She said to her friends: "Four children have I. Have no mercy on them either, lest the uncircumcised ones come and seize them alive and raise them in the ways of error. In my children, too, shall you sanctify the Holy Name of God." One of her friends came and took the knife to slaughter her son. When the "mother of the sons" saw the knife, she cried loudly and bitterly and smote her face and breast, and said: "Where is Your grace, O Lord?" With an embittered heart she said to her companions: "Do not slaughter Isaac before his brother Aaron, so that he will not see the death of his brother and flee." A friend took the boy and slew him. A delightful little child he was. The mother spread her sleeves to receive the blood, according to the practice in the ancient Temple

sacrificial rite. The lad Aaron, upon seeing that his brother had been slaughtered, cried: "Mother, do not slaughter me," and fled, hiding under a box. She had also two daughters, Bella and Madrona, modest and beautiful maidens. The maidens took the knife and sharpened it, so that it would have no notch. They extended their throats, and the mother sacrificed them to the Lord, God of Hosts, Who commanded us not to depart from His pure doctrine, and to remain wholehearted with Him.[63]

This harrowing scene—and the chronicles record many like it—expresses the values central to the martyrdoms of 1096, values invoked over and over in the various accounts. To begin with, it alludes, both through Rachel's own name and through that of her eldest son Isaac, to exemplary models of Jewish suffering and, especially, of obedience to God to the point of the sacrifice of the beloved son. Despite a deep resistance in halachic law to suicide—a resistance expressed by the denial that the mass suicide at Masada was an acceptable model for Jewish response to persecution[64]—the Jews of 1096 invoked scriptural instances where martyrdom was preferred to apostasy. These included the three Hebrews thrown into the furnace by Nebuchadnezzar in Daniel 3:1–30, and the deaths of Eleazar the scribe and of the seven sons ordered by Antiochus, martyrs whose fortitude under torture is recorded in excruciating detail in 2 Maccabees 6:21–7:42 and in 4 Maccabees 8:3–17:1. These last two are especially important passages, for they invoke not only the Hebrews of the Book of Daniel but also the binding or *'akedah* of Isaac, and focus on the religious zeal of the mother in encouraging her sons to choose their terrible deaths before enduring a similar fate herself.[65] Indeed, so powerful are these passages from Maccabees that they served the church fathers as a paradigm for Christian martyrdom, one of the earliest of the many transactions between the two religions that endows this material with a weight that is at once traumatic and ironic.[66]

Second, the chronicle passage makes it clear that these acts of slaughter are to be located within the context of the temple cult. The mother here catches the blood in her sleeves, and the knife is carefully checked—both here and throughout the other chronicle accounts—to be certain that it is, as Jewish law prescribes, without imperfection *(pegimah)*. Even when time does not permit, the martyrs choose to die in a way that defines their slaughter as a sacrifice: when the two sons of a holy man named Moses are attacked by the crusaders, "they extended their throats, and the enemy smote them" (37). And these acts of clearly ritual slaughter *(shehitah)* are throughout accompanied by the chanting of prayers. On one occasion, the martyrs "wholeheartedly affirmed the Oneness of God, . . . crying out with one mouth and one heart: 'Hear, O Israel, the Lord is our God, the Lord is One'" (34); on another, a father said to his son, "Yehiel, my son, my son, stretch out your neck before your father and I will offer you as a sacrifice to God. I will recite the benediction of Ritual Slaughter and you will respond, 'Amen'" (52).

Finally, and most important, invoked throughout the chronicles is the binding or 'akedah of Isaac. Central to the Judaic sense of obedience to the divine will, the 'akedah is used here, however, to assert the legitimacy not only of self-sacrifice but of the sacrifice of one's own children.[67] Indeed, there survives from this period a moving elegy by Rabbi Ephraim ben Jacob of Bonn in which the story of Isaac is radically revised: in Ephraim's poem, Abraham *does* sacrifice his son, who is then taken to the garden of Eden and later resurrected.[68] As Shalom Spiegel has brilliantly shown in discussing this poem and its background, the medieval idea of Jewish martyrdom now shows the impact of Christian paradigms upon this most rigorous of Jewish religious practices. This impact is also seen in the way that the self-sacrifice of the righteous, and especially the sacrifice of children, is presented in the Hebrew chronicles as a blood atonement—an idea that is marginal to traditional Jewish thought but central to Christianity.[69] Indeed, as Robert Chazan has argued, throughout these accounts we can see the impress not only of Jewish tradition but also of *contemporary* Christian culture:

> In many senses, Jewish behavior during the limited but violent persecutions of 1096 constituted a "counter-crusade," a militant Jewish response to the aggression of Christendom. Like their Christian neighbors, the Jews felt themselves caught up in a struggle of cosmic proportions; like their neighbors they were eager to make the profoundest sacrifice possible, in some instances expanding the dictates of Jewish law and exceeding the precedents of the past; like their neighbors they were certain of eternal celestial reward for their heroism. In other words, the Jews show much of the same religious frenzy that swept European society at the end of the eleventh century. When, in certain limited quarters, this general frenzy degenerated into anti-Jewish violence, the Jews under attack responded with much the same militance and readiness for self-sacrifice out of which the crusading movement had been spawned.[70]

In part because of this interaction between Christian and Ashkenazic cultures,[71] these ritual acts become a new way to fulfill the ultimate Jewish ethical commandment, the *kiddush ha-Shem* or sanctification of the Holy Name.[72]

As I have already mentioned, central to the *kiddush ha-Shem* of martyrdom is the idea—an effect of the "inward acculturation" by Jews of Christian values— that the death of the righteous is an act of atonement. But to understand the complexity of these cultural interactions we must explore this idea in more detail. There are certainly Jewish precedents for the notion that the suffering of the righteous provides atonement for the sins of Israel, in the 'akedah of Isaac, in the songs of the "suffering servant" in Isaiah 42:1–4, 49:1–6, 50:4–9, and (especially) 52:13–53:12, and in 4 Maccabees 17:21–22:

> The tyrant was punished and the homeland purified—they having become, as it were, a ransom for the sin of our nation. And through the blood of those devout ones and their death as an expiation, divine Providence preserved Israel that previously had been afflicted.[73]

But as Jon Levenson has argued, whereas early Judaism promoted the notion that the death of *every* righteous Jew atones for the sins of others, Paul revised this to a claim that was at once exclusivist and universalist. For Paul, this atonement was accomplished for all people by Jesus, but only by Jesus: Jesus is the suffering servant, not all of Israel. For Paul, in Galatians 3:14, "the blessing of Abraham might be extended to the Gentiles through Christ Jesus" but not through participation in the history and sufferings of Israel the nation, the chosen people. "Paul's Jesus does not *manifest* Isaac, He *supersedes* him," as Levenson says.[74] For Paul, the gentiles are now the children of Abraham rather than the Jews; but in order to partake of this universalism, one must leave the rejected—the people of the Torah, for whom Isaac is an exemplar—and join the chosen, the people of Christ, for whom Isaac is a prefiguration that has now been fulfilled.

Yet the 'akedah of the kiddush ha-Shem of 1096 undoes this process. Despite its precedents in Jewish tradition, it was understood by the medieval Jewish community as the entrance into Jewish culture of a new mode of religious experience. Now martyrdom was not merely passively accepted but actively sought, and this activist mode meant, in the words of Chazan, that "a radical new form of kiddush ha-Shem was introduced into Jewish history."[75] According to George Stow, "An articulated ideology equating martyrdom with the sacrifice of the Temple ritual developed only in 1096. . . . Israel had truly become the holy people, a nation of priests, itself the agnus Dei, as if in open competition with the Christian claim that Christ alone was the perfect sacrifice."[76] In one of the many moving, indeed heart-breaking elegies composed to commemorate the massacres, David bar Meshullam of Speyer presents the martyrdom as surpassing the 'akedah of Isaac and moving the history of Jewish obedience to God into a new dimension:

> [Has the like of this] ever been seen or heard? Could anyone believe such a stupefying sight? They lead their children to the slaughter as if to a beautiful bridal canopy. After this, O Exalted and Triumphant Lord, will You hold back?

> Once, long ago, we could rely upon the merit of Abraham's
> sacrifice at Mount Moriah, that it would safeguard us and bring
> salvation age after age. But now one sacrifice follows another, they
> can no longer be counted. O Living God, may the merit of their
> righteousness protect us and call a halt to our miseries![77]

In an almost explicit imitation of the blood atonement that lay at the heart
of Christianity, Jewish martyrs now became the righteous or the elect who
took upon themselves atonement for the sins of Israel. As Gershon Cohen
has explained,

> Martyrdom was not mere sanctification of the Name through faith;
> it was an atonement sacrifice, an *aqedah*.[78]

In a further imitation of the Christian idea of the Treasury of Grace, the righteous martyrs died not for their sins—on the contrary, they were the spiritual
elite—but "to create a fund of good will for coming generations."[79] To sum up,
in the words of Ivan Marcus, the *kiddush ha-Shem* of 1096 is an

> acted-out polemical riposte to Christian claims that Jesus's death
> was an atoning sacrifice. It also counters the ancient Christian
> assertion, found in the Epistle to the Hebrews, that Jesus
> represented a substitute for the Jerusalem Temple. The 1096
> acts of ritual sacrifice and suicide express a medieval Ashkenazic
> mentality that resonates with ancient Jewish ascetic and Temple
> metaphors and an awareness of living in a contemporary Christian
> culture that was derived in part from the same reservoir of ancient
> Jewish lore.[80]

The term *polemical riposte* is brilliantly apropos. Both Jews and Christians
were aware of the fact that the violence that bound the communities to each
other served as a terrible way of creating saintly martyrs for each, a process
that intensified the demonization of the other group.[81]

Perhaps most important, this form of activist, ritualistic martyrdom became a model, enacted throughout the Middle Ages, for Jewish resistance
to persecution.[82] In 1171 an accusation of ritual murder—the crucifixion by
the Jews of a Christian boy—was the pretext for the burning of the Jewish
community by Theobald, count of Blois. In the account of the episode given
by the Jewish chroniclers of Orléans (an account to be discussed in detail in
a moment), it is clear that while the forms of ritual suicide that marked the
massacre of 1096 were not observed, the willingness of the Jews to acccept
their fiery death is understood as an act of martyrdom:

From the time He gave over His people to destruction and set fire to our Temple, holy ones such as these have not been offered up as a sacrifice. These angels of the Lord went up in flame—thirty-one angels, *serafim,* who stand by the Lord. When the oppressor ordered them taken out and burned, his men said: "Let us call them and ask them. Perhaps they will abandon their god." The Jews answered unanimously: "No. We shall cling to our God, the God of Israel. Him we shall fear with all our hearts and all our souls." The Jews were taken out and the Gentiles watched them closely, perhaps one of them might waver. But the Jews said to one another: "Shall we tremble over this fire? Is not this the day for which we were chosen?" Then they said as they went forth: "Take care, lest your heart be seduced. Strengthen yourselves and let us be firm in the fear of our Creator so that our death may serve as atonement for all our sins." Indeed these are the sufferings of the community through which all Israel achieves atonement. For those burned for the sake of the Lord bring offerings for their God and become sanctified. God inhaled this sacred incense on the fourth day of the week, on the twentieth of the month of Sivan in the year 4931 [26 May 1171]. It is fitting that this day be established as a fast day for all our people. . . . it is a veritable Day of Atonement.[83]

Here, as in other incidents, the martyrs are seen as a burnt sacrifice, a holocaust offered to the Lord.[84]

In 1189, in a riot occasioned by the coronation of the crusading king Richard I, approximately thirty Jews were killed, with others taking their lives to avoid baptism. By the time Richard had left on crusade the next year, anti-Jewish riots had flared up at Lynn, Norwich, Stamford, Lincoln, Colchester, Thetford, Ospringe, and—most terribly—at York.[85] There the Jews barricaded in the castle both enacted the *kiddush ha-Shem* in its fully ritualized form at the instigation of Rabbi Yomtob of Joigny (who like many Jews had only recently arrived in England to escape the violence on the Continent) or accepted their role as a burnt offering.[86] According to Ephraim of Bonn, who recorded the event in his Hebrew chronicle,

All fled to the house of prayer. Here Rabbi Yom-Tob stood and slaughtered sixty souls, and others also slaughtered. Some there were who commanded that they should slaughter their only sons, whose foot could not tread upon the ground from their delicacy and tender breeding. Some, moreover, were burned for the Unity of their Creator [i.e., as a Sanctification of the Holy Name].[87]

Precisely these models of Jewish martyrdom—most often the ritual slitting of the throat of the victim in the manner of the temple sacrifice, but also self-immolation—are recorded throughout the Middle Ages. Poliakov provides an account from a Christian chronicler of the ritual suicide of a group of Jews at Verdun in 1320 when faced with a group of Pastoureaux, those engaged in the so-called Crusade of the Shepherds:

> The shepherds laid siege to all the Jews who had come from all sides to take refuge in whatever strongholds the kingdom of France afforded, fearful at seeing the approach of the mob. At Verdun-sur-Garonne, the Jews defended themselves heroically and in a superhuman manner against their besiegers by hurling many stones, beams, and even their own children from the top of a tower. But their resistance served to no purpose, for the shepherds slaughtered a great number of the besieged Jews by smoke and by fire, burning the doors of the stronghold. The Jews, realizing that they would not escape alive, preferred to kill themselves rather than be massacred by the uncircumcised. They then chose one of their number, who seemed the strongest, so that he might kill them. This man put some five hundred of them to death, with their consent. He then descended from the castle tower with the few Jewish children who still remained alive. He sought a parley with the shepherds and told them what he had done, asking to be baptized with the children who remained. The shepherds answered him: "Have you then committed such a crime upon your own race, and thereby seek to escape among us the death you deserve?" They killed him by quartering.[88]

Notice how quickly an act of heroic Jewish piety becomes interpreted by Christians as one of unfeeling savagery—a response that, as we shall soon see in detail, allowed Christians to justify their own cruelty by projecting it onto their victims.

In sum, the *kiddush ha-Shem* became a crucial means by which Jews throughout Europe, including England prior to the expulsions of 1290, countered the Christian debasement and rejection of their religious identity: they displayed a heroic martyrdom more uncompromising than anything in contemporary Christianity itself. As Robert Chazan has said, "The sacrifice of Jesus and its emulation by his followers throughout the ages is replaced in these Jewish narratives [of the *kiddush ha-Shem*] by the Temple ritual and its reenactment by present-day Jews. The dignity of Jewish past and present serves as guarantee for a brilliant Jewish future."[89] By not just reenacting their own traditional sacrificial practices but reenacting them in a form that was unmistakably imitative of Christian traditions, the Jews of medieval Europe not only revealed the "inward acculturation" to which minorities are so often subject but asserted the intensity of their piety in terms that Christians could not ignore.

Christians (mis)reading Jews

Not surprisingly, the response of Christians to these acts of Jewish religious martyrdom were mixed. One of the most explicit examples of Christian ambivalence is the account by William of Newburgh in his *Historia rerum Anglicarum* of the massacre that took place at York in 1190.[90] William is uncompromising in his condemnation of the disgraceful behavior of the Christians: while they claimed a religious motive for their behavior they were actually motivated by "the desire of plunder" and a frightening blood lust. This is a common reaction among clerical writers. According to Jonathan Riley-Smith, who knows the Latin sources well, "most educated churchmen found the events [in the Rhineland] abhorrent," and William was equally appalled by what took place at York.[91] Indeed, he carefully explains the official theological defense of the Jews in quoting Psalm 59:11: "Slay them not, lest my people forget." They are allowed to live among Christians, albeit in servitude, in order "to perpetuate the highly beneficial remembrance of the passion of the Lord amongst all the faithful." Yet he also insists that the Jews of York displayed an offensive opulence and that they were—and remain—a perfidious people. In trying to explain the *kiddush ha-Shem* that the Jews of York enact, he is able to recognize that they are motivated by religious zeal by having Rabbi Yomtob urge suicide as an alternative to apostasy. Not surprisingly, however, he is unable to grasp the full implications of ritual suicide, and the speech he gives to the rabbi derives in large part from the Latin translation of Josephus's account of the famous speech of Eleazar that led to the mass suicide at Masada—a speech that justifies suicide in terms that are pragmatic and stoic but on no account religious.[92] Indeed, in the medieval Hebrew translation of Josephus, Eleazar's speech led not to the suicide of the defenders but to a heroic if futile charge against the beseiging Romans.[93]

Nor is this Christian ambivalence confined to England. Mary Minty has shown that Christian chroniclers in the Rhineland understood Jewish ritual suicide as "provoked by an understandable response to Christian brutality," and that when Jews were faced with forced baptism the ritual slaughter of oneself and even of one's own children was seen as an act of heroic piety.[94] Moreover, the *kiddush ha-Shem* influenced the Franciscan debate over the forced conversion of Jewish children, and while it hardened some in their antisemitism, it led others to question whether forced conversion was really an act of spiritual beneficence. On the other side, however, Minty also shows that the knowledge that Jews would kill their own children fed antisemitic stereotypes, and emerged in exempla and especially in the representation of the Massacre of the Innocents in painting and drama—an event, we remember, whose liturgical expression is central to the *Prioress's Tale*—as an act perpetrated by Jews upon Christians. This is the same prejudicial misreading that the Prioress herself perpetuates.[95] Thus the *kiddush ha-Shem* was used to reinforce the stereotype of the cruel Jew who killed children. Indeed, although the supposition is beyond proof, it may well be that the charge of ritual murder—which first arose in England in the late 1140s and early 1150s in relation to William of Norwich—was a response to the massacres and the attendant acts of the ritual slaughter of Jewish children by their parents during the Second Crusade of 1146.[96]

What is especially cruel about these antisemitic slanders is that the Hebrew chronicles and, especially, the elegies that record these events, express the most profound grief at the death of the very children whom Christians saw Jews as murdering with cruel pleasure. In an anonymous poem about the massacre at Mainz in 1096, for instance, the poet laments:

> Oh, how the children cried aloud! Trembling, they see their brothers slaughtered; the mother binding her son, lest he profane the sacrifice by shuddering; the father making the ritual blessing to sanctify the slaughter.

> Compassionate women strangle their own children; pure virgins shriek bitterly; brides kiss their bridegrooms farewell—and all rush eagerly to be slaughtered.

> Almighty Lord, dwelling on high, in days of old the angels cried out to You to put a halt to one sacrificed. And now, so many are bound and slaughtered—why do they not clamor over my infants?[97]

And an elegy written by Rabbi Joseph of Chartres for the martyrs of York—an elegy that became part of the liturgy—focuses especially on the children as new Isaacs sacrificed by their Abrahamic fathers:

> In place of their herds they offered up their children, and they slaughtered their first-strength before their eyes.

> Those holy ones did not hold back their only children from Thee; for their father's manner they too maintained.[98]

There is much evidence that medieval Jews took special care of and pleasure in their children—far more so, perhaps, than Christians, for whom children were special objects of pity only when they could function as martyred victims.[99] Yet it was, paradoxically, just this care that led parents to slaughter their adored offspring in order to protect them from the forced baptism that would be their fate if they fell into Christian hands. Nor was this an irrational fear: there is evidence that some Christians kidnapped Jewish children from their parents in order to force conversion upon them, and Jewish children who survived the massacres of 1096 were baptized and raised as Christians.[100] It was no accident that so much of the fear that divided the Christian and Jewish communities focused on the innocent child.

As well as the chroniclers and popular representations of the Slaughter of the Innocents, there is another kind of evidence—again, especially relevant to the *Prioress's Tale*—of the Christian reaction to the Jewish *kiddush ha-Shem*. This is the religious drama. One especially provocative instance is found in the collection of plays known as the Fleury *Playbook,* most likely composed at either Blois or (more probably) Orléans in the early 1170s.[101] This is the play known as *St. Nicholas and the Jew* or *The Icon of St. Nicholas.* The story goes back to the earliest legends of the saint. A rich non-Christian entrusts his otherwise unprotected wealth to a small statue of St. Nicholas. But the wealth is then stolen by three thieves, and when the man returns home he upbraids the image for betraying him. St. Nicholas himself then appears to the thieves and threatens them into returning the wealth, whereupon the victim not only returns to his former adoration of St. Nicholas but now accepts Christianity and is baptized. Prior to the composition of the Fleury play, a dramatic version of this story was composed by Abelard's student Hilarius, and a slightly different version was also included in the vernacular verse legend by Wace, composed about 1150. Later, about 1200, it was used by Jean Bodel as the basis of his famous *Jeu de Saint Nicolas.* In all three of these accounts, the non-Christian is represented as a pagan—Hilarius calls him a *barbarus,* for Wace he is simply a *paiens,* and for Bodel he is a *rois paiiens.*[102] But in the Fleury play, and only in the Fleury play, he is a Jew. Moreoever, in the Fleury play the bereft Jew is granted an extended lament when he discovers he has been robbed.

> Alas! I'm dead! Nothing is left me! Why was I born? Why, mother, why cruel father, did you bring me into the world? Alas! What did it profit me to be born or even begotten? Why, mother nature, did you decide that I should exist, you who foresaw my grief and my sorrow? What crime should I complain about that brought me to such ruin? I who was just now wealthy, and hardly lacked anything, loaded with money, expensive clothes, gold, now I am wretched and am loaded with poverty. Used to comfort, I now don't know how to enjoy myself in the future; I would bear poverty more lightly if I had learned to bear it before. Now nothing remains of what

formerly I used to enjoy. But, not to fool myself, I did not use my head at all, so that I worshipped daily the name of Nicholas. How could I expect not to be hurt? The religion of the Christians has damaged me. So this religion shows that you, Nicholas, are indeed powerful, although not to my benefit. That gives me a reason for sadness and weeping. Nor will I cry alone and I will not, I think, lament unavenged. You will be subjected to deserved disgrace, be cut with whips. But I am tired, and for the space of a night I'll let you off. But unless by morning you restore the things that I entrusted to you, first I'll whip you, and after the whipping I'll burn you![103]

Before explicating this remarkable passage, we need to understand the historical context from which it emerges. As previously mentioned, in May 1171, for a set of complex and disgraceful reasons, Theobald, count of Blois, supported an accusation of ritual murder brought against the Jews of Blois. In the ensuing massacre, thirty-one Jews were burned. The Jewish community of Orléans took upon themselves the responsibility of recording this event and disseminating an account of it to other Ashkenazic communities. I have already cited part of their full and painful report, but must here quote another portion:

[The victims] were struck and wounded. But the more the enemy tortured them, with wounds and blows, the more these Jews strengthened and steeled their hearts to love the Lord and to remain His sacred ones. Thus they were faithful to the Lord. . . . As the day grew warm, in the morning, the fire was lit. As the flames rose, the Jews sang together; they lifted their voices sweetly. Indeed the Christians came and told us of this, asking: "What is your song that is so sweet? We have never heard such sweetness." For at first the sound was low. But at the end they raised their voices mightily, singing *Aleynu le-shabeah;* at that point the fire blazed forth. . . . Our townsmen and acquaintances, who were present, told us all these things.[104]

It should be added that there were continual complaints in ecclesiastical legislation about the loud chanting of Jews in synagogues and in funeral processions, and praying—i.e., chanting—while being immolated is virtually universal among the Hebrew accounts of these kinds of massacres.[105]

Now let us return to the lament of the Jew in the Fleury *St. Nicholas and the Jew.* To begin with, musicologists have been distressed by what they see as the ineptitude of the music of this lament. They complain of the "turgidity of pitches" and the lack of "order and balance": "on the whole," concludes one, "the music just drifts."[106] What they have failed to notice, however, although it was pointed out almost forty years ago by the Dutch musicologist Hélène Wagenaar-Nolthenius, is that this music is an attempt by a Christian composer to imitate the Hebrew hymn sung by the burning Jews.[107] This hymn is specifically the *Aleynuor Oleynu,* a prayer of adoration—a kind of verbal Sanctification of the Holy Name—that also includes the plea that God "wilt remove the abominations from the earth and heathendom will be utterly destroyed, [and] the world will be perfected under the kingdom of the Almighty." Ironically, these words—based on Isaiah 30:7 and 45:20—were wilfully misread by antisemites as an attack on Christianity.[108]

Knowing this, we can now begin to understand some of the ironies of the Jew's lament. For instance, the cry, "What crime should I complain about that brought me to such ruin?" can be seen as self-critical: "What did I do to deserve this?"—a question that is then answered later in the lament with his admission that he was foolish to trust in St. Nicholas, even more foolish to impeach his commitment to Judaism. Yet this cry is also directed against the unknown Christian thieves who have robbed him. Again, when he says, "How could I expect not to be hurt? The religion of the Christians has damaged me," he is being at once self-accusatory while also asserting that he is being hurt not just by Christians but by Christians driven on by their faith. And in the subsequent lines—"So this religion shows that you, Nicholas, are indeed powerful, although not to my benefit. That gives me a reason for sadness and weeping"—he sees St. Nicholas as behaving like a typical Christian, repaying a Jew's dutiful homage by then supporting the Christians who rob him. And in the final stanza of the lament, the author has given to the Jew a desire for vengeance that echoes with eerie specificity the cruelty that was inflicted at Blois by Christians, but inflicted not upon a mere statue or an image, as the Jew here threatens, but upon the living bodies of the Jews themselves:

> Nor will I cry alone and I will not, I think, lament unavenged. You will be subjected to deserved disgrace, be cut with whips; . . . first I'll whip you, and after the whipping I'll burn you!

The speech as a whole is by no means entirely philo-Judaic: we are not allowed to forget that the Jew is not only rich but that he has never known poverty. But this is nonetheless a powerful lament by and for the unjust suffering that Jews endured at the hands of Christians, and sung to the melody of the hymn chanted by the burning martyrs of Blois. Finally, at the end of the play, after St. Nicholas has restored his wealth to the Jew, the Jew acknowledges Nicholas's power but declines (unlike the pagans in the versions of Hilarius, Wace, and Jean Bodel) to convert: he remains a Jew, yet one who is now secure in his confidence in Nicholas's protection. What we have, in other words, is an almost utopian moment of religious harmony between the old religion and its newer offspring. The new represents the future, to be sure, but a future that—at least here, and at least for a moment—is careful to preserve rather than annihilate its past.

The effect on the Christian community of these and other massacres is also present in a sadly less complex form in the four surviving liturgical plays about the Holy Innocents, all four deriving from locations of which there is evidence of anti-Jewish violence in 1096 or contained Jewish communities vulnerable to the crusaders: Blois, Laon, Limoges, and Freising.[109] In each of these plays occurs a telling detail: the boys are not merely slaughtered by a monster "whom neither pity nor your age restrained" [quem nec pietas nec vestra coercuit aetas] (112) but are killed by a specific wound: they have their throats cut—they are *jugulati*.[110] Moreover, in all four of these plays the emphasis is less upon the martyred boys than the grieving mother, who throughout is named Rachel. So pronounced is this emphasis that Karl Young gave to all four plays the title found only in the Freising version, *Ordo Rachelis*.[111] Moreover, Rachel is presented as a specifically *Jewish* mother: her weeping is the "grief of a nation" for the loss of the "flower of Judaea" [Iudee florem patrie lacrimando dolorem!] (112), and her unwillingness to be consoled by the comforters who accompany her is an effect of her disbelief in the Christian message. In addition, she is granted a *lamentacio* or *planctus* that is powerfully moving both through its eloquence and its musical setting: Jewish grief is seen as at once inappropriate (because untempered by Christian consolation) and yet emotionally legitimate—a mixed response that witnesses to the uneasiness with which at least some Christians viewed both the violence of their coreligionists and the heroic piety of Jewish martyrs.[112] And to confirm the relevance of the *Ordo Rachelis* to our topic, in all four plays the boys not only sing immediately after their throats have been cut but are then resurrected at the end in order to sing a final antiphon in praise of Christ—a structure that parallels with uncanny specificity the narrative of the *Prioress's Tale*.

Which brings us to the final literary form that witnesses to the Christian response to the Jewish *kiddush ha-Shem:* the Marian miracle. Of these miracles, there are two that are at once antisemitic and ubiquitous: the so-called Jewish boy of Bourges and the singing clergeon that is the source of the *Prioress's Tale*. While the Jewish boy of Bourges or *Judenknabe,* as he is known in the scholarship, is not immediately relevant to the meaning of the *Prioress's Tale,* his tale provides a striking parallel to the process by which the original of the *Prioress's Tale* came into existence.[113] It tells of a Jewish boy who accompanies his Christian friend to Mass and partakes of the Eucharist. His enraged father throws him in an oven, where he is protected by the Virgin, and the father is then himself thrown in the oven and burnt to death.[114] The first appearance in the West of this originally Greek tale was in Gregory of Tours's *Libri miraculorum* of the late sixth century. With one exception, its next appearance was not until the early twelfth century, in the *Chronica* of Sigebert of Gembloux (d. 1112), who also reported the massacres of 1096 and the capture of Jerusalem in 1099.[115] Mary Minty has already proposed that this exemplum is an antisemitic response to the *kiddush ha-Shem*, and the popularity of the story—which was repeated throughout the Middle Ages—must have been connected with the idea not just of burning Jews but of Jews burning their own children.[116]

Let us now return, at last, to the Marian miracle tale of the little clergeon. The original version of the story, composed in the twelfth century and almost certainly on the Continent, can best be understood as having been written in response to the *kiddush ha-Shem* of 1146. This is especially the case when we remember that the earliest versions of the tale present the protagonist not as singing an antiphon but as *chantinga* responsorium, the *Gaude Maria*, whose last line says that the sight of the Virgin "makes ashamed the doomed Jew, who says that Christ was born from Joseph's seed."[117] This assertion was in fact common among Jewish polemicists and is widely reported in the Hebrew chronicles as having been repeated, in starker terms, by the martyrs of 1096 and 1146.[118] What is especially striking, however, is the way in which the version of the story told by Chaucer's Prioress is shaped to invoke, as its own unacknowledged indictment, the history from which it originally emerged. The tale is not only antisemitic in itself but a brutal distortion, with an almost sadistic attention to detail, of the heroic Jewish response to Christian violence, the *kiddush ha-Shem*. The *Prioress's Tale* recounts the slitting of the throat of a child by a Jew;[119] in the child's singing of the Marian antiphon, it alludes to the chanting of the Jewish martyrs as they enacted their sacrificial suicide; with the binding of the Jews by the authorities, it recalls the *'akedah* which the martyrs had reinterpreted as a form of blood atonement; it refers to the mother as a "newe Rachel" (627) in stark juxtaposition with the "torment and . . . shameful deeth" (628) to which the Jews are subjected;[120] in the invocation of "the lawe" (634) by which the Jews are punished—"Yvele shal have that yvele wol deserve" (632)—it enacts a cruel parody of the true meaning of the *lex talionis* of Exodus 21:23–25, which argues not for vengeance but precisely for a *limitation* on vengeance; and the prologue to the tale begins with a citation of Psalm 8—"O Lord, oure Lord, thy name how merveillous / Is in this large world ysprad" (453–454)—that is a verbal equivalent to the Sanctification of the Holy Name. In its definition of the clergeon's age as seven, the tale even makes relevant an Ashkenazic legal argument that "'children who cannot distinguish between good and evil,' [should] perish in the innocence of their childhood, rather than later in the guilt of an assumed Christianity."[121] The *Prioress's Tale*, in sum, is a perfect instance of the cruelest kind of antisemitism, one that turns against Jewish martyrs their own heroic piety. The best that can be said for the teller of such a tale is that she acts in ignorance—not the innocence for which she yearns, but a culturally fostered condition of being unable to understand the origins and the historical meaning of her own religion.

What did Chaucer know?

But what of the teller behind the teller? Is Chaucer also ignorant? To evade the question of authorial intention is to avoid the moral force of the issue, to avoid the consequences of literary practice by retreating into the often foggy platitudes of literary theory.[122] Could Chaucer have known about Jewish martyrdom as a form of ritual slaughter designed to sanctify the Holy Name? Could he have known that some uncharitable Christians responded not only by denying the Jewish martyrs their heroism but by distorting their pious fortitude into cruel hard-heartedness? The fact that the *Prioress's Tale* summons up this Jewish history in such remarkable detail only to misunderstand it encourages us to pursue such questions.

There are, in fact, a number of ways that Chaucer could have come to this knowledge. As we have seen, *kiddush ha-Shem* continued to be practiced by the Ashkenazim throughout the fourteenth century, as the successive waves of the plague, and the concomitant accusations of well-poisoning, led to massacres that virtually destroyed northern European Jewry.[123] As a frequent traveler to northern France in 1368–1370—the plague returned to northern Europe in 1368—Chaucer would have had the opportunity to learn of, if not to witness, anti-Jewish violence and the Jewish response.

But the most likely place for Chaucer to have learned of the *kiddush ha-Shem* was Spain. In 1366 Chaucer was granted a safe-conduct by Charles II, king of Navarre, for travel to Spain.[124] While the reason for this trip is (as usual) not stated in the document itself, it was almost certainly related to the civil war then under way between Peter of Castile and Henry of Trastamara and to John of Gaunt's Spanish ambitions.[125] Whatever role Chaucer may have played in these events, he would certainly have known that a central element of Henry's claim to the throne was the fact that Pedro had a Jewish mother, and that both Henry and his chief lieutenant, Bertrand du Guesclin, were engaged in vicious attacks upon the Jewish communities of Spain—attacks that are described with revolting enthusiasm in Cuvelier's *chanson de geste* celebrating du Guesclin.[126] Nor was anti-Jewish violence during the civil war confined to Henry and the French: a Jewish chronicler complains bitterly that the troops accompanying Pedro—which included those commanded by the Black Prince—"killed many communities" of Jews, specifically those of the towns of Villadiego and Aguilar de Campo, and brought about many (forced) conversions.[127] Again, the specific reaction of these communities to the violence inflicted upon them has not, to my knowledge, been recorded. But we do know that the Ashkenazic concept of ritual slaughter as martyrdom—*kiddush ha-Shem*— had been imported into the Sephardic communities of Spain: as early as 1165 Maimonides wrote a treatise defending the legitimacy of those who do not choose death in the face of forced accommodation to another religion, in this case Islam.[128] We also know that in the widespread massacres of 1391—at a time when John of Gaunt may have relinquished his ambitions to the throne of Castile and Léon but had sent a diplomatic mission to Castile to settle Anglo-Castilian differences[129] —the *kiddush ha-Shem* once again became a prominent aspect of an activist Jewish response to Christian violence.[130] Can we doubt that it was also present in the massacres of 1366–1367? In sum, if we are looking for a place where Chaucer could have come into contact with the *kiddush ha-Shem* that the *Prioress's Tale* so cruelly travesties, it is to Spain that we can best direct our attention. And there is one final, intriguing piece of evidence for this Spanish connection. Of the 33 versions of the story the Prioress tells, only one comes from Spain— and it sets the story in England. And of these 33 versions, only two set the story in Spain—and those two are produced in England. An Anglo-Spanish route for the story the Prioress tells is thus entirely possible.[131]

It is often thought that because the Jews were expelled from England by Edward I in 1290 that the *Prioress's Tale* could not have any relevance to the England of the 1390s. Yet as literary critics have shown, there is in fact a considerable interest in—and sympathy with—Jews in late-fourteenth-century literature. Elisa Narin van Court has urged scholars "to recognize [that] the proliferation of late-fourteenth-century Middle English narratives which directly address the issues of Jews *qua* Jews in relationship to the Christian community is indicative of a significant and ongoing interest in Jews and Judaism."[132] But if we grant such an interest, what is the reason for it? One answer can be found in the well-known ambitions of Richard II to create for himself an ostentatious and unassailable image of royal power. One of the characteristic ways in which medieval kings presented themselves as Christian defenders of their realms was by attacking the Jews. Perhaps the first medieval instance of this is the attack upon the Jews of Brie-Comte-Robert by Philip Augustus in 1192. This event occurred just after the king had returned from crusade in 1191, an expedition he had undertaken in part to confirm his status as the rightful ruler of the "most Christian" kingdom of France. By killing Jews, Philip presented himself as imbued with righteous piety—a move that was revealed as self-servingly political when a few years later he reopened the royal domain to all Jews who wished to settle there.

An English instance is the behavior of Henry III in relation to the "martyrdom" of little Hugh of Lincoln. As Joe Hillaby has shown, almost all the accusations of ritual murder were motivated by the need to create a patron saint for a Benedictine foundation that did not have one; moreover, many of these accusations coincided with monastic building projects.[133] Yet most of these efforts were failures: around neither William of Norwich nor Harold of Gloucester (presumably killed in 1168) did there develop the kind of cult the perpetrators of these legends must have anticipated, and the Jewish communities of both Norwich and Gloucester prospered despite the accusations. The exceptions to this pattern are Robert of Bury in 1181, whose success as a cult figure had to do with the royal patronage of the monastery and its immense economic and spiritual power, and Hugh of Lincoln in 1255. The Lincoln accusation succeeded in fostering a cult as did none other largely, as Gavin Langmuir has shown, because of the intervention of Henry III himself.[134] Already keen to present himself as an enemy of the Jews—he had established the *Domus Conversorum* in London for Jewish converts in 1232, a necessary charity since upon conversion a Jew's property was forfeit to the Crown— Henry took upon himself the punishment of the Jews accused of the murder. He had one Jew killed immediately; 71 others were then taken to London, of whom 18 were executed after being drawn through the streets. Nor was Henry the only English monarch to avail himself of the spiritual authority of antisemitism. After Edward I's expulsion of the Jews in 1290, Hugh was translated to a new shrine and a prominent statue representing him as a crucified child was created. Then, when Queen Eleanor died in November of that same year, two elaborate tombs were constructed for her, one at Westminster and the other at Lincoln. According to H. M. Colvin, "The trouble taken to give Queen Eleanor such elaborate memorials of stone, bronze and marble must be seen as evidence not only of Edward's devotion to her memory, but also of his desire to enhance the prestige of the English monarchy by creating visible symbols of its piety and power."[135] While the choice of Lincoln as a site for one of Eleanor's tombs was in part chance—she died at nearby Harby—it also gave Edward the opportunity, at the same time as he was expelling the unfortunate Jews from his kingdom, to confirm his status as a Christian king.

As we have seen, most of the worst anti-Jewish violence, with the exception of that connected to the plague, was prompted by crusading fervor: 1096, 1146, the English riots of 1189–1190 connected to the coronation and departure on crusade of Richard I, the Rindfleisch massacres of 1298 in the Rhineland, and so on and on. As Kenneth Stow has said, the crusaders' "goal was to purify space, the inner private one of their own minds or the outer public one of an entire society or land."[136] Edward I was himself on crusade from 1270 to 1272, and throughout his reign he maintained his intention to return to the Holy Land whenever the next domestic crisis had passed.[137] Edward II adopted the cross in 1313 (although without any real intention of going on crusade himself), and in 1332 Edward III agreed to go on crusade with Philip of France, a plan that was shelved with the outbreak of the Hundred Years' War in 1337. But the crusade in its various forms (e.g., Despenser's "crusade" against the supporters of the antipope Clement VII in Flanders) and locales (e.g., the Holy Land, the Baltic, Spain) continued to attract English adherents throughout the fourteenth century. And we can even find in late-fourteenth-century England evidence of the anti-Jewish actions that typically accompanied crusading.

The lead here was taken by the French. In 1394, for reasons that have never been explained, Charles VI expelled the Jews from his lands. The most plausible explanation is that he was responding to the crusading fervor that issued in the crusade of 1396 and the disaster of Nicopolis.[138] By having cleansed his nation of the infidel, Charles had fulfilled his role as a "most Christian king." The English nobility was also infected with zeal for crusading: several joined the duke of Bourbon's Barbary crusade in 1390, the ambitious earl of Derby campaigned in Prussia in 1390 and 1392, Chaucer's friends Clanvowe and Neville died in 1391 on what may well have been a crusading expedition or a preparatory reconnoiter for one, and Gaunt himself made plans to join the expedition of 1396.[139] Correspondingly, there are signs of an interest in making sure England was *Judenfreie*. The chronicle of Gloucester Abbey by Walter Frocester, compiled between 1382 and 1412, included a long entry about the martyred boy Harold—another failed effort at reviving a cult that had never taken hold in the first place.[140] In 1396 relics of two of the Holy Innocents were brought to England, a visible reminder of the slaughter of the young and helpless.[141] And as late as the 1420s Lydgate wrote a poem about the "martyred" Robert of Bury. But most relevant to Chaucer are the actions undertaken by Richard II, who was by no means unaware of the ideological benefits of adopting a crusading posture. Already in the winter of 1385–1386, Leo VI of Armenia, a Christian king driven from his throne by Turks, had visited Richard after having been the guest of Charles VI of France.[142] Richard granted Leo the huge pension of £1,000 per annum until his death in 1393, a pension that was actually paid. Not surprisingly, Leo wanted Richard to join Charles in a crusade: he was a colleague of the indefatigable Philippe de Mézières, who promoted the crusading Order of the Passion with relentless zeal.[143] Nor was Richard uninterested: the Wilton Diptych, for instance, has plausibly been read as a crusading icon, and Richard certainly presented himself as being deeply devoted to the cult of the Virgin.[144] Like Edward I, Richard was also devoted to Lincoln Cathedral, and in 1387, at a crucial moment in his struggle with the rebellious Lords Appellant, he and his queen, along with members of their household like Chaucer's wife Philippa, were enrolled in the cathedral confraternity.[145]

Thanks to his great-great-grandfather, Richard had no such opportunity as Charles VI to display his piety by expelling the Jews from England, "the dower of the Virgin."[146] Yet there is one telling detail that indicates that the Jews nonetheless played a role in Richard's creation of his crusading identity. While the *Domus Conversorum* was almost empty—there were only a few aged (and foreign) inhabitants—conversions still took place.

> In the year 1390, a Jew of Sicily was publicly baptized in the presence of king Richard II, at the Palace of Langley, by the Venerable Father Robert, Bishop of London; and, in honour of his royal godfather, the name of Richard was bestowed upon this convert. He was not sent to the Domus, but an annuity of £10 . . . was settled upon him for life. In addition to this, he was paid the sum of fifty marks on the day of his conversion his lot being certainly much happier than that of his confreres in the Domus.[147]

Small as this incident may be, Richard's presence, his granting of his name to the new convert, and the substantial sum he settled on him, suggests a response to the demand that he extend the borders of Christendom in a world that was in fact fast becoming far more heterogeneous, and far more dangerous to Christians, than ever before.[148] If the *Prioress's Tale* is a childish fantasy, perhaps we should see it as a fictive displacement of the equally fantastic religious ambitions which Richard seems, at least for a time, to have entertained.

Morality and sophistication

Sometime in the year 1277, as the extortions and constraints imposed on the English Jews by the crusader king Edward I were becoming more and more intolerable, a Jew named Sampson from Northampton committed an act of great courage and wit. According to the rolls of the Exchequer of the Jews, the government office charged with implementing the king's policy, Sampson "assumed the habit of a friar minor, preaching certain things in contempt of the Christian faith and the said order." As punishment Sampson was condemned to walk naked for three days through London, Canterbury, Oxford, Lincoln, and Northampton, carrying the entrails of a calf and with the flayed carcass on his neck, a sentence imposed by the archbishop of Canterbury and confirmed by the king. Whether this astonishing sentence was ever carried out remains unknown, since neither Sampson nor his two mainpernors could be found by the sheriff of Northampton. One suspects that the sheriff, who had been ordered to keep Sampson and his mainpernors imprisoned, was unwilling to participate in this barbaric and enigmatic ritual.[149]

While it was not until 1280 that it became official government policy that Jews were forced to attend conversionary sermons, usually delivered by

Dominicans, we can be sure that they had already for many years been sub-jected to a constant stream of abuse in the guise of instruction from fraternal preachers.[150] Apparently Sampson of Northampton had had enough of these sermons, but his response was not—as was elsewhere the case—to argue back either face-to-face or through tracts that met Christian arguments with rab-binic learning.[151] On the contrary, Sampson met Christian zeal with Jewish parody. One would give much to have the text of Sampson's "sermon." Per-haps it engaged in the kind of wordplay used in the *Nizzahon Vetus*, where the name *Maria* is consistently spelled *Haria*, to evoke the Aramaic word for excrement.[152] One would also like to know the audience before which he performed: given the tenor of the times, it was almost certainly meant to be exclusively Jewish. At this distance all we can know is that Sampson met uncomprehending and overbearing intolerance with parody: his mimicry was one of those "weapons of the weak" with which the oppressed so often strive to retain their dignity.[153]

The Jews of the *Prioress's Tale* have no voice at all: they are simply crea-tures possessed by Satan whose bodies perform certain actions and have other actions performed upon them. Yet not the least irony of the tale is that the Prioress herself also has no voice: she surrenders it—or so she thinks—to an institutional authority that guarantees its transcendence of the merely human and the merely historical. Yet within her mimicry, unbeknownst to her, there lurk the very voices she has sought to silence. In handing herself over to the Marian miracle and the liturgical drama she has also handed herself over to the history from which those genres sprang and to which they continue to bear witness. For these apparently most Christian of forms can never shed the Jewishness from which they emerged. Try as she might, a pure Christendom is unavailable to her: alone among the 33 versions of the tale, hers is set in an eastern country where both Christians and Jews are subordinated to a foreign, presumably Islamic sovereignty. And this inability even to imagine a pure Christianity, purged of the taint of the foreign, is Chaucer's comment on the futility of trying to escape from history. Whether the Prioress likes it or not, Christianity and Judaism are linked together not just in the past but in the present and—as we ought by now to have learned—in the future as well.

In sum, then, what the *Prioress's Tale* represents is one of Chaucer's characteristically disinterested explorations of the unpredictable interaction of history and psychology. The Prioress is at once source and effect of the intolerance and ignorance that her tale expresses. And her tale is an effect not simply of the sporadic reappearance of the crusading idea in the 1380s and 1390s, with its inevitable antisemitism, but of the whole shameful history of the Christian treatment of Jews. So grim is this history that for many in Chaucer's post-twentieth-century audience only an explicit rejection of the Prioress's prejudices could truly exculpate him from complicity in promoting her "antisemitic tract."[154] Yet Chaucer has in fact accomplished something even more effective. In trying to understand the tale he has given his Prioress, we are forced to understand the history from which it emerges and to which it makes its own contribution. Many have deplored Chaucer's willingness to allow the tale to speak for itself; but perhaps others will admire his self-restraint, not least because it invites his reader to pursue the same literary and historical pathways that led the author to the composition of this remarkable work. This self-restraint can appropriately be understood as a sign of moral sophistication.

Notes

This essay could not have been written without the generous help and support of my colleague Ivan Marcus.

1. Bernard of Clairvaux, *Epistola 391*, translated by Bruno James, *The Letters of St. Bernard of Clairvaux* (London: Burns Oates, 1953), p. 462.

2. All citations of Chaucer are from Larry D. Benson, gen. ed., *The Riverside Chaucer*, 3rd ed. (Boston: Houghton Mifflin, 1987). I have occasionally adjusted the punctuation.

3. According to Carleton Brown, "The Prioress's Tale," in W. F. Bryan and Germaine Dempster, eds., *Sources and Analogues of Chaucer's "Canterbury Tales"* (Chicago: University of Chicago Press, 1941), pp. 447–485, there are thirty-two other versions of the story in existence (none of which seems to be Chaucer's exact source, if he had one). A thirty-fourth version is identified by Santiago Gonzalez Fernandez-Corugedo, "A Marian Miracle in England and Spain: Alfonso X's 'Cantigas de Santa María' no. 6 and Chaucer's 'The Prioress's Tale,'" in Luis A. Lázaro Lafuente, José Simón, and Ricardo J. Sola Buil, eds., *Medieval Studies: Proceedings of the IIIrd International Conference of the Spanish Society for Medieval English Language and Literature* (Madrid: Universidad de Alcalá de Henares, 1994), pp. 151–175.

4. All biblical citations are from the Douay-Rheims version. The relevance of the liturgy to the *Prioress's Tale* was first explained by Marie Padgett Hamilton, "Echoes of Childermas in the Tale of the Prioress," *Modern Language Review* 34 (1939): 1–8.

5. See Patrick S. Diehl, *The Medieval Religious Lyric* (Berkeley: University of California Press, 1985), pp. 151–152.

6. In addition to the work of Hamilton (see above n. 4), *in Chaucer's Nuns and Other Essays* (New York: D. Appleton and Co., 1925), Sister Madeleva showed that the *Prologue* is heavily indebted to the Little Office of the Virgin (pp. 30–33).

7. For the Boy Bishop ceremonies, see C. H. Evelyn-White, "The Boy Bishop (*Episcopus Puerorum*) of Medieval England," *Journal of the British Archaeological Association*, n.s. 11 (1905): 30–48, 231–256; S. E. Rigold, "The St. Nicholas Tokens or 'Boy Bishop' Tokens," *Proceedings of the Suffolk Institute of Archaeology* 34 (1978): 87–101; J. M. J. Fletcher, *The Boy-Bishop at Salisbury and Elsewhere* (Salisbury: Brown and Co., 1921), and the references cited there; and for the service itself, Christopher Wordsworth, *Ceremonies and Processions of the Cathedral Church of Salisbury* (Cambridge: Cambridge University Press, 1901), pp. 52 ff.; and Francis Procter and Christopher Wordsworth, eds., *Breviarum ad usum insignis Sarum*, vol.

1 (Cambridge, 1882), cols. ccxxix–ccxlv. The Marian antiphons are identified by J. G. Davies, ed., *A New Dictionary of Liturgy and Worship* (London: SCM Press, 1986), p. 26.

8. For the citation, see Wordsworth, *Ceremonies and Processions,* p. 53. The popularity—and solemnity—of the ceremony in England is stressed by the writers cited in the previous note, and even in the classic account by E. K. Chambers, *The Mediaeval Stage,* 2 vols. (Oxford: Oxford University Press, 1903), 1: pp. 336–371, which tends to focus on the misbehavior recorded in Continental episcopal registers. For the popularity of the Boy Bishop ceremony in nunneries, see Eileen Power, *Medieval English Nunneries, c. 1275 to 1535* (Cambridge: Cambridge University Press, 1922), p. 312.

9. That medieval typological exegesis was just as ahistorical as allegorical (*pace* Auerbach et al.) is decisively argued by David Aers, *Piers Plowman and Christian Allegory* (London: Arnold, 1975), pp. 1–70. A subtle and learned exegetical reading of the tale has been provided by Sherman Hawkins, "Chaucer's Prioress and the Sacrifice of Praise," *JEGP* 63 (1964): 599–624. Hawkins's reading has been criticized by Louise O. Fradenburg, "Criticism, Anti-Semitism, and the *Prioress's Tale,*" *Exemplaria* 1 (1989): 69–115, because it colludes with the Prioress's avoidance of the historical realities of antisemitism. In this she is certainly correct—as this essay will argue in detail—yet she overlooks the fact that Hawkins's kind of typological reading is both ubiquitous throughout the Middle Ages and actively solicited by the *Prioress's Tale.* It is not simply a politically unacceptable reading to be rejected but part of the meaning of the text.

10. In "The Christ Child as Sacrifice: A Medieval Tradition and the Corpus Christi Plays," *Speculum* 48 (1973): 491–509, Leah Sinanoglou provides a wealth of instances from largely late medieval English sources of the representation of Christ as a sacrificial child.

11. The most recent proponent of this interpretation of the "greyn" is Kathleen M. Oliver, "Singing Bread, Manna, and the Clergeon's 'Greyn,'" *Chaucer Review* 31 (1996-97): 357–364. While a connection with the eucharistic wafer is unavoidable, it also seems true that the "greyn" represents more than one thing, including the martyr himself. See Sister Nicholas Maltman, O.P., "The Divine Granary, or the End of the Prioress's 'Greyn,'" *Chaucer Review* 17 (1982–1983): 163–170; and Isamu Saito, "'Greyn' of Martyrdom in Chaucer's *Prioress's Tale,*" in Takashi Suzuki and Tsuyoshi Mukai, eds., *Arthurian and Other Studies Presented to Sunichi Noguchi* (Cambridge: D. S. Brewer, 1993), pp. 31–38.

12. There is, it should be noted, one gesture toward conversion in the course of the tale. When the provost hears of the miracle of the clergeon, he "herieth Crist that is of hevene kyng, / And eek his mooder, honour of mankynde" (618–619). Insofar as we are to think of the secular power in this country as non-Christian, this would seem to indicate that the miracle has at least some conversionary impact. But in comparison to the effects wrought by Constance, Griselda, and Cecilia, the impact here is minimal.

13. Among the few critics who have discussed the links between the *Shipman's* and *Prioress's Tale,* the most perceptive are Hawkins, "Chaucer's Prioress," 621; and Jerome Mandel, *Geoffrey Chaucer: Building the Fragments of the "Canterbury Tales"* (Rutherford, N.J.: Fairleigh Dickinson University Press, 1992), 172–174. See also Ann W. Astell, *Chaucer and the Universe of Learning* (Ithaca: Cornell University Press, 1996), 184–188. For the aristocratic nature of rhyme royal, see Martin

Stevens, "The Royal Stanza in Early English Literature," *PMLA* 94 (1979): 62–76; and for its affective function, Robert O. Payne, *The Key of Remembrance: A Study of Chaucer's Poetics* (New Haven: Yale University Press, 1963), 163–170. On the same topic, see as well the shrewd comments of Alfred David, "An ABC to the Style of the Prioress," in Mary J. Carruthers and Elizabeth D. Kirk, eds., *Acts of Interpretation: The Text in Its Contexts, 700–1600: Essays in Medieval and Renaissance Literature in Honor of E. Talbot Donaldson* (Norman, Okla.: Pilgrim Books, 1982), 147–157; and Barbara Nolan, "Chaucer's Tales of Transcendence: Rhyme Royal and Christian Prayer in the *Canterbury Tales*," in C. David Benson and Elizabeth Robertson, eds., *Chaucer's Religious Tales* (Cambridge: D. S. Brewer, 1990), 21–38.

14. I am excluding here the general analogy between the Nun's Priest and "his" nuns and Chauntecleer and his sister hens: for a discussion, see Lawrence L. Besserman, "Chaucerian Wordplay: The Nun's Priest and his 'Womman Divyne,'" *Chaucer Review* 12 (1977–1978): 68–73.

15. The analogies between the clergeon and Kenelm are summarized by Beverly Boyd, ed., *Prioress's Tale*, vol. 2, pt. 20 of *The Canterbury Tales: A Variorum Edition* (Norman: University of Oklahoma Press, 1987), p. 6: "Kenelm is seven years old; he is murdered with an antiphon upon his lips; his corpse is concealed in a deep pit but discovered by a miracle and then carried into an abbey; and the king's sister, who contrived his murder, dies miserably."

16. Power, *Medieval English Nunneries*, pp. 62–64.

17. The papal attacks on the ritual murder charge have been briefly surveyed by R. J. Schoeck, "Chaucer's Prioress: Mercy and the Tender Heart," *The Bridge: A Yearbook of Judaeo-Christian Studies* 2 (1956): 239–255; for a fuller account, with translations of the relevant documents, see Solomon Grayzel, *The Church and the Jews in the XIIIth Century*, vol. 1, 2nd ed. (New York: Hermon Press, 1966); and Grayzel, *The Church and the Jews in the XIIIth Century*, vol. 2, ed. Kenneth Stow (New York: The Jewish Theological Seminary, 1989). For the civil authorities, see Robert Chazan, ed., *Church, State, and Jew in the Middle Ages* (New York: Behrman House, 1980), pp. 123–128 and passim.

18. For a full and convincing account of the stylistic and religious differences between the tales of the Prioress and the Second Nun, see C. David Benson, *Chaucer's Drama of Style: Poetic Variety and Contrast in the "Canterbury Tales"* (Chapel Hill: University of North Carolina Press, 1986), pp. 131–146.

19. For a full reading of the tale along these lines, see Corey J. Marvin, "'I Will Thee Not Forsake': The Kristevan Maternal Space in Chaucer's *Prioress's Tale* and John of Garland's *Stella Maris*," *Exemplaria* 8 (1996): 35–58.

20. The Anglo-Norman ballad of "Hughes de Lincoln," upon which Chaucer almost certainly drew, contains unmistakable suggestions of a special closeness between mother and son, a closeness that has been seen as involving incest: see Brian Bebbington, "Little Sir Hugh: An Analysis," *UNISA English Studies* 9 (1971): 3–36; repr. in Alan Dundes, ed., *The Blood Libel Legend: A Casebook in Antisemitic Folklore* (Madison: University of Wisconsin Press, 1991), pp. 72–90. The ballad is available only in nineteenth-century editions, either the *editio princeps* by Francisque Michel, ed., *Hughes de Lincoln* (Paris, 1834); or Abraham Hume, *Sir Hugh of Lincoln; or, an Examination of a Curious Tradition respecting the Jews, with a Notice of Popular Poetry Connected with It* (London, 1849).

21. I have discussed this theme in detail in "'What Man Artow?': Authorial Self-Definition in the *Tale of Sir Thopas* and the *Tale of Melibee*," *Studies in the Age of Chaucer* 11 (1989): 117–176.

22. J. A. Burrow, *The Ages of Man:* A *Study in Medieval Writing and Thought* (Oxford: Clarendon Press, 1986), p. 74. It is probable that Chaucer made the child seven, since the only other version of the story with this detail is in Middle English and is of a later date: see Margaret H. Statler, "The Analogues of Chaucer's *Prioress's Tale:* The Relation of Group C to Group A," *PMLA* 65 (1950): 898 n. 7. The difference between a reading school and a song school, and the fate of the professional chorister (decried by contemporaries), is well described by Jo Ann Hoeppner Moran, *The Growth of English Schooling, 1340–1548: Learning, Literacy, and Laicization in Pre-Reformation York Diocese* (Princeton: Princeton University Press, 1985), pp. 24, 54–61. The clergeon's education is also discussed by Bruce Holsinger, "Pedagogy, Violence, and the Subject of Music: Chaucer's *Prioress's Tale* and the Ideologies of 'Song,'" *New Medieval Literatures* 1 (1997): 157–192, who sees the violence of the tale as displaced from the violence typical of medieval pedagogy.

23. Sr. Mary Madeleva, Chaucer's *Nuns and Other Essays,* pp. 37–38.

24. Alfred David, *The Strumpet Muse* (Bloomington: Indiana University Press, 1977), pp. 209–210.

25. Ibid., p. 209.

26. Alan Gaylord, "The Unconquered Tale of the Prioress," *Papers of the Michigan Academy of Science, Arts, and Letters* 47 (1962): 634; Hawkins, "Chaucer's Prioress and the Sacrifice of Praise," p. 601.

27. For the connection between infancy and speechlessness established by the Latin etymology, see Isidore of Seville, *Etymologiae,* ed. José Oroz Reta and Manuel Marcos Casquero (Madrid: Bibliotecà de Autores Cristianos, 1982): "Infans dicitur homo primae aetatis; dictus autem infans quia adhuc fari nescit, id est loqui non potest" (XI, 2, 9 [2:40]).

28. This point is well made by Hawkins, "Chaucer's Prioress and the Sacrifice of Praise," from whom this phrase from the collect for the Mass is cited (p. 601).

29. The connection between the Virgin and miraculous speech is drawn by several other Middle English miracles of the Virgin. One recounts how the Virgin cured the cancerous throat of an otherwise speechless monk with her milk, others tell the story of a monk who could learn only the Ave Maria or of a priest who could celebrate no mass but that of Our Lady, of how lilies grew in the mouths of the corpses of dead clerks devoted to the Virgin, and of how a monk's Ave Marias were transformed into rose petals as they issued from his mouth. See Beverly Boyd, *The Middle English Miracles of the Virgin* (San Marino, Calif.: Huntington Library, 1964), pp. 123–124, 134, 141.

30. For a somewhat similar account of the style of the *Prioress's Tale,* see Richard H. Osberg, "A Voice for the Prioress: The Context of English Devotional Prose," *Studies in the Age of Chaucer* 18 (1996): 25–54. According to Osberg, "Chaucer has given the Prioress a voice that some clerical English authors adopted when addressing a female audience largely untrained in the Latin tradition and particularly when impersonating the lyrical prayers and devotions of such an audience. The voice thought appropriate for addressing religious women—rhythmical and alliterative, highly descriptive and concrete, creating strong affective responses—becomes the voice in which the Prioress answers back" (pp. 33–34). However, I differ from Osberg's view that the Prioress is in any sense "answering back" rather than simply

adopting this male-defined feminine language, and from his claim that there is nothing childish about the Prioress's language.

31. On "greyn" here as nucleus or kernel, see Hawkins, "Chaucer's Prioress and the Sacrifice of Praise," pp. 615–618.

32. See, for example, the notes to line 662 of the tale in the *Riverside Chaucer,* p. 916; and Boyd's Variorum edition, *Prioress's Tale,* pp. 160–161.

33. Piero Boitani, *The Tragic and the Sublime in Medieval Literature* (Cambridge: Cambridge University Press, 1989), pp. 177–222; Beverly Boyd, "Chaucer's Moments in the 'Kneeling World,'" in Anne Clark Bartlett et al., eds., *Vox Mystica: Essays on Medieval Mysticism in Honor of Professor Valerie M. Lagorio* (Cambridge: D. S. Brewer, 1995),pp. 99–105. Quite apart from Speght's uncorroborated claim that the "ABC" was written for Blanche, duchess of Lancaster, the poem seems to be a rosary poem, especially when seen in manuscript with each stanza headed with an illuminated initial. These initials are versions of the green "gaudes" that mark out the beads of the Prioress's rosary into decades of Ave Marias: see the note to line 159 of the *General Prologue* in the *Riverside Chaucer,* p. 805. As a rosary poem, the "ABC" is almost certainly written for a woman.

34. Sidney Sussex College, Cambridge, MS 95, described by M. R. James, *A Descriptive Catalogue of the Manuscripts in the Library of Sidney Sussex College, Cambridge* (Cambridge, 1895), pp. 76–109.

35. Benedicta Ward, *Miracles and the Medieval Mind: Theory, Record, and Event, 1000–1215,* rev. ed. (Philadelphia: University of Pennsylvania Press, 1987), pp. 142, 146, 156. In "The Miracles of Our Lady: Context and Interpretation," in Derek Pearsall, ed., *Studies in the Vernon Manuscript* (Cambridge: D. S. Brewer, 1990), pp. 115–136, Carol Meale provides a list of vernacular *Mariales* held by English monasteries (pp. 125–126). Paul Strohm's claim that the genre of the miracle of the Virgin was "almost exclusively the province of lay audiences and an object of popular circulation rather than reclusive or contemplative devotion" (*Social Chaucer* [Cambridge: Harvard University Press, 1989], p. 70) must therefore be rejected.

36. Peter Whiteford, ed., *The Myracles of Oure Lady* (Heidelberg: Carl Winter, 1990), p. 8; Meale, "The Miracles of Our Lady," p. 135.

37. My comments on the genre of the miracles of the Virgin are based on a reading of the following texts: Adgar, *Le graciel,* ed. Pierre Kunstmann (Ottawa: Editions de l'Université d'Ottawa, 1982); C. C. S. Bland, trans., *[Johannes Herolt's] Miracles of the Blessed Virgin* (London: G. Routledge, 1928); Caesarius of Heisterbach, *The Dialogue on Miracles,* trans. H. von E. Scott and C. C. S. Bland, vol. 1 (London: G. Routledge, 1929); Gautier de Coincy, *Les Miracles de Nostre Dame par Gautier de Coincy,* ed. V. Frédéric Koenig, 4 vols. (Geneva: Droz, 1955–1970); Nigel of Canterbury, *Miracles of the Virgin Mary in Verse,* ed. Jan Ziolkowski (Toronto: Centre for Medieval Studies, 1986); Whiteford, ed., *Myracles of Oure Lady;* and the excellent summaries of the 171 Middle English miracles so far identified provided by Thomas D. Cooke, "Miracles of the Virgin," section 3.I of "Tales," in Albert E. Hartung, gen. ed., *A Manual of the Writings in Middle English, 1050–1500,* vol. 9 (New Haven: Connecticut Academy of Arts and Sciences, 1993), 3177–3258, 3501–3551.

38. Brigitte Cazelles, *La Faiblesse chez Gautier de Coinci* (Saratoga: Anma Libri, 1978).

39. Ward, *Miracles and the Medieval Mind,* p. 163.

40. This group includes the miracles written by Thomas Hoccleve, "Prologue and A Miracle of the Blessed Virgin," in Israel Gollancz, ed., *Hoccleve's Works, II: The Minor Poems,* Early English Text Society e.s. 73 (London: Oxford University Press, 1925), p. 16 ff.; and by John Lydgate, "The Legend of Dan Joos," in H. N. MacCracken, ed., *The Minor Poems of John Lydgate,* pt. 1, Early English Text Society e.s. 107 (London: Oxford University Press, 1911), pp. 311–315.

41. Keith Thomas, *Religion and the Decline of Magic* (London: Weidenfeld and Nicolson, 1971), p. 76; cited by Gail McMurray Gibson, *The Theater of Devotion: East Anglian Drama and Society in the Late Middle Ages* (Chicago: University of Chicago Press, 1989), p. 41.

42. For Wyclif's hatred of the Sarum ordinal, see Archdale A. King, *Liturgies of the Past*(London: Longmans, 1959), p. 283; the citation is from Anne Hudson, *The Premature Reformation: Wycliffite Texts and Lollard History* (Oxford: Clarendon Press, 1988), p. 311. For an example of extreme formalism in prayers to Mary, see Eamon Duffy, *The Stripping of the Altars: Traditional Religion in England, 1400–1580* (New Haven: Yale University Press, 1992), p. 262.

43. Power, *Medieval English Nunneries,* p. 313, translating Chambers, *Mediaeval Stage,* 1: p. 361 n. 1.

44. I am adapting this term from Richard Pfaff's definition of what he calls "the liturgical person," by which he means "the sensibility of one whose life patterns are rooted in liturgical observance and who at the same time either studies the liturgy or makes active choices about it, or both." See Richard W. Pfaff, *Liturgical Calendars, Saints, and Services in Medieval England* (Aldershot, Hampshire: Ashgate/Variorum, 1998), p. 3. For the *Prioress's Prologue and Tale* as themselves a kind of song, see Marie Borroff, "*Loves Hete* in the Prioress's Prologue and Tale," in Robert R. Edwards and Stephen Spector, eds., *The Olde Daunce: Love, Friendship, Sex, and Marriage in the Medieval World* (Albany: State University of New York Press, 1991), 229–235.

45. For a somewhat similar reading of the Prioress, see Robert Hanning, "From EVA to AVE to Eglentyne and Alisoun: Chaucer's Insight into the Roles Women Play," *Signs* 2 (1977): 580–599.

46. Critics who argue that the miracle of the Virgin is by definition an antisemitic genre include Robert Worth Frank Jr., "Miracles of the Virgin, Medieval Anti-Semitism, and the *Prioress's Tale,*" in Larry D. Benson and Siegfried Wenzel, eds., *The Wisdom of Poetry: Essays in Early English Literature in Honor of Morton W. Bloomfield*(Kalamazoo: Western Michigan University, 1982), pp. 177–188, 290–297; Denise L. Despres, "Cultic Anti-Judaism and Chaucer's 'Litel Clergeon,'"*Modern Philology* 91 (1994): 413–427; William Chester Jordan, "Marian Devotion and the Talmud Trial of 1240," in Bernard Lewis and Friedrich Niewöhner, eds., *Religionsgespräche im Mittelalter* (Wiesbaden: Harrassowitz, 1992), pp. 61–76; and Anna Sapir Abulafia, "Twelfth-Century Humanism and the Jews," in Ora Limor and Guy G. Strousma, eds., *Contra Iudaeos: Ancient and Medieval Polemics between Christians and Jews* (Tübingen: Mohr, 1996), pp. 161–175. This is not to say that there is no connection between Marianism and antisemitism in the medieval Christian consciousness. For instance, many of the alleged instances of ritual murder were said to have taken place on one of the feast days dedicated to the Virgin: William Chester Jordan, *The French Monarchy and the Jews: From Philip Augustus to the Last Capetians* (Philadelphia: University of Pennsylvania Press, 1989), p. 18.

47. The *Tôledôt Ye'sû*, a highly influential Jewish life of Jesus written about 200 C.E., claims not only that Jesus's birth was illegitimate but that he was conceived during the period of his mother's uncleanness: see Anna Sapir Abulafia, "Invectives against Christianity in the Hebrew Chronicles of the First Crusade," in Peter W. Edbury, ed., *Crusade and Settlement: Papers Read at the First Conference of the Society for the Study of the Crusades and the Latin East and presented to R. C. Smail* (Cardiff: University College Cardiff Press, 1985), pp. 66–72. For a full account of the Jewish sense of the absurdity of the Christian doctrine of the virgin birth, and of the mistranslations of the Hebrew Bible on which its "prefigurations" were based, see David Berger, ed. and trans., *The Jewish-Christian Debate in the High Middle Ages: A Critical Edition of the Nizzahon Vetus* (Philadelphia: Jewish Publication Society of America, 1979). Andrew of St. Victor, one of the most accomplished Hebraists among the twelfth-century exegetes, in fact came to accept that Isaiah 7:14 read *"a young woman* [Hebrew *almah*] shall conceive and bear a son," not "a *virgin* shall conceive," much to the outrage of his fellow Victorine, Richard. See Jeremy Cohen, "Scholarship and Intolerance in the Medieval Academy: The Study and Evaluation of Judaism in Medieval Christendom," *American Historical Review* 91 (1986): 592-613; repr. in Jeremy Cohen, ed., *Essential Papers on Judaism and Christianity in Conflict* (New York: New York University Press, 1991), pp. 310–341; and Beryl Smalley, *The Study of the Bible in the Middle Ages* (Notre Dame: University of Notre Dame Press, 1964), pp. 112–195. See also Daniel J. Lasker, *Jewish Philosophical Polemics against Christianity in the Middle Ages* (New York: Ktav Publishing House, 1977), pp. 153–159.

48. This argument is pursued by Denise L. Despres, "Mary of the Eucharist: Cultic Anti-Judaism in Some Fourteenth-Century English Devotional Manuscripts," in Jeremy Cohen, ed., *From Witness to Witchcraft: Jews and Judaism in Medieval Christian Thought*, Wolfenbütteler Mittelalter-Studien (Wiesbaden: Harrassowitz, 1996), pp. 88–112.

49. Any discussion of Jewish-Christian relations in the Middle Ages must decide whether to describe anti-Jewish practices as *anti-Judaic* (or *anti-Jewish*) or *antisemitic*, i.e., whether they are based on religious differences or whether they define Jews as of a different species or "race" than the members of the dominant culture, even as less than human. While strict accuracy would mean using one term or the other depending on the context, and while there are plenty of exceptions, it is generally agreed that in the period from the twelfth to the fifteenth century Christian attitudes moved from anti-Judaism to antisemitism. For a summary account, see Robert Chazan, "The Deteriorating Image of the Jews—Twelfth and Thirteenth Centuries," in Scott L. Waugh and Peter D. Diehl, eds. *Christendom and Its Discontents: Exclusion, Persecution, and Rebellion, 1000–1500* (Cambridge: Cambridge University Press, 1996), pp. 220–233. It is also the case that there is an unmistakable connection between late medieval and twentieth-century antisemitism, see, e.g., Robert Chazan, *Medieval Stereotypes and Modern Antisemitism* (Berkeley: University of California Press, 1997); Gavin I. Langmuir, *Toward a Definition of Antisemitism* (Berkeley: University of California Press, 1990), pp. 55–133; Langmuir, *History, Religion, and Antisemitism* (Berkeley: University of California Press, 1990), pp. 275–305; Kenneth R. Stow, *Alienated Minority: The Jews of Medieval Latin Europe* (Cambridge: Harvard University Press, 1992), pp. 231–280; and Joshua Trachtenberg, *The Devil and the Jews* (Cleveland: Meridian Books, 1961). For these reasons I have chosen to use the term *antisemitic* throughout this essay despite its occasional inappropriateness.

50. Gilbert Dahan, "Les Juifs dans les miracles de Gautier de Coincy," *Archives juives* 16 (1980): 41–48, 59–68.

51. A. I. Bagby Jr., "The Jew in the Cántigas of Alfonso X, El Sabio," *Speculum* 46 (1971): 670–688.

52. Whiteford, *The Myracles of Oure Lady*, p. 20. In "Miracles of the Virgin, Medieval Anti-Semitism, and the *Prioress's Tale*," Frank comments on "the persistent presence of antisemitism" in the miracles (p. 178): "antisemitic tales are a commonplace in the genre, a standard, constituent element" (p. 179). But he then tells us that the percentage of antisemitic tales in the collections he studied is actually only about 7.5 percent (p. 292 n. 8).

53. Trachtenberg, *The Devil and the Jews*, passim; the scriptural source for this opinion is John 8:44.

54. See John A. Yunck, "'Lucre of vileynye': Chaucer's Prioress and the Canonists," *Notes and Queries* 205 (1960): 165–167.

55. For the Jewishness of the Holy Innocents in the mystery plays, and Herod's designation as a worshipper of Mahound, see, for example, Donald C. Baker, John L. Murphy, and Louis B. Hall, eds., *The Late Medieval Religious Plays of Bodleian MSS Digby 133 and Museo 160*, EETS o.s. 283 (Oxford: Oxford University Press, 1982), pp. 102, 108; and A. C. Cawley, ed., *The Wakefield Pageants in the Towneley Cycle* (Manchester: Manchester University Press, 1958), p. 75. This is not to say that the mystery plays as a whole are not a potent source of antisemitic propaganda: for an overview, see Stephen Spector, "Anti-Semitism and the English Mystery Plays," in Clifford Davidson, C. J. Gianakaris, and John H. Stroup, eds., *The Drama of the Middle Ages: Comparative and Critical Essays* (New York: AMS Press, 1982), pp. 328–341.

56. Philip S. Alexander, "Madame Eglentyne, Geoffrey Chaucer, and the Problem of Medieval Anti-Semitism," *Bulletin of the John Rylands Library* 74 (1992): 109–120, at 119–120. Alexander concludes that to justify the tale through hermeneutic subtlety is "fundamentally dishonest. . . . The only course of action left open is to ensure that when the *Prioress's Tale* is expounded, the basic facts of antisemitism are expounded as well" (p. 120). This is excellent pedagogical advice, but the question of Chaucer's relation to the tale remains open. Other discussions that argue for Chaucer's culpability are Robert Adams, "Chaucer's 'Newe Rachel' and the Theological Roots of Medieval Anti-Semitism," *Bulletin of the John Rylands Library* 77 (1995): 9–18; John Archer, "The Structure of Antisemitism in the *Prioress's Tale*," *Chaucer Review* 19 (1984–1985): 46–54; Albert B. Friedman, "*The Prioress's Tale* and Chaucer's Antisemitism," *Chaucer Review* 9 (1974–1975): 118–129; Emily Stark Zitter, "Antisemitism in Chaucer's Prioress's Tale," *Chaucer Review* 25 (1990–1991): 277–284; and Despres, "Cultic Anti-Judaism and Chaucer's 'Litel Clergeon.'"

57. The other is the so-called "Jewish Boy of Bourges," on which more later.

58. See, for example, Lisa J. Kiser, *Truth and Textuality in Chaucer's Poetry* (Hanover, N.H.: University Press of New England, 1991), pp. 25–41.

59. For the idea of "inward acculturation"—the absorption by an oppressed minority of the values of the dominant culture—see Ivan Marcus, "Jews and Christians Imagining the Other in Medieval Europe," *Prooftexts* 15 (1995): 209–226.

60. The best account of these events can be found in two books by Robert Chazan, *European Jewry and the First Crusade* (Berkeley: University of California Press, 1987); and *In the Year 1096: The First Crusade and the Jews* (Philadelphia: Jewish Publication Society, 1996).

61. For the latest contributions to this interesting issue, see Jeremy Cohen, "Between Martyrdom and Apostasy: Doubt and Self-Definition in Twelfth-Century Ashkenaz," *Journal of Medieval and Early Modern Studies* 29 (1999): 431–471; and his "The 'Persecutions of 1096'—From Martyrdom to Martyrology: The Sociocultural Context of the Hebrew Crusade Chronicles," *Zion* 59 (1994): 169–208 (in Hebrew, with English summary). The fullest account by a Christian is provided by Albert of Aix (Aachen), the relevant portions of whose chronicle are available in translation in Edward Peters, ed., *The First Crusade,* 2nd ed. (Philadelphia: University of Pennsylvania Press, 1998), pp. 102–104.

62. The real author of the chronicle is unknown.

63. Shlomo Eidelberg, trans. and ed., *The Jews and the Crusaders: The Hebrew Chronicles of the First and Second Crusades* (Madison: University of Wisconsin Press, 1977), pp. 35–36. Further references to this edition are given parenthetically in the text.

64. Chazan, *European Jewry and the First Crusade:* "The major instance of more radical behavior—the self-destruction of some of the anti-Roman rebels culminating in the mass suicide at Masada—was deliberately omitted from the historical tradition of rabbinic Judaism" (p. 220). Josephus's account of Masada was available to Jews in a tenth-century Hebrew translation ascribed to Joseph ben Gorion and with a title subsequently transliterated as *Yosippon, Yosifon,* or *Jossipon.* In this version the Jews do not commit suicide but march off to die fighting. For a modern Hebrew edition, see David Flusser, ed., *Sefer Yosifon,* 2 vols. (Jerusalem: Mosad Byalik, 1978–1980).

65. Other important precedents include the "ten martyrs," discussed in the *Jewish Encyclopedia* (New York: Funk and Wagnells, 1907), s.v. "martyrs"; and the four captives discussed by Gerson D. Cohen, "The Story of the Four Captives," *Proceedings of the American Academy for Jewish Research* 29 (1960): 55–131.

66. See W. H. C. Frend, *Martyrdom and Persecution in the Early Church: A Study of a Conflict from the Maccabees to Donatus* (Oxford: Blackwell, 1965), pp. 22–57; T. W. Manson, "Martyrs and Martyrdom," *Bulletin of the John Rylands Library* 39 (1956–1957): 463–484; and Arthur J. Droge and James D. Tabor, *A Noble Death: Suicide and Martyrdom among Christians and Jews in Antiquity* (San Francisco: Harper, 1992).

67. For a balanced survey of the various interpretations of the *'akedah,* see Louis A. Berman, *The Akedah: The Binding of Isaac* (Northvale, N.J.: J. Aronson, 1997); and Jon D. Levenson, *The Death and Resurrection of the Beloved Son: The Transformation of Child Sacrifice in Judaism and Christianity* (New Haven: Yale University Press, 1993).

68. Printed in *Norton World Masterpieces,* 7th ed. (New York: Norton, 1999), 1: pp. 1203–1206.

69. Shalom Spiegel, *The Last Trial: On the Legends and Lore of the Command to Abraham to Offer Isaac as a Sacrifice (The Akedah),* trans. Judah Goldin (New York: Pantheon Books, 1967). As the author of the *Chronicle of Solomon bar Simson* says: "May the blood of His devoted ones stand us in good stead and be an atonement for us and for our posterity after us, and our children's children eternally, like the 'Akedah of our Father Isaac when our Father Abraham bound him upon the altar" (p. 49).

70. Chazan, *European Jewry and the First Crusade,* p. 132.

71. This interaction has only begun to be described: see the works by Robert Chazan cited throughout this essay and especially the work of Ivan Marcus: "Jews and Christians Imagining the Other"; "From Politics to Martyrdom: Shifting Paradigms in the Hebrew Narratives of the 1096 Crusade Riots," *Prooftexts* 2 (1982): 40–52; "Une communauté pieuse et le doute: mourir pour la Sanctification du Nom *(Qiddouch ha-Chem)* en Achkenaz (Europe du nord) et l'histoire de rabbi Amnon de Mayence," *Annales: Histoire, Sciences Sociales* 49 (1994): 1031–1047; and *Rituals of Childhood: Jewish Culture and Acculturation in the Middle Ages* (New Haven: Yale University Press, 1996).

72. For a brief account of *kiddush ha-Shem*, see *The Jewish Encyclopedia*, s.v., and s.v. "martyrdom."

73. Herbert G. May and Bruce M. Metzger, eds., *The New Oxford Annotated Bible with the Apocrypha* (New York: Oxford University Press, 1977), 327–328.

74. Levenson, *Death and Resurrection of the Beloved Son*, p. 213.

75. Chazan, *European Jewry and the First Crusade*, p. 221.

76. Stow, *Alienated Minority*, p. 117.

77. T. Carmi, ed. and trans., *The Penguin Book of Hebrew Verse* (Harmondsworth: Penguin Books, 1981), p. 375.

78. Gerson D. Cohen, "Messianic Postures of Ashkenazim and Sephardim," in Max Kreutzberger, ed., *Studies of the Leo Baeck Institute* (New York: Frederick Ungar, 1967), pp. 149–150.

79. Jacob Katz, *Exclusiveness and Tolerance: Studies in Jewish-Gentile Relations in Medieval and Modern Times* (New York: Oxford University Press, 1961), p. 87.

80. Marcus, *Rituals of Childhood*, p. 7. Nor is this the only Jewish imitation of Christian religious practices. The *Memorbuchs* that were compiled with the names of the martyrs were Jewish versions of Christian martyrologies; the *piyyutor* liturgical prayers for the martyrs paralleled the liturgical feasts of the Christian saints; and, as Marcus has also shown, a new Jewish initiatory rite for children evoked the eucharistic wafer in the eating of Torah cakes ("Jews and Christians Imagining the Other in Medieval Europe," p. 222). Similarly, Jewish millenarianists copied Christian prophecies virtually verbatim: see David B. Ruderman, "Hope Against Hope: Jewish and Christian Messianic Expectations in the Late Middle Ages," in Aaron Mirsky, ed., *Exile and Diaspora: Studies in the History of the Jewish People Presented to Prof. Haim Beinart* (Jerusalem: Ben-Zvi Institute, 1991), pp. 185–202.

81. In his *vita* of William of Norwich, Thomas of Monmouth has the Jews saying insolently to the Christians, "You ought to be very much obliged to us, for we have made a saint and martyr for you. Verily we have done you a great deal of good, and a good which you retort upon us as a crime. Aye! we have done for you what you could not do for yourselves" (Thomas of Monmouth, *The Life and Miracles of St. William of Norwich*, ed. and trans. Augustus Jessopp and Montague Rhodes James [Cambridge, 1896], p. 95). See also the letter sent by the Jews of Paris to Louis VII, in which they refer to Richard of Pontoise, a reputed victim of ritual murder in 1163, as having been beatified (Chazan, ed. and trans., *Church, State, and Jew*, p. 115). For the notion of communities tied together through violence, whether real or imagined, see David Nirenberg, *Communities of Violence: Persecution of Minorities in the Middle Ages* (Princeton: Princeton University Press, 1996).

82. Alan Mintz, *Hurban: Responses to Catastrophe in Hebrew Literature* (New York: Columbia University Press, 1984): "Here lies the importance of the events of 1096: not the fact that a new form of collective behavior entered Jewish history, but

the transformation of the act, which could have remained an anomaly, into a new ideal, a norm of response to catastrophe in the imagination of Ashkenaz over the next eight hundred years, and this quite independent of the degree to which the suicides were actually imitated in deed" (p. 89). See also Cohen, "Messianic Postures of Ashkenazim and Sephardim," 115–156. For an alternative view, see Chazan, *In the Year 1096*, pp. 107–126.

83. Chazan, *Church, State, and Jew in the Middle Ages*, 301–303. For a discussion, see Robert Chazan, "The Blois Incident of 1171: A Study in Jewish Intercommunal Organization," *Proceedings of the American Academy for Jewish Research* 36 (1968): 13–31.

84. So too, during the massacres occasioned by the plague in 1348-49 the Jews of Worms and Oppenheim set fire to their district and perished in the flames: Léon Poliakov, *The History of Anti-Semitism*, vol. 1, *From the Time of Christ to the Court Jews*, trans. Richard Howard (New York: Vanguard Press, 1965), p. 111. For other examples of Jews burning themselves to death, occasionally in their synagogues, see Paul E. Grosser and Edwin G. Halperin, *Anti-Semitism, Causes and Effects: An Analysis of 1900 Years of Anti-Semitic Attitudes and Practices*, 2nd ed. (New York: Philosophical Library, 1983), pp. 105, 117, 130–131, and 139. When the crusaders captured Jerusalem in 1099 they herded much of the Jewish population into the Great Synagogue and set it afire: see Steven Runciman, *A History of the Crusades*, 3 vols. (Cambridge: Cambridge University Press, 1951), p. 287. But this event, recorded by Muslim chroniclers, seems not to have been widely reported in the West.

85. Robert Chazan, "Ephraim ben Jacob's Compilation of Twelfth-Century Persecutions," *Jewish Quarterly Review* 84 (1994): 401; Cecil Roth, *A History of the Jews in England*, 3rd ed. (Oxford: Clarendon Press, 1964), pp. 18–25.

86. The events at York have been described in detail by R. Barrie Dobson, *The Jews of Medieval York and the Massacre of March 1190* (York: St. Anthony's Press, 1974), although without attention to the meaning of the *kiddush ha-Shem*.

87. Translated by Roth, *History of the Jews of England*, p. 272.

88. Poliakov, *History of Anti-Semitism*, p. 134.

89. Robert Chazan, "The Timebound and the Timeless: Medieval Jewish Narration of Events," *History and Memory* 6 (1994): 28.

90. Richard Howlett, ed., *Chronicles of the Reigns of Stephen, Henry II, and Richard I*, Rolls Series 82, vol. 1 (London, 1884), pp. 312–322; translations in the text are by Joseph Stevenson, trans., *The Church Historians of England*, vol. 4, pt. 1, pp. 565–571.

91. Jonathan Riley-Smith, "The First Crusade and the Persecution of the Jews," *Studies in Church History* 21 (1984): 56.

92. Flavius Josephus, *The Great Roman-Jewish War: a.d. 66-70* (New York: Harper and Row, 1960), pp. 266–273. In his *Chronica*, Roger of Howden gives a much abbreviated and flatly disinterested account of the affair, although he also recognizes that the rabbi's advice is motivated by a desire to avoid apostasy: see Henry T. Riley, trans., *Annals of Roger de Hoveden* (Felinfach: Llanerch Publishers, 1997), vol. 2, pt. 1, p. 137.

93. For the *Yosippon*, the Hebrew version of Josephus, see above, n. 64.

94. Mary Minty, "*Kiddush ha-Shem* in German-Christian Eyes in the Middle Ages," *Zion* 59 (1994): 209–266 (in Hebrew). For a sermon preached around 1400 that provides an antisemitic interpretation of the Slaughter of the Innocents, see François Berier, "L'Humaniste, le prêtre et l'enfant mort: le sermon De *sanctis*

innocentibus de Nicolas de Clamages," in *L'Enfant au Moyen-Age,* Senefiance 9 (Aix-en-Provence: Imprimerie de l'Université de Provence, 1980), pp. 125–140.

95. Minty's instance of an exemplum influenced by the *kiddush ha-Shem* is that of "the Jewish boy of Bourges" ("*Kiddush ha-Shem* in German-Christian Eyes," pp. 239–241). For a discussion of this exemplum, see below, p. 535.

96. Although William apparently died in 1144, it was not until the later years of the decade—probably, indeed, after 1150—that his cult began to become popular, as Gavin Langmuir has shown, *Toward a Definition of Antisemitism,* pp. 209–236. It is no coincidence that the ritual murder charge at Bury St. Edmunds was made in 1181, after the anti-Jewish massacres of 1179–1180.

97. Carmi, trans., *Penguin Book of Hebrew Verse,* p. 373.

98. Cecil Roth, "A Hebrew Elegy on the York Martyrs of 1190," in *Transactions of the Jewish Historical Society of England* 16 (1945–1951): 213–220.

99. Ephraim Kanarfogel, "Attitudes Toward Childhood and Children in Medieval Jewish Society," in David R. Blumenthal, ed., *Approaches to Judaism in Medieval Times,* 2 vols. (Chico, Calif.: Scholars Press, 1985), 2: pp. 1–15; Magdalene Schultz, "The Blood Libel: A Motif in the History of Childhood," *Journal of Psychohistory* 14 (1986): 1–24; repr. in Dundes, ed., *The Blood Libel Legend,* pp. 273–303; and Marcus, *Rituals of Childhood,* passim.

100. For a specific example of a Jewish child kidnapped during the massacre at Rouen, and then hidden from his surviving parents in a monastery, as well as comments on this as a general Christian practice, see Norman Golb, "New Light on the Persecution of French Jews at the Time of the First Crusade," *Proceedings of the American Academy for Jewish Research* 34 (1966): 20–21, 22.

101. The Fleury plays are edited in Karl Young, *The Drama of the Medieval Church,* 2 vols. (Oxford: Clarendon Press, 1933). A facsimile of the manuscript, with transcription and annotation, is provided by Giampiero Tintori, ed., *Sacre rappresentazioni nel manoscritti 201 della Bibliothéque municipale d'Orléans* (Cremona: Athenaeum Cremonese, 1958). The translations provided in Fletcher Collins Jr., *Medieval Church Music-Dramas: A Repertory of Complete Plays* (Charlottesville: University Press of Virginia, 1976), are not reliable. That Blois rather than Fleury is the place of composition has been strongly argued by Solange Corbin, "Le manuscript 201 d'Orléans: Drames liturgiques dits de Fleury," *Romania* 74 (1953): 1–43, although the claims of Fleury have been presented by Fletcher Collins Jr., "The Home of the Fleury *Playbook*," in Thomas Campbell and Clifford Davidson, eds., *The Fleury "Playbook": Essays and Studies,* Early Drama, Art, and Music Monograph Series 7 (Kalamazoo, Mich.: Medieval Institute Publications, 1985), pp. 26–34. V. A. Kolve, "Ganymede/*Son of Getron:* Medieval Monasticism and the Drama of Same-Sex Desire," *Speculum* 73 (1998): 1014–1067, claims that "Collins effectively dismantles the claims made by Solange Corbin" (p. 1029 n. 40), which is in my opinion far from the case. While this is not the place for a full discussion, there is much other evidence, in addition to that presented by Corbin, that argues for a cathedral school in the Loire valley—either at Blois or, most likely, Orléans—as the place of composition for the plays.

102. Hilarius Aurelianensis, *Versus et Ludi, Epistolae, Ludus Danielis Belouacensis,* ed. Walther Bulst and M. L. Bulst-Thiele (Leiden: E. J. Brill, 1989), pp. 43–46; Wace, *La Vie de Saint Nicolas: Poème religieux du XIIe siècle,* ed. Einar Ronsjö (Lund: Håken Ohlsson, 1942), pp. 139, 141, lines 660, 723; Jehan Bodel, *Le Jeu de*

Saint Nicolas, ed. Albert Henry, 2nd ed. (Brussels: Presses Universitaires de Brux-
elles, 1965), p. 60, line 9.

103. The original Latin, in difficult dactylic hexameters, is in Young, ed.,
Drama of the Medieval Church, 2: pp. 346–347. I am indebted to my colleague Trau-
gott Lawler for helping me to translate this passage.

104. Chazan, ed., *Church, State, and Jew in the Middle Ages,* pp. 301–303.

105. For complaints about Jewish chanting, see Jordan, *French Monarchy and
the Jews,* p. 17; for a specific example of Jews chanting while being burned, see the
account of the massacre at Mainz in 1096 in Eidelberg, ed., *The Jews and the Crusaders,* p. 109.

106. Clyde W. Brockett, "Modal and Motivic Coherence in the Music of the
Music-Dramas in the Fleury *Playbook,*" in Campbell and Davidson, eds., *The Fleury
Playbook,* pp. 44–45.

107. Hélène Wagenaar-Nolthenius, "Der *Planctus Judei* und der Gesang
jüdischer Märtyrer in Blois anno 1171," in Pierre Gallais and Yves-Jean Riou, eds.,
Mélanges offerts à René Crozet, 2 vols. (Poitiers: Société d'Études Médiévale, 1966),
2: pp. 881–885.

108. Joseph H. Hertz, ed. and trans., *Siddur: The Authorized Daily Prayer Book*
(New York: Bloch, 1948), 208–211.

109. That there was a sizable Jewish community at Laon is shown by its inclusion among those who acceded to regulations promulgated by rabbinical synods held
in Troyes between 1150 and 1160: see Norman Golb, *Les juifs de Rouen an moyen âge*
(Rouen: Publications of the University of Rouen, 1985), p. 160. For the presence of
an obsession with Jews at Laon, one need look no further than the autobiography
of Guibert de Nogent. Since the violence of 1096 was especially marked at Rouen,
Laon's location between there and the cities of the Rhineland massacres would have
made it likely that knowledge of these events was common in the city—if, indeed,
Laon was itself spared in 1096. As for Limoges, there was enough of a Jewish community there in the late eleventh century for the well-known scholar Joseph ben
Samuel Bonfils to settle and work in the city; the Jews of Limoges suffered from
crusader violence in the thirteenth century, and Norman Golb, "New Light on the
Persecution of French Jews at the Time of the First Crusade," has shown that Jewish
communities in southern France also suffered in 1096. Freising has no record of Jewish massacres, but its proximity to the Rhineland cities and to those of Franconia,
like Würzburg, that suffered in 1146 as well as 1096, makes it likely that the massacres would have been known to the monastic community there. As well, Freising
is very close to Augsburg, where members of the Second Crusade were prevented
from attacking the Jewish community only by the intervention of the mayor and
council. One can assume that other, smaller communities in the neighborhood were
not so fortunate.

110. Quotations are from the most accomplished of these dramas, that in the
Fleury *Playbook,* and are cited from Young, *Drama of the Medieval Church,* 2: pp.
102–124.

111. Karl Young, *Ordo Rachelis,* University of Wisconsin Studies in Language
and Literature 4 (Madison: University of Wisconsin Press, 1919).

112. The notion that these plays, because part of a liturgical ritual, are transcendental actions that lack the immediacy of human emotion has been promoted by
many scholars: on the Rachel plays, see, for example, Robert Guiette, "Réflexions
sur le drame liturgique," in Gallais and Riou, eds., *Mélanges offerts à René Crozet,*

1: pp. 197–202. For Guiette, Rachel is to be understood as really being Mary, and in the plays "tout est dignité, grandeur et harmonie" (1: p. 201): the drama has "la caractère hiératique des attitudes et jusqu'à une certaine immobilité sculpturale en meme temps que sacrale" (1: p. 202). John Stevens began by arguing that Rachel is not a real Jewish mother but "a 'type' of the Church, *Ecclesia*, weeping for all her martyred sons," then moved to the recognition that the music for Rachel's laments is not in fact derived from liturgical traditions but from that of the *planctus*, which is designed to have a powerfully human emotional impact, and then finally provided a detailed account of what he called "Dramatic emotion: 'mourning Rachel.'" See John Stevens, "Music in Some Early Medieval Plays," in Francis Warner, ed., *Studies in the Arts*, Proceedings of the St. Peter's College Literary Society (Oxford: Basil Blackwell, 1968), p. 26; Stevens, "Medieval Drama," in Stanley Sadie, ed., *The New Grove Dictionary of Music and Musicians*, 20 vols. (London: Macmillan, 1980), 12: p. 37; and Stevens, *Words and Music in the Middle Ages: Song, Narrative, Dance, and Drama, 1050–1350* (Cambridge: Cambridge University Press, 1996), pp. 351–371.

113. The tale has been discussed in relation to host desecration narratives by Miri Rubin, *Gentile Tales: The Narrative Assault on Late Medieval Jews* (New Haven: Yale University Press, 1999), pp. 7–39.

114. According to Cooke in *MWME*, there are 33 versions of this tale in 68 manuscripts (9: p. 3225); to Cooke's bibliography of scholarship on the tale (3529–3530) should be added the most recent contribution, Heike A. Burmeister, *Der "Judenknabe": Studien und texte zu einem mittelalterlichen Marienmirakel in deutscher Überlieferung* (Göppingen: Kümmerle Verlag, 1998).

115. Sigebert of Gembloux, *Chronica*, ed. D. L. C. Bethmann in Monumenta Germaniae Historica, Scriptores, vol. 6 (Hannover, 1844), pp. 317 and 367–368.

116. The idea that Jewish behavior influenced either Christian antisemitic stereotypes or acts of persecution is, unsurprisingly, controversial. For some contributions to the debate set off by Israel J. Yuval, "Vengeance and Damnation, Blood and Defamation: From Jewish Martyrdom to Blood Libel Accusations," *Zion* 58 (1993): 33–90 (in Hebrew, with English summary), see the articles (in Hebrew, with English summaries) in *Zion* 59 (1994) by Jeremy Cohen, Ezra Fleischner, Mordechai Breuer, Abraham Grossman, and Gerd Mentgen, with Yuval's extended reply, which provides much insight into the meaning of *kiddush ha-Shem* both to Jews and Christians.

117. For the different versions of the tale, see Carleton Brown, *A Study of the Miracle of Our Lady Told by Chaucer's Prioress*, Chaucer Society Publications, Second Series 45 (London: Kegan Paul, Trench, Trübner, 1910); and Brown, "The Prioress's Tale," in Bryan and Dempster, eds., *Sources and Analogues of Chaucer's Canterbury Tales*, pp. 447–485 (the line from the *Gaude Maria* is translated from this chapter, p. 448 n. 1). The composition of the tale is certainly twelfth-century, but it does not appear among the English works that are the first instances of collections of Marian miracles: see R. W. Southern, "The English Origins of the Miracles of the Virgin," *Mediaeval and Renaissance Studies* 4 (1958): 176–216. The oldest surviving version appears to be in a Latin manuscript compiled in northern France (now BN lat. 18134): see Adolfo Mussafia, "Über die von Gautier de Coincy benutzen Quellen," *Denkschriften der kaiserlichen Akademie der Wissenschaft in Wien, philosophische-historische Classe* 44 (1896): 1–58, esp. 54–56.

118. This argument is repeated throughout the Hebrew crusade chronicles, where the Jews persistently refuse to accept a faith that deifies "the bastard son of a prostitute": see Eidelberg, ed., *Jews and the Crusades*, passim.

119. Of the 32 other versions of the tale, in only 7 is the boy killed by having his throat slit, and of those 7, 5 are categorized by Brown as instances of the earliest version (A), while he locates the *Prioress's Tale* in the later, C group. For the texts, see Brown, *A Study of the Miracle of Our Lady*, pp. 1–50. In his article in *Sources and Analogues*, Brown errs in his enumeration of the versions that include the detail of the throat-slitting (p. 458).

120. In "Chaucer's 'Newe Rachel' and the Theological Roots of Medieval Anti-Semitism," *Bulletin of the John Rylands Library* 77 (1995): 9–18, Robert Adams searches in vain throughout the exegetical tradition for evidence that Rachel could be considered other than as a prefiguration of Mary, and concludes that one can have no confidence that Chaucer recognized the irony. But the evidence from the liturgical drama shows that indeed Christians did recognize Rachel as a Jewish mother lamenting for a Jewish child slaughtered by a gentile, and as already mentioned, these dramas were performed in nunneries in England during Chaucer's lifetime.

121. Chazan, *European Jewry*, p. 319 n. 53.

122. Of course, authorial intention is a genuine theoretical problem, but we cannot sweep it aside in the name of some theoretical regulation like "the intentional fallacy," nor resort to currently fashionable terms like "textual unconscious": these are lexical maneuvers that beg the question. If we are truly to understand a literary work, we must at least try to determine the meaning its author was capable of—and interested in—having his text communicate.

123. For the most complete account, with an extensive bibliography, see Jean-Noël Biraben, *Les hommes et la peste en Frances et dans les pays européens et méditerranéens*, 2 vols. (Paris: Mouton, 1975–1976), 1: pp. 57–71.

124. Martin M. Crow and Clair C. Olson, eds., *Chaucer Life-Records* (Oxford: Clarendon Press, 1966), p. 64–65.

125. For the war and English involvement, see E. Russell, *The English Intervention in Spain and Portugal in the Reigns of Edward III and Richard II* (Oxford: Clarendon Press, 1955), pp. 84–148; for evidence that Chaucer's trip was undertaken to persuade, in the event successfully, the Englishman Hugh de Calvely and his troops to abandon Henry and to join the Black Prince in supporting Pedro, see Jesus L. Serrano, "The Chaucers in Spain: From the Wedding to the Funeral," at http://www.arrakis.es/~jlserrano. I am indebted to Dr. Serrano of the University of Cordoba for directing me to his website.

126. Cuvelier, *La chanson de Bertrand du Guesclin*, ed. Jean-Claude Faucon, 3 vols. (Toulouse: Editons du Sud, 1990–1991), 3: pp. 122–125.

127. The chronicle report is by Samuel Çarça and is printed (in Hebrew) in Fritz Baer, *Die Juden im Christlichen Spanien*, vol. 1, pt. 2 (Berlin: Schocken, 1936), pp. 200–201. Ivan Marcus provided me with a translation.

128. Abraham Halkin, trans., *Crisis and Leadership: Epistles of Maimonides*, ed. David Hartman (Philadelphia: Jewish Publication Society of America, 1985), pp. 13–90. For discussion, see Cohen, "Messianic Postures of Ashkenazim and Sephardim," p. 148 ff.

129. Russell, *English Intervention*, 533.

130. See, for example, José Hinojosa Montalvo, *The Jews of the Kingdom of Valencia from Persecution to Expulsion, 1391–1492* (Jerusalem: Magnes, 1993), p. 35;

and the letter from Rabbi Hasdai Crescas of Saragossa to the Jewish community of Toulouse written 19 Oct. 1391, which describes the ritual slaughters as *kiddush ha-Shem:* Franz Kobler, ed., *A Treasury of Jewish Letters,* 2 vols. (London: Farrar, Straus, and Young, 1952), 1: pp. 272–275. For discussion, with further evidence of *kiddush ha-Shem* in 1391, see Marc Saperstein, "A Sermon on the Akedah from the Generation of the Expulsion and Its Implications for 1391," in Mirsky, ed., *Exile and Diaspora,* pp. 185–202; and H. J. Zimmels, *Ashkenazim and Sephardim: Their Relations, Differences, and Problems as Reflected in the Rabbinical Responsa* (London: Oxford University Press, 1958), pp. 262–266.

131. Of the ten versions of the tale that belong to the later C group, only two have the child killed by having his throat slit: one is set in Toledo, and the other is the *Prioress's Tale;* see above, n. 119.

132. Elisa Narin van Court, "'The Siege of Jerusalem' and Augustinian Historians: Writing about Jews in Fourteenth-Century England," *Chaucer Review* 29 (1994–1995): 222. Van Court draws attention to the discussion of Jews and Judaism in Langland, Gower, the Corpus Christi plays, the two siege narratives, Mirk's *Festial* (which contains narratives of Jewish conversion), and the late-fourteenth-century manuscript that contains the only surviving copy of Peter of Cornwall's *Disputation with Symon the Jew.* See also van Court's "The Hermeneutics of Supercession: The Revision of the Jews from the B to the C Text of *Piers Plowman,*" *Yearbook of Langland Studies* 10 (1996): 43–87; and Richard Rex, *The Sins of Madame Eglentyne and Other Essays on Chaucer* (Newark: University of Delaware Press, 1995), pp. 13–26.

133. Joe Hillaby, "The Ritual-Child-Murder Accusation: Its Dissemination and Harold of Gloucester," *Transactions of the Jewish Historical Society of England* 34 (1994–1996): 69–109.

134. Langmuir, *Toward a Definition of Antisemitism,* 236–262.

135. H. M. Colvin, gen. ed., *The History of the King's Works* (London: H.M.S.O., 1963), p. 485.

136. Stow, *Alienated Minority,* p. 115.

137. Christopher Tyerman, *England and the Crusades, 1095–1588* (Chicago: University of Chicago Press, 1988), p. 231.

138. Roger Kohn, *Les juifs de la France du Nord dans la seconde moitié du XIVe siècle* (Louvain: E. Peeters, 1988), pp. 261–263.

139. For the English interest in crusading, see J. J. N. Palmer, *England, France, and Christendom, 1377–99* (London: Routledge and Kegan Paul, 1972), pp. 180–210; and Tyerman, *England and the Crusades,* pp. 288–301.

140. William Barber, trans., "The History of the Monastery of St. Peter of Gloucester," in David Welander, *The History, Art, and Architecture of Gloucester Cathedral* (Phoenix Mill, Gloucestershire: Alan Sutton, 1991), pp. 597–639.

141. Paul Olson, *The "Canterbury Tales" and the Good Society* (Princeton: Princeton University Press, 1986), p. 136.

142. Andrew Sharf, "An Armenian King at the Court of Richard II," in Pinhas Artzi, ed., *Bar-Ilan Studies in History* (Ramat-Gan, Israel: Bar-Ilan University Press, 1978), pp. 115–128.

143. Philippe de Mézières, *Letter to King Richard II,* trans. G. W. Coopland (New York: Barnes and Noble, 1976).

144. For this aspect of Richard's piety, and a discussion of the Wilton Diptych, see Nigel Saul, *Richard II* (New Haven: Yale University Press, 1997), pp.

303–308; and Dillian Gordon, *Making and Meaning: The Wilton Diptych* (London: National Gallery, 1993), pp. 59–60.

145. For an argument that the *Prioress's Tale* was written to commemorate this event, see Sumner Ferris, "Chaucer at Lincoln (1387): The *Prioress's Tale* as a Political Poem," *Chaucer Review* 15 (1980–1981): 295–321.

146. For the traditional identification of England as the *dos Mariae*, see Duffy, *Stripping of the Altars*, p. 256.

147. Michael Adler, *Jews of Medieval England*(London: Jewish Historical Society of England, 1939), 322–323.

148. There was at least one precedent for Richard's presence at the baptism of this convert: "King Louis IX of France was present . . . when 'a Jew of great renown' was baptized. This happened just before his departure in 1270 to his second and last crusade. Louis insisted that the envoys of the King of Tunisia, then in Paris, be present at the ceremony." See Joseph Shatzmiller, "Jewish Converts to Christianity in Medieval Europe," in Michael Goodich, Sophia Menache, and Sylvia Schein, eds., *Cross Cultural Convergences in the Crusader Period: Essays Presented to Aryeh Grabois on His Sixty-Fifth Birthday* (New York: Peter Lang, 1995), p. 304.

149. *Calendar of the Plea Rolls of the Exchequer of the Jews*, 3 vols. (London: H.M.S.O., 1905–1929), 3: pp. 311–312. The nakedness was presumably designed to punish Sampson for disguising himself as a friar and to show that he was circumcised; the bearing of the dead animal may represent a Christian misunderstanding of Jewish butchering practices.

150. For the institution of compulsory sermons in England, see Roth, *History of the Jews in England*, pp. 78–79. Conversionary sermons had been made compulsory in Spain in 1240, and in other European countries soon after: see Jeremy Cohen, *The Friars and the Jews: A Study in the Development of Medieval Anti-Judaism* (Ithaca: Cornell University Press, 1982).

151. For such responses, see Robert Chazan, *Daggers of Faith: Thirteenth-Century Christian Missionizing and Jewish Response* (Berkeley: University of California Press, 1989).

152. Berger, *Critical Edition of the Nizzahon Vetus*, pp. 33–34. This point is made by Jordan, "Marian Devotion and the Talmud Trial of 1240," p. 64.

153. James C. Scott, *Weapons of the Weak: Everyday Forms of Peasant Resistance* (New Haven: Yale University Press, 1985).

154. In the opinion of Albert Friedman, repeated in different words by numerous other critics, "The only way Chaucer could be wholly acquitted [of the charge of furthering anti-Semitism] would be to prove that Chaucer's tale is a bold and obvious satire of anti-Semitism and unequivocally felt as such by his audience, which certainly it is not" ("The *Prioress's Tale* and Chaucer's Anti-Semitism," p. 119).

ELIZABETH ROBERTSON

The "Elvyssh" Power of Constance: Christian Feminism in Geoffrey Chaucer's The Man of Law's Tale

Recent criticism has shown that Geoffrey Chaucer's *Canterbury Tales* are a particularly rich index of medieval culture's interest in various forms of difference. Major recent books on Chaucer have explored the importance of class—or, to use a term more suited to the Middle Ages, social status—to an understanding of Chaucer's work.[1] Another major group of critics has investigated Chaucer's complex engagement with issues of gender and sexuality.[2] Most recently, critics have called attention to racial difference in two of his *Tales—The Squire's Tale* (a romance of flying horses, magic rings, and speaking birds) for its "orientalism," and *The Man of Law's Tale* for its portrayal of the Islamic other as stereotypically monstrous, violent, and unnatural.[3] Critics have recognized not only the importance of race, class, and gender as critical categories that map difference but also the complexity of ideas produced when these categories interact with one another.[4] Current interest in that trinity—race, class, and gender—however, has tended to mask what this paper argues is a deeper source of radical otherness, at least to Chaucer, and perhaps more generally in the period: religion.

Religion's strangeness in Chaucer's work emerges powerfully, I argue in this essay, in his often neglected *Man of Law's Tale*. As one begins the tale, it appears to be first about Islam and then about suffering women, but closer inspection, especially of the tale's imagery, demonstrates that Islam is not the

Studies in the Age of Chaucer, Volume 23 (2001): pp. 143–80. © 2001 New Chaucer Society.

primary other of this tale but rather a code for an equally strong challenge to convention—apostolic Christianity as it is embedded in the feminine. By interweaving and complicating the categories of race, class, and gender (as they are understood in late medieval England), Chaucer posits a religious ideal in this tale that itself occupies the position of difference: in part, by drawing on the history of the conversion of Britain as well as Christianity's early history—apostolic Christianity as revealed in the Gospels—Chaucer presents a form of nonviolent Christianity that is less coercive, less hierarchical, and more communal than, and implicitly challenging and potentially dangerous to, the institutionalized form of Roman Christianity operating in the fourteenth-century English Church.

Religion, of course, has not been neglected in Chaucer criticism. However, because exegetical criticism so dominated early Chaucer criticism, critics have found it difficult to consider Chaucer's religion in any other way. Many postmodernist critics have therefore tended to avoid the subject of religion altogether. More recently, C. David Benson called for a reconsideration of Chaucer's Catholicism, and, in response, Linda Georgianna showed how the Protestantism of those who have studied Chaucer's religion, including the exegetical critics and the humanists who responded to them, has distorted their understanding of Chaucer' religion by leading them, for example, to ironize or dismiss specifically Catholic elements of Chaucer's work, such as his representations of miracles, and the powers of sanctity.[5] Even the most recent studies of Chaucer's religion are hindered by underexplored assumptions that his Christianity is doctrinal, conservative, uniform, and hegemonic.

Another strand of criticism of religion, most often focused on other than Chaucerian texts, has gained momentum in recent years. David Aers has been instrumental in shifting critical discussion about religion in fourteenth-century England away from the debate between the exegetical and humanist critics, and toward cultural materialism (that is, toward a more responsibly historicized, class-sensitive analysis of religion).[6] Following Aers's lead, a new body of criticism that has contributed profoundly to our understanding of religion as a cultural construct has been articulated in the work of such influential critics as Sarah Beck with, Karma Lochrie, Lynn Staley, and Nicholas Watson, although their work has been focused primarily on the drama or the writings of the mystics rather than on Chaucer.[7] Watson's call to explore the ramifications of what he has dubbed "vernacular theology" has laid the groundwork for a new appreciation of the different ways religion functions in late medieval culture.[8] Louise Fradenburg has helped us consider psychoanalytic dimensions of late-medieval English literature, but she has yet to engage fully Chaucer's religious writing from the point of view of psychoanalysis.[9] Chaucer criticism has only just begun to embrace these new historical, anthropological, psychoanalytic, and cultural approaches to the study of religion. These and other postmodernist critics have taught us that the profile of religion at any given moment responds to and is defined by that particular moment; this insight in turn allows us to revise our sense of how Christian belief and practice in late medieval England influences Chaucer's poetry and to recognize how multifaceted and historically embedded are Chaucer's representations of religion.

In *The Canterbury Tales,* Chaucer delineates a broad variety of forms of religiosity, ranging from the extreme pathos of affective piety underpinned by a disturbing foundational anti-Semitism in *The Prioress's Tale* to the eloquent understated exploration of sanctity in *The Second Nun's Tale* to the stark prosaic sermonizing of *The Parson's Tale.*[10] What these various religious tales share and what is demonstrated so richly in *The Man of Law's Tale,* I suggest, is a formation of religion itself as a category of difference intimately bound with one of the characteristic functions of Chaucer's writing itself—defamiliarization.

In *The Man of Law's Tale,* Chaucer's emphasis on the fundamental otherness of religious experience and on its capacity to defamiliarize is reinforced by the tale's engagement with other forms of difference, including race and class, but most fully, as I shall demonstrate, gender. Class, or social status, at first seems an almost invisible concern in this tale, yet we shall see that the configuration of each of the other categories of difference are in every way affected by Constance's class position as an aristocratic woman. Sheila Delany, one of the few readers to consider class and gender in the tale, exposes Constance's victimization.[11] Delany, however, in her argument that Chaucer offers Constance as a model of submission for the revolutionary participants of the English Rising, discusses class by analogy rather than by considering the ways in which social status operates literally in the tale. In her consideration of class, Delany fails to consider the particular strengths and weaknesses afforded to Constance as a member of the aristocracy. Since it was more common for women of upper rather than lower social status to become objects of exchange in foreign marriage markets, the aristocratic Constance is particularly mobile on the marriage circuit. Despite medieval Christianity's doctrinal belief in the importance of female consent in marriage, secular practice rarely solicited such consent, and in this representation Constance is no exception. Stressing her identity as a commodity while commenting on her lack of voice in her marriage, Constance laments, "Wommen are born to thraldom and penance" (line 286). Women of higher social status often had less choice in marriage partners than women of lower social status. Constance's class position both potentially severely restricts her options and affords her unusual mobility.

A full consideration of the role Christian strangeness might play in the tale has been masked by critical concern in the apparently more disturbing and shocking—though stereotypical—representation of religious difference found in the tale's opening portrait of Islam. There is no doubt that Chaucer's representation of Christianity in this tale is deeply shaped by its contrast to Islam. But if we turn our attention away from the Islamic other of the opening of the tale, and away from the class issues that allow Constance to travel to a foreign land in the first place, and toward the otherness of Constance herself, we will develop a more complex understanding of the fundamental role difference plays in the tale. Perhaps it is because of her substantial otherness that critics have had trouble talking about Constance, so much so that A. S. G. Edwards argues that there seems to be a conspiracy to avoid discussing Constance herself.[12] The habit of turning away from Constance is true not only of criticism that concludes the work is more about the teller than the tale but also of criticism that praises the tale for its celebration of Christian values. V. A. Kolve, for example, and those who agree with him (e.g., Eugene Clasby), talk about Constance as an agent of the dissemination of Christianity, one who joins a long history of men and women who have suffered for the promulgation of the Christian faith.[13] Yet most commentators on the religious issue overlook the fact that Constance, besides being a suffering Christian, is also a suffering woman. The interpretive significance of Constance's gender is virtually ignored. Chaucer's religion is inextricably bound in this tale, as in a number of other tales, with Chaucer's representation of gender, because it is through gender that he can convey religion's ultimate abject unknowability. By enriching gender through evoking concepts associated with religious others, and through linking gender with a particular form of Christianity, Chaucer is able to transcend the restrictive category of feminine identity. Cast in a rudderless boat, yet capable of positively affecting the lives of others, Constance, like the religion she embodies, resists the strictures of an ideology into which the dominant culture would like to place her.

Through the synergism of gender and religion, Chaucer is able to engage with sensitive, politically charged contemporary religious controversies, especially those raised by Lollardy, without specifying his own religious commitments. Chaucer's representation of religion in this tale intersects with a fourteenth-century cultural debate, spearheaded by the Lollards, about such issues as the appropriateness of women as preachers, the status of the vernacular Bible, the role of violence in religion, the nature of faith when unmediated by the clergy, the role of wealth in the church, and the unknowability of God. While it engages these issues, and indeed sometimes seems in sympathy with Lollardy, the tale carefully avoids embracing or reinforcing unorthodox views. On the contrary, it can be understood as completely orthodox and conventional, and in many ways engages aspects of orthodox Catholicism in direct opposition to Lollard views, such as a celebration of images, a valorization of the violence necessary for the early establishment of the Church, praise for the efficacy of miracles, and prayers to Mary and the veneration of her and the saints. In the end, however, by representing religion first and foremost as characterized by "strangeness" conveyed through feminine abjection, Chaucer allows religion here to exceed the constraints of such topical reference.

Chaucer, in sum, initially utilizes the category of race to establish ideas of strangeness, simultaneous attraction and repulsion (the "orientalist" desire described by Edward Said), and the tendency of the other to inspire violence, and then draws on contemporary concepts and practices about women to articulate an unpredictable and utopian vision of women as spiritually and politically effective.[14] We shall see, as the tale unfolds, that the expectations raised by the work's evocation of categories of race and social status, are displaced by a different, though-related, set of ideas brought out by Chaucer's intertwining of medieval concepts and practices concerning women and the "feminine" with his concept of apostolic Christianity. The fears and desires that are produced by racial categories and brought into being through class mobility are intensified by the different set of emotions evoked by a constructed "feminine" abjection. Certain particular ideas about the feminine that were current in the period—its association with motherhood, the semiotic (vs. the symbolic), submissiveness, and abjection—serve Chaucer in positing his ideal of apostolic Christianity. The idea of the Christian feminine allows for the possibility of an unconventional female agency that emanates from the ineffable powers of religion. Finally, I shall suggest, Constance not only embodies an ultimately unknowable form of religion, but also Chaucer's sense of the strangeness of poetry itself and especially of its elusive transformative potential.

Constance and the "Racial" Other

In order to establish the kind of Christian power explored in his tale, Chaucer sets the story in motion by placing Christianity in opposition to Islam. At the beginning of the tale, Chaucer uses fourteenth-century cultural stereotypes about the Islamic racial other. We must be careful in our assessment of Chaucer's racism in his use of stereotypes here, because as most critics agree, race as a category of difference is historically specific, and racial categories may convey different meanings to a medieval audience than they might to a modern one. Dana Nelson usefully summarizes the controversies over the term race:

Taken variously to stand for cultural, evolutionary, moral, metaphysical and biological difference, "race" has never been a stable idea or a fixed concept. Moreover, its enduring representation—as a scientifically documentable kind of difference—has now been thoroughly debunked: "race" is no longer recognized as a scientific category. That being so we can perhaps enter into a more critical understanding of "race." One approach might be to consider it in terms of what Michel Foucault defines as an "apparatus," namely a "formation,"

which has as its major function at a given historical moment that of responding to an urgent need.[15]

The word itself had apparently not found currency in fourteenth-century
England; the earliest recorded uses of the term from the thirteenth-century
on in Spanish, Portuguese, and French forms (*raza, race,* and *race,* respectively) seem generally to refer to a tribe or group of descendants rather than
to groups defined by shared physical characteristics, and it is not recorded in
English until after 1500.[16] Because the category of race as we understand it
today had not yet consolidated as a formation in fourteenth-century England,
it is difficult to assess precisely how the representation of race in this tale
functions for Chaucer's readers. Chaucer's notions of Islamic people are most
probably drawn primarily from literary sources and more narrowly from the
literature of the Crusades. He does not always uncritically borrow the racial
prejudices of his sources; in his *Squire's Tale* for instance, Chaucer presents a
surprisingly tolerant view of those who embrace a faith other than Christianity. In *The Man of Law's Tale,* on the other hand, he does seem to adopt the
racial stereotypes of his sources. In the majority of these sources, we find,
however, that in late medieval literature pigmentation differences were subordinated to religious difference, and those of different races were often cast in
parodic racist roles primarily because of their devotion to alternate religions.

Typical of the kind of work Chaucer might have drawn on to develop his
own ideas about the interaction of Christianity and Islam is the late twelfth-
century Middle High German *Parzival* (ca. 1197). *Parzival* is a particularly
useful literary text to consider as part of Chaucer's literary inheritance because
it is one of the few literary texts of the medieval period that includes pervasive,
although brief, meditations on the possible significations of skin color, at least
for this author. This text exemplifies the ways in which medieval literature
tended to subordinate categories of racial difference to categories of religious
difference. In addition, *Parzival* interestingly, like *The Man of Law's Tale,* utilizes "race" to explore another category of difference, that of writing itself.

The white Gahmuret's love affair with a black woman, Belacane, illustrates how skin color, although recognized in the period, was less important
in social hierarchization than class, and more importantly, religious affiliation.
Furthermore, as we shall see in *The Man of Law's Tale,* the meaning given to
"racial" difference depends on the position of the observer. Gahmuret and
Belacane mutually fear each other's different skin colors. The story begins
with Gahmuret's love affair with Belacane, whom he later abandons because
she was not baptized although he excuses himself for his ill treatment of her
by claiming that she prevented him from pursuing feats of arms. In his quest
for a mate, the hero "manege tunkele frouwen sach er bêdenthalben sîn: nach
rabvens varwe was it schin" ("saw many a dusky lady with complexions of the
raven's hue"), and he seems unconcerned about her color.[17] Belacane, however,

expresses her concern about his reaction to her color: er ist anders denne wir gevar: ôwî wan taete im daz niht wê!" ("He is of a different color than us. O I do hope he won't be offended by that").[18] The messenger reassures her that "für küneges künne erkant" ("he is known to be the kin of kings").[19] In this case, high social status over comes racial prejudice. His skin color is also of concern to her, however, as we are told, "si kunde ouch liehte varwe spehen: wan si het och ê gesehen manegen liehten heiden" ("she could also judge of fair complexions, for she had seen many a fair-skinned heathen before").[20] Nonetheless, when considering Belacane as a potential wife, Gahmuret's primary concern is not her color, but her religion: "Gahmureten dûhte sân swie si waere ein heidenin, mit triwen wîplîcher sin in wibes herze nie geslouf. ir kiusche was ein reiner touf" ("Gahmuret reflected how she was a heathen, and yet never did more womanly loyalty glide into a woman's heart. Her innocence was a pure baptism"), and in the end, "Doch was im daz swarze wîp lieber dan sîn selbes lîp" ("his black wife was dearer to him than his own life").[21]

The child that results from their liaison, Feirefiz, is described as looking like a magpie, black with white patches, "als ein agelster wart gevar sîn hâr und och sîn vel vil gar" ("like a magpie was the color of his hair and of his skin"), and is often referred to in the text as "Feirefîz der vêch gevar" ("speckled Feicefiz").[22] Feirefiz's mottled appearance gives us a glimpse into medieval ideas of miscegenation.[23] Clearly, Wolfram von Eschenbach did not know what a person of mixed race would look like. The child's mottled appearance has a further signification in the book, however, for the story of *Parzival* cannot come to a close until Feirefiz is brought into the Christian community. According to Christian ideology, all humanity is mottled. Sin is cast as dark, and manuscript illuminations and stage productions often depict the devil himself as dark-skinned. In the York cycle, for example, those who cast aspersions on the devil, who in these plays is associated especially with Islam, comment on his dark face. Feirefiz thus ultimately stands for all humanity stained with original sin whose sin can be mitigated only by entrance into the Christian community through baptism. The story is framed by the sin of the father that opens the narrative, a sin that is redeemed symbolically at the end by Feirefiz's baptism. The description of Feirefiz's skin recalls the magpie of the beginning of *Parzival* who is referred to as representative of sinful humanity. Skin color here thus signifies one's status within the scheme of Christian salvation. Feirefiz's motivation for conversion, like his skin, is mixed: he chooses to be baptized, not in order to see the Grail, but to be able to marry Repanse de Joye. Nevertheless, despite his mottled nature, Feirefiz is presented positively throughout the work. Although Eschenbach's representation of the racial other is here apparently positive, it is important, as Israel Burshatin has argued in his essay "The Moor in the Text," to recognize the presence of "racist" ideology in works that seem to represent Moors positively, because most often those positive representations are only the result of the character's potential for conversion.[24]

Wolfram makes another intriguing analogy concerning Feirefiz's skin. He describes it as "als ein geschriben permint swarz und blanc her unde dâ" ("like a parchment with writing all over it, black and white all mixed up").[25] By comparing Feirefiz's skin to a written document, Wolfram implicates Feirefiz in his own act of writing, an act that is "mixed up" with dark and white, with sinfulness and purity. It also links writing to difference itself; writing here is portrayed as hybrid, on a border, neither fully within nor fully outside the Christian community. Furthermore, its import, its potential for good or evil, is not clear.

When we turn to *The Man of Law's Tale*, we will see that Chaucer also presents writing as dangerously other. Some forms of writing—letter writing and reports—are dangerous because they distort reality; other forms (those that produce images or recount salvation history) are potentially salvific. As we shall see, this salvific potential is embodied in Constance, who like Feirefiz is a hybrid, on a border. Like Feirefiz and like the ink on a manuscript parchment skin, Constance takes the reader from the familiar into the dangerous realms of the unknown. Like the mottled child who shocks and enchants/enthralls us in his weirdness, so Constance's difference fundamentally disorients the reader.

A number of critics have observed that *The Man of Law's Tale* begins with a stereotypical and perhaps racist representation of Islamic people. In an important recent essay, Susan Schibannoff has described the motivations for the late medieval hatred of Islam, motivations that she points out stem not only from Islam's difference from but also its similarity to Christianity. Not least among the threats posed by Islam was the monotheism it shared with Christianity. The Islamic people portrayed at the opening of the tale are particularly threatening because their religion might be as powerful as Christianity. The Islamic Sultan and his mother are stereotypically portrayed as respectively naive and duplicitous, and the mother's followers are represented as exotic, cruel, and unnatural. The Sultan's monstrous mother incites the Muslims to barbarism, and their brutal behavior predictably motivates the imperialist genocide enacted by the heroine's, Constance's, father at the tale's conclusion. Clearly the tale asserts racial stereotypes in its portrait of the cunning and barbarous Islamic mother-in-law who resists the imposition of Christianity on her culture, and of the sweeping power of the Roman Christian war machine that flattens the Islamic community in revenge for its treatment of the Christian ambassadors.

However, as the tale progresses, another monstrous mother-in-law, as well as other cruel characters, torment Constance, but they are not racial others. The racism of the caricature of the Islamic mother-in-law is thus called into question by the fact that Chaucer portrays a pagan British mother-in-law, Donegild, in the same way. What Donegild shares with the Islamic mother-in-law is not a different ethnicity, but rather a different religion, for both women oppose Constance only because she believes in a religion different from their own. Race as a category here, as elsewhere in the period, is therefore complicated, if not defined by, religious affiliation. Furthermore, in this tale pagans and those of the Islamic faith are seen as interchangeable.[26] When Constance looks back on her experience, she is disturbed not so much by her contact with foreign races as by her contact with other religions. She begs her father, "Sende me namoore unto noon hethenesse" (line 1113) She applies "hethenesse" equally to her experiences in Syria and to her experiences in pagan England.[27]

If we add gender to our analysis of the racism of the opening sequence, a more complicated picture of the work's representation of difference emerges. Schibanoff also makes this observation, but her analysis leads to a very different conclusion from mine, for she argues that the racism of the tale reinforces its sexism. In discussing Constance's apparent passivity, Schibanoff argues, "Not only does Constance's behavior provide a model of female submission, but it helps the Man of Law reach a more fundamental goal in his tale: to establish and maintain woman's difference from (inferiority to) man, her otherness. . . . The Man of Law's overriding aim . . . is to preserve and enhance such difference—between women and men, East and West, Islam and Christianity, ultimately between western patriarchal culture and the Other."[28] The tale does indeed draw on "racist" stereotypes to reinforce the otherness of Constance, but in my view Constance's otherness, rather than being a mark of her inferiority, sets her apart as superior to that of any non-Christian in the tale, Eastern or Western, and furthermore is entwined inextricably with her religion.

Instead of merely applying inherited cultural stereotypes in his representations of Islam, Chaucer complicates and transforms them. On the one hand, he conventionally utilizes stereotypes as he represents Roman Christianity's imperialist conquest of the racial other, Islam. On the other hand, he also depicts Islam's colonizing impulses vis-à-vis Constance. Constance is portrayed from the point of view of Islamic observers as a stranger, the foreign other. Syrian merchants see her first, and their description of her initiates the plot. As Schibanoff argues, in contrast to its sources, the tale here expresses the commonalities between the Syrians and the Romans, even though a momentary anxiety occurs when "the sultan's councillors doubt that a Christian emperor would allow his daughter to marry under 'Mahoun's' law, 'By cause that ther was swich diversitee / Bitwene hir bothe lawes' (lines 220–21)"; this diversity is easily overcome.[29] Following the impulses of a number of late medieval theologians, Chaucer represents Islam as not dissimilar to Christianity; for example, the Sultan's counselors use reason to convince the Sultan to convert, a representation in keeping with medieval theological respect for the rationality of Islam. In the tale this respect is indicated in the narrator's acknowledgment that those who follow Islam consider it to be a "sweete" law (line 223) compared to the "deere" law of Christianity (line 237).[30]

The underlying dangers of similitudes emphasized in these opening sequences extend to the text's representation of the imperialist impulses shared equally by East and West. Like Christians motivated by the desire to conquer and possess foreign lands, the Sultan desires to possess this exotic other, Constance (lines 186–89):

> . . . this Sowdan hath caught so greet plesance
> To ban hir figure in his remembrance,
> That al his lust and al his bisy cure
> Was for to love hire. . .

If he cannot "han Custance withinne a litel space, / He nas but deed" (lines 208–9). His lust for this idealized image pushes him to the point of relinquishing his own religion. Here Chaucer paints a portrait of possessive desire that blinds and obscures values in a way that is analogous to the racism of the violent Christian conqueror desirous to overcome the heathen other. The other in this case is not a person of color, however, but Constance—a woman of a different faith, and from the point of view of the Syrians, of a different race. The central "racial" other in this opening sequence, then, is arguably not the Islamic mother-in-law, but Constance. Thus, Chaucer here uses the category of race to emphasize, first, Christianity's power and, second, its strangeness, for it is not only Constance's experiences in a foreign land that are at issue here but also her experiences as a foreigner bringing with her a foreign religion—to a land presented from the point of view of those who reside within it.

Chaucer represents the Islamic other as dangerously the same not only in monotheism but also in imperialist impulse—an impulse toward colonizing desire, awakened by storytelling itself. These opening stanzas entwine medieval orientalism with a subtle elucidation of the potentially dangerous effects of "tidynges," (reported accounts of things seen). The poem opens with a description of a company of merchants in Syria "That wyde-where senten hir spicerye, / Clothes of gold, and satyns riche of hewe" (lines 136–37). These merchants who trade in spices and luxury goods, their "chaffare," also trade in stories, for they return to Syria with tales (lines 178–82):

> For whan they cam from any strange place,
> He wolde, of his benigne curteisye,

Make hem good chiere, and bisily espye
Tidynges of sondry regnes, for to leere
The wondres that they myghte seen or heere.

In this passage the usual orientalist expectations are reversed in that the
Syrian Sultan desires to know more about the exotic West, rather than being
the object of the curious desire of the West.

These opening passages tell us that desire for the other is inspired not
only by Constance's image but also significantly by the report or "tidings" of
her, that is, by the outsized image of her coming not from a single human
source but from "sondry regnes," from the exotic collective authority culled
from many realms. Chaucer distinguishes the person from the collective image of her. The merchants first hear a report of the "renoun / Of . . . dame
Custance" lines (150–51). After hearing of her virtues, they then see her.
Upon their return, their report of Constance inspires the Sultan to desire "To
han hir figure in his remembrance" (line 187); "telling" inspires a colonialist
desire to see and possess the image in his mind. "Tidynges" not only evoke a
desire to possess but also are strong enough to inspire conversion. Chaucer
here represents storytelling as both powerful and dangerous, recalling Wolfram von Eschenbach's ambivalent representation of writing cast as racial
other. Given the fact that the larger work within which *The Man of Law's Tale*
appears is a series of told stories, perhaps Chaucer is here drawing our attention to the power of writing itself, suggesting that an encounter with writing
can be considered an encounter with a category of difference. Writing can be
understood to inspire the fears, resistances, desires, and transformations that
are commonly evoked by other categories of difference or encounters with
the strange.

In this case, stories ultimately have the power to convert. Like Feirefiz,
the Sultan's motivation for conversion is a worldly one; and like Feirefiz, an
image inspires an act of faith that has the potential to be salvific. The Syrian
Sultan feels the need for salvation as he asks his counselors to "Saveth my lyf
. . . / To geten hire that hath my lyf in cure" (lines 229–30). Although on one
level he simply uses a secular courtly convention by describing a beloved as a
cure for lovesickness, the Sultan's unconscious reference to salvation also suggests at another level the salvific potential offered by the Christian Constance.
The Sultan little realizes that from a Christian point of view, Constance's
requirement that he convert before marrying might literally save his life. In
some senses, the Sultan is on the "right" road to Christianity because he has
already responded with an act of faith, faith in the report of Constance.

The interplay between report, image, and desire here anticipates *The
Man of Law's Tale*'s interest in secondhand reports, narrative, argument, and
rhetoric, all set in opposition to the much more effective persuasiveness of

imagery itself—and, as we shall see, these oppositions are played out through the interplay of gender and Christianity that fully emerges in the second half of the work. The tale becomes increasingly interested in the power of the image in Christian pedagogy; and here what is said of Constance, what her image can convey by report, is linked to God: "And al this voys was sooth, as God is trewe" (line 169), the narrator asserts of other people's assessment of her virtue. Thus, the veracity of Constance's reputation is here compared to the truth of God, a comparison that both increases her exotic desirability and reinforces the "oriental" qualities of God. Casting God in orientalist terms is not foreign to the medieval tradition. As is said in the *Ancrene Wisse,* the hope offered by Jesus "is a swete spice."[31] Dealing in spices, the merchants inadvertently stumble upon the agent of the "true" Christian God. Thus, in the opening lines of the tale, Chaucer interweaves race and gender in order to establish the power of Constance as an embodied Christianity who inspires both violence and desire.

Constance and the Agency of Strangeness

Those who have studied the representation of gender in the tale, however, do not grant Constance any power. Dinshaw, for example, in her brilliant analysis of the narrator's problems with female power in his portrait of the incestuous mothers-in-law, concludes that Constance is a nothing, "an essential blankness that will be inscribed by men."[32] Jill Mann, whose reading comes closest to mine, nonetheless fails to see the peculiarly feminine, if not feminist, aspects of Constance's power.[33] Delany, in her argument that Chaucer uses this tale as an allegory of contemporary class issues, concludes that Constance is merely passive. Schibanoff, in the most recent assessment of gender in the tale, similarly dismisses Constance as a reinscription of medieval ideals of the submissive female.[34]

    In contrast to many feminist critics, my view is that Constance holds power, but unlike the Christian apologists, I see Constance's power as problematic because of her gender. It is difficult to talk about the power Constance holds because she does not participate in systems we know, although her power, as Kolve, Benson, and Clasby demonstrate, emanates from her Christianity. In contrast to other kinds of Christian power, and in spite of her status as a daughter of an emperor, Constance's power is buttressed neither by institutional religion nor by the state. Having suppressed her class origins, Constance converts others without the violence associated with imperialist, hegemonic Christianity. Her Christian power, when combined with gender, finally becomes radically other; its force resides in its otherness, and it operates from the margins. If we consider the tale's representation of otherness as a locus of both repulsion and desire, it is Constance who is the central and productive "other" of the tale. Like racial others, Constance, as an embodiment of a foreign religion in foreign lands, is the site of such desire (all who see her want to possess her) and repulsion (many who see her want to hurt her). Her otherness as a woman combined with her otherness as a religious minority (a Christian in an Islamic country, then in a pagan country), is central to the tale's representation of apostolic Christianity as a potentially dangerous, "elvish," unknowable force. Furthermore, it is within the strangeness and mystery of apostolic Christianity that Constance's agency resides.

Critics tend to measure Constance's power in terms of that exhibited by the other women in the tale, the violent mothers-in-law. In their condemnation of what they see as Chaucer's endorsement of female submissiveness in the figure of Constance, Delany, Dinshaw, and Schibanoff all conclude that Chaucer reinforces his views by presenting women who do exhibit power as monstrous. The narrator criticizes both women for their mannishness (the Islamic mother-in-law is called unwomanly and Donegild a virago). Critical understandings of the mothers-in-law tend to assume, however, that in these passages Chaucer criticizes women, I would like to offer an alternative reading by arguing that here Chaucer criticizes not women, but rather a certain kind of masculinity present in either men or women, one that uses power for its own selfish purposes. Chaucer's description of the Islamic mother-in-law as a "feyned womman" (line 362), and later of Donegild as "mannysh" (line 782), thus signals Chaucer's intuitive recognition that gender is constructed. He criticizes not only the fact that these women attempt to seize power but also the kind of masculine power in which they are invested, one marked by violence, deception, and cruelty. Such violent, tyrannical, "male" power seems suspect even when wielded by the Christian heroes of the tale. For example, as an agent of conversion, Constance's rudderless boat sailing between the powerful war machines bent on revenge (lines 953–966) is far more effective than that army which brings not conversion but mass destruction.[35] And Constance, although powerless in some senses, brings a powerful ruler, Alla, to his knees. Might not Chaucer be drawing our attention to the negative consequences of male-identified violence and proposing instead nonviolent religion? For her part, Constance never advocates violence, even when it seems justified. Alla commands the death of the false knight—but Constance "hadde of his deeth greet routhe" (line 689).

Chaucer seems aware of the social construction not only of femininity but of masculinity as well. While violence is associated with the masculine, it is not *essential* to masculinity as formulated by Chaucer. Indeed, with the exception of his own act of vengeance, Alla seems to be "feminized" and contrasted with the mannish mothers-in-law. He is, for example, inspired to excessive, perhaps "feminine" tears: "This Alla kyng hath swich compassioun, / As gentil herte is fulfild of pitee, / That from his eyen ran the water doun" (lines 659–61). By his "feminine" feeling, as David Benson has noted, Alla is brought to his knees in awe of Constance's faith.[36]

Although most critics agree that Constance has no agency in the tale, Chaucer's representation of Constance's apparently passive submissiveness is more complex than it first seems. Constance's relationship to action is obscure. She inspires extreme and often irrational violence in others, but she herself is neither an instigator nor a perpetrator of that violence. She triumphs over others, but she chooses neither to suffer nor to triumph. Rather than being obedient, Constance seems outside of law. The primal image of her in a rudderless boat in the sea reinforces her unknowable, anarchic power. Whether or not Constance can be called active or passive therefore seems indeterminate.

Indeed, Chaucer seems intent on obscuring her agency. Critics often bolster their assessment of Constance as passive by pointing to the fact that Chaucer changed his sources to diminish Constance's involvement in action. Chaucer's revisions to his sources do not erase her agency, however, but rather problematize it. In Trivet's and Gower's earlier versions of the story, for example, Constance purposely places the would-be rapist at the edge of the boat and then prays for aid from God. In Chaucer's version, on the other hand, Mary comes to her aid unasked, and Constance's involvement in the overthrow of the rapist is ambiguous. Chaucer tells us, "For with hir struglyng wel and myghtily / The theef fil over bord al sodeynly" (lines 921–22). The language is double here: it gives the reader the opportunity to attribute the fall both to God and to Constance's struggle. Later in the work, Chaucer treats the incident when her son Maurice goes to meet her father in a way that veils Constance's active participation in the event. The sources tell us she sends Maurice to Alla. Chaucer's narrator obscures Constance's agency. We are told first only that she might have sent the boy and second that it was at least at her command that the boy stares at his father (lines 1009–15):

> Som men wolde seyn at requeste of Custance
> This senatour hath led this child to feeste;
> I may nat tellen every circumstance—
> Be as be may, ther was he at the leeste.
> But sooth is this, that at his moodres heeste
> Biforn Alla, durynge the metes space,
> The child stood, lookynge in the kynges face.

Constance's power and effectiveness are revealed not through her actions so much as through her face. As the work progresses, her face becomes the site of signification for others. The tale's repeated use of the imagery of sight underscores the importance not just of seeing that face but of understanding it properly. The story is set in motion, as we have noted above, by the reported sighting of Constance. As the story unfolds, characters observe Constance, some for good and some for ill, but seeing her incites desire in all of them. When Constance first sets foot in Northumberland, her example, indeed simply the sight of her, inspires pity, devotion, service, and love, despite her obscure origins: "She was so diligent, withouten slouthe, / To serve and plesen everich in that place, / That alle hir loven that looken in hir face" (lines 530–32). In a passage of sweet irony, Constance urges Hermengyld to give a blind Briton back his sight in the name of Christ. Although we never know whether or not the Briton's sight is restored, Constance's power is revealed in this scene around issues of sight. As the tale puts it, the constable is "abasshed of that sight" (line 568) and only after observing the same does he ask to hear Christ's lay: "And so ferforth she gan oure lay declare / That she the constable, er that it was eve, / Converteth" (lines 572–74). Alla is moved to believe in Constance's innocence "Whan he saugh so benigne a creature" (line 615). Others defend her "For they han seyn hire evere so vertuous" (line 624). The senator praises Constance by saying "Ne saugh I nevere as she" (line 1025). Satan, on the other hand, "Saugh" (line 583) all her perfection and then incited the knight to kill Hermengyld. The would-be rapist is part of a crowd that "gauren" on her ship (line 912). To judge Constance's power solely in terms of her activity or passivity overlooks the ways other kinds of power are revealed in the tale. As we see in these events, Constance's inner being is conveyed not by how she herself acts, but rather by her effect on others.

Constance is initially praised as a "mirour of alle curteisye" (line 166), that is, as someone or some idealized object of desire who merely reflects, a point that to Dinshaw suggests Constance's nonexistence in the text. But Constance's face is more than a mirror, for it generates power, the power to convince Alla of her probable innocence, and, more important, the power to convert. Dinshaw further argues that the thrice repeated image of Constance's pale, corpselike face is further evidence of her nothingness. But the image of her deathly pale face (line 645) can serve other functions. First, it enhances Constance's abject unknowability in that the paleness signifies her ghostliness, a kind of marginality that places her on the border between life and death. Donegild furthers the impression of Constance's otherworldliness. She objects to her son's marriage to so peculiar a person—"Hir thoughte a despit that he sholde take / So strange a creature unto his make" (lines 699–700)—and in her invented letter hopes to capitalize on that difference by associating her with other forms of strangeness, namely the supernatural. She labels Constance an elf, an appellation that suggests her affiliation with the world of spirits as much as with the world of humans: "The mooder was an elf, by aventure / Ycomen, by charmes or by sorcerie" (lines 754–55).

Although we know this is a slanderous fiction, the attribution articulates the potential fear her difference can inspire in others. To describe her as "elvish" and as one who uses charms is to articulate her power, and although we as readers know that she is not an elf, her mystery fascinates and engages all who encounter her both within and without the tale.

The ambiguity of Constance's nature is further enhanced by the oft-noted generic confusion of the work, for she is at once a heroine from the romance deeply involved in the secular world and sexualized as a wife and a mother and an asexual heroine from the saint's life. Indeed the narrator responds to the confusion inspired by her secular saintliness in his passage about Alla and Constance's intercourse on their wedding night (lines 708–14):

> They goon to bedde, as it was skile and right;
> For thogh that wyves be ful hooly thynges,
> They moste take in pacience at nyght
> Swiche manere necessaries as been plesynges
> To folk that han ywedded hem with rynges,
> And leye a lite hir hoolynesse aside,
> As for the tyme—it may no bet betide.

Critics have often commented upon the odd combination of prudishness and prurience in this passage, but Chaucer is also arguably drawing our attention here to the problems of secular sanctity, and thus ultimately to the challenge facing those trying to integrate the spiritual with the mundane.

The narrator's description of Constance's arrival in Northumberland further emphasizes her mystery. When she lands at Northumberland, the constable finds first "the tresor that she broghte" (line 515), surely a sign that might convey her identity. The narrator does not reveal the nature of this treasure. Its status as treasure might enhance the Constable's open reception of Constance. But we do not know whether treasure signifies a monetary or a symbolic value, or both. If it's monetary, the Constable might conclude that Constance is an aristocrat whose recovery might offer him future reward. Or the treasure might only be symbolic; for example, it might simply be a wooden cross. Perhaps it is both monetary and symbolic—for example, a gold cross. Like us, the Constable is unable to discern her meaning from the treasure that travels with her. Surely, however, the unknowable treasure reinforces her intriguing attractiveness.

The Constable must then rely on verbal exchange to determine Constance's identity. Constance, however, proves also to be linguistically strange—that is, she speaks a corrupt language, not even that of the people whose land she has entered. Nonetheless, she is understood. As is characteristic of her, her strangeness does not prevent her from communicating even across languages:

"In hir langage mercy she bisoghte.... A maner Latyn corrupt was hir speche, / But algates therby was she understonde" (lines 516, 519–20). As an agent of conversion, Constance is translatable, despite her foreignness. Her universal linguistic power is perhaps again hinted at rather indirectly when the false knight swears upon "A Britoun book, written with Evaungiles" (line 666), for Constance is protected in this scene by the sudden appearance of a British form of the Gospels. At the time of the conversion of Britain, where might such a text have come from? Is this a version of the Gospels written in British hands or a translation of the Gospels into British? Given the controversy concerning English Bibles in Chaucer's own day, the presence of this "underground" Bible reinforces Constance's mysterious power.[37] Nonetheless, like the Bible, Constance's speech can universally be understood.

Constance conveys meaning not only by words but by gesture, for her first act is to kneel and pray that the Constable kill her. Constance is aware of the long history of danger induced by the arrival of a foreigner on native shores. By articulating abjection, however, Constance disarms the Constable's fear of her difference. It is not gesture alone that makes Constance understandable, for besides kneeling down, she continues to speak to the Constable in her strange language, further and deliberately obscuring her origins: "She seyde she was so mazed in the see / That she forgat hir mynde, by hir trouthe" (lines 526–27). In Chaucer's sources, Constance must hide her family origins, fearful of the pursuit of her incestuous father. Chaucer's elimination of the fear of incest serves to reinforce Constance's obscure motivations and origins. An acknowledgment of her father as emperor of Rome, through an announcement of her class affiliations, would immediately categorize her and limit her. In Chaucer's version, Constance's obscurity thus reinforces her mysterious association with God, and her unconventional agency emanates from that alliance.

Constance as Bertha: Apostolic Christianity and Fourteenth-Century Christianity

Why should Chaucer here, as elsewhere in *The Canterbury Tales*, choose to embody Christianity in a woman? What does he achieve by embodying Christianity in a female rather than a male body? One answer is that Christian women in history have exerted a variety of powers as mystics, virgin martyrs, and proselytizers of Christianity, and although Constance is none of these overtly, in some ways she is all of these. Furthermore, by embodying Christianity in a woman of the past, Chaucer is able to safely engage controversial contemporary issues without seeming to do so. Women's historical experience in Christianity is complex, as Caroline Bynum and others have so ably demonstrated, and Christianity seems to have both oppressed women and afforded women a range of power.[38] In the secular world, as members of the fourth estate, women are both integral to the culture's functioning and excluded from its power structure, yet manage to exert influence despite or perhaps through their marginality. In *The Man of Law's Tale*, Chaucer uses Constance's secular marginality and ambiguous status within Christianity to construct a kind of Christianity that is itself also marginal.

That women's power is severely constrained within medieval secular society is suggested in both the Prologue and the Tale. The *Prologue*, in its long list of Chaucerian stories of classical women abandoned by men, reminds the reader of the ways in which secular patriarchy repeatedly betrays women. The *Tale* itself reinforces the idea of the culture's objectification of women in its representation of Constance's treatment by most, although not all, of the men she encounters in her travels. Those women who are able to exert power within secular culture seem only to be able to do so by forfeiting their gender, that is, by becoming mannish. In this tale, the marginal position is the only place where women can maintain their integrity. While it may appear from certain perspectives to be weakness, marginality in some ways grants power. As Helene Cixous writes, it can be "a position of maximum maneuverability . . . a border in which outmoded male logic ceases to speak."[39] And who has more mobility in this tale than Constance? In her border position as a Christian in a pagan land she does succeed in overthrowing an outmoded pagan logic. And, as David Raybin points out, Constance, even when on land, never stays far away from the border, from the sea whence she emerged.[40] Marginality, then, can enhance rather than weaken Christianity's power.

Constance's gender contributes to Chaucer's delineation of Christianity in yet another way. He may well be invoking in his portrait of Constance a historical woman who also effected a major conversion without violence: Bertha, the Frankish bride who facilitated the conversion of Anglo-Saxon England, thus restoring the earlier forms of Christianity present among the Roman Britons.[41] Her marriage to Aethelberht took place on the condition that she be allowed to bring her priests with her. She brought with her a Frankish bishop named Liudhard, and Christian observances took place in the king's household almost nine years before Augustine's mission. Bertha did not demand that Aethelberht convert, nor did he convert until some years after Augustine's landing in Britain in 597, but that conversion ultimately changed the face of England. We do not know if Chaucer was aware that Bertha was memorialized at Canterbury in the font dedicated to her in the church of St. Augustine, but at the very least he may have known of Bertha's role in English national Christianity. Female and religious power were thus closely intertwined in England's history from its beginnings. This focus on the role gender plays in British religious history further delineates the superior otherness of Constance's religion as one that emerges and flourishes specifically in Britain; and as Schibanoff also points out, that British form becomes authorized in the tale by its ultimate links to Rome through Maurice, Constance's son, who eventually becomes the new emperor of Rome.

Like Bertha, Constance converts without violence and without coercion. Most of the men in the tale, Constance's father and his ambassadors, are far less successful in their forceful attempts at conversion than is Constance in her nonviolent teaching. In this work, conversion is a mystery rarely achieved by force. Christianity is associated with violence, the violent revenge Constance's father takes for the killing of the Christian ambassadors, for example, or the punitive hand that appears from heaven; but this violence is not primarily in the service of conversion, nor is it perpetrated by Constance. While the miraculous hand does effect conversion, its occurrence is motivated by a need to protect Constance. Conversion seems to be inspired by observation of an example and seems to be a matter of time and choice. Constance's image is far more forceful than even a fleet of ships.

It would be a mistake to dismiss these qualities as conventional. The nonviolent ideal Chaucer advocates here is by no means a complacent one. Christian power is disturbing in the tale. It inspires extreme violence in others, including murder and attempted rape, and its operation depends on the suffering of an innocent woman. Chaucer embodies these unsettling qualities in an apparently helpless woman who is also a mother, therefore enhancing their shock value. And just as Constance's timeless devotion to faith continually disrupts the various forms of secular corruption she encounters, so the tale distrusts and disrupts the reader's assumptions about the nature of power itself. In this tale, Christianity's power finally resides in what its characters perceive to be its otherness, and this form of Christianity operates from the margins.

This textual construction of a marginal form of Christianity reflects apostolic Christianity's marginal status in the fourteenth century, when institutionalized religion had moved far from the original tenets of the Christian faith. The apostolic Christianity described here is most definitely in the world (Constance is not a nun or a saint) but not of the world. In keeping with early apostolic Christianity, her religion is communal and nonhierarchical and ties are formed horizontally rather than vertically, in a structure of ascending power. She, Hermengyld, and Hermengyld's husband, the constable, form horizontal bonds that even affect their sleeping arrangements, so that Hermengyld and Constance share a bed. Conversion to her religion is effected through prayer and the expounding of the new law rather than by coercion, although violence occurs around her and sometimes to those who try to interfere with her. Thus, the hand that appears from heaven to smite the false accusing knight, although followed by the conversion of those who witnessed the event, is preceded by Alla's inclination toward Constance because of her appearance, a predisposition that causes him to inquire further into her case.

As opposed to the Christianity represented by her father, Constance's religious ideal is a force of personal transformation rather than an institutional power. In this personalized and nonhierarchical form of religion, Chaucer here recalls the religion practiced by Christ and the apostles in the Gospels.

The role the apostolic church did or should play in the institutionalized church was not of course a neutral topic in the fourteenth century. A variety of groups and individuals from the strictly heretical to the potentially heretical embraced this ideal, and Chaucer's purposes in his evocation of such an ideal are virtually impossible to pinpoint.[42] The friars embraced such an ideal, and Chaucer's thoroughgoing satire of the corruption of the friars throughout his work shows both his scathing assessment of Franciscanism and his disappointment with ideals not inconsonant with his own.[43] Perhaps more to the point is the number of specific aspects of Constance's religiosity that suggest affinities with fourteenth-century debates concerning Lollardy.[44] A woman converting those around her through her prayers and explications of doctrine evokes one of Lollardy's cherished tenets: that anyone—even women and the uneducated laity—can preach. A late-fourteenth-century commentary objects to the influence of such notions in this way: "Ece iam videmus tantam disseminacionem evangelii quod simplices viri et mulieres et in reputacione hominum laici ydiote scibunt et discunt evangelium et quantum possunt et sciunt docent et seminant verbum Dei" ("Behold now we see so great a dissemination of the gospel that simple men and women, and those accounted ignorant laymen in the reputation of men, write and learn the gospel, and, as far as they can and know how, teach and scatter the word").[45] Furthermore, another commentary specifically condemns a young London virgin for conducting the mass. The former comment aptly describes Constance, a woman who is not a saint, or an authorized visionary, but who nonetheless spreads the gospel. Chaucer skirts the question of Constance's explicitly priestly actions, but nonetheless her effectiveness as a disseminator of the gospel and as an agent of conversion is clear. By placing Constance firmly in the past, Chaucer avoids directly affirming a woman's ability to preach, while at the same time he is able to allude to a controversial issue of his day.

Other less-obvious tenets also surface when the tale is scrutinized closely, yet they too emerge only incompletely.[47] One of the most politically charged debates inspired by the Lollards was one familiar from earlier Franciscan ideals, that servants of the church should live in poverty. The status of church poverty is nowhere explicitly present in the tale, but the tale is preceded by a long, seemingly irrelevant, disquisition on poverty in the voice of the Man of Law in the prologue to the tale. Placing this commentary on the ills of poverty in proximity with his evocation of the ideals of apostolic Christianity in the figure of Constance tantalizes with its dual potentially heretical and strictly orthodox valences, but finally eludes explication, not least because of the fact that these views are espoused not by Chaucer directly, nor by a member of the clergy, but by a man of law. Furthermore, the function of this speech within the prologue is complex, and its relationship to the *Tale* is in no way specified.[48]

A second elusive issue engaged by Lollards and the tale is the role of violence in the service of the church. One of the twelve conclusions of the Lollards clearly takes a position against violence in the church: "þe tende conlusiun is þat manslaute be barayle or pretense lawe of rythwysnesse for temperal cause or spirituel withouten special revalaciun is expres contrarious to þe newe testament . . . þis conclusiun is opinly provid be exsample of Cristis preching here in erthe, þe qwiche moste taute for to love and to have mercy on his enemys, and nout to slen hem."[49] As I have argued above, Constance eschews violence. On the other hand, the Bishops, in their assessment of Lollard views, stress that violence is acceptable in those cases when absolutely necessary, that is, when justified by special revelation. Perhaps the special intervention of God's minister who slays Constance's accuser would be justified by the Bishops, who argue, "Also we graunten þat it is leveful to sle men in dome and in batellis, if þo þat doun it han autorite and leve of God."[50] Presumably, the emissaries from Rome have God's authority. The tale, in the end, has it both ways in its representation of violence: Constance eschews violence, but plenty of violence occurs in her wake. In addition, although she herself neither advocates nor participates in revenge against her potential Islamic in-laws, the tale does without commentary portray a vicious, relentless revenge enacted righteously by her father and emanating directly from Rome (see lines 960–66). The extreme violence of the unnatural Islamic others incites justified retribution from the center of Christian faith, Rome. Is Chaucer obliquely criticizing the calls to violence that emanate from Rome, or is he validating the justice of revenge, thus reinforcing the conventional medieval European attitude toward the Islamic other? Chaucer allows for either interpretation.

The *Tale* also engages other issues debated by the Lollards. The Lollards repeatedly stress the unknowability of God, a position that is, I shall demonstrate more fully later in this essay, also stressed by the Man of Law, who asserts repeatedly the limits of human knowledge of God in statements such as "Crist . . . / By certaine meenes ofte . . . / Dooth thyng for certein ende that ful derk is / To mannes wit" (lines 479–82). But that unknowability is praised not by Chaucer, but by the Man of Law, one whose understanding of his subject matter is shown to be repeatedly inadequate. Is Chaucer parodying Lollard views here or protecting himself from criticism by mediating those views?

The role of mediation is itself a Lollard concern, for Lollards argued in favor of an unmediated relationship with God. Constance articulates her faith without mediation. We as readers, however, learn of her faith through the mediation of the Man of Law. And one could argue that the Man of Law's mediation only interferes with an understanding of Constance's mysterious powers. One can't say that Chaucer criticizes the mediation of the clergy here, since the Man of Law is not a clergyman, yet Constance's unmediated knowledge of God anchors the tale. Perhaps it was allowable in the late fourteenth century to celebrate unmediated access to God in figures from the past, in saints, for example. Constance, however, is not a saint, although she is placed firmly in the historical past.

On the other hand, the tale might also be construed as advocating positions in direct opposition to Lollard views. Lollards were accused of rejecting the veneration of Mary and the cult of the saints. The eleventh point in the Bishops' accusations is "þat it is not leful to praye to seint Marie neiþer seientis seying þe latanye or oþer orisouns, but onli to God men owen to preie."[51] This tale clearly, however, revels in a form of Marian spirituality. Constance repeatedly prays to Mary and miraculous rescues result from her prayers. Furthermore, Constance is aligned with saints and her behavior is saintly. If one considers the Bishops' responses to Lollard condemnations of Marianism more closely, one can see that Constance's Marianism might actually engage the very points under contestation, for they write: "Also we graunten þat it is boþe leveful and medeful to preie to oure Lady and to alle halowus, so þat þe entent of oure preiour be do principally to Goddes worschipe. And in oure preiouer we schulden not þenke þat oure lady or oþer seyntis mowun graunte any þing of hemself, but þei knowen Godis wille and preien þat it be fully don and so þer preier is herde."[52] In each of Constance's prayers she acknowledges God's power and the history of salvation in Mary. She asks Mary to take pity on her child in memory of her own suffering in witnessing Christ's death. She does not ask for the miracles of such distaste to the Lollards.

That Chaucer hints at questions of urgent contemporary concern only to elude any clear articulation of those questions only reinforces the ineffability of the Christian ideal he portrays in the tale, an ideal that disturbs as much as it comforts. The Christianity represented here disturbs not so much in itself—indeed, the images of Constance praying in Northumberland are peaceful—but rather because of the difficulty of conversion and because of the violence it inspires in others. It is Christianity's alien quality—a category of difference—that to others is frightening. On the other hand, it also provides a model for the acceptance of the strange. For example, when Alla learns that his child is purportedly a monster, rather than reject that child, he welcomes him as a product of God's will. Constance herself accepts difficulty because of her faith. Christianity thus provides access to understanding of what is inscrutable and often painful. Apostolic Christianity and conversion to it propels the convert into the realm of the abject, a realm of strangeness that is both attractive and repellent.[53]

Image as Power: Imagery, Rhetoric, and the
Female Reproductive Body

The mystery of Christian power as embodied in Constance is reinforced by the work's insistence on the primacy of the image over the word, the repudiation of verbal for iconic force. Consider, for example, the fact that the written word twice fails to achieve its purpose in the story in the letters of the messenger; indeed these letters reinforce how susceptible the written word is to distortion and manipulation. The image, although ineffable, does not distort meaning. As V. A. Kolve has so ably demonstrated, images of Constance dominate her story—images that evoke other well known images.[54] For example, as she leaves Syria, Constance prays to the cross, and it is the image of her, helpless, that dominates here. She is repeatedly associated with both Mary and Christ and thus with innocence and excessive pain and suffering. Images comparing her to Mary evoke our pity; for example, as she leaves Northumberland with her small chid, she stands on the shore and prays, recalling images of Mary's suffering, as in the lines "Hir litel child lay wepyng in hir arm, / and knelynge, pitously to hym she seyde" (line 834 ff.). Furthermore, the poem is permeated with images of Constance floating rudderless in the "salte see." The narrative produces a series of tableaux and images that are overdetermined and offer more meaning than the narrative can make sense of. Chaucer teases our imaginations with heavily loaded and ultimately obscure imagery. For example, what do we make of the image of the bloody knife placed between Hermengyld and Constance when they are in bed together—a knife that evokes Mark's sword in the story of Tristan and Isolde? Or, as mentioned earlier, how do we interpret the image of a British Bible in a pagan court? These images finally are evocative rather than decodable.

Like Kolve, I agree that Chaucer's portrait of Constance invokes a body of familiar images, primarily Marian images, and that these images have pedagogical power and range in their ability to convey complex doctrinal issues to both literate and nonliterate audiences. But where Kolve (and others who have studied the Christian pedagogical power of medieval imagery such as Eamon Duffy and Margaret Miles) read such images as serving a univalent orthodoxy, I believe Chaucer's use of this store of familiar religious imagery produces neither complacency nor a sense of the familiar. Rather, Chaucer teases and challenges us by calling up familiar associations in his descriptions of Constance, only to defamiliarize these associations by emphasizing her departure from the stereotype. Images of Constance make us uncomfortable precisely because she, Constance, is not Mary or a saint, despite her similarities to both, but rather a secular heroine, a commodity on the aristocratic marriage market, and the producer of an heir who will become powerful to both church and "state." The Christian lesson conveyed by her image is thus complicated by her class and gender. Furthermore, her secular status forces us to realize the difficulties of bringing a certain kind of religious idealism into practice in the midst of a variety of conflicting hegemonies. These images produce discomfort not only in themselves (for example, in the pathos of the tableau of a victimized mother and child) but also in the violent and irrational responses they inspire in others, from lust, to envy, to desire for God.

Chaucer's assertion of the allurements and dangers of the image evokes a contemporary controversy about imagery articulated in various medieval discourse, but perhaps most polemically by the Lollards. Typical of Lollard distrust of images is the Bishops' eleventh and twelfth accusations "þat it is not leful to preye to seint Marie neiþer seientis, scying þe latanye or oþer orisouns, but onli to God men owen to preie"and "þat neiþer crosse ne ymages peynted or graven in þe worschip of God or any oþer seyntis in þe chirche schuld be worschipid, and, þouȝ a man sauȝe before him þe same crosse wereon Crist suffered deþ, he schulde not worschipe it, for, as it is seid, al þat worschipen þe crosse or ymages ben cursed and done mawmentri."[55] Constance, in praying directly to the cross, seems to engage in just the sort of idolatry condemned by some Lollards: "O cleere, o welful auter, hooly croys, / Reed of the Lambes blood ful of pitee, /... Victorious tree, proteccioun of trewe, /... Me kepe"(lines 451–62). The Bishops defend such prayer, however, by arguing that images can be worshipped if they serve God's purposes, "men mowen levefuliche worschippe hem in sum manere, as signes or tokones; and þat worschipe men done to hem, if þei loven hem and usen hem to þat ende þat þei ben ordayned fore."[56] Images function in a variety of ways in the *Tale,* and might be said to evoke both sides of the debate. At the very least, Chaucer indicates his awareness of the contemporary debate about images by emphasizing the troubling force of images.

Part of the complexity of images is conveyed when they are linked to gender. The dominant image of the tale is of Constance floating in a rudderless boat. Kolve has shown how pervasive this image is in his discussion of the ship of the church and/or the ship of the soul floating in the sinful sea.[57] Kolve has overlooked, however, how evocative this image is as a specifically gendered one. Luce Irigaray has powerfully explored the ways in which the image of water has particular resonance for women, evoking other cultural ideas of women as fluid, lacking in boundaries, and uncontainable, cultural concepts of the feminine that have their roots in medieval medical views.[58] Chaucer seems to draw on these cultural constructions of gender to reinforce his concept of the timeless uncontainability of his form of Christianity.

Constance's association with imagery that has the power to convert without violence is in opposition to the far less persuasive language of both the narrator and the men like him in the story who repeatedly try, but fail, to know the causes and nature of things. Like Dinshaw, I would argue that the law of men is under scrutiny in this tale. But unlike Dinshaw, I would argue that the different law of a woman, the "law" represented by Constance through imagery, comments on and resists the "law of men." The narrator himself comments upon the insufficiency of men's wits to predict the future: "mennes wittes ben so dulle / That no wight kan wel rede it atte fulle" (lines 202–3). Christ's work, the Man of Law reminds us, "ful derk is / To mannes wit" (lines 481–82), but to at least one woman's wit, to the knowledge of Constance, appears to be less obscure. It is impossible to determine, of course, how gender specific Chaucer' use of "men" is in these passages, but at the very least he describes a system of knowledge most commonly expounded by men. The narrator ridicules the Syrian's inadequate attempts to know things, but Chaucer lets the reader know that he is, and that we should be, skeptical of the Man of Law's attempts to know and understand; that is, the Man of Law's rhetorical interpolations, which provide lists of classical and biblical precedents for Constance's life, are seen by some critics as so excessive as to point to Chaucer's satire of the religious life; to others they are seen as simply dull, a sign of Chaucer's lack of interest in his subject.[59] Chaucer may indeed be satirizing the Man of Law's rhetoric, but that alone does not mean that he is also satirizing Constance. The Man of Law continually tries—and fails—to authorize and appropriate Constance's experience, a religious experience that is finally inexplicable in words. Ultimately Constance's experience goes beyond the wit of the men she encounters in her tale, or even that of the narrator who tries to contain her with his legalistic epistemology.[60] The Man of Law's rhetoric is shown to be inadequate to the understanding of the ineffable, which Chaucer assigns in this tale to Christianity and Constance.

Constance is difficult to know in part because she inhabits a different temporal reality from the Man of Law, and even from those she encounters in the tale, for Constance lives in the realm of liturgical time. As David Raybin points out in his essay on Constance and history, Constance presents a challenge to conventional time schemes.[61] That we should attend carefully to the meaning of time is signaled in the Introduction to the *Tale*, where the host warns the pilgrim not to waste time: "Leseth no tyme, as ferforth as ye may. / Lordynges, the tyme wasteth nyght and day" (lines 19–20). The link between time and gender represented in the *Tale* is anticipated in the Introduction by the host's comparison of lost time to the breaking of a woman's hymen (lines 28–31)—a passage whose significance in terms of men's law has been illuminated by Dinshaw:

> "But los of tyme shendeth us," quod he.
> It wol nat come agayn, withouten drede,
> Namoore than wole Malkynes maydenhede,
> Whan she hath lost it in hir wantownesse.

Tale telling is seen as profitable when it does not waste time. The Man of Law, describing his storytelling as required by law, and agreeing to the host's request, says,

> "... ich assente;
> ... Biheste is dette, and I wolde holde fayn
> Al my biheste, I kan no bettre sayn
> For swich lawe as a man yeveth another wight,
> He sholde hymselven usen it, by right ..." (lines 39–44)

He then promises to tell a tale in prose. Of course the story that follows is not in prose but in rhyme royal, a metrical pattern that complicates the timing of the presentation of the story.

The Man of Law tells a history, one very self-consciously committed to linear time, but Constance's story defies such linearity, for hers is a story of repetition and circularity, one that begins and ends in the same place—Rome, at the home of her father. This kind of double time scheme, one that encompasses both linear and liturgical time, is common in medieval works, but Constance's gender enhances her association with liturgical time, because as a woman she is associated with birth and regeneration, repetition and cycles. These attributes contribute to the definition of what Kristeva calls "monumental" or "women's time."[62] That time intersects with the world of "cursive" time occupied by the Man of Law, but finally transcends it.

Constance is thus associated with ineffability, timelessness, repetition, circularity, generation, fluidity, and obscured agency and how she acts as a mediator for transcendence. Many of these qualities, while not necessarily gender determined, are gender linked. According to medieval physiology, they are seen as essential to women.[63] Aristotle, for example, defines women as essentially fluid and naturally drawn to water. Commentaries on Genesis circulating in the Middle Ages stress that as a consequence of the Fall, women are prone to suffering. Chaucer seems to question such essentialism in his exposure of a brutal marriage economy that reduces women to voiceless agents, in his condemnation of the "mannishness" of the mothers-in-law, and in his celebration of the "womanishness" of a man, Alla. The Man of Law's rhetoric, on the other hand, defines a world that is bound by time, certain knowledge, intrusiveness, containment, boundaries, and control of the female body (through incest, marriage contracts, and the like).

Constance's ineffability, her "elvishness," resides not so much in her gender as in her ability to convert, to turn people from one system of belief to another without exerting any force. It is perhaps significant that the other use of the word "elvish" in *The Canterbury Tales* appears in the *Sir Thopas–Melibee Link,* where the host describes Chaucer: "He semeth elvyssh by his contenaunce" (Prologue to *Sir Thopas*, line 703). One of Chaucer-the-narrator's key features is his unknowability, but perhaps his elvishness is not so much in his appearance as in what he does, that is, in his poetry, writing that also converts without violence. In *The Man of Law's Tale*, Chaucer seems invested in one kind of poetry; elsewhere in *The Canterbury Tales*, he explores others.[64] In this tale, however, Chaucer seems to privilege the power of the image—specifically the Christian image—to convert. That Chaucer's poetics is also at issue in this tale is suggested by the prologue with its concern with profitable use of time, its list of Chaucer's works, and its praise of stories as riches that counter poverty. Just as the Syrians obtained access to Constance through the stories of merchants, so the Man of Law heard this story from merchants. Stories and Constance are thus both valuable commodities of exchange–and like women on the marriage market, subject to distortion and corruption (e.g., incest).

To conclude, *The Man of Law's Tale* intertwines the categories of race, class, and gender in complex ways in order to articulate the ineffability of a noninstitutionalized early form of Christianity that proselytizes through example and communal exchange, that is powerful as much through its mystery as through its exertion of force, and that is cyclical and repetitious as much as it is teleological. Constance succeeds in converting those around her to this form of Christianity through her example, that is, through what others observe in her. By embodying conversion in a female rather than a male body, Chaucer is able to construct a form of Christianity that is marginal; that is, he is able to separate spirituality from its contemporary institutionalization. Since what is fundamental to the spiritual is a belief in the other, Constance's gender as a marker of marginalized difference is crucial to Chaucer's exploration of the nature of the spiritual. Our introduction to Constance explains how she becomes a commodity to the Syrian merchants, one among the other riches of their trade, rich satins, cloths of gold, and spices. She is the exotic other coveted in the West as well as the East, as any spice would be. If we consider the etymology of the word *spice*, her affinity to this particular commodity becomes even more readily apparent, for *spice* originates from the Latin *species*, "look" or "appearance."[65] Like the spices used, perhaps most significantly, to embalm the dead, Constance is the spice that can overcome death, and through contemplation of her image, the viewer turns away from the deadly pale realm of mortality and toward a transcendent realm. A concrete manifestation of the power of the image lies in the female reproductive body. As the tale comes to a close, the mother herself becomes less significant in the story as her child, Maurice, emerges into adulthood and takes on his assigned role as leader of the church and state. Yet Constance's face remains reflected in her son's visage, a reminder of the female contribution to that patrimony and of the force of the female other that latemedieval secular marriage practices and hegemonic Christianity can neither fully acknowledge nor erase. When Maurice is first seen "lookynge in the kynges face" (line 1015), the boy's image evokes the emperor's memories (lines 1025, 1030–33):

> Ne saugh I nevere as she . . .
> Now was this child as lyk unto Custance
> As possible is a creature to be.
> This Alla hath the face in remembrance
> Of dame Custance.

"Whan Alla saugh his wyf" he weeps, he knew her at first sight, and she swoons "in his owene sighte" (lines 1051 and 1058).

What might we conclude about Chaucer's religious poetics as manifested in *The Man of Law's Tale*? Chaucer places the image in this tale at the boundary of the known. Chaucer's religious poetry, then, like Constance's face, takes us beyond the familiar, beyond the social—the world of hierarchies and exchanges that so constrain and determine the self—and to another strange world.[66]

NOTES

1. Paul Strohm, *Social Chaucer* (Cambridge, Mass.: Harvard University, 1989), and Lee Patterson, *Chaucer and the Subject of History* (Madison: University of Wisconsin Press, 1991).

2. Carolyn Dinshaw, *Chaucer's Sexual Poetics* (Madison: University of Wisconsin Press, 1989), and Elaine Tuttle Hansen, *Chaucer and the Fictions of Gender* (Berkeley: University of California Press, 1992).

3. *The Squire's Tale* has been the subject of a number of talks on the category of "race" in Chaucer at the Medieval Institute Meetings of the past few years; *The Man of Law's Tale* was first commented upon in terms of issues of "race" by Glory Dharmaraj in "Multicultural Subjectivity in Reading Chaucer's "Man of Law's Tale," in *Medieval Feminist Newsletter* 16 (1993): 4–8, and more recently and comprehensively by Susan Schibanoff in "Worlds Apart: Orientalism, Antifeminism and Heresy in Chaucer's Man of Law's Tale," *Exemplaria* 8.1 (1996): 59–96.

4. The call to bring together race, class, and gender was first sounded by African American feminists in such essays as Hazel Carby's "White Woman Listen! Black Feminism and the Boundaries of Sisterhood," which appeared first in *The Empire Strikes Back:Race and Racism in 70s Britain* (Birmingham: Centre for Contemporary Cultural Studies, 1982), pp. 212–35, and then again in her *Cultures on Babylon: Black Britain and African America* (New York: Verso, 1999), pp. 67–92. For an interesting recent collection of essays that brings psychoanalysis, race, gender, and history together, see Elizabeth Abel, Barbara Christian, Helene Moglen, eds., *Female Subjects in Black and White: Race, Psyhconansalysis, Feminism* (Berkeley: University of California Press, 1997). In their introduction to this collection, which sprang from a conference, the editors tell us that the subject they had not considered in formulating the conference was the greater importance African American

spirituality, rather than psychoanalysis, would play for the African American feminist critics, further evidence to my mind for the need to add religion to our current critical trinity. The relationship between psychoanalysis and religion—especially from an historicist perspective—deserves further consideration. For an important early consideration of the theoretical implications of the interplay between the three categories, see Gayatri Spivak, "French Feminism in an International Frame," in *In Other Worlds* (New York: Routledge, 1988), pp. 134–53. Patricia Parker and Margo Hendricks were among the first to historicize the study of race, class, and gender in their important collection *Women, "Race" and Writing in the Early Modern Period* (New York and London: Routledge, 1994). For a specific study of the difficulties the critic faces in bringing the three categories together in an analysis of a literary text, see Margaret Ferguson, "Juggling the Categories of Race, Class and Gender in Aphra Behn's *Oroonoko*," *Women's Studies* 19 (1991): 159–81, reprinted in the Hendricks and Parker collection.

5. C. David Benson, "Introduction," and Linda Georgianna, "The Protestant Chaucer," in Benson and Elizabeth Robertson, eds., *Chaucer's Religious Tales* (Cambridge: Boydell and Brewer Press, 1990), pp. 1–11; 55–70.

6. Almost all of the work of Aers on Langland and Chaucer as well as other medieval English writers has argued for such a position. For one example see *Community, Gender and Individual Identity: English Writing 1360–1430* (London: Routledge, 1988). For a recent study of religion in late medieval culture, see his and Lynn Staley's book, *The Powers of the Holy: Religion, Politics and Gender in Late Medieval English Culture* (University Park: Pennsylvania State University Press, 1996).

7. See Sarah Beckwith's *Christ's Body: Identity, Culture and Society in Late Medieval Writings* (London and New York: Routledge, 1993) and her forthcoming *Signifying God: Social Relation and Symbolic Act in York's Play of Corpus Christi*. Beckwith's work is of particular importance because it demands of literary critics a deeply theorized as well as meticulously researched historical mode of analysis of religion. For Lynn Staley's work see, for example, her book with David Aers or her own *Margery Kempe's Dissenting Fictions* (University Park: Pennsylvania State University Press, 1994). For one of the earliest feminist historicist studies of Kempe, see Sarah Beckwith, "A Very Material Mysticism: The Medieval Mysticism of Margery Kempe," in David Aers, ed., *Medieval Literature: Criticism, Ideology and History* (Brighton: Harvester Press, 1986), pp. 34–57, and for a full-length feminist study see Karma Lochrie's influential *Margery Kempe and Translations of the Flesh* (Philadelphia: University of Pennsylvania Press, 1991). My earlier book, *Early English Devotional Prose and the Female Audience* (Knoxville: University of Tennessee Press, 1990), also takes a feminist historicist approach to the study of religion in medieval England. Much of the work on religion in recent years has grown out of the influential book by Caroline Bynum, *Holy Feast and Holy Fast: The Religious Significance of Food to Medieval Women* (Berkeley: University of California Press, 1987), responded to directly by David Aers and Lynn Staley in their book and most recently by Nicholas Watson in his essay "Desire for the Past," in *SAC* 21 (1999): 59–98. Watson also responds in this essay to Kathleen Biddick's important call to medievalists in her critique of Bynum to broaden our sensitivity to categories of difference in her "Gender, Bodies, Borders: Technologies of the Visible," *Speculum* 68 (1993) [*Studying Medieval Women: Sex, Gender, Feminism*, ed. Nancy F. Partner]; 389–418; revised and reprinted in her *The Shock of Medievalism* (Durham, N.C.: Duke University Press, 1998), pp. 135–62.

8. "Nicholas Watson, "Censorship and Cultural Change in Late Medieval England: Vernacular Theology, the Oxford Translation Debate, and Arundel's Constitutions of 1409," *Speculum* 70 (1995): 822–63.

9. See Louise Fradenburg, "Voice Memorial: Loss and Reparation in Chaucer's Poetry," *Exemplaria* 2 (1990): 169–202, and "'Be not Far from me': Psychoanalysis, Medieval Studies and the Subject of Religion," *Exemplaria* 7(1995): 41–54.

10. For a variety of essays on Chaucer's religious tales, see my and David Benson's *Chaucer's Religious Tales*. For discussions of the affective piety of *The Prioress's Tale*, see my "Aspects of Female Piety in the Prioress's Tale," in *Chaucer's Religious Tales*, pp. 145–60; reprinted in Steve Ellis, ed., *Chaucer: The Canterbury Tales* (London: Longman, 1998), pp. 189–208; Louise Fradenburg, "Criticism, Anti-Semitism, and the Prioress's Tale," *Exemplaria* (1989): 69–115; Judith Ferster, "'Your Praise is Performed by Men and Children': Language and Gender in the Prioress's Prologue and Tale," *Exemplaria* 2 (1990): 147–49; and Bruce Holsinger, "Pedagogy, Violence and the Subject of Music: Chaucer's Prioress's Tale and the Ideologies of Song," *New Medieval Literatures* 1(1999): 157–92.

11. Sheila Delany, "Womanliness in the Man of Law's Tale," in *Writing Woman* (New York: Schocken Books, 1983), pp. 36–46.

12. A. S. G. Edwards, "Critical Approaches to the *Man of Law's Tale*," in Benson and Robertson, eds., *Chaucer's Religious Tales*, pp. 85–94.

13. V. A. Kolve, *Chaucer and the Imagery of Narrative: The First Five Canterbury Tales* (Stanford, Calif.: Stanford University Press, 1984), pp. 297–358; Eugene Clasby, "Chaucer's Constance: Womanly Virtue and the Heroic Life," *ChauR* 13 (1979): 221–33; C. David Benson, Introduction to *Chaucer's Religious Tales*, pp. 1–7.

14. Edward W. Said, *Orientalism* (New York: Vintage Books, 1979).

15. Dana Nelson, *The Word in Black and White: Reading "Race" in American Literature, 1638–1867* (New York: Oxford University Press, 1993), p. viii. Henry Louis Gates also usefully summarizes ways we might consider the category of race. He writes that "'race' has become the trope of ultimate, irreducible difference between cultures, linguistic groups, or practitioners of specific belief systems, who more often than not have fundamentally opposed economic interests." See Henry Louis Gates, Jr., "Writing, 'Race,' and the Difference It Makes," in his *Loose Canons: Notes on the Culture Wars* (New York: Oxford University Press, 1992). For a recent excellent study of the necessity for historical specificity in the analysis of "race," see David Nirenberg, *Communities of Violence: Persecution of Minorities in the Middle Ages* (Princeton, N.J.: Princeton University Press, 1996). For an excellent provocative study of medieval ideas of skin color and justified violence, see Bruce Holsinger, "The Color of Salvation: Desire, Death and the Second Crusade in Bernard of Clairvaux's *Sermons on the Song of Songs*," in David Townsend and Andrew Taylor, eds., *The Tongue of the Fathers: Gender and Ideology in Twelfth-Cenrury Latin* (Philadelphia: University of Pennsylvania Press, 1998).

Another useful source for the study of race in medieval England is Jean Devisse and Michel Mollat, *The Image of the Black in Western Art*, vol. 2, pts. 1 and 2 (New York: William Morrow and Company, 1979). A useful summary of the controversies about the origins and development of the term *race* is Nicholas Hudson's "From 'Nation' to 'Race': The Origin of Racial Classification in Eighteenth-Century Thought," *Eighteenth-Century Studies* 293 (1996): 247–64.

For a general introduction to Islam in the Middle Ages and the Early Modern period, see Norman Daniel, *Islam and the West: The Making of an Image*

(Edinburgh: Edinburgh Press, 1960), and his *The Arabs in Medieval Europe* (London: Longmans, 1975), and the older, but still useful Samuel Chew, *The Crescent and the Rose: Islam and England during the Renaissance* (New York: Octagon Press, 1965). A more recent, though controversial, study is that of Bernard Lewis, *Christians, Muslims and Jews in the Age of Discovery* (New York: Oxford University Press, 1995). An older but still useful study of the role of Arabic in medieval literary history is Dorothy Metlizki's *The Matter of Araby in Medieval England* (New Haven, Conn.: Yale University Press, 1977). See also the more recent book by Maria Rosa Menocal, *The Arabic Role in Medieval Literary History* (Philadelphia: The University of Pennsylvania Press, 1987), as well as her newly published *Cambridge History of Arabic Literature*. For a recent theoretical consideration of feminism and Islam, see Anne Emmanuelle Berger, "The Newly Veiled Woman: Iragaray, Specularity, and the Islamic Veil," *Diacritics* (spring 1988): 93–120. This essay engages fully some of the problems of Specularity and Islam, especially in the recent move by some Islamic women to choose to take on the *hijab*.

16. See Verena Stolcke's discussion of the history of the term in "Invaded Woman: Gender, Race and Class in the Formation of Colonial Society," in Hendricks and Parker, *Women, "Race," and Writing*, pp. 272–86.

17. The Middle High German text is taken from Karl Lachmann's newly revised student edition of *Parzival in Wolfram von Eschenbach* (Berlin: Walter de Gruyter and Co., 1998) and the English translation from Wolfram von Eschenbach, *Parzival,* trans. Helen M. Mustard and Charles E. Passage (New York: Vintage Books, 1961). The German is from p. 22, lines 4–6; the translation from p. 12.

18. Lachmann, ed., *Parzival,* p. 24, lines 8–9; translation, p. 13

19. Ibid., p. 24, line 17; translation, p. 13.

20. Ibid., p. 31, lines 3–5; translation, p. 18.

21. Ibid., p. 30, lines 10–14, and p. 56, lines 21–22; translation, pp. 17, 31.

22. Ibid., p. 59, lines 27–28, and p. 785, line 6; translation, pp. 33, 406.

23. This representation of the child of miscegenation as mottled recurs in Lady Mary Wroth's *Urania*. See Kim F. Hall, *Things of Darkness: Economies of Race and Gender in Early Modern England* (Ithaca, N.Y.: Cornell University Press, 1995).

24. Israel Burshatin, "The Moor in the Text: Metaphor, Emblem and Silence," in Henry Louis Gates Jr., ed., *"Race," Writing and Difference* (Chicago: University of Chicago Press, 1985), pp. 117–37.

25. Lachmann, ed., *Parzival,* p. 751, lines 22–27; translation, p. 390.

26. Schibanoff points out that pagans or infidels usually posed a lesser threat to Christianity than Islam in the ideology of the period because it was so clearly defined as the Other, whereas Islam was uncomfortably close to Christianity in its monotheism. See her discussion in "Worlds Apart," p. 65.

27. Schibanoff (ibid., p. 70) argues that late medieval texts "troped the familiarity of Islam . . . not to mute the threat of the new religion to Europe, but to intensify it, to increase rather than reduce the 'pressure' it created upon the occidental mind . . . [T]he pressure posed by the heretic as proximate Other [here the heretic is one who embraces Islam] had to be released." Here Schibanoff, following Dollimore, makes an extremely important case about the dangers of similitude. One might argue that the Islamic people in *The Man of Law's Tale* are all the more dangerous in their similarity to the pagans. It is also true that all of the Islamic accusers of Constance are destroyed, whereas only some of the pagans are. Most of the pagans are redeemable because of their potential convertability. Nonetheless, individual pagans

and individual Islamic antagonists are represented as similar or, as in the case of the mothers-in-law, virtually interchangeable in the tale.

28. Ibid., p. 63.

29. See ibid., p. 79. The Chaucer is taken from Schibanoff's citation of it and from Larry Benson, gen. ed., *The Riverside Chaucer* (Boston: Houghton Mifflin Company, 1987), MLT 220–21. All further quotations from the tale are taken from this edition and will be cited parenthetically in the text.

30. In a response to this paper, my student, Wahid Omar, suggested that the description of Islam as sweet only reinforces its orientalist representation; here the religion of Islam is presented as another spice.

31. J. R. R. Tolkien, ed., *The Ancrene Wisse: Corpus Christi College Cambridge 402* (Oxford: Oxford University Press for the Early English Text Society, 1962), p. 43.

32. Carolyn Dinshaw, "The Law of Man and Its 'Abomynacions,'" in *Chaucer's Sexual Poetics* (Madison: University of Wisconsin Press, 1989), pp. 65–87.

33. Jill Mann, "Suffering Woman, Suffering God," in *Feminist Approaches to Geoffrey Chaucer* (Atlantic Highlands, N.J.: Humanities Press, 1991), pp. 128–64.

34. Schibanoff, "Worlds Apart."

35. I am grateful to David Benson for alerting me to this striking contrast.

36. David Benson made this point to me in conversation.

37. This passage is very difficult to interpret since Chaucer is vague about the meaning of British Gospels. Is it a potentially heretical text, and why then does the knight swear on it? Does a hand smite him from heaven because he swears falsely or because he swears falsely upon a nonstandard translation of the Bible? Is the knight being associated with heresy? We do not know if the book belongs to him or the court. If it belongs to the court, then perhaps Chaucer is making a point here about the power of British—that is, English—Bibles. For an analysis of the complex status a Bible can have in foreign culture, see Homi K. Bhabha, "Signs Taken for Wonders: Questions of Ambivalence and Authority under a Tree Outside Delhi, May 1817," in *The Location of Culture* (New York: Routledge, 1994), pp. 102–22.

38. See Bynum, *Holy Feast and Holy Fast*, my *Early English Devotional Prose*, and more recently, Aers and Sraley, *Powers of the Holy*.

39. Verena Conley, review of *Helene Cixous: Writing The Feminine*, in *Rocky Mountain Review* 40. 1–2 (1986): 97. Conley's statement succinctly summarizes the arguments about marginality's powers. For a more detailed discussion of the strategic powers of the marginal position, see the debate about essentialism in *The Essential Difference: Another Look at Essentialism*, ed. Naomi Schor and Elizabeth Weed, in *differences* 1.2 (1988). Naomi Schor's essay in that volume, pp. 38–58, "This Essentialism Which Is Not One: Coming to Grips with Irigaray," is especially useful in this regard. See also Gloria Anzaldua's discussion of the power of the hybrid living in a borderland in her *Borderlands/La Frontera* (San Francisco: Aunt Lute, 1987).

40. David Raybin, "Cuscance and History: Woman as Outsider in Chaucer's 'Man of Law's Tale,'" *SAC* 12 (1990): 69. The essay as a whole concerns Constance's liminality and the intersection of her timeless Christian essence with the earthly world of business.

41. See Bertram Colgrave and R. A. B. Mynors, eds., *Bede's Ecclesiastical History of the English People* (Oxford: Clarendon Press, 1969), ch. 25, pp. 72–79.

42. For a recent essay arguing that multiple kinds of heretical activity and various forms of radical theology were present in fourteenth-century England, see

Kathryn Kerby-Fulton, "Prophecy and Suspicion: Closet Radicalism, Reformist Politics, and the Vogue for Hildegardiana in Ricardian England," *Speculum* 75.2 (2000): 318–41.

43. For a general discussion of Chaucer's attitude toward the friars, see Penn R. Szittya, *The Antifraternal Tradition in Medieval Literature* (Princeton, N.J.: Princeton University Press, 1986), pp. 231–46. For a more recent discussion of the friars in late medieval England, see Lawrence M. Clopper, *"Songs of Rechelesnesse:"Langland and the Franciscans* (Ann Arbor: University of Michigan Press, 1997).

44. Chaucer's possible interest in Lollardy has been much discussed in recent conferences (for example, in Kate Crasson's essay on *The Second Nun's Tale* and Lollardy), but published work on Chaucer and Lollardy is not extensive. Alcuin Blamires summarizes the state of Lollardy in the 1390s, arguing that "what Gower called 'this newe secte of Lollardie' was a public issue in the 1390's . . . Chaucer himself—even more than Gower—had reason to be sensitive to the controversy, given his connections with both John of Gaunt (a notable patron of Wyclif at first, and reputedly a champion of the Wycliffite call for a vernacular Bible) and with a group of men in Richard II's service nowadays dubbed 'The Lollard Knights.' " See Alcuin Blamires, "The Wife of Bath and Lollardy," *MAE* 58.2 (1989): 224–42.

45. Quoted in Margaret Aston, "Lollard Women Priests?" *Journal of Ecclesiastical History* 31 (1980): 442.

46. See ibid., p. 456.

47. For a discussion of the general tenets of the Lollards, see Anne Hudson, *The Premature Reformation: Wycliffite Texts and Lollard History* (Oxford: Clarendon Press, 1988), especially her summaries of the theology, ecclesiology, and politics of the Lollards, pp. 278–390.

48. I am grateful to Kirsten Otey for pointing out the possible Lollard tinge this passage might carry for Chaucer's audience.

49. Anne Hudson, ed., *Selections from English Wycliffite Writing* (Toronto: Medieval Academy of America, 1997), p. 28.

50. Ibid., p. 23.

51. Ibid., p. 19

52. Ibid., p. 23

53. For a discussion of Kristeva's theory of the abject, see Julia Kristeva, *Powers of Horror: An Essay in Abjection,* trans. Leon S. Roudiez (New York: Columbia University Press, 1982). Those readers who have been repelled by Constance's hyperbolic submission have failed to recognize the psychological power of this abject realm. This form of religion can invite the convert to turn away from the limited realm of the symbolic and toward the realm of the Kristevan preverbal semiotic.

54. Kolve, Margaret Miles, and, most recently, Eamon Duffy have shown how pervasive Christian imagery is to the teaching of doctrine. See Eamon Duffy, *The Stripping of the Altars: Traditional Religion in England,* 1400–1580 (New Haven, Conn., and London: Yale University Press, 1992), and Margaret Miles, *Image as Insight: Visual Understanding in Western Christianity and Secular Culture* (Boston: Beacon Press, 1985).

55. Hudson, ed., *Selections*, p. 19.

56. Ibid., p. 23.

57. See Kolve's chapter, "The Rudderless Ship and the Sea," in *Imagery of Narrative,*pp. 297–358.

58. The association of women and fluids permeates Irigaray's work, but see, for example, her *Amante marine de Friedrich Nietzsche* (Paris: Minuit, 1980).

59. See Edwards's review of the criticism in "Critical Approaches."

60. To put this argument in Kristevan terms, Constance embodies the semiotic realm, an embodiment reinforced by gender and her representation as a mother, and this semiotic realm can be approached but not contained by the symbolic realm articulated by the Man of Law.

61. Raybin, "Custance and History," pp. 65–84. He discusses Constance's association with Augustinian notions of time and the Man of Law's specific uses of time in the beginning of his essay.

62. Julia Kristeva, "Women's Time," in *The Kristeva Reader,* ed. Toril Moi (New York: Columbia University Press, 1986), pp. 187–213.

63. For summaries of medieval medical and theological views of women as well as references to specific Aristotelian medical sources and analyses of them, see "Medieval Views of Female Spirituality," in my *Early English Devotional Prose,* pp. 32–43, and my "Medieval Medical Views of Women and Female Spirituality in the *Ancrene Wisse* and Julian of Norwich's *Showings,*" in Linda Lomperis and Sarah Stanbury, eds., *Feminist Approaches to the Body in Medieval Literature* (Philadelphia: University of Pennsylvania Press, 1993), pp. 142-67.

64. For a demonstration of this variety of style, see C. David Benson, *Chaucer's Drama of Style* (Chapel Hill: University of North Carolina Press, 1986).

65. I am indebted to Timothy Morton for alerting me to this origin and for general discussions about the range of meanings invoked by the word spice.

66. This essay began as a response to an energizing conversation with Winthrop Wetherbee at a New Chaucer Society meeting many years ago where we disagreed about Constance's agency in the tale. I thank him for sharpening my focus and for his enthusiastic encouragement of my argument. I gave a short version of this paper at the New Chaucer Society Meetings in Canterbury in 1990 and then a longer version specifically engaging the question of race at an MLA session on that topic in medieval studies organized by Linda Lomperis in San Francisco in 1991. I would also like to thank David Aers, Mark Amsler, A. S. G. Edwards, Sharon Farmer, Bruce Holsinger, Gerda Norvig, Karen Palmer, Carol Pasternak, Elihu Pearlman, Jeffrey Robinson, Karen Robertson, and Dana Symons for their responses to this essay. Finally, I would like to thank the two anonymous readers for the journal for their generous and informative suggestions.

FIONA SOMERSET

"Mark him wel for he is on of po": Training the "Lewed" Gaze to Discern Hypocrisy

When Chaucer's narrator in the prologue to the *Canterbury Tales* points to the "farsed" "typet," "fyr-reed face," and voice "as smal as hath a goot" of the Friar, Summoner, and Pardoner, he is marking for his audience reliable indicators, written on the body for all to read, of the past behavior and present dispositions of his three most hypocritical clerics.[1] The bodies of the Friar, Summoner, and Pardoner advertise their habits quite openly—and not just for assiduous readers of physiognomy treatises or experts in the clerical discourse of hypocrisy, but, through the combined weight of Chaucer's implications, for any reader who can take a hint.[2] That Chaucer is tapping into well established discourses of antifraternalism and anticlericism here has been amply documented.[3] What I want to examine, with Chaucer as my pretext, is the particular kind of anxiety about the discerning of clerical hypocrites, and especially their discernment by *laymen*, or the "lewed," that comes to the fore in many late-medieval English writings.[4] A good example of the sort of concern about lay discernment that I am talking about, and of a typical device for dispelling it, shows up at what for clerics is an embarrassingly public moment in 1395, when the *Twelve Conclusions* of the Lollards, a manifesto posted on the doors of St. Paul's cathedral and the Westminster parliament building, ostensibly aims to make this capacity for discernment available to all.

English Literary History, Volume 68 (2001): pp. 315–334. © 2001 The Johns Hopkins University Press.

143

The 1395 *Twelve Conclusions* and Roger Dymmok's voluminous *Reply* each "mark" their opponents for the wider lay audience they invoke.[5] They promise to show laypeople, the less well-educated readers they project as their audience, how to tell clerics who merely bear the appearance of sanctity from the veritably holy—how to tell "them" from "us." But when it comes to it, the *Twelve Conclusions* and the *Reply* deflect their attention, and that of their readers: rather than providing practical instruction in a method of discernment that would enable laypeople to tell true Christians from hypocritical ones, they instead descend into sexual innuendo of a kind that sorts oddly with the reasoned arguments and authoritative citations of scholastic discourse that they direct at one another. In contrast to the reasoned, lucid argument the *Twelve Conclusions'* writers set forth in, for example, their discussion of idolatrous worship, the Lollards bolster their claim that "men of holi chirche" and especially members of "privat religions" are false Christians with the accusation that those men practice sodomy; and they provide their readers with this proof: "Experience for þe priue asay of syche men is, þat þei like non wymmen; and whan þu prouist sich a man mark him wel for he is on of þo."[6] Near the end of Roger Dymmok's point-by-point *Reply* to every nuance and every implication of the *Conclusions'* arguments—a manner of proceeding in marked contrast to his usual practice of reporting, translating, and then refuting in meticulous detail what his opponents have written—when he comes to providing evidence of just why his opponents are hypocritical, Dymmok suggests that heretics teach women to make their bodies common property: "Docent namque mulieres nulli petenti ex caritate negare corpora sua, que doctrina, si licita credatur, aufert uerecundiam de fornicacione" [For they teach women for charity to deny their bodies to no petitioner; and this teaching, if it were thought legitimate, would remove all shame from fornication].[7] From the promise to train the "lewed" gaze to distinguish true Christians from hypocrites there never follows, for either side, a logically laid out scheme of instruction accessible to less educated readers. Instead, the "lewed" gaze is retrained, displaced, and directed elsewhere.

The sort of reluctance to deliver promised enlightenment that these two works exhibit is very common among late-medieval English works written by educated clerical writers, nearly always in the vernacular, for lay audiences. These works set up a particular kind of relationship between writer and reader. The writer presents himself as an educated cleric, though he often leaves his precise institutional position obscure or distances himself from traditional clerical practices. He projects an uneducated lay audience. And he purports to give that audience new information not previously available to them. The reluctance these writers exhibit when it comes to delivering the information they have promised is scarcely surprising. "The Age of Chaucer," as literary historians have been accustomed to call it, was also the time when vernacular writings presenting knowledge of various kinds—encyclopedic works, advice manuals, popular and pseudo-scientific writings, commentaries, polemic tracts, and so on—were for the first time becoming available in English, and when that availability itself was in many cases becoming a topic of controversy.[8] For as long as vernacular learning continues to seem novel or even unprecedented, an offer of this sort poses the central dilemma for an educated writer making new or previously reserved kinds of information potentially available to a wider audience. The writer wants to parade his possession of specialized knowledge, to demonstrate his expertise, in order to show that he and his writing deserve attention. But he runs the risk of passing on "clergie," or learning, in such a way that he transfers his own capabilities to his audience and renders himself and even his writing dispensable.[9] Above all, the promise to train laypeople to discern clerical hypocrisy is perilous for its writer because that promise potentially subjects the writer himself to the process it recommends. If fulfilled, this promise could make it possible for the lay audience to judge not just the clerical writer's opponents, but the writer himself.

Nor is clerical reluctance the only obstacle to writers fulfilling their promise to train the laity in the discernment of hypocrisy. "Proving a man," as the *Conclusions* recommends, is not a straightforward task readily accessible to rational analysis and forthright exposition. From the outward appearance someone presents to the world we can have no direct, trustworthy access to their inward thoughts and intentions; nor can we immediately assess character and disposition. The reason why we need to be warned about the hypocrite is precisely that the intentions he hides beneath the whitewash of outer dissembling are not readily accessible to surface examination. Conversely, if discernment is not easy, neither is concealment. The surface appearance of the body cannot be fully subjected to conscious control. Instead, that body's dispositions and practices leave marks on its surface: traces of past actions, present thoughts, and persistent habits that conflict with the image its person—or the person whose it is—would like to project.

Both of these difficulties are truisms of medieval physiognomy.[10] Like palmistry, astrology, geomancy, onomancy, uroscopy, and other pseudo-sciences that enjoyed burgeoning popularity in late-medieval England, physiognomy promises a new sort of vernacular "clergie"—in the sense of "learning"—giving access to previously inaccessible knowledge.[11] Physiognomy treatises attempt to forge from the hints the body provides a method of discerning character and disposition based on a clerically conceived and conferred scheme of information. The information these treatises give is presented as fascinating, marvellous, allowing unprecedented access to truth by means of a key to interpreting what cannot be concealed. While any attempt to conceal one's vices may be locally successful, no one who is embodied can

entirely control his overall outward appearance—as, for example, John Metham points out, in an aside of his own in his translated treatise:

> Sum-tyme yt happyth that scolerys the qwyche stody in vnyuersyteys
> at her frendys fyndyng, qwan thei perseyue that of ese her nekkys be
> pleyn and ful off qwyete and off rest, and that this tokyn ys opyn and
> vycyus, be craft thei make her nekkys stabyl and rugh, that ys to sey,
> ful of schrynkys; but her craft holdyth noght, for-as-myche as thei
> hyde in that parte, the werkyng of nature schewyth on odyr partys.[12]

The "werkyng of nature" can never be so thoroughly hidden in every part
that an expert cannot see the truth. Yet all the same, lay readers of physiognomies are not offered the opportunity to become experts themselves. These
treatises seek to instill a continued dependence on clerical learning, and on
clerics as its necessary proponents, by repeatedly urging difficulties in interpreting the evidence they set forth, difficulties which necessitate recourse to
the authority of clerics.

The exemplum of Hippocrates and Philemon with which many treatises
in the *Secretum* tradition begin nicely epitomizes the lay/clerical relation they
promote.[13] With some small variations, the story goes something like this:
Hippocrates's students take his portrait to Philemon, the master of physiognomy, and after studying the portrait Philemon pronounces that it shows
the face of a lecherous beguiler. The students indignantly tell Philemon that
the portrait depicts Hippocrates; but Philemon defends himself, saying that
he is simply reporting what he sees. The students return to Hippocrates and
tell him what has happened. To their surprise, Hippocrates acknowledges
that Philemon is quite right in his interpretation of his disposition. Here
is Hippocrates's instructive explanation, quoted from what Manzalaoui calls
the "Ashmole version":

> Certaynly, Philemon told you trouth and left behynd no lettre.
> Sothly, sithen Y saw and considred þe foule and reprouable
> disposicion, I ordeyned and stablisshed my soule to be kyng vpon
> my body and withdrow it fro the bad inclinaciouns, and Y had
> victorie and put resistence ayens my concupiscence[14].

This exemplum shows the infallibility of physiognomy: the great masters
agree. But at the same time this very infallibility is shown to require and
depend upon recourse to the most authoritative clerics available for endorsement and proper interpretation: the students are confused until Hippocrates
resolves the apparent contradiction for them. The principles of physiognomy
are not sufficient in themselves, especially in the hands of the untrained.

What is more, Hippocrates's explanation itself becomes an occasion for exhorting readers to aspire to a moral ideal, and this moral application, this turning inward on the recipient/reader of the information supplied, becomes the pretext for including the physiognomy treatise amidst the advice, ostensibly for princes, provided by the *Secretum Secretorum*.[15] Information also intended to enable the prince to discern the character of his servants and associates becomes an occasion for the prince—or any lay reader—to reflect upon and perhaps reform his own character. The very difficulty of the feat Hippocrates has accomplished in overcoming his disposition and ruling over his body underlines the ordinary reliability of physiognomy. And it is a cleric that provides the ideal exception of *regal* self-control—"I . . . stablissed my soule to be kyng vpon my body . . . and Y had victorie"—which, unusual and difficult to analyse as it is, makes it necessary for all readers, princely or not, to continue to rely on the interpretative authority of clerics.

In his pastoral manual *Handlyng Synne*—aimed at parish priests of the sort who need to know how to administer confession and provide basic instruction for their parishioners, but also (and at scarcely any greater remove) at a lay audience able to read the manual themselves—Robert Mannyng also includes a physiognomy treatise of a sort, one that yet more guardedly preserves the interpretation of inner intent from bodily appearance as a privy process accessible only to the clergy.[16] Mannyng interpolates his physiognomy treatise—not found in the *Manuel des Pechés*, the source for the bulk of his material—into his discussion of how the sacrament of the altar ought to be understood, consecrated, and received. Placed there, his treatise functions not just to train the lay gaze inward, but to deflect it from a possible occasion for lay judgment of clerics.

The sacrament of the altar had long been an occasion for discussions of lay discrimination. Since the Fourth Lateran Council of 1215, it had been the responsibility of every lay person to assess whether they were in a fit state to receive the Eucharist at least once a year, at Easter. Before receiving the Eucharist, all men and women were expected to examine their consciences, confess their sins to their parish priest, and receive absolution.[17] That is the more familiar sort of lay discrimination associated with the sacrament of the altar, but in addition, and since long before 1215, laypersons were also sometimes expected to assess the disposition and actions of their priest.

Provision for lay assessment of priests arises in the section of the first part of Gratian's *Decretum* devoted to clerical celibacy, D 26–34. In D 32 c. 6 Gratian considers to what extent fornicating priests ought to be permitted to perform their duties—or are even capable of doing so. He concludes that such priests can, despite their sinfulness, efficaciously perform the sacraments; but that nonetheless, any priest *known* to engage in fornication should be deprived of his office. How precisely this is to be accomplished is not clear; but lay persons certainly have a role to play: they are the ones who will know of the priest's activities, and they themselves are expected to refuse his services, or even to intervene so as to deprive him of his ministry:

> Attamen decessores nostri Nicolaus et Gregorius a missis sacerdotum . . . fideles abstinere decreuerunt, et ut peccandi licentiam ceteris auferrent, et huiusmodi ad dignae penitentiae lamenta reuocarent. Scribit enim predecessor noster Gregorius Radulfo et Bertolfo ducibus inter cetera: "Offitium simoniacorum et in fornicacione iacentium scienter nullo modo recipiatis, et quantum potestis tales a sanctis ministeriis, ut oportuerit, prohibeatis" etc.[18]

> [Nonetheless our predecessors Nicholas and Gregory decreed that the faithful should shun the masses of priests . . . both so as to remove the license for sinning from others, and so as to recall them to repentance. Moreover, our predecessor Gregory wrote to the lords Radulphus and Bertholf, among other things, "You should in no way knowingly accept the service of simoniacs or those mired in fornication, and so far as you are able, you should (as is fitting) prevent them from engaging in sacred ministry."]

In England, where the church was always concerned to protect itself from the incursion of secular governance, it seems likely that addressing the recommendation "you should . . . prevent them from engaging in sacred ministry" to secular lords would be especially unpalatable to the church hierarchy.[19] And indeed, although the Fourth Lateran Council also includes a decree about priestly continence which was cited by most English bishops who promulgated the Lateran decrees in the decades following 1215, although those promulgations often include some reference to D 32 c. 6 as well, nowhere in any of the versions of the decrees promulgated in England that address the question of priestly continence have I found any reference to the recommended behavior of the laity. There are a few references to the public scandal caused by priests' behavior, but no discussion of how laypeople who know their priest has a concubine should behave: the responsibility for reform always belongs to church officials.[20]

Unsurprisingly, however, Wycliffite citations of D 32 c. 6 do not maintain the same silence with regard to the laity. The tract *De Officio Pastorali* emphasizes that it is better for laymen to decline to accept spiritual service from such a priest and withdraw their tithes on their own initiative rather than to rely on the archdeacon to impose fines after he has been informed of the notorious sin, because any such fines would end up being paid out of their tithes anyway.[21] *The Twenty-Five Articles* affirms the orthodox position that a priest in deadly sin is capable of performing the sacraments, even though doing so adds to his sin, and even suggests that parishioners unaware of their priest's sinfulness can receive the good effect of those sacraments. But for this writer, "if his synne be open, þo pepul owes nout to receyve sacramentus of hym, leste consent to his synne make hem parteners in peyne": that lay persons know of the priest's sin is all that is necessary for them to be *obliged* to refuse his services: inaction is equivalent to participation in the sin.[22] And *The Dialogue Between a Knight and a Clerk* cites D 32 c. 6, then extends it to cover all kinds of sins by priests:

> bi þe popes lawe no man schuld here a prestes messe þat he wist had a lemman or a woman taken into his howse be wai of syn//ne; ne no suche preste schuld synge no messe ne rede no gospell ne no pistel at messe ne dwell among clerkes. And ʒit more he ne schuld take no parte of holi chirche godes. And bi þe self skill a preste schuld haue all sich vengeaunce for all dedeli synnes, or elles ʒe mot sai þat liccherie es gretter dedeli synne þan ony o þer synne. And þat nis noʒt so þe.[23]

For Wycliffites, then, laymen are responsible for superintending the virtue of their ministers by the same pastoral logic that explains why priests are responsible for their parishioners—and to the same, or even a greater, extent.

Mannyng's treatment of the sacrament of the altar swiftly puts the issue of the priest's virtue to rest: he argues that sinful priests can efficaciously consecrate the host, adding that they do so to the greater harm of their own souls, but makes no reference to the knowledge or consequent spiritual state of their parishioners.[24] Instead Mannyng focuses almost exclusively on the issue of discerning—and, by means of the effect of his exemplum on its potential audience, teaching them to discern for themselves—whether parishioners about to receive the host have the proper disposition for doing so. Mannyng's physiognomist is a parish priest graced with "gode dyscrecyoun." At the priest's specific request, following upon prayers about his parishioners that give evidence of his pastoral concern for them, God supernaturally confers upon him the special ability to see his parishioners' sins in their faces:

> ʒyt preyde he god of more grace
> þat he myghte knowe hem by face,
> þe whyche receyuede hyt wrþyly
> And whyche to haue hyt were wrþy.
> And god graunted hym hys wyl
> To knowe þe gode fro þe yl.

þe folk þat to þe prest went
For to receyue þe sacrament,
Of some þe faces were as bryght
As þe sunne ys on dayes lyght.
And some here vyseges al blake
þat no þyng myght hem blakkere make.
And some were as rede as blode,
Staryng ryght as þey had be wode.
And some were swolle þe vysege stout
As þogh here yen shuld burble out.
And some gnapped here fete & handes
As dogges doun þat gnawe here bandes.
And some had vyseges of meselrye,
And some were lyke foule maumetrye.

At the priest's further request, God also provides an interpretative key:

ȝyt preyd he god wyþ gode entent
þat he myghte wyte what al þat ment.
And god almyghty louede hym weyl
And wld shewe hym eurydeyl.
"þo men þat are so bryght
As þe sunne on dayes lyght,
þo men are ȝyt yn charyte
And clene of synne & wrshype me.
þo men þat were so blake
þat no þyng myghte hem blakkere make,
þey are lechours foul wyþ ynne
And haue no wyl to leue here synne.
þo men þat were rede as blode,
þey are yrous & wykked of mode,
Here euen crysten for to slo
Wyþ deþ or wyþ pyne do wo.
þo þat þou saye wyþ swolle vysage,
þey are enuyous ouer outrage.
And þo þat gnapped here fynger endes
Are bakbyters bytwyxe frendes.
þo þat þou saye meselles by syght,
þey loue more gode þan god almyght.
þo þat þou saye lyke maumetrye,
On wrly þyng þey most affye.
More loue þey gode þat he haþ sent

pan pey do hym þat al hap lent.
þese maner men are ȝyt yn wyl
Yn here synne to lyue styl;
And þarfore shal þe sacrament
On hem aske hard iuggement,
þat þey haue receyued hyt vnwrþyly
And serued þe fend hys enemy."[25]

The privy "informacion" Mannyng presents here is available directly only to an especially virtuous priest who has specifically requested it. Once this "clergie" has been conveyed, at two removes, by Mannyng to his readers, it becomes not a system of discernment that parishioners can implement in judging others, but a scheme of pastoral instruction applicable to their own inward states: what the priest alone can see, and what Mannyng's readers receive, are outward manifestations of the parishioners' inward states. For Mannyng's readers, this catalogue has the same sort of didactic function as any catalogue of personifications of the seven deadly sins: it serves as moral instruction by rendering the inward states it describes more easily recognizable.[26] Mannyng's exemplum of priestly "dyscrecyoun" reserves that discretion to its priest; but insofar as it may convey discretion to lay readers, it exhorts them to turn it upon themselves and use it—with the help of priests—to discern their own spiritual states in order to attain the knowledge that will help them save their own souls.

We have already seen from the *Twelve Conclusions* that Wycliffites can be as diversionary as the most insouciant cleric when explaining how laymen may discern hypocritical clerics. They can also be remarkably straightforward, however.[27] A tract entitled by its editor "Of Dominion" bases its contention that laymen may judge clerics on what seems a quite precise reversal of the common clerical tactic of diversion employed by Mannyng: if laymen are expected, indeed required, to examine the state of their own souls, the writer argues, then of course they may apply the same skills to discerning whether the clergy who serve them are worthy of their office. The tract lays out for an inexperienced audience precisely the means by which valid judgements can be arrived at and invalid ones avoided. First listing three kinds of invalid judgement that all should avoid, it then recommends two methods of valid judgement that anyone can apply: judgement by the senses, and judgement by conscience.

[S]um good iugement is of mennes out-wittis, as þei iugen whiche mete is good & whiche mete is yuel, & sum men iugement is of mennes witt wiþinne, as men iugen how þei schal do, by lawe of conscience; as cristen men schal iuge to whom þei done here almes, and þat þei feden nouȝt fendis children among here owne heed.[28]

But the example the tract gives here for the valid judgement conscience can deliver already indicates the direction the argument will take: in this tract the whole apparatus of lay discrimination is quite firmly harnessed to the writer's polemic end. From the argument that worldly men *can* judge clerics it follows directly that they *shall* judge them: shall judge them to be corrupt, and shall withdraw their alms. Although it may accidentally have the effect of teaching its readers skills of critical questioning, no polemic, not even this one, can afford to leave them space to decide for themselves.

Perhaps polemic must always function to exact the assent of its audience; but Chaucer is not writing polemic, nor participating in any direct way in the discussion about discerning hypocrisy that I have been examining. In the *Canterbury Tales* hypocrisy is both less, and more, apparent on the surface than the sorts of polemical and informational writings we have been examining would suppose. One pilgrim in the *Canterbury Tales*, more than any other, plainly experiences his outward appearance as an inescapable signifier of his inner depravity, a signifier which renders his shame all too visible:

> A somonour was ther with us in that place,
> That hadde a fyr-reed cherubynnes face,
> For saucefleem he was, with eyen narwe.
> As hoot he was and lecherous as a sparwe,
> With scalled browes blake and piled berd.
> Of his visage children were aferd.
> Ther nas quyk-silver, lytarge, ne brymstoon,
> Boras, ceruce, ne oille of tartre noon,
> Ne oynement that wolde clense and byte,
> That hym myghte helpen of his whelkes white,
> Nor of the knobbes sittynge on his chekes. (1.623–636)

Although the Summoner introduced here in the *General Prologue* has tried every available remedy, no medicine can ameliorate his appearance. The Summoner within the *Friar's Tale*, whose intended likeness to the Summoner on the pilgrimage the Friar reinforces by means of repeated gestures toward the pilgrim-Summoner in the opening section of his tale and indeed throughout the course of fragment 3, is at least equally interested in bodily alteration.[29]

Larry Scanlon, when discussing the *Friar's Tale*, shows how Chaucer adapts the exemplum that is the core of the Friar's narrative so that it stages just the kind of lay appropriation of clerical authority that (I have been suggesting) clerical vernacular writers who offer a lay audience an opportunity for judgement always want to avoid: the Summoner is condemned by a single humble virtuous lay woman whose curse is not merely an arbitrary manifestation of demonic power (as it is in other versions) but a judicious legislative act in which the Summoner participates by testifying against himself. Furthermore, the Summoner is not a rapacious lay official, as in other versions, but a cleric, even if of a very worldly kind.[30] But the Summoner's trouble in Chaucer's version goes beyond his inescapable entrenchment in language that literally means what it says: in addition, he resents—and is preoccupied with—being trapped in a body that inextricably signifies what he truly is.

How the Summoner feels burdened by his body is most evident just after the Devil's truthful self-revelation. Fascinated by the Devil's aptitude for thoroughgoing physical self-misrepresentation, the Summoner ignores the explicit warning he is given here:

> I am a feend; my dwellyng is in helle,
> And heere I ryde aboute my purchasyng,
> To wite wher men wol yeve me any thyng.
> My purchas is th' effect of al my rente.
> Looke how thou rydest for the same entente,
> To wynne good, thou rekkest nevere how;
> Right so fare I, for ryde wolde I now
> Unto the worldes ende for a preye. (3.1447–1455)

Not for a moment does the Summoner consider that he might *be* that prey. Instead, he fixes his attention exclusively on the Devil's deceptive bodily appearance:

> "A!" quod this somonour, "benedicite! What sey ye?
> I wende ye were a yeman trewely,
> Ye han a mannes shap as wel as I;
> Han ye a figure thanne determinat
> In helle, ther ye been in youre estat?" (3.1456–1460)

And he continues to badger the Devil with questions on this one point. In reply to the Summoner's eager further questions—again keeping his own attention on the warning the Summoner ought to be receiving—the Devil goes on to explain that although he has no determinate shape in hell, he can alter his body at will so as to present the appearance best calculated to ensnare his prey:

> "Nay, certeinly," quod he, "ther have we noon;
> But whan us liketh we kan take us oon,
> Or elles make yow seme we been shape;

> Somtyme lyk a man, or lyk an ape,
> Or lyk an angel kan I ryde or go."
>
> ....
>
> "For we," quod he, "wol us swiche formes make
> As moost able is oure preyes for to take." (3.1461–1465,
> 1471–1472)

Although the Devil speaks the truth here, and his words contain a warning, what he promises is also the best possible "forme" by which to ensnare the Summoner. Rather than rejecting his "felaweship," the Summoner asks questions about the Devil's specialized, supernatural "clergie" of deception, in the pursuit of a misdirected intent that causes him to overlook the true "informacion" that could have saved him. What intensely fascinates the Summoner from the moment of the Devil's truthful self-revelation onward, what misdirects the Summoner's attention so thoroughly that he entirely overlooks the consequences for himself of the Devil's "informacion," is that the Devil's consummate hypocrisy extends further than any human's can, to the kind of full control over his bodily appearance that the Summoner can only wish he could attain. The Summoner ignores the Devil's broad hint, and even the explicit warning that soon follows—"But o thyng warne I thee, I wol nat jape: / Thou wolt algates wite how we been shape" (3.1513–1514)—single-mindedly intent on his attempt to forge as close a fellowship with the Devil as he can, with a view to learning the secrets of his method and sharing his winnings.

But although the Summoner repeatedly reinforces their fellowship by insisting on his similarity, even brotherhood, with the Devil—and the Devil plays along—the Summoner is not nearly as similar as he would hope and as the Devil pretends.[31] The Summoner is a "layman" in the face of the Devil's "clergie," so to speak, not only as concerns the capacity for physical dissimulation, but also in the more usual area of lay/clerical distinction we began by investigating: the discernment of intention. The Summoner does have an almost instinctual, animal perceptiveness that aids him in his pursuit of profit:

> ... in this world nys dogge for the bowe
> That kan an hurt deer from an hool yknowe
> Bet than this somnour knew a sly lecchour,
> Or an avowtier, or a paramour,
> And for that was the fruyt of al his rente,
> Therfore on it he sette al his entente. (3.1369–1374)

But in other areas he shows himself to be remarkably dim. It is not just the Devil's intentions he overlooks in his bedazzlement with the twin hopes of profit and bodily alteration. He also mistakes the intentions of the carter the two of them meet, excitedly urging the Devil to seize him and his horses too without waiting to see if he means what he says:

> Herken, my brother, herkne, by thy feith!
> Herestow nat how that the cartere seith?
> Hent it anon, for he hath yeve it thee,
> Bothe hey and cart, and eek his caples thre. (3.1551–1555)

However, the Devil's superior abilities in discernment do not, in this case, make use of supernatural faculties. His recommended method of assessing the carter's "entente" invokes God but makes use of no ability out of the ordinary:

> "Nay," quod the devel, "God woot, never a deel!
> It is nat his entente, trust me weel
> Axe him thyself, if thou nat trowest me;
> Or elles stynt a while, and thou shalt see
>
> ....
>
> Heere may ye se, my owene deere brother,
> The carl spak oo thing, but he thoghte another." (3.1555–1558,
> 1567–1568)

No revelation, divine or demonic, is required. Instead, the Devil does what even the humblest layman knows how to do: aware that people do not always mean what they say, he considers the sum of their statements and actions in different circumstances over an extended period of time. The Devil understands that outward appearance does not reveal as much as someone like the Summoner might hope, or fear, that it does.

Chaucer's insistence on common sense is quite similar to that of the Wycliffite writer of "On Dominion," although very differently directed: like that writer he recasts the relationship between divinely inspired or marvellous "clergie" and uneducated, ignorant "lewedness" that we have found in physiognomic treatments of the lay discernment of hypocrites. In the *Friar's Tale,* the experiential evidence that proves the relationship between intentions and actions is easily available to any layman, while the Summoner's hankering after clerical expertise is if anything the source of his obtuseness. So fixated upon appearances and surfaces is the Summoner, to the exclusion of the long-term consistency of words and actions, that he fails to notice his own unwitting self-revelation when he challenges the old woman, and in his boasting to the Devil just beforehand:

> "I wole han twelf pens, though that she be wood,
> Or I wol *sompne* hire unto oure office;

And yet, God woot, of hire knowe I no vice,
But for thou kanst nat, as in this contree,
Wynne thy cost, taak heer ensample of me."
....
"I have," quod he, "of *somonce* here a bille;
Up peyne of cursyng, looke that thou be
Tomorn bifore the erchedeknes knee
T'answere to the court of certeyn thynges." (3.1576–1580, 1586–
1589; my emphases)

None of the Summoner's earlier claims that he was a "yeman," no attempt at physical disguise, can stand up against his unwitting acknowledgements (indicated by my emphases) of his profession. Indeed, the Summoner's abilities are inferior not just to those of the Devil, but also to those of the lay widow he is challenging here. Shut up tight in her house, she no less than the Devil can readily discern that the Summoner should not be trusted, and without even seeing his face.

As Chaucer moves from his earlier role as my pretext for this investigation of hypocrisy in the "Age of Chaucer" to my focus in this conclusion, I want to stress that Chaucer's use of the discourse of hypocrisy does not participate directly in the concerns with lay discernment felt by polemical and informational writers. Yet the way Chaucer puts those concerns to another use can help us to understand them better; in particular, he can show us that retraining the lay gaze upon the stigmatized habits (nonetheless no more easy to discern than hypocrisy) of a writer's opponents, and lay retraining toward apprehensive, clerically directed self-regard, have more in common than polemical and informational writings can admit.

All three of Chaucer's most hypocritical churchmen, the Pardoner, Friar, and Summoner, are in a way constructions as artificial as the stigmatized opponents imagined by the polemicists we examined earlier. Chaucer, like the polemicists (though to different ends), imagines figures who actively espouse hypocrisy and are also thoroughly devoted to concealment. The Pardoner parades hypocrisy through aggressively strident vaunting of his verbal prowess despite, or all the more because of, his moral depravity in an inadequate attempt to conceal physical insecurity, figured by his thinly spread locks of hair. The Friar and Summoner pose a different sort of extreme case: each is devoted to concealing physical depravity and hypocrisy at the same time. The Friar sumptuously clothes over (literally and metaphorically, through fine words and good manners) a body and character that are nonetheless figured forth in his apparel (the knife-farced tippet) and stripped bare by rage.[32] The Summoner, concerned that his face reveals him, is fascinated by the possibility of bodily redisposition and thus utterly imperceptive of what he might do to render his hypocrisy less apparent, even though this goal occupies his attention to the extent of complete eclipse of its possible achievement.

It remains the case, however, that no readers, no writers, really *want* to be the consummate hypocrite, let alone the hypocrite inadequate to the task of concealing himself. Active espousal of hypocrisy, or thoroughgoing devotion to concealing it, is a special case. Instead, it is far more usual to fear being labeled as a hypocrite, or (sometimes self-defensively) to point the finger at others. When the lay gaze is retrained, it is often displaced into scapegoating in terms of stigmatized habits or roles no more easily recognizable than hypocrisy, but at least equally feared. And this retraining is also easily turned inward, toward fear about the often difficult project of discerning one's own motives and character. What the Summoner in particular lays bare is the coercively normative influence exerted by condemnation of others and apprehensive self-regard, whether they work together or apart.

Notes

1. *Canterbury Tales,* in *The Riverside Chaucer,* 3rd ed., gen. ed. Larry D. Benson (Oxford: Oxford University Press, 1987), 1.233, 624, 688. Hereafter cited parenthetically by fragment and line number.

2. Work on Chaucer's use of physiognomical lore has largely focused on the Latin treatises and has for the most part used them as an interpretative key to the symbolism of Chaucer's physical descriptions. The first such investigation was that of Walter Clyde Curry, *Chaucer and the Medieval Sciences,* rev. ed. (New York: Barnes and Noble, 1968), esp. 56–70. See also John Block Friedman, "Another Look at Chaucer and the Physiognomists," *Studies in Philology,* 78 (1981): 138–52; and Laurel Braswell-Means, "A New Look at an Old Patient: Chaucer's Summoner and Medieval Physiognomia," *The Chaucer Review,* 25 (1991): 266–75. For a similar interpretative approach, this time using the Middle English physiognomy of John Metham (which I will cite in a very different connection below), see Oze E. Horton, "The Neck of Chaucer's Friar," *Modern Language Notes,* 48 (1933): 31–34. Useful historical introductions to the professions of these three pilgrims (and hence to just how they are hypocritical in their actions) appear in *Chaucer's Pilgrims; An Historical Guide to the Pilgrims in* The Canterbury Tales, ed. Laura C. and Robert T. Lambdin (Westport, Conn.: Greenwood Press, 1996); see the entries by Karl T. Hagen ("A Frere Ther Was, A Wawntone and a Merye," 80–92), James Keller ("A Sumoner Was Ther With Us In That Place," 300–13), and Elton E. Smith ("With Hym Ther Rood a Gentil Pardoner," 314–23). Hypocrisy is commonly a central concern in anticlerical and antifraternal writings; for further references see the next note.

3. Selective references from an extensive corpus: Jill Mann places all three portraits in the context of medieval literary satire in *Chaucer and Medieval Estates Satire: The Literature of Social Classes and the* General Prologue *to the* Canterbury Tales (Cambridge: Cambridge University Press, 1973), pp. 37–54, 137–144, 145–152; on antifraternalism in academic as well as literary contexts see Penn R. Szittya, *The Antifraternal Tradition in Medieval Literature* (Princeton: Princeton University Press, 1986), esp. 231–246, which focuses on the *Summoner's Tale;* on anticlericalism more generally, and on changes in the antifraternal tradition, see Wendy Scase,

"Piers Plowman" and the New Anti-Clericalism (Cambridge: Cambridge University Press, 1989).

4. The ramifications of this anxiety, and the kinds of writing in which it is most prominent, are the focus of my book *Clerical Discourse and Lay Audience in Late Medieval England* (Cambridge: Cambridge University Press, 1998). The present article, and its companion piece focusing on Chaucer's Friar and the friar of the *Summoner's Tale,* 'As just as is a squyre': The Politics of 'Lewed Translacion' in Chaucer's *Summoner's Tale"* (*Studies in the Age of Chaucer,* 21 [1999]: 187–207), aim to show how this anxiety manifests itself in Chaucer's work—and how that work, because its purposes are neither polemical nor informational, can deploy anxiety about lay discernment in a way that reveals its implications all the more clearly.

5. The *Twelve Conclusions* is most conveniently available in the well-annotated edition of Anne Hudson, included in Selections from *English Wycliffite Writings* (Cambridge: Cambridge University Press, 1978). Roger Dymmok's *Reply* has been printed under the title *Rogeri Dymmok Liber Contra Duodecim Errores et Hereses Lollardorum,* ed. H. S. Cronin (London: Wyclif Society, Trübner, 1922). For a discussion of the evidence for publication, dissemination, and response to both works, as well as a detailed treatment of Dymmok's most extended explanation (drawn mainly from pseudo-Chrysostom) of how hypocrites may be discerned, see Somerset, *Clerical Discourse,* 103–34.

6. For the discussion of idolatrous worship, see Hudson, 27; for the quotations, see 25.

7. *Reply,* 311–312. All translations are my own.

8. On new kinds of vernacular knowledge produced through translation and adaptation of academic and other Latin sources, see essays by Andrew Galloway including: *"Piers Plowman* and the Schools," *The Yearbook of Langland Studies,* 6 (1992): 89–107, "Gower in his Most Learned Role and the Peasants' Revolt of 1381," *Mediaevalia,* 16 (1993): 329–347, "Chaucer's Former Age and the Fourteenth-Century Anthropology of Craft: The Social Logic of a Premodernist Lyric," *ELH,* 63 (1996): 535–553. For an anthology of new kinds of vernacular knowledge, see *Popular and Practical Science of Medieval England,* ed. Lister M. Matheson (East Lansing, Mich.: Colleagues Press, 1994); on the importance of the vernacular to the Wycliffite heresy, see Margaret Aston, "Wycliffe and the Vernacular," in her *Faith and Fire: Popular and Unpopular Religion, 1350–1600* (London: Hambledon Press, 1993), pp. 27–72; and Anne Hudson, "Lollardy: The English Heresy?" in her *Lollards and Their Books* (London: Hambledon Press, 1985), pp. 141–163; see also Somerset, *Clerical Discourse,* 3-21, and on Trevisa's translations 62–100 and the other scholarship cited there.

9. See Scase for a lucid explanation of this "rhetorical breakdown," as she terms it (165–173).

10. Most Middle English physiognomies either appear in or derive from translations of the immensely popular *Secretum Secretorum,* the work supposedly written as a manual of instruction and advice by Aristotle for Alexander the Great. See *Secretum Secretorum: Nine English Versions* (vol. 1, Early English Text Society o.s. 276, ed. M. A. Manzalaoui [Oxford: Oxford University Press, 1977], pp. ix–l) for an introduction to the Arabic and Latin versions of the work, their relationship to the French and English versions, and a description of the contents and manuscripts of the nine texts he includes. Especial interest in the Physiognomy is demonstrated by the Latin versions: many divide the text such that the Physiognomy section forms

its own separate section or even transcribe the Physiognomy separate from the rest of the text (xvii). Of Manzalaoui's nine English versions, the second is a fragment including only the Physiognomy and Onomancy sections, the third, the "Ashmole," contains the expanded Physiognomy first found in the Latin tradition (see also xviii, sec. E), the fourth is also a full text including a Physiognomy, the eighth is a printed version including the Physiognomy, and all other versions are fragmentary or incomplete and do not include the Physiognomy (xxiv-xliii; on the expanded Latin version see xvii).

Additional English versions (all, except Hay, including a Physiognomy) are *Lydgate and Burgh's Secrees of Old Philosoffres*, Early English Text Society e.s. 66, ed. R. Steele (London: Trübner, 1894); *Three Prose Versions of the Secreta Secretorum*, Early English Text Society e.s. 74, ed. R. Steele (London: Trübner, 1898); *The Prose Works of Sir Gilbert Hay*, vol. 3, Scottish Text Society n.s. 21, ed. J. A. Glenn (Edinburgh: Scottish Text Society, 1993); and *The Works of John Metham*, Early English Text Society o.s. 132, ed. H. Craig (London: Trübner, 1916), pp. 118–145 (includes a *Secretum*-derived Physiognomy separate from the rest of the *Secretum*). For more recent scholarship focusing on the manuscripts and content of Middle English and Middle Scots versions, providing editions of more full or partial versions, and corroborating Manzalaoui's suggestions about independent interest in the Physiognomy itself, see: George R. Keiser, "Filling a Lacuna in a Middle English 'Secretum Secretorum,'" *Neuphilologische Mitteilungen*, 96 (1995): 381–388, esp. 382–383; J. Sanderson, "A Recently-Discovered Poem in Scots Vernacular: Complections of Men in Verse," *Scottish Studies*, 38 (1987): 49–68; S. Mapstone, "The Scots Buke of Phisnomy and Sir Gilbert Hay," in *The Renaissance in Scotland: Studies in Literature, Religion, History, and Culture Offered to J. Durkan*, ed. A. A. Macdonald, M. Lynch, and I. B. Cowan (Leiden: 1994), pp. 1–32; Paul Acker, "The Missing Conclusion of *The Book of Physiognomy*," *Medium Aevum*, 54 (1985): 266–270. Acker discusses and provides a revised edition and the conclusion to a Middle English physiognomy derived from another Latin source and previously edited from an incomplete copy in *The World of Piers Plowman* (ed. Jeanne Krochalis and Edward Peters [Philadelphia: University of Pennsylvania Press, 1975], pp. 218–228). For another, as-yet unnoticed physiognomy in Middle English not derived directly from the *Secretum* tradition, see 319 and n.16.

11. The editors' prefaces and the authors' prologues to the materials included in Matheson, *Popular and Practical Science*, show the range of available material and the kinds of claims that were made for it.

12. "Physiognomy," in *Works of John Metham*, 135–136.

13. For some versions of the exemplum see *Secretum* 10–11, 90, 197–198, 376–377; *Lydgate and Burgh's Secrees*, 2479–2520; *Three Prose Versions*, 38, 113, 217–218; *Works of John Metham*, 118–119.

14. *Secretum*, 90.

15. Certainly works in the advice-to-princes, or *Fürstenspiegel*, tradition were frequently presented to kings and princes. But even the limited available evidence of manuscript ownership and dissemination indicates that they enjoyed a much wider distribution, in the vernacular and even in Latin, among those aspiring to display regal self-control (even if only through ownership of a copy of the treatise). See Judith Ferster's recent summary of the evidence and scholarship in *Fictions of Advice: The Literature and Politics of Counsel in Late Medieval England* (Philadelphia: University of Pennsylvania Press, 1996), pp. 178–185. On the characteristics and

readership of what he terms the "public exemplum," that is, an exemplum focusing on matters of state, in the *Fürstenspiegel* tradition and elsewhere, see Larry Scanlon, *Narrative, Authority, and Power: The Medieval Exemplum and the Chaucerian Tradition* (Cambridge: Cambridge University Press, 1994), pp. 81–87 (Scanlon's analysis of the *Friar's Tale* will be discussed below). Much groundbreaking work on the advice-to-princes tradition in England and its relation to better-known court poetry by writers like Chaucer and Gower was done by Richard F. Green in *Poets and Princepleasers: Literature and the English Court in the Late Middle Ages* (Toronto: University of Toronto Press, 1980).

16. Citations will be made by line number from the most recent edition, Robert Mannyng of Brunne, *Handlyng Synne,* Medieval and Renaissance Texts and Studies 14, ed. Idelle Sullens (Binghamton, New York: Center for Medieval and Early Renaissance Studies, 1983). Still useful for its parallel text edition (however partial) of Mannyng's principal source is *Robert of Brunne's "Handlyng Synne," A.D. 1303, with those Parts of the Anglo-French Treatise on which it was Founded, William of Wadington's "Manuel des Pechiez,"* 2 vols., Early English Text Society o.s. 119, 123, ed. Frederick J. Furnivall (London: Trübner, 1901, 1903). Mannyng has been cited most often by critics interested in oral and popular culture, exempla, or penitential manuals; his embedded physiognomy treatise has never to my knowledge received any attention. Representative studies would include John M. Ganim, "The Devil's Writing Lesson," in *Oral Poetics in Middle English Poetry,* ed. Mark C. Amodio (New York: Garland Publishing, 1994), pp. 109–112; Nancy Mason Bradbury, "Popular Festive Forms and Beliefs in Robert Mannyng's *Handlyng Synne,*" in *Bakhtin and Medieval Voices,* ed. Thomas J. Farrell (Gainesville: University Press of Florida, 1995), pp. 158–179; Brian S. Lee, "'This is no Fable': Historical Residues in Two Medieval *Exempla,*" *Speculum,* 56 (1981): 728–760; Fritz Kemmler, *Exempla in Context: A Historical and Critical Study of Robert Mannyng's* Handlyng Synne (Tübingen: Narr, 1984); D. W. Robertson, "The Cultural Tradition of *Handlyng Synne,*" *Speculum,* 22 (1947): 162–185; Lee Patterson, "The 'Parson's Tale' and the Quitting of the 'Canterbury Tales,'" *Traditio,* 34 (1978): 331–380. For an attempt to analyze the "penitential politics" of the poem, particularly with regard to its treatment of women, see Cynthia Ho, "Dichotomize and Conquer: 'Womman Handlyng' in *Handlyng Synne,*" *Philological Quarterly,* 72 (1993): 383–401.

17. For the text of the decree that imposed this universal requirement, *Omnis utriusque sexus,* see X 5.38.12, in *Corpus Iuris Canonici,* 2 vols., ed. Aemilius Friedberg (Leipzig, 1879; reprint, Graz, 1959), 2: cols. 887–888. For a synopsis of all the decrees of the Lateran Council and an investigation of their subsequent publication and implementation in England, see Marion Gibbs and Jane Lang, *Bishops and Reform,* 1215–1272, *With Special Reference to the Lateran Council of 1215* (Oxford: Oxford University Press, 1934; reprint, London: Frank Cass, 1962), pp. 180–128, 94–179.

18. For D 32, see *Corpus Iuri Canonici,* 1: cols. 116–122. See especially c. 6, cols. 117–119, and for this quotation col. 118.37–46.

19. For a general introduction to the conduct of and points of conflict in relations between church and state in later medieval England, see R. N. Swanson, *Church and Society in Late Medieval England* (Oxford: Blackwell, 1989), esp. pp. 1–26, 89–139, 140–190; and also W. A. Pantin, *The English Church in the Fourteenth Century,* Medieval Academy Reprints for Teaching 5 (Toronto: University of Toronto Press, 1980), esp. pp. 9–102, 126–129.

20. For versions of the 1215 decree on priestly continence issued in England later in the thirteenth century, see David Wilkins, *Concilia Magnae Britanniae et Hiberniae*, 4 vols. (London, 1737; reprint, Brussels, 1964), 1:573, 581, 590, 607, 609–610, 616, 635, 638, 653, 661, 672–673, 692, 705–706, 716–717. See also Gibbs and Lang, 126–129.

21. *De Officio Pastoralis*, chap. 19, in *The English Works of Wyclif Hitherto Unprinted*, ed. F. D. Matthew, Early English Text Society o.s. 74 (London: Trüber, 1880), pp. 435.

22. *The Twenty-Five Articles*, no. 18, in *Select English Works of John Wyclif*, 3 vols., ed. Thomas Arnold (Oxford: Clarendon Press, 1869–1871), 3:486.

23. *The Dialogue Between a Knight and a Clerk*, MS Cosin V iii 6, ff 12v-14, University of Durham Library. The page break is marked by "//"; modern punctuation supplied. Folios 12v and 14r were adjacent in the original manuscript; in its present binding the manuscript is interleaved with a seventeenth-century transcription and thus appears on alternating folios. For a description see Hudson, "A Lollard Quaternion," in *Lollards and their Books*, 193–200.

24. *Handlyng Synne*, 1083–1084, 10155–10158.

25. *Handlyng Synne*, 10199–10218, 10225–10256.

26. On medieval catalogues of the seven deadly sins, see Morton W. Bloomfield's comprehensive survey, *The Seven Deadly Sins: An Introduction to the History of a Religious Concept with Special Reference to English Literature* (East Lansing: Michigan State College Press, 1952).

27. See 315–316 above. Kantik Ghosh perceptively notes in his thesis that the Wycliffite (and, in turn, anti-Wycliffite) hermeneutic focus on authorial intention led to a corresponding concern with the intentions of interpreters and thus produced *ad hominem* refutations focusing on the opponent's hypocrisy rather than the invalidity of his argumentation. His examination of the pervasive tendency in the *English Wycliffite Sermons* to focus on discerning hypocrisy in opposing interpreters, rather than weighing interpretations against one another on other hermeneutic grounds, is particularly valuable. See Kantik Ghosh, *"Authority" and Interpretation in Wycliffite, Anti-Wycliffite and Related Texts, c. 1375–c. 1430* (D. Phil. thesis, University of Cambridge, 1995), chap. 4, 120–163, esp. 125–131. These Wycliffite polemics on hypocrisy for the most part illustrate the usual clerical attitude to lay discernment. So does Dymmok's *Reply*, which I discuss in far greater detail in *Clerical Discourse* (131–134). For a survey of the various kinds of instruction that Wycliffites provide, and crossreferences to a range of examples, see *Clerical Discourse* (15–16).

28. "Of Dominion," in *English Works of Wyclif*, 291.

29. The Friar's aside in the opening stages of his tale, "For thogh this Somonour wood were as an hare, / To telle his harlotrye I wol nat spare" (3.1327–28), explicitly links the Summoner on the pilgrimage with his counterpart within the tale, as does his reference to the pilgrimage Summoner in his conclusion: "Lordynges, I koude han toold yow, quod this Frere, / Hadde I had leyser for this Somnour heere" (3.1645–46). For the developing rivalry between the Friar and Summoner, and how the Friar attempts to fuel that rivalry by offending *this* Summoner in particular— and succeeds—see also 3.829–856, 1256–1297, 1329–1337, 1665–1671.

30. Scanlon, 147–160.

31. The Devil is of course first to address the Summoner as "brother" and assert their similarity (3.1395–96), but the Summoner is more than happy to play along after the Devil has proposed a fellowship based on profit (3.1399). See also

3.1410, 1413, 1417, 1419, 1423–1424, 1434, 1452, 1527–1529. In "'As just as is a squyre,'" I suggest that Friar John in the *Summoner's Tale* aspires to the same sort of lay status that the squire in the tale evidently possesses; in the *Friar's Tale* too it seems that the Summoner aspires to the apparent status of his lay counterpart the yeoman/Devil (see esp. 3.1524). J. Lachlan Mead has suggested in "Military Practice and Chivalric Ideology" (paper delivered at the 33rd International Congress on Medieval Studies, Kalamazoo, Mich., May 1998) that owing to changes in the organization of the military, yeomen in the later fourteenth century increasingly aspired to the same sort of status as squires. He analyzes the accoutrements of the Yeoman in the *General Prologue* to suggest that Chaucer means this yeoman to display precisely these sorts of new aspirations. In correspondence in May 1998, Mead suggests that the same is certainly true of the *Friar's Tale* yeoman; I thank him again for discussing the matter and suggesting references. If Mead's argument is accepted, then both tales, rather than just the *Summoner's Tale,* present members of the clergy aspiring to lay status and service of a kind particularly controversial during the course of Wycliffite/anti-Wycliffite conflict. On this point of controversy, see Hudson, "*Hermafodrita* or *Ambidexter*: Wycliffite Views on Clerks in Secular Office," in *Lollardy and the Gentry in the Later Middle Ages,* ed. Margaret Aston and Colin Richmond (Stroud, Gloucestershire: Sutton Publishing, 1997), pp. 41–51, and Somerset, *Clerical Discourse*, 116–120.

32. My more detailed discussion of the Friar as well as the friar within the *Summoner's Tale* appears in Somerset, "'As just as is a squyre.'"

LOUISE M. BISHOP

"Of Goddes pryvetee nor of his wyf": Confusion of *Orifices in Chaucer's* Miller's Tale

Other critics have connected the word "pryvetee" in the *Miller's Tale*, referring to both human genitalia and secrets, to the Biblical story of Moses seeing God's "back parts" (posteriora).[1] There appears to be general agreement that the complex of secrets, genitalia, and divinity points to many levels of meaning in the *Tale*, including a parody of the *Knight's Tale*[2] and an invocation of theological commonplaces such as the Holy Family.[3] I would suggest an even more challenging and terrifying, certainly blasphemous and heretical reading of the Tale's meaning, taking a different tack from Frederick Biggs and Laura Howes to tie Chaucer's purposeful confusion to epistemological questions and, in turn, gender issues. This train of thought inflects the word pryvetee's purposeful confusion between "secret" and "genitalia" with a Biblical story in Exodus 33: God, after hiding Moses in a rock's cleft, shows him His back parts. Augustine's commentary on the Biblical episode illuminates the *Tale's* connections between (and confusion about) the body and knowledge. The *Tale's* confused orifices—backsides taken for mouths—parody the Bible story's concern with the unseen and seen, and Augustine's understanding of the Bible story as an allegory of the means and limits of human knowledge. By successfully concatenating divine and female "pryvetee," the *Tale* plays with concepts of bodily knowledge by alluding to divine genitalia. Combining confused orifices—holes—and

Texas Studies in Literature and Language, Volume 44, Issue 3 (Fall 2002): pp. 231–247.
© 2002 University of Texas at Austin (University of Texas Press).

163

the desire to "know" in its varied intellectual and bodily meanings with purposeful punning on "secret" and "private parts" leads to a blasphemous conclusion—or purposeful lack of conclusion—about God's private parts. Alison's escape from injury in the *Tale* forms part of this complex of meaning. The connection between divine knowledge and the knowing of women's secrets—so powerful a theme in the *Wife of Bath's Tale*[4]—here finds a different "end."

"Pryvetee" first appears in the *Tale's* prologue as the Miller advises the Reeve, and everyone else who is listening, "An housbonde shal nat been inquisityf Of Goddes pryvetee, nor of his wyf."[5] Twice more in his tale the Miller repeats the phrase "Goddes pryvetee": first, in John's nervous apostrophe to Saint Frideswyth after he has been advised of Nicholas's plight (1.3454); and then in Nicholas's caution to John while telling him about the impending flood (1.3558). The word "pryvetee" and its variants, such as "pryvely," appear seven more times, describing various secret communications, such as Alison's advice to Nicholas to be secretive around John (1.3295) and John's telling Alison about the plan with the tubs, a "pryvetee" of which "she was war, and knew it bet than he" (1.3603–3604). The word and its variants become a leitmotif through the tale, alerting us to the comedy inherent in domestic secrets and the misprision and misuse of divine ones, no matter how mistaken they—the characters or the secrets—may be. Significantly, the leitmotif begins by yoking "Goddes pryvetee" with that of a "wyf": divine secrets join women's secrets. The *Miller's* introductory link between God and wife suggests a way to read the *Tale's* complex of confused orifices and bodily knowledge.

The *Tale's* narrative concern with bottoms—Alison's, Nicholas's, John's concern for Alison's, Absolon's preoccupation with Alison's—suggests that Chaucer's audience could catch, each time the *Tale* uses "pryvetee," the word's other meaning: not only "secrets," as above, but "private parts" or genitalia[6]—how to know a boy from a girl. Earlier critics of the Tale may have shied from so indecent a pun, but current criticism accepts and trades on the pun's vitality.[7] The pun on "secrets" and "private parts" provides feminist critics a way to unmask the patriarchal strategies embedded in this *Tale* specifically, and in the fabliau mode generally.[8] Those strategies are themselves connected to epistemological questions, as Bums asserts:

> In many key instances fabliau women's speech reveals the extent to which male protagonists' claims to absolute knowledge are based on an anxiety about sexual difference, calling into question the authority of the fabliau narrator's pretense of knowing women. [39]

Feminist critics have noticed the *Tale's* anxieties about gender definition, and others have investigated the material practices and ideologies associated with the body and gender in the Middle Ages.[9] In the theological sphere, perhaps the most challenging problem—one which motivated its own feast day and affected artists' renderings of the infant Jesus—is the corporeal nature of the Son of God. Orthodoxy uses the "proof" of Jesus's corporeality, the very basis of the Corpus Christi feast, to face heterodox threats to the role of Christ's literal body in salvation ideology. Besides this basic theological issue, bodily knowledge in a "scientific" sense was a topic of discussion in the Middle Ages, analyzing what the body "proves" through its five senses and how the body's senses can be, and are, fooled.[10] Without belaboring an obvious point, it is important to recognize this intellectual intersection between the facts of knowledge gained through the body and the role of the body in Christian salvation ideology. Only when we remember the body's role in the production of knowledge and salvation can we appreciate the complex intellectual joke Chaucer makes by conflating the body, knowledge, and divinity. In this light we can evaluate the literary weight of the *Miller's Tale*'s pun on God's private parts.

In her treatment of the *Miller's Tale* Laura Kendrick provides clear examples of fourteenth-century visual artists' preoccupation, not with God's, but with Christ's genitals." Those genitals prove Jesus's corporeal nature and, as Kendrick says,

> In such paintings, the Christ Child no longer needs to hold a scroll symbolizing the Old Testament in his hand to remind us that he is the incarnate Word, that the text of his flesh is the key to understanding God's intentions. The transparent veil reveals the nude body behind it or falls away to discover God's pryvetee in a material, physical representation of the abstract sense of St. Paul's words.[13]

Kendrick points out that "God the Father's private parts were as taboo in the late fourteenth century as today".[11] Nevertheless, artists' concern with Christ's genitalia cannot help, trinitarianally speaking, but make a theologically aware audience think of God's bottom, if only to banish as quickly as possible so rude a thought. Humor about human "private parts"—the very essence of the *Miller's Tale*'s confused orifices, mouths and bottoms—and the invocation of God's "privity," comparing it to that of a"wyf," spectacularly de-sublimates pryvetee's pun on "secret" and "private." Recognizing the pun contrasts the human desire for certainty with the absolute depth of divine knowledge in a linguistically playful, if doctrinally disturbing, way.

It is in this context of calibrating the text's playful and disturbing pun on God's privates that the Biblical story of Moses seeing God's backside, and Augustine's analysis and use of the Biblical passage, provides further meaning for Chaucer's *Tale*. God has a face that no one can see and live, according to

Exodus 33. After the Israelites' apostasy and Moses's smashing of the tablets containing the Ten Commandments, Moses and God "make up":

> Moses said, "Show me your glory, I pray." And he [God] said, "I will make all my goodness pass before you and will proclaim before you the name 'The Lord'; and I will be gracious to whom I will be gracious, and will show mercy on whom I will show mercy. But," he said, "you cannot see my face; for no one shall see me and live." And the Lord continued, "See, there is a place by me where you shall stand on the rock; and while my glory passes by I will put you in a cleft of the rock, and I will cover you with my hand until I have passed by; then I will take away my hand and you shall see my back parts [posteriora mea]; but my face [Vaciem] shall not be seen" (Exodus 33:18–23).[12]

Notice that, in an episode wherein Moses cannot see God's "face," the hidden and secret are conflated with seeing—and knowing (or not knowing)—God's "pryvetee": His face, and by extension His front side, are off-limits to human sight and knowledge. Moses's knowledge of God cannot be complete; human knowledge is different from divine knowledge. Significantly, what Moses does get to see—and know—are God's back parts. The Latin plural, for a punning mind, is important. Posteriora mea can be euphemistically glossed as the singular "back" only by ignoring grammatical number and human anatomy. Certainly those back parts include legs and shoulders, but "back parts" inescapably suggests buttocks, what we call the backside.[13] Moses can see God's backside, but he cannot see—or know—God's face or His front side. Moses's expressed desire to see and to know God can be only partially met.

Not surprisingly, and in line with a general tendency towards decorum (an attitude that characterizes Augustine's time as much as that of early Chaucer critics, if not our own), Augustine counsels in his *Exposition on the Book of Psalms* a figurative interpretation of God's backside, admonishing his reader not to think literally but allegorically:

> And from these words there ariseth another enigma, that is, an obscure figure of the truth. When I have passed by, saith God, thou shalt see My back parts; as though He hath on one side His face, on another His back. Far be it from us to have any such thoughts of that Majesty! . . . But forasmuch as the Lord was about to take flesh in due time, so as to appear even to fleshly eyes, that healthfully He might cure the soul within, since thus it was needful that He should appear, foretelling this . . . By His Face He meant

His former estate, and in a manner by His back parts, His passing from this world by His Passion. . . . [14]

Augustine, like the *Miller's Tale*'s early critics, intends to cut off any speculation on God's bodily form, including his private parts, front or back, by allegorizing the incident, and warning his audience not to think about God's body. The warning, while needed, can hardly be heeded, since even the readers of exegesis are situated as bodily creatures, created in God's image, and their greater theological sophistication, such as a belief in a unified Trinity, only adds to an inability to "forget" God's body. In other words, Augustine's reading of the passage, far from diminishing the importance of these corporeal themes, such as the linking of knowledge to the body, foregrounds the very centrality of God's body, as fourteenth-century painters had foregrounded Christ's genitals. Almost in spite of himself, Augustine's rationale participates in and depends on the necessity of human, bodily understanding to explain the Incarnation and salvation history.

Augustine was obviously aware of this inherent contradiction between the need to explain salvation in terms of a real body and, owing to Trinitarian orthodoxy, the importance of keeping God disembodied. He includes in *On the Trinity* the same warning he had given in his commentary on Psalm 138—not to take "backside" too literally:

> For we should not become so enveloped in the murkiness of the flesh as to think that the face of the Lord is invisible but His back is visible . . . Far be it from us to think any such thing of Him in the form of God! Far be it from us to think that the Word of God and the Wisdom of God has a face on one side and a back on the other, as the human body, or that it undergoes any change at all either in appearance, motion, time, or place![15]

That attitude, of course, reveals Augustine's desire to cleanse the episode of a meaning it too easily—and inescapably—has. Instead, Augustine counsels an allegorical reading: "By His Face He meant His former estate, and in a manner by His back parts, His passing from this world by His Passion." For Augustine, God's face typifies his divine nature, his back parts typify the Passion, and the allegory of God's passing his hand over Moses refers to the two periods of history, before and after the crucifixion. Since the Passion could not have happened without Christ's corporeal nature, we can complete the syllogism that Augustine suggests despite himself: God's backside symbolizes Christ's corporeality. Elsewhere Augustine more explicitly calls God's behind a metaphor for Christ's flesh. In his commentary on Psalm 120, Augustine makes the following equation: "What are His back parts?

and the Word was made flesh, and dwelt among us"; and, after a disquisition on bodily resurrection, "What meaneth, see His back parts? Believe in His resurrection."[16] *De Trinitate* also connects God's backside with Christ's body.

> And as a matter of fact the words which the Lord later says to Moses . . . are commonly and not without reason understood to prefigure the person of our Lord Jesus Christ. Thus, the back parts are taken to be His flesh, in which He was born of the Virgin and rose again, whether they are called back parts [posteriora] because of the posteriority of His mortal nature, or because He deigned to take it near the end of the world, that is, at a later period.[17]

Equating God's backside with Christ's flesh fills out Augustine's earlier allegory of God's back parts; after all, what makes the son the Son is his flesh.

Warnings against literalist reading, coupled with equating fleshly nature with the backside, make the rude humor of the *Miller's Tale* all the more delicious as well as blasphemous—even though Christ has a backside, we are not supposed to think about it, either. On the other hand, the backside seems ubiquitous in medieval art. As the backside typifies the flesh, so bottoms provide profane humor in much art of the Middle Ages. Art historian Michael Camille notes this humor in manuscript margins and misericord faces.[18] The success of the backside as a metonymy for human flesh depends on theological sources, such as Augustine's exegesis, for its suggestiveness and power. The body, the flesh, and the bottom are not far removed from the most elevated theological discussions, even in Augustine's warnings against such literal thinking.

In letter 147, explaining to Paulina the difference between bodily and inward sight, Augustine deals with "seeing is believing," and, in trotting out the passage from Exodus, obliquely refers to God's backside as a figure for the church:

> Again, in ancient times, in the case of the faithful servant of God, Moses, who was destined to labor on this earth and to rule the chosen people, it would not be surprising that what he asked was granted: that he might see the glory of the Lord, to whom he said: "If [I] have found favor before thee, show me thyself openly." He received an answer adapted to present conditions, that he could not see the face of God, because no man could see Him and live; thus God made clear that the vision belongs to another and better life. In addition to that, the mystery of the future Church of Christ was foreshadowed by the words of God. Doubtless, Moses represented in himself the type of the Jewish people who would believe in

Christ after His Passion, and that is why it says: "When I shall pass, thou shalt see my back parts," and the rest which is there said, by an admirable mystery which foretells the Church to come. But it would take too long to discuss this now. [19]

As in his other commentaries, Augustine equates God's front and back with the Old and New Law. Considering the length of the letter, Augustine's reluctance to elucidate his equation of the church with God's backside is surprising. Perhaps his lacuna serves the same purpose as his warnings in other commentaries not to take God's back and front literally. More important for our purposes, this letter of Augustine's treats the concept of knowledge and human reliance on the senses with a brief disquisition on the metaphor of "seeing":

Although there are five senses in the body—seeing, hearing, smelling, tasting, touching—of these, sight is attributed especially to the eyes, but we use this word also of the others. Not only do we say, "See, how bright it is,' but also "See, what a noise," "See, what a smell," "See, what a taste," "See, how hot it is." [20]

The confluence in Augustine's letter between his invocation of the Exodus story (along with his unusual lacuna) and his meditation on how bodily senses provide knowledge reveals his association of the Exodus story with the realm of human knowledge, located for Augustine in the power to "see" as both word and action. In his allegorical renderings, Augustine connects the passage from Exodus with the role of the literal body, especially sight, in human understanding. Augustine's letter 147 explains to Paulina the difference between bodily and inward sight, in an attempt to answer her question whether God can be seen by bodily eyes; he also treats the difference between spiritual and corporeal sight in *The Literal Meaning of Genesis*.[21] In both works, Augustine uses the passage from Exodus to explain spiritual sight, and to assess the body's role in attaining knowledge. When Augustine thinks "body" and "sight," he thinks of the Biblical passage from Exodus, with its shimmering, if inappropriate, image of God's *posteriora* and uses the confluence of seeing and knowing in his attempt to explain the differences between spiritual and bodily sight. Again, the body is foundational to and used for human understanding, even as spiritual understanding is the orthodox goal.

If for Augustine, the passage in Exodus figures God's "back parts" as a metaphor for corporeality, His face for divinity, and Augustine fits that corporeality into the larger question of relying on the body's senses for knowledge, Chaucer's humor plays upon Augustine's exegesis by emphasizing bottoms and using confused body parts to "expose" the limits of human knowledge. Nicholas and Absolon learn to their regret that the human backside does not provide incontrovertible knowledge of person, place, or thing. Chaucer makes laughable the importance of vision to knowledge by subverting visual and bodily knowledge in the *Tale:* bottoms are taken for faces in more than one instance. Furthermore, the *Tale,* like Augustine's exegesis, uses conflated senses to illustrate confounded human knowledge. The synesthesia Augustine outlines to explain the power of sight in the passage from Letter 147 cited above echoes in the *Tale*'s final episode, the blinding fart:

> This Nicholas anon leet fle a fart
> As greet as it had been a thonder-dent,
> That with the strook he [Absolon] was almoost yblent;
> And he was redy with his iren hoot,
> And Nicholas amydde the ers he smoot. (1.3806–3810)

Absolon, who had earlier kissed Alison's behind, thinking it her face, here exacts his revenge, having prepared a hot poker. But Nicholas, Alison's lover, humorously takes Alison's place at the window and receives Absolon's punishing stroke, with only a fart between Absolon's arrival and Nicholas's burned bottom. The passage alludes to four of the five senses, from smelling and hearing the fart, to its capacity to blind, and then to the sensation of burning. The one sense this passage avoids had been the center of Absolon's earlier mistake when he kissed Alison's backside "ful savourly" (1.3735). Blind as he is, Absolon still makes his way to his fell purpose, misdirected as it may be, while Nicholas has his own vacuum of understanding, having misunderstood Absolon's intent. Chaucer uses sensual confusion to poke fun at the limits of human knowledge in the same way that Augustine uses linguistic synesthesia—seeing a smell—to foreground how humans use and abuse sensual vocabulary to recognize—or kick against—knowledge's limits.

We do not need Augustine's exegesis to see that the *Miller's Tale* emphasizes the body: no surprise for a fabliau. Nicholas grabs Alison's haunch bones (1.3279), and balances his own on the shot window (1.3803). Alison's white apron sits "Upon hir lendes, ful of many a goore" (1.3237). Absolon's talents include body care: "Wel koude he laten blood, and clippe and shave." (1.3326). The Tale depends on bodily desire for its inception, and on backsides for its humor. More importantly, the Tale consistently makes fun of the limits of human knowledge, from John's misunderstanding his wife, his boarder, and the Bible, to Absolon's confusion regarding backsides and love. But the greatest confusion in the *Miller's Tale* does not just come from flesh; it comes more specifically from holes.

Holes show up everywhere in the *Tale*'s details, from architectural holes—windows (1.3694, 1.3708) and doors (1.3432)—to the cat hole John's servant uses to spy on Nicholas (1.3440–3441). Clothes have holes: the windows on

Absolon's shoes (1.3318), the gores in Alison's apron (1.3237). And bodies have holes: the lovers' kissing mouths (1.3305); Absolon's singing mouth, sweetened with cardamom and licorice (1.3690); Alison's kissed anus (1.3734–3735) and Nicholas's burned one (1.3812). These orifices are confused: cat holes become peep holes, windows become doors, mouths become anuses and anuses become wounds.[22] The *Tale's* humor depends on this confusion to direct our attention to the incompleteness of human knowledge and amplify the meaning of the *Tale's* indecent puns on God's and a wife's "pryvetee."

A hole—an aperture or opening—appears in the Bible episode in Exodus 33. God tells Moses the conditions under which he may see His backside: Moses will stand in a "cleft of the rock" as God's "glory passes by." "Cleft of the rock" translates the Vulgate's foramen petrae. Foramen is "an opening or aperture produced by boring, a hole" and, in late Latin, "a cave."[23] The Biblical story, then, also has its hole. For Augustine in *On the Trinity,* however, it is not a hole, but a watchtower, from a textual confusion in the Old Latin Bible between specula and spelunca. Augustine's watchtower could have prompted the power of his association between the Exodus 33 story and the importance of sight to human knowledge, as evidenced in his meditation on sight in Letter 147. Whether formamen, spelunca, or specula, Moses's "hidey hole"—a place where looked-for knowledge is circumscribed, only partially given, despite (or because of) human desire—seems of a piece with the many holes in Chaucer's *Tale* and the humorous limitations of and confusions about many of them.[24]

Augustine never explicitly refers in his commentaries to what Moses cannot see, God's secret, private parts and, while paradoxically insisting on the backside as a figure for the flesh, simultaneously warns the reader: "Far be it from us to have any such thoughts of that Majesty!" Augustine's warning reminds the reader of the *Miller's Tale* of its Prologue's advice to "chese another *Tale,*" a paradoxical kind of insistence, foregrounding that which it ostensibly counsels against, as does Augustine's warning. The object of Augustine's warning is both God's front side—utterly hidden, secret, forbidden—and God's backside—circumspectly but dangerously a figure for human fleshly nature. The nature of Augustine's warning—its link between the body and knowledge—provides a telling parallel to Chaucer's own warning about reading an obscene *Tale* with many confusions about bottoms and holes.

Chaucer transforms Augustine's decorum into the *Miller's* joke. But the Miller himself reveals his own ignorance of anatomy, in particular female anatomy, when he confuses the "holes" of Alison's female body.

Derk was the nyght as pich, or as the cole,
And at the wyndow out she putte hir hole,

> And Absolon, hym fil no bet ne wers
> But with his mouth he kiste hir naked ers
> Ful savourly, er he were war of this (1.3730–3735)

Which hole? Alison's sense of balance would have to be rather remarkable were she to hang only her anus, and not her vagina, out the shot window. But, since Absolon gets a mouthful of hair, he apparently didn't kiss her backside and miss her vagina, as the Miller has with his singular noun.[25] While Nicholas is obsessed with Alison's private parts, and the Miller, in telling his tale, shifts continually between holes and "pryvetee," the Miller himself reveals his confusion about, and maybe even his ignorance of, female anatomy. The *Tale* thus hints at the impossibility of a man knowing a woman's private parts, as well as her secrets—as did the yoking of "Goddes pryvetee" with that of a "wyf" Elaine Hansen and E. Jane Burns generalize the Miller's confusion into that of patriarchy, and lament another patriarchal appropriation of women's bodies. But the Miller's confusion about Alison's private parts, as noted by both critics, echoes the Miller's, Moses's, and indeed everyone's, ignorance of God's private parts.

The episodes at the shot window with their intentional confusions of holes and bodies parody God's display to Moses, making us all too aware of the limits of human knowledge. What is the secret knowledge God keeps from us? Karma Lochrie and Elaine Hansen base their readings of the *Miller's Tale* on patriarchy's hidden paradigm of male homosocial bonding, where women exist only as a means of exchange between men. For Lochrie, God's privity equals this once-secret patriarchal strategy: "'Goddes pryvetee' is really the subject of Nicholas's plan to fool John, who knows better than to inquire into it (1.3454)" (298). Yet, as Burns points out, the thing not "known" in the *Miller's Tale* is Alison's "front." Nicholas "privily" grabs her aproncovered "queynte" as she, keeping her orifices confused, tells him he can't have a kiss. Later, Absolon mistakes her behind for her face, and the Miller tells us about the singular hole she hangs out the window (1.3732). On the one hand, Alison's "front" is well-known, as welcoming as can be but not as welcoming as that of the *Tale's* analogues;[26] on the other, it is as mysterious to the reader's eye as is God's, and baffles the *Tale's* other characters as well. The unknowability of "Goddes pryvetee" in Exodus— the face refused to Moses or, more tellingly (by analogy to the "back parts"), the "front parts" of God—becomes the ostensibly self evident, yet persistent mystery of Alison. The *Miller's Tale* thus blasphemously—and deliciously—elevates Alison's private parts and their unknowability to the level of God's. Lochrie notes Alison's disappearance by the end of the poem, but I suggest that another disappearing character is ever present: God. The *Tale's* parallel between a wife's secrets and God's—and a wife's privates and God's—subverts complacent masculinity as does the *Tale's* hilarious narrative, especially in the case of Nicholas's punishment. As the Exodus story, and even Augustine's exegesis makes clear, God's privates—his front parts—are beyond man's comprehension. Could the confusion of mouths, bottoms, and other holes, along with the unknowability of a wife's as well as God's privates, imply that His too might be feminine?[27] In a *Tale* saturated with a confusion about holes and their purposes and meaning, can we be so sure how many holes God has, even as we are surely not supposed to think of such things, or read such tales?

The *Miller's Tale* doesn't mention, even euphemistically, the male genitalia: instead the *Tale,* either despite or because of all its confused orifices, mystifies the male anatomy.[28] The movie rating system used in the United States until recently said the same thing: only a visible penis earned a movie an X rating.[29] Western culture has surrounded the penis with fearsome sanctity for centuries. We can read that fearsome sanctity in God's refusal to let Moses see Him: no human can see his face and live. The earthly version of God's front is Christ's genitalia, and that appurtenance is celebrated in fourteenth-century art. The *Tale* equates the mystery of God's privates not with Nicholas's, but with a "wyf"'s, Alison's, the one character in the *Tale* who receives no punishment. While the *Miller's Tale* from the very first mention of "pryvetee" punningly elevates female genitalia to the level of the divine, at the same time it humorously alludes to Augustine's exegesis concerning the limits of human knowledge as foundational to the identity mechanisms of the human frame, beginning (and ending) with the difference (or lack thereof) between male and female. The *Miller's Tale* gives its readers the mystery and power of unknowable woman: the mystery of her orifices, utterly confusing even to the ostensibly initiated, and the mystery of her power, situated, unlike (or like) the divine's, in a triumphant "Tehee."

Notes

1. See Frederick M. Biggs and Laura L. Howes, "Theophany in *The Miller's Tale,*" Medium Aevum 65.2 (1996): 269–279, and their very kind note. My appreciation to Elizabeth Scala for her exceptionally perceptive criticism of this essay and invaluable assistance, and to John Rumrich, editor of *TSLL.*

2. See *A Variorum Edition of The Works of Geoffrey Chaucer, Volume II (The Canterbury Tales),* Part 3: the *Miller's Tale,* ed. Thomas W. Ross, 37–41 for a general overview of the relationships between the *Knight's Tale* and the *Miller's Tale.*

3. See, for instance, Robert Kaske, "The Canticum Canticorum in the *Miller's Tale,*" Studies in Philology 59 (1962): 479–500.

4. For a tantalizing reading of such secrets, see Kanna Lochrie, "Don't Ask, Don't Tell: Murderous Plots and Medieval Secrets," in *Premodern Sexualities,* ed. Louise Fradenburg and Carla Freccero (New York: Routledge, 1996), 137–152. For the most important feminist reading of sacred flesh, see Sarah Beckwith, *Christ's*

Body: Identity, Culture, and Society in Late Medieval Writings (New York: Routledge, 1993).

5. Geoffrey Chaucer, "The Miller's Prologue," *The Riverside Chaucer, Third Edition,* ed. Larry D. Benson (Boston: Houghton Mifflin, 1987). fragment 1, lines 3164–3165. All further citations of the *Miller's Prologue* and the *Miller's Tale* are taken from this edition.

6. See "privete" in the *Middle English Dictionary,* part of the online *Middle English Compendium* (accessed February 21, 2001, http://ets.umdl.umich.edu/cgi/m/mec/med-idx). The word's primary meaning as "secret" appears as early as the Ancrene Riwle and continues with fourteenth-century citations from Chaucer, Gower, the Wyclif Bible, and Richard Rolle. Meaning "genitalia," the word appears, among other places, in the *Monk's Tale,* the Wyclif Bible, and the "Charters of the Abbey of Holy Ghost," all from the late fourteenth century.

7. Peter Beidler usefully surveys the fortunes of the *Miller's Tale* in his article "Art and Scatology in the *Miller's Tale," Chaucer Review* 12 (1977): 90–91. Besides Howes and Biggs's study, see Katarina Wilson, "Hagiographic (Dis)Play: Chaucer's *The Miller's Tale,"* Auctor Ludens: *Essays on Play in Literature,* eds. Gerald Guinness and Andrew Hurley (Philadelphia: Benjamins, 1986), 37–45; Thomas J. Farrell, "Privacy and the Boundaries of Fabliau in the *Miller's Tale," ELH* 55 (1989): 773–795; and Britton J. Harwood, "The 'Nether Ye' and its Antitheses: A Structuralist Reading of *The Miller's Tale," Annuale Medievale* 21 (1981): 5–30.

8. E. Jane Burns's assessment of bodily jokes in fabliaux locates male authors' references to female genitalia within a frame of ignorance about female sexuality: Burns adopts Irigaray's model of patriarchal strategies to silence woman through the "penis eye." See "A Close Look at Female Orifices in Farce and Fabliau," Chapter 1 of *Bodytalk: When Women Speak in Old French Literature* (Philadelphia: University of Pennsylvania Press, 1993). Similarly, Elaine Tuttle Hansen's assessment of the tale starts with its misogyny: she sees the tale as both misrepresenting female sexuality and, because of male fear of the feminine, replacing the female with the male, as Nicholas replaces Alison in the final scene: "By deflecting attention from Alisoun's threatening self-exposure as he does—blurring the focus to begin with by the use of the word 'hole,' and then replacing Alisoun altogether—the Miller mystifies and averts the threats that any representation of female sexuality seems to entail: the feminization of the man who tells 'queynte' stories, as well as both the homoerotic and self-mutilating aspects of male competition for the 'queynte' of a woman" ("'Women-as-the-Same' in the A-Fragment," Chapter 8 of Chaucer and the Fictions of Gender [Berkeley: University of California Press, 1992], 236) Karma Lochrie sees the tale's triangular relationships as evidence of patriarchy's "secret" mode that makes "woman" exclusively the result of men's economic transactions ("Women's 'Pryvetees' and Fabliau Politics in the *Miller's Tale,"* Exemplaria 6 [1994]: 287–304).

9. The body as a category of literary investigation has motivated a great number of feminist studies in the 1990s. Besides Beckwith, *Christ's Body* (see note 4), see also the essays in *Feminist Approaches to the Body in Medieval Literature,* eds. Linda Lomperis and Sarah Stanbury (Philadelphia: University of Pennsylvania Press, 1993); *Writing on the Body: Female Embodiment and Feminist Theory,* eds. Katie Conboy, Nadia Medina, and Sarah Stanbury (New York: Columbia University Press, 1997); *Framing Medieval Bodies,* eds. Sarah Kay and Miri Rubin (Manchester: Manchester University Press, 1994).

10. One of many places to find this issue explored, albeit somewhat later than the *Miller's Tale,* is the work of Nicholas of Cusa: see the new edition of his works, *Nicholas of Cusa: Metaphysical Speculations,* volumes 1 and 2, ed. Jasper Hopkins (Minneapolis: Arthur J. Banning Press, 2000).

11. "Reading for Sentence versus Reading for Solas: A Broadening Example," chapter 1 in Laura Kendrick, *Chaucerian Play: Comedy and Control in the Canterbury Thies* (Berkeley: University of California Press, 1988), 5–19. Kendrick's argument relies on Leo Steinberg, *The Sexuality of Christ in Renaissance Art and in Modern Oblivion,* 2nd ed. (University of Chicago Press, 1996).

12. *The New Oxford Annotated Bible* (Oxford University Press, 1991) with the insertion of "back parts" to reflect the Latin plural. The Vulgate reads, "Qui ait: Ostende mihi gloriam tuam. Respondit: Ego ostendam omne bonum tibi, et vocabo in nomine Domini coram te: et miserebor cui voluero, et clemens ero in quem mihi placuerit. Rursumque ait: Non poteris videre faciem meam: non enim videbit me homo, et vivet. Et iterum: Ecce, inquit, est locus apud me, et stabis supra petram. Cumque transibit gloria mea, ponam te in foramine petrae, et protegam: tollamque manum meam, et videbis posteriora mea: faciem autem meam videre non poteris," *Biblia sacra: iuxta Vulgatam versionem,* eds. Boniface Fischer and Robert Weber (Stuttgart: Deutsche Bibelgesellschaft, 1983).

13. It is also possible that verses 20 and 23 use *faciem* as a euphemism for *penis,* in light of the Biblical prohibition against seeing a father's naked penis; so Noah curses his son Ham for seeing his father's nakedness (Genesis 9:20–28).

14. Expositions on the Book of Psalms (Oxford: John Henry Parker, 1857), vol. 6, 197–198; Migne PL 37: 1788–1789: "Et ex his verbis natum est alterum (aenigma, id est obscura quaedam figura rerum. Cum transiero, posteriora mea videbis, dicit Deus; quasi ex alia parte habeat faciem, ex alia dorsum. Absit a nobis tale aliquid de illa Majestate sentire . . . Sed quia erat Dominus opportuno tempore carnem suscepturus, ut oculis etiam cameis propter salubritatem curandae intus mentis appareret, quando ita apparere opus esset . . . Faciem suam dixit, prima sua? et quodam modo posteriora sua, transitum de hoc mundo passionis suae."

15. *The Trinity,* translated by Stephen McKenna, C.S.S.R. (Washington, D.C.: Catholic University ofAmerica Press, 1963), 89; Migne PL 42:866, "Neque enim tanto carnis nubilo debemus involvi, ut putemus faciem quidem Domini esse invisibilem, dorsum vero visibile; quandoquidem in forma servi utrumque visibiliter apparuit; in forma autem Dei absit ut tale aliquid cogitetur: absit ut Verbum Dei et sapientia Dei ex una parte habeat faciem ex alia dorsum, sicut corpus humanum, aut omnino ulla specie vel motione sive loco sive tempore commutetur."

16. Book of Psalms, vol. 5,478; Migne PL 37: 1609–1610, "Posteriora ejus quae sunt? Et Verbum caro factum est, et habitavit in nobis . . . Quid est, Vide posteriora ejus? Crede in resurrectionem ejus."

17. *The Trinity,* 85; Migne PL 42: 863, "Non incongruenter ex persona Domini nostri Jesu Christi praefiguratum solet intelligi, ut posteriora ejus accipiantur caro ejus, in qua de Virgine natus est, et mortuus, et resurrexit; sive propter posterioritatem mortalitatis posteriora dicta sint, sive quod eam prope in fine saeculi, hoc est, posterius suscipere dignatus est."

18. *Image on the Edge* (Cambridge: Harvard University Press, 1992), 40–46.

19. Letters, translated by Sr. Wilfrid Parsons, S.N.D. (New York: Fathers of the Church, Inc., 1953), 200; Migne PL 33: 610–611, "Quanquam et illi fidelissirno antiquo famulo Dei Moysi, mirum nisi in hac terra laboraturo, populumque

ilium adhuc recturo concessum est quod petivit, ut claritatem Domini videret, qui dixerat: Si inveni gratiam ante te, ostende mihi tcmetipsum manifeste. Accepit enim in praesentia congruum responsum, quod faciem Dei videre non posset, quam nemo videret, et viveret; hoc modo significante Deo alterius potioris vitae illam esse visionem. Deinde in verbis Dei, futurae Christi Ecclesiae mysterium figuratum est. Gestavit quippe Moyses typum populi Judaeorum, in Christum passum postea credituri; ideo dictum est illi, Cum transiero, posteriora mea videbis: et caetera quae ibi dicunter, mirabili sacramento praenuntiant Ecciesiam post futuram, unde modo longum est disputare."

20. Letters, 176; Migne PL 33: 599, "Nam cum sint quinque corporis sensus, cernendi, audiendi, olfaciendi, gustandi, tangendi; visus quidern in eis praecipue oculis attributus est, verum tamen hoc verbo utimur et in caeteris. Non enim tantum dicimus, Vide quid luceat; sed etiam, Vide quid sonet, Vide quid oleat, Vide quid sapiat, Vide quid caleat."

21. *The Literal Meaning of Genesis, Ancient Christian Writers,* no. 42, translated by John Hammond Taylor, S.J., vol. 2 (New York: Newman Press, 1982), pp. 217–219; Migne PL 34: 245.

22. The description of Alison as a weasel also fits the theme of confused orifices: "Some say that they [weasels] conceive through the ear and give birth through the mouth, while, on the other hand, others declare that they conceive by mouth and give birth by ear," *The Book of Beasts,* ed. T. H. White (New York: G. P. Putnam, 1954), p. 92.

23. "II. Transferred in genitive, an opening, hole, cave (late Latin): petrae Vulgate Exodus 33:22; id. Jeremiah 13:4," *A Latin Dictionary,* eds. Charlton T. Lewis and Charles Short (Oxford: Clarendon Press, 1879, imp. 1975), s.n. "foramen." Intriguingly, but probably not aptly, R. E. Latham's *Revised Medieval Latin Word-List from British and Irish Sources* (London: Oxford University Press for the British Academy, 1965) includes a 1473 use of foramen to mean "window-pane."

24. The King James/Revised Standard Version's translation of foramen or spelunca as "cleft" tries to negotiate the confusion among these words' meanings and ends up inadvertently giving us the image of a backside's cleft.

25. Hansen also notes the ambiguity of the word "hole" (226) and helpfully explicates the words"hole" as well as "eie" in Middle English.

26. The Variorum includes four analogues, in all of which the wife has two or three lovers, including, for the "Italian novellino," "a Genoese, a priest, and a smith" (5–6).

27. The joke here seems related to the "nothing" assessment of the female anatomy by the male, a most frequent pun in Shakespeare's plays, not to mention Freudian analyses.

28. Peter Beidler notes that Alison's equipoise and Absolon's cry of "a beard!" contrast the part of Nicholas's anatomy, besides his "toute," that would have confronted Absolon at the window (95–96). Hansen takes this picture one step further and points out how close Nicholas comes to castration in the final scene (235). Beidler's and Hansen's essays alert us to the male privates as important "hidden" parts of the *Miller's Tale.*

29. For an informative history and analysis of the "visible penis," see Linda Williams, *Hard Core: Power, Pleasure, and the Frenzy of the Visible* (Berkeley: University of California Press, 1989).

WORKS CITED

Augustine of Hippo. *Expositions on the Book of Psalms.* Oxford: John Henry Parker, 1857.

——. *Letters.* Translated by Sr. Wilfrid Parsons, S.N.D. New York: Fathers of the Church, 1953.

——. "The Literal Meaning of Genesis." *Ancient Christian Writers* no. 42. Vol. 2. Translated by John Hammond Taylor, S.J. New York: Newman Press, 1982.

The Trinity. Trans. Stephen McKenna, C.S.S.R. Washington, D.C.: Catholic University of America Press, 1963.

Beidler, Peter. "Art and Scatology in the *Miller's Tale.*" *Chaucer Review* 12 (1977): 90–91.

Eds. Boniface Fischer and Robert Weber. *Biblia sacra: iuxta Vulgatam versionem.* Stuttgart: Deutsche Bibelgesellschaft, 1983.

Biggs, Frederick M., and Laura L. Howes. "Theophany in *The Miller's Tale.*" *Medium Aevum* 65.2 (1996): pp. 269–279.

Bums, E. Jane. *Bodytalk: When Women Speak in Old French Literature.* Philadelphia: University of Pennsylvania Press, 1993.

Camille, Michael. *Image on the Edge.* Cambridge: Harvard University Press, 1992.

Chaucer, Geoffrey. *A Variorum Edition of The Works of Geoffrey Chaucer. Volume II (The Canterbury Tales), Part 3: the Miller's Tale.* Ed. Thomas W. Ross. Norman: University of Oklahoma Press, 1983.

——. *The Riverside Chaucer.* Third Edition. Ed. Larry D. Benson. Boston: Houghton Mifflin, 1987.

Conboy, Katie, Nadia Medina, and Sarah Stanbury, eds. *Writing on the Body: Female Embodiment and Feminist Theory.* New York: Columbia University Press, 1997.

Farrell, Thomas J. "Privacy and the Boundaries of Fabliau in the Miller's Tale." *ELH* 55 (1989): pp. 773–795.

Hansen, Elaine Tuttle. *Chaucer and the Fictions of Gender.* Berkeley: University of California Press, 1992.

Harwood, Britton J. "The 'Nether Ye' and its Antitheses: A Structuralist Reading of *The Miller's Tale.*" *Annuale Medievale* 21 (1981): pp. 5–30.

Kay, Sarah, and Miri Rubin, eds. *Framing Medieval Bodies.* Manchester: Manchester University Press, 1994.

Kendrick, Laura. *Chaucerian Play: Comedy and Control in the Canterbury Tales.* Berkeley: University of California Press, 1988.

A Latin Dictionary. Eds. Charlton T. Lewis and Charles Short. Oxford: Clarendon Press, 1879, imp. 1975.

Lochrie, Karma. "Don't Ask, Don't Tell: Murderous Plots and Medieval Secrets," *Premodern Sexualities,* ed. by Louise Fradenburg and Carla Freccero, pp. 137–152. New York: Routledge, 1996.

——. "Women's 'Pryvetees' and Fabliau Politics in the *Miller's Tale,*" *Exemplaria* 6 (1994): pp. 287–304.

Lomperis, Linda, and Sarah Stanbury, eds. *Feminist Approaches to the Body in Medieval Literature.* Philadelphia: University of Pennsylvania Press, 1993.

New Oxford Annotated Bible. New York: Oxford University Press, 1991.

Nicholas of Cusa. *Nicholas of Cusa: Metaphysical Speculations.* Two volumes. Ed. Jasper Hopkins. Minneapolis: Arthur J. Banning Press, 2000.

Steinberg, Leo. *The Sexuality of Christ in Renaissance Art and in Modern Oblivion.* 2nd Edition. Chicago: University of Chicago Press, 1996.

White, T. H., ed. *The Book of Beasts.* New York: G. P. Putnam, 1954.

Williams, Linda. *Hard Core: Power, Pleasure, and the Frenzy of the Visible.* Berkeley: University of California Press, 1989.

Wilson, Katarina. "Hagiographic (Dis)Play: Chaucer's *The Miller's Tale*," *Auctor Ludens: Essays on Play in Literature.* Eds. Gerald Guinness and Andrew Hurley. Philadelphia: Benjamins, 1986. pp. 37–45.

RICHARD FIRTH GREEN

Changing Chaucer

Let me begin by apologizing for the somewhat gnomic quality of my title. It's the result of a scholarly subterfuge I suppose most of us have practiced at one time or another: the trick of being noncommittal when asked to provide the title for a paper we're still months away from writing. If, last January, I was pretty sure I wanted to talk to you today about forms of metamorphosis in Chaucer, I was still unsure whether to choose *The Franklin's Tale* or *The Canon's Yeoman's Tale* as my primary text. The first, with its shapeshifting black rocks, would, I felt, be an appropriate choice for a talk in Boulder, Colorado, though I discovered to my chagrin not only that Chaucer himself never uses the word "boulder," but that in Middle English it invariably denotes something we would probably refer to as a cobblestone, certainly nothing that could possibly be construed as a potential hazard to coastal shipping. The alchemical transformations of *The Canon's Yeoman's Tale*, then, were looking like the better bet as the subject for a talk in a city that was, after all, founded on a gold rush, when I was struck by line 751. It offered me, I suddenly realized, the opportunity to move beyond alchemy itself into a wider consideration of Chaucerian metamorphosis. Let me read it to you in its immediate context:

Studies in the Age of Chaucer, Volume 25 (2003): pp. 27–52. © 2003 Duke University Press.

> Whan we been there as we shul exercise
> Oure elvysshe craft, we semen wonder wise,
> Oure termes been so clergial and so queynte. (VIII [G]:750–752)[1]

I might equally well have stumbled across line 842 from the same tale:

> Nay, nay, God woot, al be he monk or frere,
> Preest or chanoun, or any oother wyght,
> Though he sitte at his book bothe day and nyght
> In lernyiag of this elvysshe nyce loore,
> Al is in veyn, and parde, muchel moore. (VIII [G]:839–843)

The key word shared by both these passages is, of course, *elvysshe:* alchemy is an elvish calling and the alchemist's expertise is elvish. Now Chaucer famously describes himself as elvish in the prologue to *Sir Thopas,* and that passage has garnered a certain amount of critical attention (from John Burrow among others),[2] but these two appearances of the word have excited far less comment. Beth Robertson, for instance, in her recent piece on Constance's "elvyssh" power, alludes to the Thopas prologue but not the *Canon's Yeoman's Tale.*[3] Most critics, if they notice the lines at all, seem to believe that *elvysshe* is merely a synonym for "devilish,"[4] though Lee Patterson and Lisa Kiser are notable exceptions. Patterson calls *elvysshe* a "loaded" term that draws attention to "the analogy between the poet and his alchemical yeoman" (an important insight, though not one I shall be exploring this afternoon);[5] for Kiser, it suggests "the ease with which people can be led to believe in illusion as if it were truth" (for my immediate purposes, a more promising line of thought).[6]

Now, for some reason modern editors have been uncomfortable with the Canon's Yeoman's unequivocal statement that the alchemist's expertise is an elvish one. They evidently don't want to believe that he says what he quite patently does say. Skeat, substituting connotation for denotation, glosses both occurrences of *elvysshe* as "mysterious (but used in the sense of foolish)";[7] Robinson glosses the second only as "strange [and foolish]"; Baugh gives "weird, strange" for the first, and "mysterious [(and) foolish]" for the second; Pratt gives "mysterious, weird," and Benson, "strange, mysterious" for both; while Schmidt offers "strange, weird" for the first and simply "strange" for the second. Finally, the Oxford *Chaucer Glossary* offers "mysterious" for both occurrences, though its definition is graced with a question mark. The *Middle English Dictionary* (never one to stick its neck out in such matters), despite having found six citations to justify its rendering the word elsewhere as "belonging or pertaining to the elves; possessing supernatural skill or powers" dutifully glosses both the Canon's Yeoman's uses of the word as "mysterious, strange." I have found only three exceptions to this intimidating scholarly consensus: both Maurice Hussey and John Fisher remain in the realm of connotation, but at least in the right corner of that realm, it seems to me: the first glossing both instances of the word as "supernatural" and the second (glossing the first only) as "mysterious, magical." Finally, while A. C. Cawley glosses the *elvysshe* of line 751 as "mysterious," the *elvysshe nyce* of line 842 he renders somewhat tautologously as "[silly] elvish." Here, then, is a useful demonstration of the limitations of statistical proof in the humanities: *elvysshe* in these passages is glossed as "mysterious" a total of thirteen times, as "strange" eight times, and as "weird" four times, but only once each as "supernatural" and "magical," and once (correctly, if redundantly) as "elvish." This final gloss, though it may well be a slip on Cawley's part, is, I believe, the only adequate one: *elvysshe* does mean "elvish," or, in other words, the craft of alchemy, says the Canon's Yeoman, is a fairy craft. In fact, "faery-like, fantastick" is precisely the gloss given these passages by Thomas Tyrwhitt in 1778, and this, or some variant of it, was standard in all the major Victorian editions except Skeat's: Edward Moxon (1843), Thomas Wright (1853), Robert Bell (1854), Richard Morris (1872) and Alfred Pollard (1898).[8] I shall return later to the interesting question of why this simple proposition seems to have been so difficult for Skeat and his successors to accept, but first I must try to show why I believe Chaucer means what he says here.

The word *fairy* in Middle English regularly refers to a place or region, the abode of those creatures known to the French as *fées* (Latin, *fata*): *fées* in other words, live in *fé-erie*.[9] Though *fairy*, influenced perhaps by the native word *ferli*,[10] might also be used as a synonym for a "marvel" or "wonder" (and indeed is so used, at least twice, by Chaucer himself),[11] and sometimes in a more generalized sense as "magic," it does not seem to be used to denote an actual creature, a fairy, much before the middle of the fifteenth century.[12] Nor, as far as I can see, is it used unambiguously an as adjective: in Middle English one referred to a "fairy knight" much as we now refer to a "New York policeman," that is to say *fairy* in such phrases was primarily appositional not adjectival. The standard word in Chaucer, as in most other Middle English writers, for what we generally call a fairy was *elf*, and, if he felt himself in need of an adjective, the one Chaucer would have found nearest to hand was *elvish*. The denotative meanings of "elvysshe craft" and "elvysshe loore," then, are "a skill, or knowledge, exercised by (or resembling one exercised by) the fairies." But to say this is merely to beg a further question: "Why is an alchemist like a fairy?" But before I attempt an answer I want us to be quite clear about the kind of fairy we are talking about here.

What Chaucer calls elves were what C. S. Lewis, sounding very like his friend J. R. R. Tolkien, called "high fairies"—though in actuality many medieval commentators would have thought of these beings as the lowest (in the hierarchical sense) of the fallen angels.[13] Keith Thomas has pointed to a common tendency among chose who discuss fairies to assign them to the past, and in order to show that this has always been the case he cites the opening lines of *The Wife of Bath's Tale*,[14] yet we don't have to go back "manye hundred yeres" before Chaucer's time to find a writer willing to acknowlege fairies as his contemporaries. Gervase of Tilbury writing at the beginning of the thirteenth century has left us a succinct account of them in his *Otia Imperialia*;[15] after paraphrasing a passage from Augustine's *City of God* (15:23) on *incubi* (which he breaks off when Augustine begins to express skepticism), he writes:

> For, indeed, we know that this has been daily proved by men of unimpeachable reputation, because we have heard of certain lovers of these kinds of spirit (which are called *fada*), and how, when they committed themselves in marriage to other women, they died before they intermingled themselves in carnal coupling with their consorts. And we have observed that most enjoyed the highest state of worldly fortune, but when they extricated themselves from the embraces of this kind of fairy, or spoke of them in public, they lost not only worldly prosperity but even the paltry comfort of life itself.[16]

Such fairies in other words were human in appearance and scale, and were capable of engaging in social and sexual intercourse with human beings. Originally they seem to have been regarded as beneficent or at least admirable creatures, though they were early demonized in Christian tradition.[17] But when Shakespeare paired Oberon with the mischievous Puck or had Titania send her diminutive servants to steal honey bags from the humble bee he unfortunately promulgated a confusion between these high fairies and other very different kinds of spirit that has lasted down to our own day.

There is no question that, unlike Shakespeare, Gervase regarded his *fata* as quite distinct from the kind of household spirits that Shakespeare's probable informant, Reginald Scot, calls *virunculi terrei*, "such as was Robin good fellowe, that would supplie the office of seruants."[18] The more benevolent of such spirits Gervase calls *portuni* (ed. Banks and Binns, pp. 674–677). Though of diminutive stature, they are capable, like Robin Goodfellow, of assisting with household chores, but, while generally harmless, they do seem to find some amusement in leading benighted travelers astray.[19] The more mischievous, on the other hand, he calls *folletti* (English *foliots*). These "inhabit the houses of simple rustics" and are given to throwing sticks, stones, and domestic utensils about; though capable of human speech, their appearance is nonhuman (ed. Banks and Binns, pp. 98–99). Beliefs of this kind were certainly common enough in Chaucer's day, but though there were a number of English terms for such spirits (the most common seems to have been *gobelyn*),[20] *elf* was not one of them.

Though an Englishman, Gervase of Tilbury himself nowhere employs a latinized form of the Germanic word *elf*,[21] but in an earlier discussion of *incubi* (which, following Geoffrey of Monmouth, he describes as "impure spirits dwelling between the moon and the earth, . . . their nature partly that of humans and partly of angels"), he adds that "when they wish, they assume human shape and lie with women. Of these Merlin, who (as the *Historia Britonnorum* tells us) had a mother, but no human father, is said to have been conceived." He then adds, "we know that many such things are seen daily."[22] A very late thirteenth-century writer Robert of Gloucester gives us much the same account of Merlin's origins, but he, significantly, does use the word *elf*:

> He [Vortigern] esste at is clerkes . were it to leue were.
> þe clerkes sede þat it is . in philosofie yfounde .
> þat þer beþ in þe eyr an hey . ver fram þe grounde .
> As a maner gostes . wiȝtes as it be .
> And me[n] may ȝem ofte an erþe . in wilde studes yse .
> & ofte in mannes forme . women hii comeþ to .
> & ofte in wimmen fourme . hii comeþ to men al so .
> Þat men clupeþ eluene (lines 2747–2754)[23]

So, too, does the *South English Legendary,* a closely related text.[24] In a description of the ranks of the fallen angels, it gives a similar account of these creatures, but adds some intriguing details:

> And ofte in forme of womman . in moni deorne weie
> Me sicþ of hom gret companie. boþe hoppe & pleie
> þat eleuene beoþ iduped . Þat ofte comeþ to toune
> And bi daie muche in wode beoþ . & biniþre upe heie doune
> Þat beoþ of þe wrecche gostes . þat of heuene were inome
> And mony of hom a Domesday : ssolleþ ȝute to reste come (lines 253–258)[25]

That Chaucer himself associated elves with *incubi* is proved by his juxtaposition of the two terms in the opening lines of *The Wife of Bath's Tale.* The author of *Dives and Pauper,* writing in the early fifteenth century, shows that this was a common association: "And þe fendis þat temptyn folc to lecherie ben mest besy for to aperyn in mannys lycnesse & wommanys to don lecherye with folc & so bryngyn hem to lecherie, & in speche of þe peple it arn clepyd eluys. But in Latyn whan þei aperyn in þo

lycnesse of man it arn clepyd *incubi,* and whan þei aperyn in þo lycnesse
of woman it arn clepyd *succuby.*"[26]

Now that we have some idea of what kind of creature is denoted by
the phrase *elvysshe lore,* it is time finally to return to the question "why is an
alchemist like a fairy?" Actually this riddle turns out to be considerably sim-
pler than "why is a raven like a writing desk?" and when we ask ourselves how
what Alan Fletcher has recently called "the discourse of fairyland"[27] resembles "the discourse of alchemy," the similarities appear really quite striking.
For one thing, alchemists, like fairies, are liminal figures, both geographically
and culturally, hovering around the edges of established communities and
established beliefs. In a well-known passage, Chaucer describes his Canon's
natural habitat as "the suburbes of a toun":

> Lurkynge in hernes and in lanes blynde,
> Whereas thise robbours and thise theves by kynde
> Holden hir pryvee fereful residence,
> As they that dar not shewen hir presence. (VIII [G]. 658–661)

Like his master, the Canon's Yeoman also belongs, in Judith Herz's words,
"to no particular place," a Protean man "who must shift about the world
seeking an identity."[28] Finally, the second alchemist is equally rootless:

> On his falshede fayn wolde I me wreke,
> If I wiste how, but he is heere and there;
> He is so variaunt, he abit nowhere. (VIII [G]. 1173–1175)[29]

Culturally, too, alchemists were outsiders, even potential proto-revolu-
tionaries. As John Reidy pointed out in 1972, "no alchemist ever seems to
have been a genuine member of the establishment."[30] Some, indeed, like
Chaucer's "Arnold of the Newe Toun," a follower of Joachim of Flora, were
even involved in revolutionary movements that brought them to the notice of
the Inquisition (Reidy, p. 46), though by and large, as Sheila Delany points
out, alchemy was an even more marginal social phenomenon than heresy.
Still there is no mistaking, as Delany puts it, "the subversive orientation" of
alchemical practice in general nor of Chaucer's alchemists in particular.[31]
For John Scattergood, the "suburban tenements of those who were by choice
and necessity outsiders" represents "the potential for growth and change and
the energy to turn the world upside-down."

The cultural liminality of *fairies* scarcely needs elaborating—indeed, for
Diane Purkiss in a recent book this becomes one of their defining characteristics: "a fairy is someone who . . . presides over the borders of our lives, the
seams between one phase of life and another,"[32] but in a geographical sense,

too, fairies are marginal figures, appearing suddenly (rather as Chaucer's Canon and his Yeoman do) in "wilde studes," "in wode," and "upe heie doune," though also capable of making clandestine visits to human habitations: "þat ofte comeþ to toune." Their own dwelling places lie beyond the pale of the civilized world (though, for all that, they are not uncivilized in themselves). Almost always one must cross water to reach them, and sometimes, as in the romances of *Huon of Bourdeux*, *Partenope of Blois*, or *Reinbrun*, they lie at the very margins of Christendom itself, in far-off Asia Minor or even Africa. In French romance *fées* generally inhabit splendid castles buried deep in the woods (Bercilak's castle in *Sir Gawain and the Green Knight* conforms to this type). In the insular tradition, however, fairies are quite as likely to live, as in *Orfeo*, *Reinbrun*, *Thomas of Ercledoune*, and Marie de France's *Yonec*,[33] in underground kingdoms. entered through a cave, and such a locus is confirmed in non-romance English sources. The normally skeptical William of Newburgh, for instance, has left us a vivid account of a local countryman (a *rusticus*), returning late and slightly drunk from visiting a friend, who stumbles upon "a large well-lit dwelling crowded with men and women reclining at table, as at a formal feast" located inside a nearby hillock (*proximo tumulo*).[34] This subterranean dimension to elvish lore may well have deepened its alchemical associations in Chaucer's mind.

Fairy beliefs, like alchemy, hovered at the very edge of orthodox thought. Unwilling to reject them outright, most churchmen rationalized fairies into minor devils (rather as, we might remember, the Yeoman demonizes his alchemists),[35] a position that even a Wycliffite preacher might be prepared to contemplate:

> And summe dremen of þes feendis [of the loweste rank] þat summe
> ben elues and summe gobelynes, and haue not but litil power to
> tempte men in harme of soule; but siþ we kunne not proue þis ne
> disproue þis spedili, holde we vs in þe boundis þat God telliþ vs
> in his lawe. But it is licli þat þes feendis haue power to make boþe
> wynd and reyn, þundit and lyȝttyng and oþir wedrus.[36]

Far more radical is the *South English Legendary*'s speculation that many of these "wrecche gostes . þat of heuene were inome . . . a Domesday ssolleþ ȝute to reste come."[37] The romances are sometimes eager to enfold fairies within the bosom of the church. The hero of Marie de France's *Yonec*, for example, despite living in an underground kingdom and being able to turn himself at will into a hawk, protests to his lady that he is a true Christian.[38] Melusine (p. 31) and *Desire*'s fairy mistress[39] are similarly insistent on their own religious orthodoxy, while Sir Partenope is reassured to hear his invisible lady, whose bed he happens to be sharing at the time, swear by the Virgin Mary.[40] In much the same vein, Oberon presents Huon of Bordeaux with a magic cup, whose powers are activated by making the sign of the cross over it.[41] However, such passages smack strongly of rationalization, and the popular view is probably better represented by *Thomas of Erceldoune* (lines 201–220) and its descendant, the ballad *Thomas Rymerr*:[42]

> O see not ye yon narrow road,
>   So thick beset wi thorns and briers
> That is the path of righteousness,
>   Tho after it but few enquires.
>
> And see not ye that braid braid road
>   That lies across yon lillie leven?
> That is the path of wickedness,
>   Tho some call it the road to heaven.
> And see not ye that bonny road
>   Which winds about the fernie brae?
> That is the road to fair Elfland,
>   Whe[re] you and I this night maun gae. (Child 37A: 12–14)

I know of no text that so vividly exemplifies the marginal status of elvish lore, approached only by way of this third path unmapped in orthodox Christian cartography.[43] Whether dabbling in such lore implied a "subversive orientation," analogous to that we have noted in connection with alchemical practice, is rather more difficult to determine, but a riot that occurred in Kent in 1451 suggests that this might not be an altogether preposterous speculation: in a curious precursor of the events leading to Robert Walpole's notorious Black Act, a hundred men invaded the deer park of Humphrey Stafford, Duke of Buckingham, at Penshurst, and disguised with long beards and blackened faces, stole 82 beasts, "*nuncupantes se esse servientes Regine del Faire* [proclaiming themselves to be the servants of the Queen of Fairy].[44] It is amusing to imagine these poachers as precursors of another set of dissidents as well: modern British environmental protesters apparently refer to their acts of sabotage against construction equipment as "pixieing."[45]

Closely related to the sense of marginality shared by these two discourses is their common concern with secrecy. Again, Chaucer's Yeoman cites Arnold of Villanova: "'For this science and this konnyng,' quod he, / 'Is of the secree of the secretes, parde.'" (VIII [G]. 1446–1447). Thomas Norton tells us that the alchemist must jealousy protect this secret of secrets from all but a single trusted pupil:

When age shal greve hym to ride or go,
One he may teche but then nevir no mo,
For this science most evir secrete be. (lines 235–237)[46]

If (as William Thynne and Elias Ashmole suppose) Norton learned his craft from George Ripley, his master was a poor role model, for only a few years later Ripley was offering the same secret to Edward IV:

For like it you to trust that truly I have found,
The perfect way of most secret Alchymie,
Which I will never truly for marke nor for pound
Make common but to you, and that conditionally,
That to your selfe you shall keepe it full secretly.[47]

The irony of proclaiming occult knowledge in so public a place seems lost on both these authors,[48] though, as Joseph Grennen pointed out in 1965, the empty admonition to secrecy is so widespread in alchemical treatises as to constitute something of, in Ernst Curtius's sense of the term, a *topos* (lines 309–311);[49] it is certainly one Chaucer himself employs in the *Canon's Yeoman's Tale*.[50]

A similar epistemological paradox occurs in Gervase of Tilbury's account of fairies, for those who spoke of their fairy mistresses in public, he tells us, lost "even the paltry comfort of life itself." But in that case, we might wonder what they had been doing telling Gervase's informants about them. In fact a proscription against revealing the name or the existence of a fairy lover is a commonplace in the romances, though, like Helen Cooper's "magic that does not work,"[51] such prohibitions rarely seem to be rigidly enforced in practice. English readers will be most familiar with this motif from Thomas of Chestre's retelling of Marie de France's *Lanval*,[52] but it also appears in a French analogue to *Lanval* called *Graelent* (lines 311–312), in another Breton lai called *Tydorel*, in which a fairy lover who has been making regular nocturnal visits to the hero's mother disappears for ever after he has been accidentally glimpsed by a knight of the court (l. 214), and in yet a third, *Desiré*, where even the hero's revelation of his fairy mistress in the privacy of the confessional endangers their future happiness together (lines 371–372).[53] Among the longer romances, *Partenope of Blois* makes particular use of this motif; Partenope's mother's inquisitiveness leads him to break his mistress's command ("þys loue be-twyn vs shall be kepte preve" [l. 1826]), and almost destroys the relationship.

If alchemy might easily be imagined as elvish in both its cultural situation and its epistemological status, it was also akin to the fairy world in the elusive nature of the rewards it promised.

> The philosophres stoon,
> Elixer clept, we sechen faste echoon;
> For hadde we hym, thanne were we siker ynow.
> But unto God of hevene I make avow,
>
> ....
> For al oure sleighte, he wol nat come us to. (VIII [G].862–867)

Two of these rewards are almost identical in both the discourse of alchemy and the discourse of fairyland: unlimited wealth and the prolongation of life. Though the power to turn base metal into gold might be the most celebrated of the philosopher's stone's properties, for Thomas Norton it is was rather the prospect of its extending his life that made it most desirable:

> For above all erthlye thynge
> I mooste desire & love connynge;
> And for the red stone is preseruatife,
> Moost precious thynge to length my life,
> The rede stone, saide I, is levire to me
> Then all were Golde that I wolde so to be. (lines 2595–2600)

George Ripley expresses a similar disdain for filthy lucre, but evidently still found comforting the notion that the stone would support him into an extreme old age:

> And if thou had not at the beginning to fill a spoon,
> Yet maist thou them so multiply both white and red.
> That if thou live a 1000. yeres, they shall stand thee in sted.[54]

Like Norton, Ripley seems to have lived a good long life, though still far short of the millennium he'd apparently been hoping for.

It is not difficult to show that the elusiveness of the philosopher's stone was matched in the middle ages by a similar belief in evanescent fairy gold. The worldly prosperity of those who enjoyed the embraces of fairies is mentioned by Gervase of Tilbury, as is its propensity to vanish as soon as its source was revealed.[55] Again, Thomas of Chestre's *Launfal* offers the example that will be most familiar to readers of Middle English: Triamour gives Launfal a magic purse, but as soon as he reveals her existence to Guivevere it loses its power (lines 733–736). Similarly a gold ring given to Desiré by his lover vanishes from his finger when he mentions her to his confessor. The lavish munificence of the fairies is almost a commonplace in the romances we have been discussing, as is its conditional nature and its association with danger, but these motifs can also turn up in some rather unexpected places: in Sir

John Mandeville's account of the Castle of the Sparrowhawk in Armenia, for example,[56] or in Adam de la Halle's thirteenth-century farce, the *Jeu de la Feuillée*.[57] They even make an appearance in the fabliau *Le chevalier qui fist parler les cons*, where one of three grateful fairies endows the knight with inexhaustible wealth.[58] Perhaps the oddest manifestation of these motifs is in a set of Latin exercises, composed for use in Exeter Grammar School around 1450. One of these reads:

> A general rumour is spreading among the people that the spirits of the air, invoked by necromantic art to find mines of gold, silver, azure, and other treasures hidden in the ground, have appeared in bodily form, stirring up great tempests in the air which are nor yet calmed, it is believed, nor allayed.[59]

Of course, this should no more be regarded as the record of an actual event than the sentence from the Victorian traveler's phrase-book, "our postillion has been struck by lightning," but it does presumably represent the kind of thing that someone might credibly have said.

If the philosopher's stone prolonged human life, so too did contact with the fairies. The fairies themselves were, of course, famously long-lived, as C. S. Lewis recognizes when he calls them the *longaevi* (pp. 122 ff.), a term he found in Martianus Capella (echoed later by Bernardus Silvestris). Oberon, a son of Julius Caesar, tells Huon of Bordeaux that "I shall never seme elder than thou seest me now" (p. 74), and whenever fairies appear in romance they seem to enjoy this gift of eternal youth.[60] It is perhaps less often recognized that they also have the power to bestow this gift on their mortal companions. After what he believes to have been only a three-day stay with his fairy mistress, Guingamour returns home to discover that more than three hundred years have passed, that the king, his uncle, is long dead, and his castle lies in ruins.[61] Similarly, in *Thomas of Ercledoune*, when the hero complains about being sent home after what he, too, thinks has been only three days, he learns that the truth is rather different:

> "Lufly lady, now late me bee,
> ffor certis, lady, I hafe bene here
> Noghte bot þe space of dayes three."
> "ffor sothe, Thomas, als I þe telle,
> þou hase bene here thre ȝere and more;
> Bot langere here þou may noghte dwelle." (lines 282–287)

Where a disillusioned Guingamour had returned to his fairy refuge, True Thomas, after this briefer temporal disruption, lives out the rest of his life among humankind.

If the discourse of alchemy and the discourse of fairyland resemble one another in their shared marginality, their obsession with secrecy, and the nature of the rewards they dangle before their initiates, their most obvious point of resemblance, of course, is their common concern with transformation. In the case of alchemy this hardly needs to be demonstrated: the transmutation of metals to which the alchemical enterprise was directed arose from a profound engagement with the fact of mutability; to appreciate what the alchemists were doing, says Sherwood Taylor, "we must think ourselves back to the position of the intelligent man [or woman] viewing changes in things and changes in himself and focusing his mind not so much on the details of the individual changes as on the idea of change."[62] With fairyland, however, the proposition may need little more elaboration. Paradoxically, for creatures that enjoy a state of perpetual youthfulness, the very substance of fairies seems inherently unstable: as John Gower writes of Medea as she is cursing Jason: "In sondri wise hir forme changeth, / She semeth *faie* and no womman."[63] Thus it is that the old can appear young, as in *The Wife of Bath's Tale*, for instance, and the young old, as in *Thomas of Erceldoune* (or vice versa). Even more striking, in view of the oft remarked changes in the Canon's Yeoman's complexion,[64] is the frequency with which fairies also undergo shifts of colour. Bercilak in *Sir Gawain and the Green Knight* is an obvious instance, but so typical is such chromatic instability that when the narrator encounters the protean figure of "Prevy Thought" in the late-fifteenth-century allegory *The Court of Love* he is immediately reminded of fairyland:

> "Yon is," thought [I], "som spirit or som elf,
> His sotill image is so curious:
> "How is," quod I "that he is shaded thus
> With yonder cloth, I not of what colour?" (lines 1270–1273)

Petitcrû, the dog from Elfland that Tristram sends as a present to Ysolt, is similarly polychrome: no one "could relate or record its shape or appearance, for however one looked at the dog it displayed so many colours that no one could discern or fix them,"[65] and in Malory the ring that Lyories lends to Sir Gareth for the Tournament at the Castel Peryllous endows him with a similar quality: "at one tyme [he] semed grene, and another tyme at his ageynecomyng he semed blewe. And thus at every cours that he rode to and fro he chaunged his colour, so that there myght neyther kynge neyther knyghte haue redy congnyssaunce of hym."[66]

A further aspect of fairy lore that may resonate with *The Canon's Yeoman's Tale* is the belief, in George Puttenham's words, "that the Fayries vse to steale the fairest children out of their cradles, and put other ill fauoured in their places, which they called changelings, or Elfs."[67] Latham claims that this belief was peculiar to late-sixteenth-century England,[68] but Jean-Claude Schmitt has found traces of it throughout Europe from the thirteenth century onward,[69] and has used it brilliantly to explicate Etienne de Bourbon's curious description of the cult of Saint Guinefort, the Holy Greyhound; evidently, this cult fed on a popular conviction that the canine saint was able to restore stolen babies to their heartbroken parents. Though there appear to be no direct references to changelings in England before the mid sixteenth century, indirect evidence for such a belief is provided by the use of the Middle English noun *conjoun*, cognate with a rare French word *chanjon*, meaning "changeling."[70] Although it often seems to be little more than a vague term of abuse (the *Middle English Dictionary* offers "fool, nincompoop, worthless person, rascal . . . a lunatic, . . . a brat"), there are enough places where it is used of children, particularly in contexts where there might be a question about their parentage, to suggest that its original sense still clung to it. Thus in the *Auchinlech of Arthour and of Merlin*, the young Merlin is twice called *conioun* (lines 1071, 1217),[71] and in the *Chester Play*[72] it is used by Cain of his brother Abel (2:601) and by Herod of the infant Christ. This last example is especially pertinent:

> Alas, what presumption should move that peevish page
> or any elvish godlinge to take from me my crowne?
> But, by Mahound, that boye for all his greate outrage
> shall die under my hand, that elfe and vile [congion]. (8:325–328)

It may seem farfetched to associate this particular aspect of elvish lore with the clever substitutions by which the second Canon gulls the chantry priest, but we might recall that alchemical theory envisaged the engendering of minerals by processes closely analogous to human and animal procreation: after all, the philosopher's stone was imagined to be the progeny of a quite literal "chemical wedding" between sulfur and mercury. As Del Kolve has shown, in visual representations of this wedding the image of sexual congress could scarcely be more explicit.[73]

A final aspect of transmutation in the discourse of fairyland is the belief that fairies have the ability to change human beings into animals and even inanimate objects. Again, direct evidence for this belief is scanty but its existence can be inferred from a number of sources. The early-fourteenth-century *Fasciculus Morum* reproves "those superstitious wretches who claim that at night they see the most beautiful queens and other girls dancing in the ring with Lady Diana, the goddess of the heathens, who in our native tongue ate called *elves*" (p. 579).[74] It then continues: "and they believe that these can change both men and women into other beings [*in alias naturas transformare*] and carry them with them to *elvenland*." John Gower (*Confessio*

Amantis, 5:4937–5162) tells the story of a peasant who tries to rescue a man that had fallen into a pit by lowering down a rope to him, but who at his first attempt rescues instead an ape that had also been trapped in the pit:

> But whan he sih it was an Ape,
> He wende al hadde ben a jape
> Of fairie, and sore him drad. (lines 5001–5003)

Evidently the simple peasant thinks he has rescued a man who has been transformed into an ape. Similarly, in the *Second Shepherd's Play* Mak tries to pass off the stolen sheep that has just been discovered by its rightful owners as a baby transformed by the fairies:

> He was takyn with an elfe,
>   I saw it myself;
>   When the clok stroke twelf
> Was he forshapyn. (4:616–620)

Finally, in the ballad of *Tam Lin,* Janet's lover gives her detailed instructions on how to win him back from the fairies and warns her about the transformations that they will employ to try and frustrate her:

> They'll turn me in your arms, lady,
>   Into an esk and adder;
> But hold me fast, and fear me not,
>   I am your bairn's father.
>
>
> They'll turn me into a bear sae grim,
>   And into a lion bold;
> But hold me fast, and fear me not,
>   As ye shall love your child.
> ....
> And last they'll turn me in your arms
>   Into the burning gleed;
> Then throw me into well water,
>   O throw me in wi speed
>
> And then I'll be your ain true-love,
>   I'll turn a naked knight;
> Then cover me wi your green mantle,
> And cover me out o sight. (Child, 39A: sts. 31–35)

At root, the alleged power to transform (minerals, in the case of the alchemists, and living creatures, in the case of the fairies) is, I believe, what linked these two discourses for Chaucer, so that *The Canon's Yeoman's Tale* may be read as a late manifestation of what Carolyn Walker Bynum has recently called "the facination with rules of change that permeate[d] twelfth- and thirteenth-century discussions of the natural world."[75] If Gerald of Wales could discuss werewolves in terms of sacramental transubstantiation (Bynum, p. 107), Chaucer can certainly consider alchemy in the light of fairyland. Many of the epiphenomena these discourses share (their liminality, their subversiveness, their secrecy) can be traced to a common concern with metamorphosis, and clearly that was what linked them in the mind of the sixteenth-century skeptic Reginald Scot, who treats both in his *Discouerie of Witchcraft*. (Incidentally, Scot evidently regarded Chaucer as a kindred spirit: he quotes both the Wife of Bath and the Canon's Yeoman with approval.) Here, for instance, is Scot on alchemical transmutation:

> Let the dealers in Alumystrie vnderscand, that the *verie* nature and kind of things cannot be changed, but rather made by art to resemble the same in shew and likenesse: so that they are not the *verie* things indeed, bur seeme so to be in appearance: as castels and towers doo seeme to be built in the clouds. (pp. 368–369)

And here are his views on a story about a man turned into an ass:

> But where was the yoong mans owne shape all these three yeares, wherin he was made as asse; It is a certeine and a generall rule, that two substantiall formes cannot be in one subject *simul & simel*, both at once. . . . The forme of the beast occupied some place in the aire, and so I thinke should a man doo also. For to bringe the bodie of a man, without feeling, into a thin airie nature, as that it can neither be seene nor felt, it may well be vnlikelie, but it is *verie* impossible. (p. 98)

Scot's views on alchemical transformation would have been perfectly orthodox in the middle ages; they were held by Avicenna (as he acknowledges), but also by such authorities as Thomas Aquinas and Giles of Rome.[76] His views on biological transformation are more radical in that he denies even the possibility of an airy simulacrum,[77] but in essence his claim that anything like genuine material transformation is impossible would have been shared by such doctrinal heavyweights as Gratian and Aquinas.[78] Aquinas, indeed, in his *Commentary on the Sentences* draws an explicit comparison between the impotence of both alchemists and devils to "induce substantial forms."[79]

I hope that by now enough has been said to show that in the late middle ages the discourse of alchemy and the discourse of fairyland shared a considerable amount of common ground and that there is every reason to take the Canon's Yeoman literally when he describes alchemy as an "elvysshe craft" and as "elvysshe lore." I would like to conclude by considering briefly why this simple proposition appears to have been so difficult for recent editors to accept. What qualities might seem to divide these discourses in the minds of modern readers, and what are the implications of such a division? Well, in the first place we tend to see alchemy as belonging squarely with learned, literate discourse (as the coda to the *Canon's Yeoman's Tale* itself, with its references to Arnold and Senior, makes clear), while the discourse of fairyland appears largely popular and oral, and can now be only painstakingly reconstructed from scraps of information culled from romances, ballads, sermons, tracts, and anecdotes. As a corollary to this, while most will recognize an element of magic in alchemy, such magic may well seem different in kind to the magic of fairyland, the natural, scientific magic that Richard Kieckheffer distinguishes from popular, demonic magic.[80] (We might notice in passing, however, that if Langland associates alchemy with learned necromancy,[81] our Exeter schoolroom text makes a similar connection between necromancy and fairies.)[82] This contrast might also take on a gendered aspect, so that Susan Crane's useful distinction between "uncanny women" and "subtle clerks" may similarly serve to separate for us the Wife of Bath's nostalgia for a "land fulfild of fayerye" from the Canon's Yeoman's "clergial" talk of "citrinacioun / . . . cementyng and fermentacioun" (lines 816–817). A distinction might equally be drawn in terms of Marxist analysis, the fairy magic of the Wife of Bath and the Canon's Yeoman's alchemy forming opposite sides of the same historical coin—the first, in Louise Fradenburg's words "a vision of everything lost under capitalism,"[83] the second, as Peggy Knapp has recently written, "gesturing towards a capitalism yet to come."[84] However, as soon as we seek to situate these two discourses in history (as the Marxist critic must inevitably do), an even more fundamental disjunction raises its head.

One of the earliest, and in many ways still the most challenging, of modern critics of *The Canon's Yeoman's Tale* is Charles Muscatine. For Muscatine (as for Lynn Thorndike), alchemy was a precursor of modern chemistry and Chaucer's rejection of alchemy as "blind materialism" contains "a germ of wry prophesy in it."[85] In other words, where the discourse of fairyland might have looked to the past the discourse of alchemy is speaking the language of the future:

> The dogged refusal to admit the intractability of matter, one of the virtues to which we owe so much of our civilization, is here represented by a group of sooty figures sifting and picking for

salvage in a pile of refuse. He who cheers them on is a fool. In the light of later history, indeed, the poem is reactionary. This kind of alchemy gave us chemistry (p. 221).

Muscatine's phrase *"this kind of* alchemy" is intended to set the practice of Chaucer's canons against the kind of philosophical alchemy that regarded matter as hylozoic (p. 218). But does such a distinction really hold? For me, the yeoman's breathless inventory of technical terms suggests something quite different: the futility of his master's attempts to contain and control matter that was, indeed, "instinct with life":

> Thise metals been of so greet violence
> Oure walles mowe nat make hem resistence,
> But if they weren wroght of lym and stoon;
> They percen so and thurgh the wal they goon.
> And somme of hem synken into the ground—
> Thus han we lost by tymes many a pound—
> And somme are scaterd al the floor aboute;
> Somme lepe into the roof. (lines 908–914)

If the descendant of medieval alchemy (applied, as well as theoretical) must be sought among the modern sciences, it was conceptually far closer to genetic engineering than inorganic chemistry. But, in fact, the immense gulf dividing the mentality of the alchemist from the scientist cannot be papered over by any such superficial resemblances.

Lee Patterson, to whose 1992 Biennial Chaucer Lecture this one is in many ways but a footnote, recognizes the difficulty of treating alchemy as simply a "prelude to chemistry," but he still wants to read it as "a site where modernizing values could take root," and Chaucer's own interest in it as thus anything but "reactionary." With this last point I am wholeheartedly in agreement, but I still have difficulty accepting even Patterson's more muted account of the alchemical project: "the non-existence of the philosopher's stone," he writes, "lured alchemy into a quest without a goal" (p. 47), and, a little later, "if alchemy is progressive, then, its dynamism cannot be understood in the usual terms by which scientific progress is measured" (p. 49). Patterson recognizes that alchemical knowledge was not, like modern science, aggregative, but, like Scattergood, he still finds in its commitment to technology the potential to transform society. On the contrary, I suggest, the alchemical project was studiously regressive, not progressive, and its goal, at least in terms of its own discourse, seemed far from unattainable.

Most will naturally assume that medieval alchemists saw themselves as building upon knowledge gained by their predecessors and advancing the project step by step toward a distant goal. But, as Sherwood Taylor puts it, "on the whole [alchemy] looked backward where modern science looks forward. The alchemist believed thar the 'ancients' knew the secrets of the work and could perform it, and his principal endeavour was to understand the meaning of their books" (p. 12). Nothing could better exemplify such an attitude than John Gower's discussion of alchemy in Book IV of the *Confessio Amantis*:

> This Ston hath pouer to profite.
> It makth multiplicacioun
> Of gold, and the fixacioun
> It causeth, and of his habit
> He doth the work to be parfit
> Of thilke Elixer which men calle
> Alconomie, as is befalle
> To hem that *whilom* weren wise.
> By *now* it stant al otherwise;
> Thei speken faste of thilke Ston.
> Bot hou to make it, *nou* wot non,
> After the sothe experience. (4:2572–2583)

By contrast, modern science, as Taylor says, "looks forward to the time when her efforts will make known the things that have never been known. To those who made her she looks back with respect, with honour, but not with any belief that their works contain hidden secrets to be unraveled for her enlightenment" (p. 12).

Moreover, it is a mistake to suppose that the medieval alchemist, like the modern scientist, was striving for an imaginable but as yet unrealizable goal—that the philosopher's stone, in other words, was the medieval equivalent of nuclear fusion, or a cure for HIV/AIDS. Though we may now know that this particular goal was unattainable, or at least hugely impractical, the striving, we might suppose, was the same, then as now. But this is emphatically not how the alchemists themselves saw it: many among them had, they believed, achieved the stone, and not just in the distant past. Chaucer's French contemporaries, Nicholas and Peronelle Flamel, were alleged to have succeeded; so, too, were two fifteenth-century Englishmen, Thomas Norton and George Ripley. In fact, Norton's great-grandson Samuel tells us that in Edward IV's time, no less than seven men, including his great-grandfather and Ripley, possessed the secret of alchemy.[86] Sherwood Taylor regards it as "the central problem" of alchemy that "apparently sincere alchemical writers do claim success and describe in detailed and pretty consistent language how they obtained the white and the red stone and carried out transmutations" (Taylor, pp. 90–91). In other words, to imagine that medieval alchemists saw themselves as using practical experiments to test an as yet unproven hypothesis is to view them in the distorting mirror of modern empirical science.

On this reading, medieval alchemy can lay claim to no particularly privileged status as "a site where modernizing values could take root"; there is no obvious reason why the discourse of fairyland, for instance, should not offer an equally hospitable (or inhospitable) site, and indeed, judging by his two uses of the word "elvysshe" in *The Canon's Yeoman's Tale*, for Chaucer himself it functioned in precisely this way. Chaucer's skeptical attitude to "elvysshe lore" is widely recognized: the satirical opening lines of *The Wife of Bath's Tale*, the all-too-human deities in *The Merchant's Tale*, the onlookers' various attempts to explain the steed of brass in *The Squire's Tale*, the naturalistic explanation for the vanishing rocks in *The Franklin's Tale*, and the absurd quest for an elf-queen in *Sir Thopas*, all suggest that Chaucer was deeply suspicious of such popular beliefs, but that he should have regarded alchemy in the same way appears on the surface rather more surprising. A man who could write a technical manual on the astrolabe and who evinces, as Scott Lightsey has recently shown, a fascination with "the mechanical marvels that were part of late medieval court life,"[87] might be expected to have shown a similar fascination with alchemy. In fact, he must at one time have done so. The weight of detailed technical information in *The Canon's Yeoman's Tale* can only have been acquired by someone who felt a genuine intellectual curiosity about alchemy. At the time that he borrowed from Jean de Meun the image of turning ferns into glass as a parallel to the one of the marvels of *The Squires Tale* (V [F].253–257), he may well have shared the Frenchman's confidence in the alchemist's ability to understand and harness the principles of change: "arquemie est ars veritable," Jean de Meun had declared flatly.[88] If so, by the time he came to write *The Canon's Yeoman's Tale* disenchantment had clearly set in. To suggest this is certainly not to espouse Brink's old conjecture that Chaucer himself had once been gulled by a crooked alchemist,[89] merely to speculate that he felt he could no longer sustain an old enthusiasm—a speculation for which Donald Howard's reading of the poem offers some support.[90] Viewed in this way, the bitterness of *The Canon's Yeoman's Tale* is not the mark of a reactionary who thinks he glimpses in the alchemist's furnace a nightmare future consecrated to a technologized materialism, it is the disillusionment of a genuine inquirer who has come to recognize the discourse of alchemy as no less "slidynge" a science than the illusory discourse of fairyland. However it may have looked to Walter Skeat, alchemical transformation for Chaucer was neither "mysterious" and "strange" nor "weird"; it was a mere figment of the imagination. It was, in a word, all-too-literally, "elvysshe."

Notes

1. All Chaucer references are to *The Riverside Chaucer,* 3rd ed., ed. L. D. Benson et al. (Boston: Houghton Mifflin, 1987).

2. "Elvish Chaucer," in *The Endless Knot: Essays in Old and Middle English in Honor of Marie Borroff,* ed. M. Teresa Tavoramina and R. F. Yeager (Cambridge: D. S. Brewer, 1995): 105–111.

3. "The 'Elvysshe' Power of Constance," *SAC* 23 (2001): p. 178.

4. I.e., Bruce A. Rosenberg, "Swindling Alchemist, Antichrist," *Centennial Review* 6 (1962): p. 577.

5. "Perpetual Motion: Alchemy and the Technology of the Self," *SAC* 15 (1993): p. 55; see also David Raybin, "'And pave it al of silver and of gold': the Humane Artistry of the Canon's Yeoman's Tale," in *Rebels and Rivals: The Contestive Spirit in the Canterbury Tales,* ed. Susanna Greer Fein, David Raybin, and Peter Braeger (Kalamazoo: Medieval Institute, 1991), pp. 189–212, and Mark Bruhn, "Art, Anxiety, and Alchemy in the *Canon's Yeoman's Tale,*" *ChauR* 33 (1999): 288–315.

6. *Truth and Textuality in Chaucer's Poetry* (Hanover, N.H.: University Press of New England, 1991), p. 145.

7. The sense of "foolishness" evidently became attached to *elvysshe* from its juxtaposition with *nyce* at line 842.

8. Wright's Percy Society edition (1847–1851) was printed without a glossary but, following Moxon's example, subsequent reprintings simply appended Tyrwhitt's glossary (see E. P. Hammond, *Chaucer: A Bibliographical Manual* [London: Macmillan, 1908] pp. 138, 212, 509); Bell glosses "like a fairy," Morris, "fairy-like, supernatural," and Pollard, "elflike" (though a 1919 reprint has "aerial").

9. Cf. "Gawain . . . / Though he were comen ayeyn out of Fairye" (*SqT* 95–96).

10. Cf. "Me befel a ferly, of fairie me pouȝte" (Pr. 6); *Piers Plowman: The A Version,* ed. George Kane (London: Athlone Press, 1960), p. 175.

11. I.e. *MerchT* 1743, *SqT* 201 (cf. *SGGK* 240).

12. *The Chaucer Glossary* glosses *fayerye* (at *WBT* 872 and 859, and *MerchT* 2039) as "magic creatures," though in none of these instances is this meaning unavoidable. The English prose translation of *Melusine* (ca. 1500), however, clearly uses the word to denote a creature: "the whiche somme called Gobelyns / the other ffayrees, and the other 'bonnes dames' or good ladyes" (7–9); ed. A. K. Donald, EETS ES 68 (London, 1895), p. 4.

13. *The Discarded Image: An Introduction to Medieval and Renaissance Literature* (Cambridge: Cambridge University Press, 1964), p. 130. For a more recent study of these "high fairies," see Laurence Harf-Lancner, *Les Fées au moyen âge* (Paris: Champion, 1984).

14. *Religion and the Decline of Magic: Studies in Popular Belief in Sixteenth- and Seventeenth-Century England* (1971; Harmondsworth: Penguin Books, 1973), p. 726.

15. On Gervase himself, see H. G. Richardson, "Gervase of Tilbury," *History* 46 (1961): 483–486.

16. Ed. and trans. S. E. Banks and J. W. Binns (Oxford: Clarendon Press, 2002), p. 730.

17. H. Stuart, "The Anglo-Saxon Elf," *Studia Neophilologica* 48 (1976): 313–319.

18. *The Discouerie of Witchcraft* [STC 21864] (London, 1584), p. 521.

19. Cf. *Les Évangilles des guenouilles,* ed. Madeleine Jeay (Montréal: Les Presses de l'Université de Montréal, 1985), p. 141 (lines 2296 ff.).

20. Cf. *Dives and Pauper*'s attack on such superstitions "as settynge of mete or drynke be nyȝt on þe benche to fedyn Al-holde [eiþer gobelyn]," ed. Priscilla H. Barnum, 2 vols., EETS, 275, 280 (London, 1976–1980), I: 157; and a Middle English sermon's mention of "alle suche [that] been led al nyȝt with gobelyn, and erreth hider and thider," cited in G. R. Owst, *Literature and Pulpit in Medieval England,* 2d ed. [Oxford, Blackwell; 1966], p. 113).

21. For the etymology of *elf,* see Claude Lecouteaux, *Les Nains et les elfes au moyen âge,* 2d ed. (Paris: Imago, 1997), pp. 121–123.

22. Ed. Banks and Binns, p. 96.

23. *The Metrical Chronicle of Robert of Glouester,* ed. W. A. Wright, 2 vols., Rolls Series (London, 1887), 1:196.

24. O. S. Pickering, "*South English Legendary* Style in Robert of Gloucester's *Chronicle,*" *Medium Ævum* 70 (2001): 1–18.

25. Ed. Charlotte D'Evelyn and Anna J. Mill, 3 vols., EETS OS 235, 236, and 244 (London, 1956 and 1959), 2:410.

26. Ed. Barnum, 2:118.

27. "*Sir Orfeo* and the Fight from the Enchanters," *SAC* 22 (2000): 158–162.

28. "The Canon's Yeoman's Prologue and Tale," *Modern Philology* 58 (1961): 231.

29. Cf. Senior's injunction to his fellow alchemists to "shun the society of men" *[abborre conventum hominum];* quoted in Joseph E. Grennen, "Chaucer and the Commonplaces of Alchemy," *Classica et Mediaevalia* 26 (1965): 311.

30. "Alchemy as Counter-Culture," *Indiana Social Srudies Quarterly* 24 (1971–1972): 49.

31. "Run Silent, Run Deep: Heresy and Alchemy as Medieval Versions of Utopia," in *Medieval Literary Politics: Shapes of Ideology* (Manchester: Manchester University Press, 1990), p. 11.

32. *At the Bottom of the Garden: A Dark History of Fairies, Hobgoblins, and Other Troublesome Things* (New York: New York University Press, 2001), p. 4.

33. *Sir Orfeo,* ed. A. J. Bliss, 2d ed. (Oxford: Clarendon Press, 1966), lines 347–354; for *Reinbrun,* see *The Romance of Gay of Warwick,* ed. Julius Jupitza, EETS ES 42, 49, and 59 (London, 1883–1891), 3:657 (st. 78); *Thomas of Erceldoune,* ed. Ingeborg Nixon (Copenhagen: Akadernisk Forlag, 1980), 1:38–39 (lines 169–172); for *Yonec,* see Marie de France, *Lais,* ed. Alfred Ewert (Oxford: Blackwell, 1963), pp. 90–91 (lines 345–356).

34. *The History of English Affairs, Book 1,* ed. and trans. P. G. Walsh and M. J. Kennedy (Warminster: Aris and Phillips, 1988), pp. 118–121 (chap. 28). Cf. Ralph of Coggeshall's account of the green children of Woolfpits in his *Chronicon Anglicanum,* ed. J. Stevenson, Rolls Series (London, 1875), pp. 118–120; Gerald of Wales on the adventures of Eliodor in his *Itinerarium Kambriae,* ed. James F. Dimock, *Opera Omnia VI,* Rolls Series (London, 1868), pp. 75–78; and Gervase of Tilbury on the antipodeans (ed. Banks and Binns, pp. 242–245). For seventeenth-century survivals of this tradition, see John Aubrey, *Remaines of Gentilisme and Judaisme,* ed. James Britten, Folklore Society 4 (London, 1881), pp. 30 and 123.

35. See John Gardner, "*The Canon's Yeoman's Prologue and Tale:* An Interpretation," *Philological Quarterly* 46 (1967): 1–17.

36. *English Wycliffite Sermons, I,* ed. Anne Hudson (Oxford: Clarendon Press, 1983), p. 686. Chaucer himself might have been prepared to concede this much; cf. his association of "ayerissh bestes" with bad weather in the *House of Fame* (lines 964–969).

37. See W. P. Ker, "The Craven Angels," *MLR* 6 (1911): 85–87.

38. *Lais,* p. 85 (lines 149–152).

39. *Lais féeriques des XIIe et XIIIe siècles,* ed. Alexandre Micha (Paris: Flammarion, 1992), p. 128 (lines 386–390).

40. *The Middle English Versions of Sir Partenope of Blois,* ed. A. Trampe Bödtker, EETS ES 109 (London, 1912), p. 36 (lines 1341–1347; cf. lines 1883–1893).

41. *The Boke of Duke Huon of Burdeux,* ed. S. L. Lee, EETS ES 40 and 41 (London: 1884–1883), p. 76.

42. *The English and Scottish Popular Ballads,* ed. Francis James Child, 5 vols. (Boston: Houghton Mifflin, 1882–1898), 1:317–329.

43. Cf. Thomas D. Hill, "'The Green Path to Paradise' in Nineteenth-Century Ballad Tradition," *Neuphilologische Mitteilungen* 91 (1990): 483–486.

44. *Documents Illustrative of Medieval Kentish Society,* ed. F. R. H. Du Boulay (Ashford: Kent Archaeological Society, 1964), p. 255.

45. Andy Letcher, "The Scouring of the Shires: Fairies, Trolls, and Pixies in Eco-Protest Culture," *Folklore* 112 (2001): 151.

46. *Ordinal of Alchemy,* ed. John Reidy, EETS 272 (London, 1975), pp. 11–12.

47. "The Epistle . . . written to King Edward the 4," st. 5, from *The Compound of Alchymy (1591),* ed. Stanton J. Linden (Aldershot: Ashgate, 2002), p. 90.

48. There are six fifteenth-century manuscripts of Ripley's *Compound* and two of Norton's *Ordinal;* see, *A Manual of the Writings of Middle English,* gen. ed. Albert Hartung, Vol. 10, Pt. 25 (*Works of Science and Information*), ed. George R. Keiser (New Haven: Connecticut Academy of Arts and Sciences, 1998), pp. 3193 and 3791.

49. "Chaucer's 'Secree of Secrees': An Alchemical 'Topic'," *Philological Quarterly* 42 (1963): 562–566; also the same author's "Chaucer and the Commonplaces of Alchemy," *Claisica et Mediaevalia* 26 (1965): 309–311.

50. The Yeoman himself makes a similar admonition even as he offers to betray alchemical secrets to the pilgrims (line 643), the first canon berates him for this breach of confidence (line 696), and the second prepares to gull the chantry priest by dangling before him the prospect of initiation into arcane mysteries (lines 1136–1139).

51. Helen Cooper, "Magic That Does Not Work," *Medievalia et Humanistica: Studies in Medieval and Renaissance Culture* ns. 7 (1976): 131–146.

52. *Sir Launfal,* ed. A. J. Bliss (London and Edinburgh: Nelson, 1960), lines 361–365.

53. See *Lais féeriques,* ed. Micha, pp. 36, 164, and 126.

54. "Recapulatio totius operis praedicti," st. 9; ed. Linden, p. 84.

55. For seventeenth-century survivals of this tradition, see Aubrey, *Remaines of Gentilisme,* ed. Britten, pp. 29 and 102.

56. *Mandeville's Travels,* ed. M. C. Seymour (Oxford: Clarendon Press, 1967), p. 108 (lines 17–21).

57. Ed. Jean Dufournet (Gand: Éditions scientifiques, 1977), p. 74 (lines 659–663 and 667–669).

58. *Nouveau recueil complet des fabliaux,* ed. Willem Noomen and Nico Van Den Boogaard, 10 vols. (Assen/Maascricht: Van Gorcum, 1983–1998), 3:163 (lines 206–213).

59. Nicholas Orme, "An English Grammar School ca. 1450: Latin Exercises from Exeter (Caius College MS 417/447, Folios 16v–24v)," *Traditio* 50 (1995): 280 (C20).

60. Despite religious hostility, the beauty and nobility of the elves remained proverbial throughout the middle ages; see, e.g., the description of Candace in *The Wars of Alexander* (ed. Walter W. Skeat, EETS ES 47 (London, 1886), p. 263): "Scho was so faire & so fresche . as faucon hire semed, / An elfe oute of an-othire erde / ot ellis an Aungell" (lines 5257–5259); or the goddesses who vie for the judgment of Paris in *The Seege or Batayle of Troye* (ed. Mary Elizabeth Barnicle, EETS OS 172 (London, 1927), p. 40): "In þat forest weore gangand / ffoure ladies of eluene land" (lines 507–508).

61. *Lais féeriques,* ed. Micha, pp. 96–97 (lines 596–608).

62 F. Sherwood Taylor, *The Alchemists* (1952; St. Albans: Granada, 1976), p. 16.

63. *Confessio Amantis,* 5:4104–4105, in *The English Works of John Gower,* ed. G. C. Macaulay, 2 vols. EETS ES 81 and 82 (London, 1900–1901), 2:58.

64. See Joseph E. Grennen, "Chaucer's Characterization of the Canon and His Yeoman," *Journal of the History of Ideas* 25 (1964): 279–281.

65. *The Saga of Tristram and Ísönd,* trans. Paul Schach (Lincoln: University of Nebraska Press, 1973), p. 95. Cf. *Le Roman de Tristan par Thomas,* ed. Joseph Bédier (Paris: SATF, 1902), 1:218–219.

66. *Caxton's Malory,* ed. James W. Spisak, 2 vols. (Berkeley and Los Angeles: University of California Press, 1982), 1:189 (Bk.7, Chap. 29). Cf. "The Boy and the Mantle" (Child 29: sts. 11 and 12).

67. *The Arte of English Poesie,* ed. Gladys Doidge Willcock and Allice Walker (Cambridge: Cambridge University Press, 1936), p 173.

68. Minor White Latham, *The Elizabethan Fairies* (New York: Columbia University Press, 1930), p. 150.

69. *The Holy Greyhound: Guinefort, Healer of Children Since the Thirteenth Century,* trans. Martin Thom (1979; Cambridge: Cambridge University Press, 1983), pp. 74–82.

70. See P. M[eyer], "*Chanjon,* enfant changé en nourrice," *Romania* 32 (1902): 452–453.

71. *Of Arthour and of Merlin, I,* ed. O. D. Macrae-Gibson, EETS 268 (London, 1973), pp. 83 and 93 (cf 1. 1110, p. 87).

72. *The Chester Mystery Cycle, I,* ed. R. M. Lumiansky and David Mills, EETS SS3 (London, 1974).

73. "Chaucer's *Second Nun's Tale* and the Iconography of Saint Cecilia," *New Perspectives in Chaucer Criticism,* ed. Donald M. Rose (Norman: Pilgrim Books, 1981), pp. 155–156.

74. *Fasciculus Morum: A Fourteenth-Century Preacher's Handbook,* ed. and trans. Siegfried Wenzel (University Park: Pennsylvania State University Press, 1989).

75. *Metamorphosis and Identity* (New York: Zone Books, 2001), p. 90.

76. See William R. Newman, ed., *The Summa Perfectionis of Pseudo-Gerber* (Leiden: Brill, 1991), pp. 30–35.

77. CE *Discouerie,* p. 516. Also Stuart Clark, "The Scientific Status of Demonology," in *Occult and Scientific Mentalities in the Renaissance,* ed. Brian Vickers (Cambridge: Cambridge University Press, 1984), p. 368.

78. *Decretum Magistri Gratiani,* ed. Emil Friedberg, *Corpus Iuris Canonici* 1 (Leipzig: Tauschnicz, 1879), pp. 1032–1036 (2nd pt. cause 26, question 5. c. 14); *Summa theologiae,* gen. ed. Thomas Gilby and T. C. O'Brien, 60 vols. (London: Eyre and Spottiswoode; New York: McGraw-Hill, 1964–1976), 9:31–41 (1a, 51, 1–3).

79. Newman, ed., *Pseudo-Gerber,* pp. 30–31.

80. *Magic in the Middle Ages* (Cambridge: Cambridge University Press, 1989), pp. 8–10.

81. *A Text* (ed. Kane), XI: 159–161.

82. Michael D. Bailey ("From Sorcery to Witchcraft," *Speculum* 78 [2001]: 960–990) has recently argued that the common and elite traditions were gradually coming together in the fourteenth century and that this coalescence lies behind the European witchhunts of the later fifteenth and sixteenth centuries.

83. "The Wife of Bath's Passing Fancy," *SAC* 8 (1986): p. 51.

84. "The Work of Alchemy," *Journal of Medieval and Early Modern Studies* 30 (2000): 576. See also Britton J. Harwood, "Chaucer and the Silence of History: Situating the Canon's Yeoman's Tale," *PMLA* 102 (1987): 338–350.

85. *Chaucer and the French Tradition* (Berkeley and Los Angeles: University of California Press, 1960), pp. 217 and 221.

86. Ed. Reidy, p. xxxviii.

87. "Chaucer's Secular Marvels and the Medieval Economy of Wonder," *SAC* 23 (2001): 289.

88. *Le Roman de la rose,* ed. Daniel Poirion (Paris: Garnier-Flammarion, 1974), p. 433 (l. 16084).

89. *History of English Literature (Wyclif, Chaucer, Earliest Drama, Renaissance), Vol. 2. Pt. 1,* trans. W. C. Robinson (New York: H. Hoit, 1893), p. 181.

90. See Donald R. Howard, *The Idea of the Canterbury Tales* (Berkeley and Los Angeles: University of California Press, 1978), pp. 292–298.

LIANNA FARBER

The Creation of Consent in the Physician's Tale

In a remarkable moment of the *Physician's Tale* Virginia consents to her own death, asking her father Virginius to kill her: "Yif me my deeth, er that I have a shame," she implores him (VI 249).[1] This moment, like all those when Virginia speaks, appears neither in Chaucer's stated source, Livy's history, which Chaucer may or may not have known, nor in his unstated source, Jean de Meun's *Roman de la Rose*, which Chaucer most certainly did know.[2] This particular addition arises from Virginius's response to the evil judge Apius's demand that Virginia be handed into his custody. As Virginius understands the situation, he is faced with a terrible choice for his daughter: to hand her to Apius "in lecherie to lyven" (VI 206), or to kill her, ending her life before Apius can take her virginity. What is remarkable about this moment in the *Physician's Tale* is not so much that Virginius decides it is better for his daughter to be dead than dishonored (taking her head to save her maidenhead, as some have explained the pun),[3] but instead that Virginia herself agrees with this decision. Virginia's consent to her own death, added to the story by Chaucer, is only one improbable moment in a tale generally considered faulty, but it is, I believe, a crucial moment. In this essay I will argue that the primary question that drives this tale is what might lead a

The Chaucer Review, Volume 39, Number 2 (2004): pp. 151–164. © 2004 Pennsylvania State University.

203

young woman to decide that death is preferable to loss of virginity and to agree to her own death.

While some Chaucerians have simply condemned the *Physician's Tale* (it is, one succinctly stated, "the faultiest" of the *Canterbury Tales*), many more have analyzed the problems with the tale, providing a variety of diagnoses.[4] Noting that the story as told in Livy's history and the *Roman de la Rose* is explicitly political, Sheila Delany has argued that in the *Physician's Tale* Chaucer introduces political ideas but is subsequently unwilling or unable to treat them as the plot develops.[5] Angus Fletcher also sees the tale as moving away from the question of explicitly political authority, but contends that it takes up questions of writerly and historical authority.[6] Linda Lomperis contends that the authority in question is authority over bodies, and she reads in the tale a split between the physical body and metaphysical questions of virginity and mortality.[7] Derek Pearsall, Jill Mann, and Lee Patterson focus upon the issue of genre, seeing the tale as a saint's life that has been grafted onto a political story.[8] Anne Middleton believes the genre in question is instead the exemplum and argues that the tale is a demonstration of the exemplum's inability to consider moral ambiguity.[9] These disparate readings, some dismissing the *Physician's Tale*, others lauding it, and still others taking a more neutral stance towards its aesthetic success, all point to a fundamental sense of disunity that readers experience in the tale, whether between the politics claimed and those written, between mind and body, between genres, or between our expectations for genre and its own limits. From different perspectives and for different reasons, all contend with what seems an incommensurability of parts—the long encomium to Virginia's virtue, the also long, seeming digression on governesses and parents, the sudden moment when Virginius beheads his daughter, his even more sudden and seemingly unmotivated advocacy that Claudius be pardoned, and the hasty ending that treats none of the issues in the story itself—and their failure to fit properly together. The disproportion or disunity of the tale that these readings note is not, furthermore, a function of its basic plot, as we can readily see from the far more harmonious versions of the story told by Livy, Jean de Meun, John Gower, and Giovanni Boccaccio.[10] The disunity, whether intentional, salutary, or a terrible mistake, arises instead from the way Chaucer tells the story and most particularly from the additions that he makes to it.

In this essay I will argue that Chaucer's additions and changes to his source material, which create the disunity or disproportion of the tale, are consistent. All, I will argue, work to turn the tale away from the theme of justice (the explicit point of the story in the *Roman de la Rose*) and toward the idea of what shapes a person and how she comes to understand and experience the world, even to the point of agreeing that she should die. The changes, I believe, move toward exploring what we would today call "ideology," whether we use the standard modern definition of a person's imaginary relationship to her actual conditions of existence, or whether we instead use Chaucer's question of why a person might consent to her own death. While I conclude that the tale is in this sense broadly political, I arrive at this conclusion through a method that is formal. My argument is not about politics per se, but about the ways that Chaucer's changes and additions work to set up a framework for calling our attention to how Virginia reaches her decision when she agrees that she should die and to why she might make that decision. I therefore examine in turn the changes Chaucer makes to the story before explaining what I take to be their import, because I believe that they achieve this import only when read together.

The changes Chaucer makes can be divided into three main parts: first, the long discursus by and about Nature on the formation of Virginia's particular beauty and virtue; second, the abstract discussion of the responsibility governesses and parents bear for the children in their charge; and third, the scene where, after hearing Apius's judgment, Virginius comes home to tell Virginia what transpired and Virginia agrees to her own death. The first two parts of this scheme are completely original with Chaucer; in the third part he moves the action from the public sphere of the open court to the private sphere of Virginius's house, where he has Virginius not only perform the act of beheading but also discuss the action with Virginia—it is here that Chaucer adds Virginia's voice to the story. Chaucer's modifications, however, start even before this scheme, with the way the tale begins.

In the *Roman de la Rose* the story, after a nod to Livy, begins with Apius.[11] Such a starting point makes sense since Jean uses it to illustrate the evils of justice gone wrong. Chaucer, after a nod to Livy, begins instead with Virginius, by calling him a knight, which establishes his role in society, and then showing that Virginius has all that a secular knight needs to be good: he is "[f]ulfild of honour," a virtue that is both personal and public, "and of worthynesse" (VI 3), the catch-all virtue, used also for the knight in the *General Prologue,* which shows not a particular quality but instead that he deserves whatever he has as well as his rank. This general desert presumably encompasses the many friends of whom we next learn, magnifying our sense of his public virtue, and "greet richesse" (VI 4), a detail that not only confirms his station but also, as the story progresses, shows us that his problems do not stem from an inability to pay an appropriate sort of a bribe, and that, unlike Apius, Virginius either would not or could not use his influence through friends and wealth to change the situation in which he will find himself. Virginius's status and good character, rather than the character of the judge, thus frame the story.

Although the discussion then moves to Virginius's daughter, it moves to her not in herself, through a discussion of her general qualities (the way we met Virginius) but instead through a discussion of her relationship to Nature. Nature has, of course, a constitutive hand in forming every person. Here the narrator's interest lies in showing that Nature could do no more for any person than she did for Virginia:

> For Nature hath with sovereyn diligence
> Yformed hire in so greet excellence,
> As though she wolde seyn, "Lo! I, Nature,
> Thus kan I forme and peynte a creature,
> Whan that me list." (VI 9–13)

Throughout her hypothetical speech and the contemplation of Virginia's beauty that follows Nature's imagined direct discourse, the emphasis is upon Nature's agency: Nature forms and paints, we are told five times in eleven lines; Nature shapes all creatures and decides "What colour that they han or what figures" (VI 28); Nature did her best with Virginia. The speech, given by Nature, emphasizes her own self primarily. She presents Virginia as a showpiece of her own craft. The encomium thus implies a causal link between nature and character.

The next paragraph about Virginia begins again with Nature's agency before moving into a discussion of Virginia's manner and virtue. The shape of the paragraph implies the possible guiding hand Nature has in her virtue, even while Virginia's manner and character are presented as possibly her own. The narrator begins the enumeration of Virginia's virtues by giving her his all-encompassing approval ("In hire lakked no condicioun / That is to preyse" [VI 41–42]) to let us know that if we happen to think of an unmentioned virtue the omission should be attributed to narratorial negligence rather than a hidden fault. With that disclaimer comes a list, which ends by noting that she finds polite ways to excuse herself from inappropriate situations, neither offending others nor compromising herself.[12] This characteristic stands out as particularly important because it is the one place in the catalogue where Virginia clearly determines her own actions, where the agency is entirely her own:

> And of hir owene vertu, unconstreyned,
> She hath ful ofte tyme syk hire feyned,
> For that she wolde fleen the compaignye
> Where likly was to treten of folye. (VI 61–64)

By the time we have come to this point we have learned that every beauty and virtue that could be given to Virginia upon her creation has been given to her, and we see here that in instances where she, by her own agency, can avoid situations that might become "ful perilous" (VI 69), as the narrator, a few lines later, calls these gatherings, she removes herself. We are thus presented with two potentially complementary explanations for virtue and virtuous behavior, one emphasizing the role of nature, the second a person's own decisions.

Rather than using these explanations alone as background to the plot, the narrative moves to an abstract account of the importance of governesses. The passage has been read as a comment upon Katherine Swynford, Chaucer's sister-in-law who was governess of John of Gaunt's daughters, his mistress, and finally his wife, and her potential role in the elopement of one of her charges.[13] While contemporaries may have seen the discussion as politically pointed, it also works to provide another account for the creation of virtuous behavior. The narrator addresses governesses directly:

> And ye maistresses, in youre olde lyf,
> That lordes doghtres han in governaunce
>
> ....
>
> Thenketh that ye been set in governynges
> Of lordes doghtres oonly for two thynges:
> Outher for ye han kept youre honestee,
> Or elles ye han falle in freletee,
> And knowen wel ynough the olde daunce,
> And han forsaken fully swich meschaunce
> For everemo. (VI 72–73, 75–81)

The narrator begins by using the word "governaunce," which for Chaucer had primarily political connotations as well as the more general meaning of having a controlling or determining influence over events or people.[14] After planting the seeds of this potential analogy between governesses and rulership, the address moves away to assert two reasons that women might be entrusted to this job: they have either maintained their virtue or, having fallen, have a superior understanding of how to guard against similar falls in others. A woman's effectiveness as a governess, therefore, is entirely covered by matters of virtue. We have already seen, of course, that lack of virtue was not Virginia's problem, so whatever befalls her clearly cannot be blamed upon her governess, but the narrator takes the opportunity of discussing the already exonerated governess to make clear the stakes in having *governaunce* over a young woman:

> Looke wel that ye unto no vice assente,
> Lest ye be dampned for youre wikke entente;
> For whoso dooth, a traitour is, certeyn.
> And taketh kep of that that I shal seyn:

Of alle tresons sovereyn pestilence
Is whan a wight bitrayseth innocence. (VI 87–92)

The language here turns explicitly political. Although the governess gov-
erns, innocence is placed in the role of the sovereign or principle that could
be betrayed. Such a betrayal turns one into a traitor, and not just any traitor
but the worst possible sort. The passage makes less clear the relationship
between "assente" and "wikke entente." If you assent to vice you will be
damned for your wicked intent, but whether you are held responsible even if
your intent was not wicked is left ambiguous. The passage establishes that
treason, however, arises from the betrayal of innocence whatever the intent
behind that betrayal.

Speaking of those who have governance over innocence, the narrator
does not stop at governesses but turns next to parents, who also fill that role:

Ye fadres and ye moodres eek also,
Though ye han children, be it oon or mo,
Youre is the charge of al hir surveiaunce,
Whil that they been under youre governaunce. (VI 93–96)

If governesses have charge only of matters of virtue, parents' responsibilities
are not so limited: their purview extends instead to all aspects of protecting
their children. The term *governaunce* links what the narrator will say about
parents to what has been said about governesses, making clear that the subject
is not parents versus governesses so much as the role each has in governing
children. The narrator goes on to warn parents where they might go wrong:

Beth war, if by ensample of youre lyvynge,
Or by youre necligence in chastisynge,
That they ne perisse. (VI 97–99)

We thus see that parents teach not only by instruction but also by example
and by omission. Unlike governesses, parents cannot rest content with
guarding virtue, but must live exemplary lives and chastise children if they
go wrong. To omit either of these elements in parenting sets up parents, too,
as potential *traitours* to innocence.

Not content with this analogy, the narrator turns to another before moving back to the particular story of Virginia:

Under a shepherde softe and necligent
The wolf hath many a sheep and lamb torent.

Suffiseth oon ensample now as heere,
For I moot turne agayn to my matere. (VI 101–104)

Here the parents are rather conventionally depicted as the shepherds of
innocence whose negligence can lead to the destruction of the lambs whatever the "intent" behind the negligence (and here that negligence seems
almost entirely removed from the "wikke entente" attributed earlier to the
betrayal of innocence). The analogy turns briefly from the political to the
pastoral in order to emphasize that any harm that may come to children is
the responsibility of the parents who should guard them. To say that one
example here and now is enough implies that another may follow later, elsewhere, as indeed it does in the story of Virginia. At the same time, we can
read the last couplet as an indication that one example, the story of Virginia,
must suffice to illustrate the proverbial wisdom about sheep, shepherds, and
wolves, because the narrator must now move on to that story.

Many have noted the seeming incongruity of these passages. Brian Lee
defends this incongruity against its critics, although he calls the passages a
digression, by noting that as "the subject of the tale is the guardianship of a
young girl, . . . the digression, though long, is not inappropriate."[15] This defense, logical as it is, does not answer Middleton's charge that the emphasis
on governesses and parents in these passages is

> theoretically inappropriate. Their stress on the passive malleability
> of youth contrasts strangely with the moral self-sufficiency we have
> already heard praised in Virginia; and the peculiar absence of any
> mention of love as the root of parental discipline runs counter to
> the whole burden of Nature's speech.[16]

While Middleton sees these contradictions as appropriate because they
point out the limits of the exemplum form, I would argue that they are
important because they demonstrate at work not a linear argument, in
which the elements proceed from conclusions established along the way, but
instead an inclusive list that presents all possible answers regardless of their
relationship to each other. Any of these elements could account for behavior; all are possible explanations of virtuous action. In writing about the
causes of behavior, Chaucer posits a number of plausible answers. The long
introduction to the matter of the tale provides four different accounts of the
causes behind virtuous behavior: it may be given by nature; it may arise from
an individual's own agency; it may be a result of the *governaunce* applied by
governesses; or it may come from the rule and tending of parents. Virginia is
placed very specifically within this theoretical framework: Nature has done
everything possible to "forme and peynten" her well (VI 21); she exercises

her own agency wisely; and she has no governess. Only the influence of parents is left, then, as a locus for behavior that might seem, to us, wrong or ill-considered. As the narrator moves, finally, from this long introduction to the story of Virginia, then, he has brought us back full circle to Virginius, the very place he began.

From here the plot of the story follows the *Roman de la Rose* through Apius's refusal to hear Virginius's case for his own paternity, along the way calling Apius's plan "how that his lecherie / Parfourned sholde been" (VI 150–151) a "conspiracie" (VI 149), employing again the political diction we find throughout the warnings to adults. Where in the *Roman de la Rose* Virginius acts immediately in the open court,[17] in the *Physician's Tale* he instead goes home to sit in his hall,

> And leet anon his deere doghter calle,
> And with a face deed as asshen colde
> Upon hir humble face he gan biholde,
> With fadres pitee stikynge thurgh his herte,
> Al wolde he from his purpos nat converte. (VI 208–212)

While his obstinacy clearly cannot be condoned, it must be contrasted with Apius's lecherous "conspiracie," even if both end in the "betrayal" of Virginia. His face, dead as cold ashes, is a detail akin to a blush in Chaucer—a sign of genuine emotion that cannot be feigned. Furthermore, the narrator presents us with the information about Virginius's interior state and explicitly tells us that he feels struck through the heart—a feeling that either does or does not exist and is not subject to manipulation.[18] By identifying this emotion as "fadres pitee," furthermore, Chaucer explicitly links Virginius's feelings to his role as a parent, the role in which he is supposed to provide guidance for his daughter.

Virginius's love and emotion cannot be in question, then, when he addresses his daughter:

> "Doghter," quod he, "Virginia, by thy name,
> Ther been two weyes, outher deeth or shame,
> That thou most suffre; allas, that I was bore!" (VI 213–215)

In Jean de Meun's telling of the story, Virginius, seeing that he had no choice but to submit to Apius, exchanged "shame for injury" and beheaded Virginia, neither voicing his reasoning nor consulting her or anyone else.[19] In Chaucer's story, however, Virginius quite clearly presents his daughter with an either/or decision: either death or shame.[20] These alternatives are problematic because there would presumably be many other ways to deal with the situation: Virginia could run away; she could go into hiding; Virginius could stall for time while he called together all their friends who were pointedly mentioned when we were introduced to Virginius; and on and on. The idea of course is not really that Virginia and her father could follow these options (since being fictional, they cannot "do" anything), but instead that the choice Virginius presents to his daughter is blatantly false. Its falseness is highlighted not only by the way Virginius was presented at the beginning of the tale, but also by Virginia herself. Virginia has good reason to question an alternative so severe, which she does: "Goode fader, shal I dye? / Is ther no grace, is ther no remedye?" (VI 235–236). She first asks, in other words, for a solution that invokes religious justice and privilege: is there no grace? Her second question, "is there no remedy?" could be a reiteration of the first, but it also queries whether a more practical solution might be sought—"could not something else be done?"—pointing us to the obvious conclusion that indeed many other things could be done.

Virginius's answer, however, is definitive: "No, certes, deere doghter myn" (VI 237). Virginia asks if she may complain, swoons twice, rises,

> and to hir fader sayde,
> "Blissed be God that I shal dye a mayde!
> Yif me my deeth, er that I have a shame;
> Dooth with youre child youre wyl, a Goddes name!"
> (VI 247–250)[21]

In asking for her death, Virginia accepts both the dichotomy Virginius proposes (death or shame) and his governance over her (he should do his will with his child).[22] It turns out, audiences of the story other than the Host tend to agree, that this is bad governance, perhaps mirroring Apius's own even without the "wikke entente," but Virginius's plea for Claudius's clemency at the end, which Chaucer includes even as he rushes through the story, shows us that Virginius himself cannot be considered "unworthy" even if he does misuse his sovereign powers over his daughter. Furthermore, in placing Virginia's acceptance of her father's interpretation alongside her acceptance of his right to govern her, Chaucer makes clear that the responsibility does not lie entirely with Virginius: Virginia embraces her father's logic as well as his power and, voicing both, consents to her own death.

In the *Physician's Tale*, then, Chaucer tells of a young woman who actively believes she must die because she accepts both her father's understanding of her situation and his right to govern her. Chaucer changes the story of Apius and Virginius to make it work through the shaping influences on character and action that might lead to Virginia's decision. There is Nature, which can "forme and peynte" but not teach; there are virtue and good behavior, which Virginia possesses; there is the possible influence of a governess, which does not in this case affect her; and there are parents, who must teach by example and by chastising when appropriate. *The Physician's Tale* shows us the very bad example Virginius's conclusion about his daughter sets for her and its shocking result. Chaucer's original "beginning" for the story, which takes up over a third of its whole, works to set up an experiment with one carefully controlled variable—parental teaching—and the tale shows us how this one variable can overcome all else by creating Virginia's consent to her own death. Given these variables, she recognizes her father's governance and asks to die.

Critics have tended to de-emphasize the weight of Virginia's voice. Middleton, expressing a sophisticated form of a common critical stance, writes that since Virginius has already decided that Virginia must die, offering her the chance to speak emphasizes her role as an object. Virginius here, she argues, tries to take the place of Nature.[23] This argument, however, depends upon the idea that Nature was "right" and the passage about parents was "wrong." It also minimizes the importance of Virginia's agency—an aspect of her character that Chaucer emphasizes when he explains how she found ways to remove herself gracefully from potentially inappropriate situations. I cannot see any reason for Chaucer to add words that he did not mean, whether in praise of Virginia or in her voice. That Virginius had made up his mind could not have prevented Virginia from disagreeing with him, even if her disagreement would not have changed the outcome. These facts, as well as a reading that sees the introductory material as cumulative rather than right and wrong, lead me to take seriously Virginia's words. This moment also, I believe, makes problematic Fletcher's argument that "Virginia's virtuous behavior places her outside of traditional power structures," even as Virginius, by recognizing Apius's governance, "relegitimates the very hierarchies that Virginia's portrait has dispelled."[24] Virginia herself recognizes her father's governance. Although Apius knows that her virtue would make her unwilling to submit to his advances, these advances would not normally be a form of his judicial power. By conceiving his plot with Claudius, he turns them into a form of judicial authority, and he clearly does expect her to submit to this (now judicial) authority or there would be no point to his plan.

In showing us the way consent can be created, Chaucer does not entirely erase the political themes of his source material, even if he does transpose them. The crucial scene of the story moves, as I have noted, from the public sphere to the private, but rather than understanding this shift as a way of omitting politics from his story, I believe we must see it as a way of positing a broader idea of what constitutes politics than we find in his sources. Chaucer uses explicitly political language in his discussion of governesses and parents and their control over their charges, and in his description of Apius's plan. This diction is not simply residual. Jean de Meun calls Apius a traitor; Chaucer, in the material he adds, moves the idea of treachery from the realm of judges to that of governesses and parents.[25] Such political language works in two ways. In the first instance, it poses Innocence, an abstract quality that resides in young people, as sovereign, in order to compare any negligence to treason. The rest of the story points to the idea that leading a young woman to agree to her own death might indeed be considered negligent. This analogy broadens the political sphere, which in turn allows Chaucer to venture upon an analysis of the ways treason and betrayal work. Treason and betrayal are, as we have seen, the words Chaucer uses in connection with his discussion of *governaunce*. In this tale, betrayal and treason do not work by giving away secrets or plotting to kill the sovereign. Instead, they work through miseducation and negligence that might lead the sovereign (in this case personified Innocence in the figure of Virginia) into believing her own destruction is her best option.

At the same time, this political language encourages us to see Virginia as exemplifying not only virginity but also the political subject. Virginia is under the control of her father, who believes he has her best interests in mind even if we believe he does not, and of Apius, who definitely does not mind her interests at all. In this case she agrees with her father and believes she makes the right decision because of the way he presents choices to her ("outher deeth or shame").

Chaucer thus has good reason to use a young woman, not a man, as the most fitting way to represent people as a whole, and particularly as the most fitting way to represent men. Men, in the political realm, are on the whole not powerful agents, but subject to others, some of whom care about them and many of whom think only of their own needs. The young woman, whom all recognize as having little power over the fate of her own body, is in this case the proper allegorical embodiment of men, who, Chaucer seems to say, do not have so much power as they think they do, especially when they agree with those who hold real power over them.[26] The question for them, as for Virginia, is one of what creates their agreement.

The point, then, in calling the *Physician's Tale* an exploration of ideology is to emphasize that when Chaucer told a political story he did not tell it as a story about the outward administration of judgment and justice, as his sources did. In the *Physician's Tale* politics and governance instead become the process of getting people to agree with you; the process of creating consent. Virginius does this through the choices he presents to his daughter. Governance as it most affects us every day, as the *Physician's Tale* illustrates, is not so much a question of good judges and bad judges (although good judges and bad judges are a part of it), but instead a question of who controls the ways we learn to think and what power we have over the people and systems who have this control. If Virginia continued to refuse her father and Virginius cut off his daughter's head despite her protests, this tale would be an easy story of tyranny. Virginia, however, not only did not refuse the person who had the most direct claim to control her actions, she actively agreed with him and his assessment of her own best interest. The story thus presents two kinds of bad governors: in Apius we see the crudely bad, who ultimately has to flee; in Virginius we see the unknowingly bad, who first persuades his daughter that she should die and then persuades the crowd that they should not kill Claudius. Virginius's success at governance lies not in his ability to make judgments but in his ability to describe reality in such a way that others, most particularly his own daughter, come to agree with him. In the *Physician's Tale* such agreement is created so comprehensively that Virginia not only agrees that her father should kill her, she also reaches the same conclusion as her father that they have no other choice. The tale poses the question of what might make a young woman agree to her own death, and then answers it by stressing the way those who have control over her educate her and teach her to understand reality. In doing so, it depicts the processes that create consent.

Notes

I would like to thank Derek Pearsall, John Watkins, and the editors of *The Chaucer Review* for their helpful comments on earlier drafts of this paper.

1. All quotations from *PhyT* are from *The Riverside Chaucer*, ed. Larry D. Benson, 3rd edn. (Boston, 1987).

2. Livy, *From the Founding of the City: Books Three and Four*, trans. B. O. Foster, in *Livy II*, Loeb Classical Library 133 (Cambridge, Mass., 1967), pp. 142–167. All references are to this edition. Guillaume de Lorris and Jean de Meun, *Le Roman de la Rose*, ed. Félix Lecoy, 3 vols. (Paris, 1965–1970), 1:5559–5628. All references are by line number to this edition. There is no conclusive evidence that Chaucer did know Livy's writing—he includes no details from Livy that do not also appear in the *Roman de la Rose*—although the negative case is clearly impossible to prove. For an assessment of the evidence that does exist, see Bruce Harbert, "Chaucer and the Latin Classics," in *Writers and Their Background: Chaucer*, ed. D. Brewer (Athens, Ohio, 1975), pp. 137–153. For the argument that Chaucer knew Bersuire's French translation of Livy, see William H. Brown, Jr., "Chaucer, Livy, and Bersuire: The Roman Materials in *The Physician's Tale*," in *Festschrift for Robert P. Stockwell from His Friends and Colleagues*, ed. Caroline Duncan-Rose and Theo Vennemann (London, 1988), pp. 39–51.

3. See, for example, R. Howard Bloch, "Chaucer's Maiden's Head: *The Physician's Tale* and the Poetics of Virginity," *Representations*, 28 (1989): 113–134, at 113.

4. The quotation is from Nevill Coghill, "Chaucer's Narrative Art in the *Canterbury Tales*," in *Chaucer and Chaucerians: Critical Studies in Middle English Literature*, ed. D. S. Brewer (London, 1966), pp. 114–139, at 126, but he is by no means alone in this opinion. See also, for example, Charles Muscatine, *Poetry and Crisis*

in the Age of Chaucer (Notre Dame, 1972), pp. 138–139; E. Talbot Donaldson, ed., *Chaucer's Poetry* (New York, 1958), p. 927; and Derek Pearsall, *The Canterbury Tales* (London, 1985), pp. 277–279. Others have instead lauded the tale for being bad, which they see as an intentional strategy on the part of Chaucer. See, for example, John Gardner, *The Poetry of Chaucer* (Carbondale, Ill., 1977), p. 297; D. W. Robertson, Jr., "The Physician's Comic Tale," *Chaucer Review*, 23 (1988): 129–139; and Emerson Brown, Jr., "What is Chaucer Doing with the Physician and His Tale?" *Philological Quarterly*, 60 (1981): 129–149.

5. Sheila Delany, "Politics and the Paralysis of Poetic Imagination in *The Physician's Tale*," *Studies in the Age of Chaucer*, 3 (1981): 47–60.

6. Angus Fletcher, "The Sentencing of Virginia in the *Physician's Tale*," *Chaucer Review*, 34 (2000): 300–308.

7. Linda Lomperis, "Unruly Bodies and Ruling Practices: Chaucer's *Physician's Tale* as Socially Symbolic Act," in *Feminist Approaches to the Body in Medieval Literature*, ed. Linda Lomperis and Sarah Stanbury (Philadelphia, 1993), pp. 21–37.

8. Derek Pearsall, *The Life of Geoffrey Chaucer* (Oxford, 1992), pp. 264–266; Jill Mann, *Geoffrey Chaucer* (Atlantic Highlands, N.J., 1991), pp. 143–146; and Lee Patterson, *Chaucer and the Subject of History* (Madison, Wisc., 1991), pp. 368–369. John Hirsh makes a similar argument when he contends that *PhyT* is "virtually" "a modern, secular rewriting of the *Second Nun's Tale*" ("Modern Times: The Discourse of the *Physician's Tale*," *Chaucer Review*, 27 [1993]: 387–395, at p. 390).

9. Anne Middleton, "The *Physician's Tale* and Love's Martyrs: 'Ensamples Mo Than Ten' as a Method in the *Canterbury Tales*," *Chaucer Review*, 8 (1973): 9–32.

10. Gower's version of the story is in *Confessio Amantis*, VII 5131–5306, in G. C. Macaulay, ed., *The Complete Works of John Gower*: II, *The English Works* (Oxford, 1901); Boccaccio's version is in chapter 58 of *De mulieribus claris*, in Giovanni Boccaccio, *Famous Women*, ed. and trans. Virginia Brown (Cambridge, Mass., 2001), pp. 242–249. Like Chaucer, Boccaccio cites Livy but seems to follow Jean de Meun; Gower seems instead to follow Livy's version.

11. Jean de Meun frames the story as an example of evil judges and thus first introduces Apius, who makes his sergeant give false testimony against Virginia, since he knows he can have her no other way (*RR*, 5559–5568). Virginia is thus explicitly the object of Apius's attention while Apius is the subject of the story. Livy, for whom the story is an illustration of the degeneration of justice that preceded and precipitated the Roman revolution of 449 B.C.E., also begins with Apius, who is the subject of both the first sentence and the story: "Appius Claudium virginis plebiae stuprandae libido capit" (Appius Claudius was seized with the desire to debauch a certain maiden belonging to the plebs) (142). He thus makes explicit from the beginning the political point about the struggle between the patriciate and the plebs that he uses the story to illustrate.

12. Brian Lee defends this list, which many have found excessive, on the grounds that "as her possession of a remarkably complete set of virtues is Virginia's most significant characteristic, Chaucer was bound to enumerate them" ("The Position and Purpose of the *Physician's Tale*," *Chaucer Review*, 22 [1987]: 141–160, at p. 142).

13. John Tatlock calls these connections "conjectural but respectable" (*The Development and Chronology of Chaucer's Works* [Gloucester, Mass., 1963], p. 150). Nevill Coghill accepts them as the probable reason Chaucer created the passages, which he finds artistically unnecessary ("Chaucer's Narrative Art," pp. 126–128).

Helen Cooper sums up the current consensus sensibly when she writes: "Since Chaucer's sister-in-law was both the mistress of John of Gaunt and the governess to his daughters, it is hard to believe that the lines on guardianship . . . were written entirely ingenuously; but if Chaucer wrote them with any more specific topical reference in mind, the sentiments are too generalized to enable it to be recovered" (*Oxford Guides to Chaucer: The Canterbury Tales* [Oxford, 1989], p. 248).

14. The *MED* confirms these definitions, but the evidence it provides for general usage is, in this context, circular since its earliest examples come from Chaucer's writing. Chaucer uses the word, in both the more specifically political sense and the more general sense, fifty-nine times in his writing. See *MED*, s.v. *governaunce;* Christopher Cannon, *The Making of Chaucer's English: A Study of Words* (Cambridge, 1998), p. 302.

15. Lee, "Position and Purpose," pp. 141–142. Fletcher also argues for the passage's importance, but on very different grounds: he believes it demonstrates the tale "getting away from the Physician" and thus highlights the problems of authorial authority he argues are central to the tale ("Sentencing of Virginia," 303).

16. Middleton, "*Physician's Tale* and Love's Martyrs," p. 20.

17. In Livy's story, too, all of the action, including a speech by Virginia's fiancé (a character absent from Jean de Meun and Chaucer's stories), takes place in public. For Livy the public nature of the actions is an important part of their point.

18. John Hirsh similarly reads this scene as emphasizing Virginius's distress, but reaches the very different conclusion that "Virginia's death is presented as calamitous less because of the physical violation of her body than because of the pain it will cause her father" ("Modern Times," pp. 387–388).

19. "[S]i change honte por domage" (*RR*, 5602); instead he immediately cut off her head and presented it to the judge before all in the open court ("tantost a la test coupee / et puis au juige presentee / devant touz en plein consitoire," *RR*, 5607–5509).

20. For a different reading of this choice, see Bloch, where he argues that Virginia has already been defiled by the fact of Apius's gaze and is thus already subject to the shame Virginius posits ("Chaucer's Maiden's Head," pp. 116–118).

21. For discussions of Chaucer's use of the story of Jephthah's sacrifice of his child from Judges 11:29–40, explicitly mentioned in lines 240–241, see Middleton, "*Physician's Tale* and Love's Martyrs," pp. 22–23; Lee, "Position and Purpose," p. 156; and Cooper, *Oxford Guides,* p. 248.

22. For the argument that the lines are significant because they are presented in social rather than religious terms, see Hirsh, "Modern Times," pp. 387–388.

23. Middleton, "*Physician's Tale* and Love's Martyrs," pp. 20–22.

24. Fletcher, "Sentencing of Virginia," p. 305.

25. "Traïstres" is the word Jean uses for Apius (*RR*, 5585). Rather than repeating the charge of treachery when describing Apius, Chaucer instead inserts the idea of conspiracy.

26. This technique of using a young woman as the figure who most properly represents all people because of the obvious limitations on her abilities to act freely is one that I believe Chaucer uses often, most notably in *KnT, MLT,* and *CIT.*

PETER W. TRAVIS

Thirteen Ways of Listening to a Fart: Noise in Chaucer's Summoner's Tale

Consonance is a mixture of high and low sound falling pleasantly and uniformly on the ears. Dissonance, on the other hand, is a harsh and unpleasant percussion of two sounds coming to the ear intermingled with each other. For as long as they are unwilling to blend together and each somehow strives to be heard unimpaired, and since one interferes with the other, each is transmitted to the sense unpleasantly.

Boethius[1]

[Music] is herald, for change is inscribed in noise faster than it transforms society. . . . Listening to music is listening to all noise, realizing that its appropriation and control is a reflection of power, that it is essentially political.

Jacques Attali[2]

When we listen to the poetry of Chaucer's words, we listen to meaningful sounds as well as to sounds that are culturally coded to carry little or no meaning. As medieval grammarians explained it, when we attend to *vox articulata literata*, to transcribable and humanly understandable speech, we are also committed to suppressing various kinds of *sonus*—sonic vibrations and percussive explosions that threaten nevertheless to resonate on a subphonemic level of significance. A similar form of discrimination,

Exemplaria: A Journal of Theory in Medieval and Renaissance Studies, Volume 16, Number 2 (Fall 2004): pp. 323–348. © 2004 Pegasus Press.

repression, and purification happens when we listen to music. Music, as medieval and modern theoreticians have maintained, is essentially disso-nance harmonized, sounds mathematically arranged into an order of ulti-mately concordant significance. But this concordance is always achieved by a form of cultural proscription, by determining that certain sounds are insig-nificant noises that if unrepressed would otherwise disrupt the decorum of harmonic design. It is perhaps not surprising that the same prescriptive discriminations between meaningful and anti-meaning sounds in language and in music are also found in traditional models of the body politic, where dissonance generated by a discordant element is likely to be classified as a violation of the authorized harmonics of the orderly state.

In this essay I intend to explore the politics of sound in Chaucer's poetry by focusing specifically on that sonic reality which classical theories of har-mony are so intent on circumscribing, containing, and suppressing. This sonic reality is noise. Noise, as a metaphor of social disorder, historical discord, and aesthetic dissonance, is of course audible throughout western literature. But what is striking in Chaucer's poetry is the degree to which Chaucer fore-grounds noise as a richly problematic and political sign. Rather than merely the antithesis of aesthetic harmony and social *concordia,* explosive noise in Chaucer seems to contain its own counter-harmonics.

The better to hear this counter-harmonics, it is helpful to open the field of auditory aesthetics by acknowledging from the outset that all sounds, even the most dissonant, are culturally coded and humanly significant. A persua-sive demonstration of this general proposition is Richard Leppert's *The Sight of Sound: Music, Representation, and the History of the Body,* a study of musical instruments and music making represented in various eighteenth- and nine-teenth-century paintings. In his first chapter Leppert sets out four premises:

> 1) ... sounds surround us, helping to construct us as human subjects and to locate us in particular social and cultural environments;
> 2) ... sounds produced or manipulated by humans result from conscious acts and hence carry a semantic and discursive charge;
> 3) ... all sounds—even those not produced by humans but 'merely' heard by them—can be read or interpreted;
> 4) ... sounds are a means by which people account for their versions of reality: as it was, is, and/or might be. That is, people do not employ sounds arbitrarily, haphazardly, or unintentionally—though the "intentionally" haphazard may itself constitute an important sort of sonoric discourse.[3]

Leppert's major contention is that the paintings examined in his study are all works of art depicting "the alliances between human desire, on the one hand, and the manipulations of power, on the other"; as such, these paintings instantiate class-inflected social tensions within "sonoric landscapes over stakes that are in every sense always already political."[4] Drawing upon Leppert's premises, my contentions here are similar: I believe that Chaucer's poems are "sonoric landscapes" wherein sound carries a discursive, and indeed political, charge. At certain moments throughout his career Chaucer chose to foreground the noise of history as well as the politics of noisy resistance in order to provide his readers an "auditory" position from which to appreciate noise as a possible herald for change. Within the noisy contexts of Chaucer's verse there are four sonic explosions that are unusually closely related in their scholarly/literary heritage: the canon-like emanation of sound from Sklaundre's trump of brass in *The House of Fame;* the huge "noyse" of political debate in *The Parliament of Fowls;* the massive fart in *The Summoner's Tale;* and the murderous noise made by "Jakke Straw and his meynee" in the narrator's account of the fox chase in *The Nun's Priest's Tale.*

In this paper, while alluding to the other three sonic eruptions, I wish to focus on the hermeneutic problems posed by just one of Chaucer's noisy explosions: the fart detonated at the center of *The Summoner's Tale.* My major purposes in analyzing this fart at such great length are two-fold. I intend to celebrate the fart's power as an extremely complex political sign. Furthermore, by arguing against a narrowly historical decryption of this fart, I want to shift our hermeneutics away from the restraints of premature allegorical closure and move in the direction of allowing a text to contain and radiate all the contradictory meanings and associations that come to the critic's mind.

As is well known, in *The Summoner's Tale* a friar named John has for many years been bilking a sick freeholder named Thomas, all the while promising to restore him to good health via the ardent prayers of his brethren in the friary. Midway through the tale, Thomas's long-repressed ire is so ready to explode that he finally promises the friar he will give him a treasured gift, but only on one condition: that he divide the gift evenly among all the members of his convent. Groping eagerly in Thomas's sickbed under the "clifte" of Thomas's "buttok" until he reaches Thomas's "tuwel," Friar John receives the gift directly into his hand: "Ther nys no capul, drawynge in a cart, / That myghte have lete a fart of swich a soun" (*CT* 3.2150–51).[5] The friar is instantly nonplussed—not, as one would expect, by the "material" gift itself, but rather by the impossibility of its equal division. Intent on keeping his word, however, he anxiously carries his metaphysical conundrum from Thomas's house all the way to the manor house of the "lord of that village" (*CT* 3.2165). Presented with this baffling sophistical problem in "ars-metrike[s]" (CT 3.2222), everyone in the seigniorial household—lord, wife, squire, and "ech man" (*CT* 3.2287)—is invited to gloss the churl's *impossibilium.*

The lord proceeds to process the difficulties of the dilemma at length, both intensively and extensively. That is, his thoughts begin in a pre-linguistic silence of internal deliberation (*CT* 3.2218–27); they then suddenly explode into public discourse with the locution "Lo . . . !" (*CT* 3.2228); thereafter, expanding into open air, his words amplify to such a pitch that each of his last three utterances is graced by editors with an exclamation mark (*CT* 3.2228–42):

> The lord sat stille as he were in a traunce,
> And in his herte he rolled up and doun,
> "How hadde this cherl ymaginacioun
> To shewe swich a probleme to the frere?
> Nevere erst er now herde I of swich mateere.
> I trowe the devel putte it in his mynde.
> In ars-metrike shal ther no man fynde,
> Biforn this day, of swich a question.
> Who sholde make a demonstracioun
> That every man shold have yliche his part
> As of the soun or savour of a fart?
> O nyce, proude cherle, I shrewe his face!
> Lo, sires," quod the lord, "with harde grace!
> Who evere herde of swiche a thyng er now?
> To every man ylike? Tel me how.
> It is an inpossible, it may nat be.
> Ey, nyce cherl, God lete him nevere thee!
> The rumblynge of a fart, and every soun,
> Nis but of eir reverberacioun,
> And evere it wasteth litel and litel awey.
> Ther is no man kan deemen, by my fey,
> If that it were departed equally.
> What, lo, my cherl, lo, yet how shrewedly,
> Unto my confessour to-day he spak!
> I holde hym certeyn a demonyak!
> Now ete youre mete, and lat the cherl go pleye;
> Lat hym go honge hymself a devel weye!"

CT 3.2216–42

Duplicating the interior/exterior production of Thomas's rude *sonus* at the level of *vox*, the lord's corporeal rumblings and vocal ventilations eventually come to naught, and so it is left to his ingenious squire to find a solution to the friar's perplexing problem.

A twelve-spoked cartwheel, he suggests, needs to be positioned under the nostrils of the friary's twelve brothers spaced equidistantly around its rim. With Thomas donating his sonic gift at the wheel's hub, the twelve fraternal scholars will be able to receive equally the fart's sound and odor. But, the squire insists, Friar John in all fairness should be placed directly under the "nave," and there receive the fart's "firste fruyt, as resoun is" (*CT* 3.2277). And on this note, *The Summoner's Tale* comes to its end, leaving the image of the actualization of the equitable division of this diabolical gift to resonate in the reader's mind.

For several decades of Chaucer criticism *The Summoner's Tale* has been appreciated as a brilliant example of anti-mendicant satire, which of course it is. However, after the publication of Lee Patterson's *Chaucer and the Subject of History* in 1991, it has become apparent that the closing scenes of the tale also give expression to certain political agendas that violently confronted each other in the 1381 Uprising. Audible in the language attending Thomas's ironized gift, Patterson discovers, is the rebels' cry for material equality: "every man shold have yliche his part" (*CT* 3.2227). Similarly, the lord's response to Thomas's demand reiterates upper-class incomprehension and disbelief: "To every man ylike? Tel me how. / It is an inpossible; it may nat be" (*CT* 3.2230–31). Just as a fart cannot be "departed equally," neither, according to the dominant social classes, can the goods of this world. For Patterson, this scene provides a "brief allegory" of the seigniorial reactions to peasant demands articulated in the Uprising. However, once Chaucer takes cognizance of these demands, he apparently retreats from considering their implications. That is, once the squire offers his ingenious cartwheel solution, we are witnessing, according to Patterson, the "translation of Thomas's challenge back into the dehistoricizing language of antifraternal discourse."[6] This translation works at two levels. It dramatizes the historical phenomenon of the rebels' political demands being "displaced and finally appropriated to the traditional structure of medieval society"; it also serves as "an allegory of Chaucer's own practice of articulating but finally containing the voice of political protest."[7] And this containment, Patterson insists, is final. As he did at the end of *The Miller's Tale* (Chaucer's boldest foray into radical politics, according to Patterson), here at the end of *The Summoner's Tale* the poet retreats into a position he never again leaves: a politically unmarked and "socially undetermined subjectivity . . . that stands apart from *all* forms of class consciousness."[8]

Patterson's argument that *The Summoner's Tale* contains a rare moment where Chaucer can be observed, if not directly naming the most disquieting historical event in his lifetime, at least evoking that rebellion by citing key words in its political manifestos, marks a significant turn in the general mentalité of Chaucer criticism. Traditionally seen as either timelessly apolitical or politically indistinguishable from his conservative acquaintances, Chaucer may indeed be revealing within these scenes a moment of "radical" political sympathy. But, then again, he may not. Instead of revealing his own singularly personal reading of the Revolt, he may be more interested as a poet in transforming the fart's sonoric environs into a cornucopian text embodying a rich array of interpretative positions.

Persuaded entirely by Patterson's insistence that the ending of *The Summoner's Tale* directly evokes dominant discourses surrounding the Revolt, I want to amplify the range of critical listening by tuning into a wider variety of locutions that may all be encoded in this dense noise. To understand the fart in as nuanced a fashion as possible, it is helpful to recall that in Chaucer's *The House of Fame* history is disclosed to be nothing but sounds—percussive sounds emanating from history's actors, mingled with percussive sounds emanating from history's reporters. The sonic chaos of the House of Fame combined with the sonic chaos of the House of Rumor proves that all those who declaim the meaning of history are also contributors to history's making; consequently, history itself is nothing more nor less than a contestation of conflicting voices, a concatenation of sounds. In a strikingly similar fashion, Steven Justice in his excellent study *Writing and Rebellion: England in 1381* arrives at a determination parallel to that advanced by Chaucer in *The House of Fame*. The Peasants' Revolt of 1381, Justice finds, was in no small part an extended battle over the meaning of verbal utterances, with the peasants striving to make their voices audible and recordable as human voices, and the chroniclers managing wherever possible to reduce the rebels' locutions to the level of noise and inarticulate sounds. The chroniclers' "trope of noise," writes Justice, was "there to deny, take away, obscure, and otherwise render inaudible anything the rebels might have *said*—by speech, script, or purposeful action—and jumble all their words and actions into undifferentiated *sound*" (emphases in the original).[9] Thus the central problem in *The Summoner's Tale*, I suggest, is not simply the political intention of a rebellious sound, but, as with the Revolt itself, the politics of its aural reception and aural repression.

Thus a major part of the interpretative task posed by Thomas's fart is to appreciate its complexity as a noise that invokes, contains, and projects a concatenation of historical words, sounds, and actions. And also embedded in the significance of this noise, I insist, are the explanatory glosses provided by Thomas, Friar John, and the village lord. These glozing activities encircling the fart continue to radiate outward, embracing the figure of the squire, the figures of the twelve friars, and then (beyond the rim of the *Tale*) all those who strive to interpret the great noise at its center. The general critical strategies I am advancing thus differ from Patterson's methods of historical and biographical allegoresis. In its presumption that Chaucer takes one "radical" look at "history" and then returns to "literature" and the safe haven of a "socially undetermined subjectivity," Patterson's allegory, while insightful, remains cautiously circumscribed and self-contained. Or, to put it another way, Patterson compresses the signifying parameters of the fart in *The Summoner's Tale* into what we can infer to be true about Chaucer's political persuasions as they relate to specifically cited social agendas contested in the Revolt. My own concerns are in fact not focused upon Chaucer's privately held political beliefs (which may well be impossible to locate), but rather upon the shared hermeneutics of historical dissonance provided by this publicly repeated fart, a hermeneutics, I have suggested, that is embodied in the noise itself as well as in the circular image of the wheel that contains it.

The cartwheel surrounding the fart is semiotically as important as the noise released at its center. Throughout the Middle Ages the circle's geometric perfection served as an icon of the harmonic perfections of music, human or divine. In Martianus Capella's *The Marriage of Mercury and Philology*, for example, the liberal arts figure of Harmony (i.e., Music) carries a shield that is "circular overall, with many inner circles," and from these circles emanates the enchanting music of the spheres[10] The figure of the circle was also closely associated with the scientific understanding of sound itself, the basic element of both music and language. In *De musica*, Boethius famously compares the production and dispersion of a sound to the movement of concentric circles in a pond formed by a stone thrown into its center:

> First it causes a wave in a very small circle; then it disperses clusters of waves into larger circles, and so on until the motion, exhausted by the spreading out of waves, dies away. The latter, wider wave is always diffused by a weaker impulse. Now if something should impede the spreading waves, the same motion rebounds immediately, and it makes new circles by the same undulations as at the center whence it originated.[11]

Medieval poets rang many changes on Boethius's foundational sonic image. Dante, for example, in the opening lines of *Paradiso* 14, describes the sound waves of St. Thomas's voice repercussing from the center of his mind to its rim and then back again:

> Dal centro al cerchio, e sì dal cerchio al centro,
>   movesi l'acqua in un ritondo vaso,
>   secondo ch'è percossa fuori o dentro:
> ne la mia mente fé sùbito caso
>   questo ch'io dico, sì come si tacque
>   la glorïosa vita Tommaso. . . .

Paradiso 14.1–6

> From centre to rim, and again from rim to centre, the water in
> a round vessel moves, according as it is struck from without or
> within; this, as I tell it, dropped suddenly into my mind as soon as
> the glorious living soul of Thomas was silent.[12]

While the collision of waves produced by percussions both "from without and
from within" might have resulted in a tempest of rough waters, the effect of these
sanctified sounds blending in the "ritondo vaso" of Dante's mind proves to be
the purest of spiritual harmonies. Such harmony is appropriate, for St. Thomas
and Dante are presently within the sphere of the sun, the site of mathematical
order, reason, and harmony. However, Dante next ascends to the heaven of
Mars, the planet of discord par excellence. But even here harmony ultimately
reigns. While these martial cantos are rife with allusions to historical dissonance, most notably the cacophonies of Florentine urban violence recounted
in Canto 16, Dante manages to hear, quite amazingly, an ineffable melody
"which held me rapt, though I followed not the hymn" (*Paradiso* 14.122–23).
The music's ultimate source proves to be Christ's crucified body imposed upon
a cross of stars intersecting the dome of heaven, a "sweet lyre" whose "holy
strings" are invisibly strummed by the "right hand of heaven" (*Paradiso* 15.5–6).
As Jeffrey Schnapp explains in his erudite study of these "historical" cantos,
The Transfiguration of History in the Center of Dante's Paradise, the invisible
instrument of Christ's body serves as "a scandalous countersign to anarchic
discord of the human city," staging a utopian integration of the "heterogeneous
strings of the city of man into the transcendent unity of the sign of Christ in
anticipation of history's end.[13] Counterposing the gently percussive words of
St. Thomas with the percussive instrument of Christ's sweet passion, and the
"ritondo vaso" of Dante's mind with the circles of the heavenly spheres, Dante's
Christian faith manages to hear, even in the din of urban revolt and in the
clamor of historical dissonance, the harmonies of divine love.

But Chaucer hears nothing of the kind. *The House of Fame,* to consider
briefly one important example, is a poem of a thousand noises. In many
ways a sustained response to the transcendent harmonies of Dante's audi-
tion of salvation history in the *Commedia, The House of Fame* is a serio-comic
representation of Chaucer's skeptical reading of political history as a cha-
otic mix of sounds that refuse to blend together into any harmonic design.
To advance his proposition that history is noise, Chaucer employs the Boethian stone-in-water trope, but in a radically different way from Dante. As
he ascends into the stratosphere in *The House of Fame,* Geoffrey is instructed
by his eagle-mentor that all human speech is created by an act of percussion the effects of which amplify in space like the concentric circles formed
by a stone thrown into water. By the end of the eagle's protracted lecture,
Geoffrey is well prepared to bear aural witness to the ideal realization of

Boethius's sonic circles in the divine harmonies of the heavenly spheres. Instead, however, his ears are suddenly assaulted by a noise of such magnitude that even at a mile's distance he finds its impact deafening. "[W]hat soun is it lyk?" asks the quizzical eagle, and Geoffrey answers:

> "Peter, lyk betynge of the see,"
> Quod y, "ayen the roches holowe,
> Whan tempest doth the shippes swalowe,
> And lat a man stonde, out of doute,
> A myle thens, and here hyt route;
> Or elles lyk the last humblynge
> After the clappe of a thundringe,
> Whan Joves hath the air ybete.
> But yt doth me for fere swete."

HF 1034–1042

Notwithstanding Boethius's authoritative pronouncement that "sound is fainter to someone standing at a distance," the noise emanating from the House of Fame, even a mile away, is so overwhelming that Geoffrey finds he can describe it only by analogy—like an angry tempest beating against rocks, or else like thunder "Whan Joves hath the air ybete." In marked contrast to the limpid wavelets of Boethius's undulating pool and the plangent rings of Dante's aural memory, these cataclysmic "tidyngs" attack the human auditor with the aggressive force of an oceanic typhoon.

Chaucer twice again uses the Boethian trope to dramatize the force of history, both past and present, as a militant and dangerous noise. Having left the pandemonium of classical history in the House of Fame, Geoffrey hears the noise of present-day history emanating from the House of Rumour, a spinning airborne labyrinth of ever-shifting oral ejaculations that together make such a volume of concentrated sound that the impact is audible halfway around the world. If heard on earth, Geoffrey realizes, the percussive effect of this noise would be as powerful as the blast of a cannon, even to the distant listener:

> And therout com so gret a noyse
> That, had hyt stonden upon Oyse,
> Men myghte hyt han herd esely
> To Rome, y trowe sikerly.
> And the noyse which that I herde,
> For al the world ryght so hyt ferde
> As dooth the rowtynge of the ston
> That from th'engyn ys leten gon.

HF 1927–1934

Chaucer captures the percussive force of history once again, this time in the very center of the House of Fame, as Aeolus's trumpet of brass blasts out the noxious tidings of Sklaundre, or ill-fame, "[a]s swifte as pelet out of gonne":

> [Aeolous] gan this trumpe for to blowe,
> As al the world shulde overthrowe,
> That thrughout every regioun
> Wente this foule trumpes soun,
> As swifte as pelet out of gonne
> Whan fyr is in the poudre ronne.
> And such a smoke gan out wende
> Out of his foule trumpes ende,
> Blak, bloo, grenyssh, swartish red,
> As doth where that men melte led,
> Loo, al on high fro the tuel.
> And therto oo thing saugh I wel,
> That the ferther that hit ran,
> The gretter wexen hit began,
> As dooth the ryver from a welle,
> And hyt stank as the pit of helle.

HF 1639–1654

Boethius's dropped stone has now been transformed into a militant projectile of aural destruction. Shot through an odiferous cannon, the pellet explodes with such force from the cannon's "tuel" (end-hole) that the scope of its sonic boom increases, *contra* Boethius, the further it travels. In the sound-wars of *The House of Fame*, the dissonance of history clearly undoes the consonance of harmony at every turn.

But does this mean that for Chaucer the noise of history defies human understanding, or that it is devoid of contemporary political significance? I think not. Consider briefly a second example. Chaucer's *The Parliament of Fowls* is framed by circles of music-making harmony, from the *musica mundana* of the heavenly spheres to the "roundel" sung by the mating birds at the poem's end. But at the poem's center there is a "huge . . . noyse" (*PF* 312), the source of which turns out to be a raucous parley held on St. Valentine's day among a community of birds. Approaching the noise, Geoffrey discovers that there are several sociolects audible in the debate, ranging from the animaloid squawks of the lowest orders, to the bourgeois parlance of the middle class, to the elegant poetry of the aristocrats. But which class and whose desires are least disruptive of the harmony, the "commune profyt," of the state? The lower-class birds may be "more loudly discordant and more gross," writes conservative critic David Chamberlain but, he continues, "the tercels are the center of interest, they are socially more obliged to create 'pes' and 'accord', and yet they are the 'welle' of discord, the *contrary of the spheres*."[14] A critical position which hears the *voces populi* as if they were positively aligned with the music of the spheres would thus seem to place the poem's political sympathies, at least in part, with the commoners. And indeed, because the lower-class birds' complaints verge on active rebellion, several recent studies have suggested that the class debate in *The Parliament of Fowls* alludes directly even though perhaps ambivalently to the social discontent that gave rise to the Peasants' Revolt of 1381.[15]

The only place in his entire corpus where Chaucer unambiguously cites the Peasants' Revolt, however, is in the middle of his rhetorical tour de force, the fox chase in *The Nun's Priest's Tale*. The entire barnyard world makes raucous noise in its collective pursuit of the fox—men, women, dogs, cow, calf, hogs, ducks crying, geese flying, bees swarming, horns blowing, "howp[ing]" and "powp[ing]"—"It semed as that hevene sholde falle" (*CT* 7.3374–3401). Yet in the the middle of this carnival of sounds, the narrator suddenly exclaims:

So hydous was the noyse, a, benedicitee!
Certes, he Jakke Straw and his meynee
Ne made nevere shoutes half so shrille
Whan that they wolden. any Flemyng kille,
As thilke day was maad upon the fox.

CT 7.3393–3397

The narrator's comparing the noise of those pursuing the fox to the noise made by "Jakke Strawe and his meynee" as they slaughtered Flemings is one of the most perplexing tonal shifts in all of Chaucer's poetry. And yet, in light of Chaucer's recurring association of noise with social resistance and historical tidings, the disequlibrating auditory experience of political revolution within all these other sounds should not be a complete surprise. What *The Nun's Priest's Tale* uniquely denies its readers is the support of an icon that may be found in Chaucer's other sonoric landscapes: an encircling wheel that provides a measure of interpretative control.

It is the particular variant of this icon, the cartwheel of *The Summoner's Tale*, that I now wish to honor. It obviously works somewhat like the margins of Boethius's pool and the "cerchio" of Dante's mind; it invokes the outermost rim of the heavenly spheres, the *primum mobile;* it attempts to contain the centrifugal circles of "air ybroke," returning its own centripetal locutions back toward the center. Yet what is most distinctive about this wheel is its twelve-spoked design (Dante's starcrossed orb of heaven may be a distant analogue), and the position of twelve friar-scholars as exegetical recipients of the great rushing of wind.

Thus, in deference to Chaucer's iconic and subphonemic instructions, I will provide in the next few pages the same number of contending positions vis-à-vis the fart that the image of the twelve-spoked cartwheel invites and parodies. My major purpose in defining these twelve positions is to demonstrate how the *vox confusa* of the Revolt, resisting the codifications of any single-minded allegoresis, discovers much of its meaning in the dissonance among its multifarious interpreters, including the rebel-actors themselves. The result, inevitably, is a wide variety of locutions, all of them potentially "political," all pertinent to Thomas's disruptive fart. After completing the hermeneutic circle of these twelve readings, I will then attempt to answer a question that seems to hover at the cartwheel's very center: is there any central theme that succeeds in harmonizing the dissonant readings of a noise which by its very nature resists the hegemonic politics of critical harmony? In other words, is there a thirteenth way of listening to this fart?

• • •

Spoke One. Thomas, the fart's originator, appears to be a peasant: at least he is called a "cherl" a total of ten times in the *Tale*. But what is his actual social status, and does it matter? All material evidence indicates that he is neither poor nor indentured, but rather an independent and rather wealthy freeholder who has his own "meynee" (*CT* 3.2156). Initially, therefore, it seems unlikely that Thomas would identify himself with the demands expressed in the Peasants' Revolt for personal freedom and material equality. However, as Justice illustrates in *Writing and Rebellion,* a great many of the insurgents were already freeholders whose public insistence that peasants be given *libertas* was in certain ways a symbolic rallying cry rather than an economic program.[16] In an act of free self-naming, the rebels collectively identified themselves as peasants, choosing, Justice explains, "the rural laboring class . . . as a focus around which they could arrange diverse ambitions."[17] Thus some of the tensions at the center of the Peasant's Revolt are dramatically reflected in the political/linguistic issue of Thomas's being properly, or improperly, called a "cherl."

• • •

Spoke Two. As Anne Hudson has argued in *The Premature Reformation,* twentieth-century readings of Wycliffite thought as providing a proto-communist theory of property are readings based on scant evidence. Assuredly, Wyclif believed that "the just" would wish to share their spiritual or temporal goods with others, but these "just" are for Wyclif otherworldly conceptions of perfect charity rather than human individuals living on earth.[18] Thus, to smell a Marxist in the Lollard wind of *The Summoner's Tale* appears to be an act of creative misprision. Nevertheless, Wyclif's critique of the materialism of the endowed church coincided with the rebels' belief, recorded in the *Anonimalle Chronicle,* that "the goods of holy church should not be in the hands of . . . any churchmen, but that they should have their sustenance alone, and the rest of their goods should be divided among parishioners."[19] Thus the ideal of a redistribution of goods from church to parish could easily have been generalized, in the minds of some rebels, into a more radical equalization of *all* material wealth.

• • •

Spoke Three. As Wendy Scase has demonstrated in *Piers Plowman and the New Anti-Clericalism,* extremely heated debates raged among monks, friars, and seculars in the late fourteenth century as to whether or not the ideal of commonly held property forbade or legitimized a religious orders' accumulation of wealth.[20] Chaucer's satire not only addresses this urgent contemporary issue, I suggest, but also gives voice to one of the rebels' major complaints, ecclesiastical materialism. Calling the first partition of Thomas's fart the "firste fruyt" is, of course, an indelicate allusion to the long tradition of tithing. Thus Patterson may well be mistaken in assuming that the ending of *The Summoner's Tale* effects a "translation of Thomas's challenge back into the dehistoricizing language of antifraternal discourse."[21] Only a purely formalist sensibility (which Patterson strenuously eschews) should be able to view all forms of anti-mendicant satire as belonging to a "literary," "dehistoricizing," and "apolitical" genre. In certain local contexts, in other words, pieces of antifraternal satire such as *The Summoner's Tale* may well be targeted against specific abuses, such as those ecclesiastical excesses that were seen as one cause catalyzing the Peasants' Revolt.

• • •

Spoke Four. In an excellent study of the social classes of *The Summoner's Tale,* Linda Georgianna reveals how the friar's attempt to sustain with Thomas a "horizontal," cash-nexus, and secular "brotherhood" is a modernizing social gesture. This self-serving attempt at bourgeois social leveling is itself a sullying of the penitential association to which both Thomas and his wife belong, a lay confraternity attached to Friar John's convent.[22] By *Tale's* end, however, both spiritual and social economies are turned inside out: first, by the hierarchical positioning of the fart (the "cherl" on top); and then by "the vertical relations of older feudal practices" in the lord's manor, where, for example, gifts are given instead of money as signs of personal esteem.[23] Thus vertical, horizontal, spiritual, material, collective, personal, feudal, and capitalist dynamics are all mingled inside the social exegetics and body language of this increasingly complicated "political" fart.

• • •

Spoke Five. For more than thirty years, the twelve-part division of the fart has been interpreted as a profanation of the iconographic representations of the descent of the Holy Spirit to the twelve apostles at Pentecost.[24] The lower-body language of the fart is undoubtedly a parody of the Holy Spirit's ghostly afflatus, that great rushing of wind with tongues of fire. But to what degree are the two utterances, one sacred (*vox dei*) and the other profane (*vox populi*), actually opposed to each other? And to what degree is the parody a top-down critique of the material by the spiritual? For some auditors, it may indeed be possible to hear in Thomas's *sermo humilis* the voice of one utopian ideal of *communitas* speaking to another, the community of saints unified in the body of Christ. In Thomas's great rushing of wind, it may even be possible to hear reverberations of John Ball's famous revolutionary question: 'Whanne Adam dalfe and Eve span, / Who was þanne a gentil man?"[25] At any rate, because the discourses of Chaucer's doubting Thomas and the Holy Spirit are equally non-verbal and glossolalic, both discourses require an unusual degree of auditory creativity to calibrate the parodic interplay between their political and their anagogic meanings.

• • •

Spoke Six. Although it may at first seem blasphemous, the polyvalence of Thomas's fart in this regard is strikingly similar to the polyvalence of Christ's body as it was represented and understood in the late Middle Ages. In her study of the role of Christ's body in the city of York and especially in the York mystery plays, Sarah Beckwith provides a compressed outline of its many competing registers:

> [T]he body of Christ . . . does not simply operate according to static binary opposition: divinity versus humanity. Rather it catches in its network of association a range of oppositions that, because they are mutually constructed through the way the body of Christ conflates them, provide nuance, add to, and so defer any final signification. Christ's body alludes to numerous oppositions: inner and outer, transcendent and immanent, spirit and flesh, male and female, left and right, up and down, noisy and silent, just and unjust, passive and active, noumenal and phenomenal, public and private, hierarchical and collective, unified and multiplicitous, and so on.[26]

Similarly, it could be argued that the network of associations inhering in and adhering to the fart of The Summoner's Tale is a complex semiotic site embracing oppositions whose relative significance is constantly being contested and revalorized.

• • •

Spoke Seven. Now that we are halfway around the hermeneutical circle, we should honor the intellectual lightheadedness of the entire enterprise, for part of the fart-and-cartwheel's satiric thrust is obviously directed against *any* form of elevated discourse. The "demonstratioun" of the solution to this "probleme" in posterior analytics is clearly a send-up of scholastic choplogic, of all manner of "ars-metrikes," and of liberal-arts learning in general. The lord's squire is a "kervere" who, like Plato's philosopher-king, believes it is possible to cut Reality at the joints: thus the lord's educated household praises him for speaking "As wel as Euclide [dide] or Ptholomee" (*CT* 3.2289). English peasants, however, would typically have responded by using less abstract, but equally expressive, language. Among the medieval *illiterati*, as Aron Gurevich has shown, the "disinclination for abstract concepts" was by no means a deficiency, but rather a conscious way of organizing experience within a less generalized and socially elevated discourse.[27] The fart thus can be seen as a noise organizing peasant experience and expressing their revolutionary sentiments in a lower yet extremely powerful linguistic register.

• • •

Spoke Eight. The fart's rhetorical strains of opposition between material substance and immaterial essence are also embodied in the linguistic logic of the tale's central pun. A medieval French verbal game helps make the point:

> DEMANDE. Comment partiroit on une vesse en douze parties?
> RESPONSE. Faittes une vesse sur le moieul d'une roe, et douze personnes ayent chascun son nez aux xii trous, et par ainsi chascun en ara sa part.

> QUESTION: How can one divide a fart into twelve parts?
> ANSWER: Make the fart in the middle of a wheel, with twelve people, each with his nose between the twelve spokes (lit: in the twelve holes), so that each shall thus get his share.[28]

In *The Summoner's Tale*, as Richard Firth Green has insightfully suggested,[29] Chaucer may be using a similar English riddle, "How do you part a farthing into twelve?" Mindful that a farthing is next to worthless—literally a penny cut into fourths—the traditional respondent is expected to have no answer.

Thomas, however, responds to Friar John's question "What is a ferthyng worth parted in twelve?" (*CT* 3.1967) by brilliantly transposing the meaning of "ferthyng" from the economic to the meta-physical. The English courtly audience, undoubtedly familiar with the riddle (the French analogue is found in a collection of courtly verbal games), would have appreciated the cleverness of this intellectual joke. But would they also have appreciated the novel "ymaginacioun" of its churlish author, who "shrewedly" has created a "question" which no one had heard "Biforn this day"? Chaucer is careful to model at least two responses for his readers: either the so-called peasant is stupid, or he is extremely intelligent. The village lord's first explanation is that Thomas was momentarily possessed by a demon: "I trowe the devel putte it in his mynde." But once the peasant's problem is solved, all (except for the silent friar) agree that "subtiltee / And heigh wit made hym speken as he spak; / He nys no fool, ne no demonyak" (*CT* 3.2290–92). Thomas, the churlish freeholder, ultimately comes across as a devilishly clever intellectual.

• • •

Spoke Nine. If this landed freeholder has the intellectual subtlety to pose a highly sophisticated problem concerning the equal division of a sound, we should recall that Chaucer himself had been extensively trained, as had all his reasonably well-educated readers, in precisely how to determine whether a musical tone (which is, admittedly, different from a single sound) is evenly divisible. This problem and its rational, mathematical solution constitute the entirety of book 3 of Boethius's *De Musica*, of which I quote a very small part:

> The first numbers containing the tone are 8 and 9. But since these follow each other in natural sequence in such a way that there is no mean number between them, I multiply both these numbers by two, which, of course, is the smallest I can use. This makes 16 and 18. Between these a number, 17, falls naturally. Thus 18:16 is a tone, but 18 compared to 17 contains the latter wholly plus 1/17 part of it. Now 1/17 part is naturally smaller than 1/16 part, so the ratio contained in the numbers 16 and 17 is larger than that between 17 and 18. Let these numbers be set out in this manner: let 16 be A, 17 C, and 18 B. . . .
>
> But since the ratio 18:17 follows next after 17:16, we should see whether, multiplied by two, it will not fill a tone. The term 18 contains 17 plus one part of 17. So if we produce another number in relation to 18 with the same ratio that 18 has to 17, it will be 19 and 1/17 part. But if we produce a number situated in the sesquioctave ratio in relation to the term 17, it will make 19 and 1/8

part. An eighth part is larger than a seventeenth part, so the ratio of numbers 17 and 19 1/8 is larger than that comprised of 17 and 19 1/17 (which, of course, consists of two continuous 18:17 ratios). Thus, two continuous ratios of 18:17 are seen not to complete one tone. Therefore, 18:17 is not a half tone, since these terms, when duplicated, do not fill a whole; they do not form halves, for a half, when doubled, is always equal to that of which it is half.[30]

Considering the difficulty of determining whether a single tone can be divided equally, it is no wonder that dividing into twelve equal parts the discontinuous ratios of an atonal, or multitonal, noise would seem an *impossibilium* to all but the most brilliant, and perhaps hubristic, medieval scholars.

• • •

Spoke Ten. But a fourteenth-century intellectual interested in parts and wholes might ask, would any sound so divided be *part* of a sound or a *full* sound? The branch of medieval philosophy known as mereology, the study of parts and wholes, would take such an issue into the deepest recesses of logic, and then into physics, metaphysics, and theology. To keep matters uncomplicated, let us simply turn to *The Consolation of Philosophy.* Lady Philosophy, by way of emphasizing that worldly wealth is a finite good as opposed to the limitless nature of the *summum bonum,* asserts that it is impossible to distribute one's riches perfectly. She illustrates her precept by using a familiar analogy: "And certes a voys al hool (that is to seyn, withouten amenusynge [diminution]) fulfilleth togydre the herynge of moche folk. But certes your rychesses ne mowen noght passen unto moche folk withouten amenusynge; and whan they ben apassed [have passed away], nedes they maken hem pore that forgoon tho rychesses."[31] In other words, whereas worldly wealth is diminished in proportion to the number of individuals who divide it, this is not true of the Platonic Absolute, the *summum bonum:* just as all auditors hear equally "a voys al hool," so may all share equally in the Idea of the Good.[32]

• • •

Spoke Eleven. As a requital to Boethius's Platonic defense of his family property, it is useful to recall that it is the "savour" of Thomas's fart, as well as the "soun," that must be divided equally. Mindful of the economic and political symbolism of eating in literature (and in life), the emphasis in *The Summoner's Tale* upon the provision and consumption of food, as the friar moves from Thomas's table to his lord's table, is significant. The lord of the village dismisses the posed question of social/material equality by calling the friar to his meal: "Now ete youre mete, and lat the cherl go pleye" (*CT*

3.2241). The relationship of the squire to his lord is also expressed via food: the squire's foremost duty is to "karf[en] his [lordes] mete" (*CT* 3.2244). With all of this concentration on the social semiotics of the service of food, the *qualitas* of the fart's "savour" may be an incontrovertible sign of its owner's ill-health or well-being. Since Thomas's major complaint is that he has been physically sick for years, the symptomatic "stynk" of his fart provides an unpleasant critique of the English economic body.

•••

Spoke Twelve. After circling through these eleven theoretical positions, we need to re-emphasize the fart's powers of self-reification: the fart is a fart is a fart, and as a literal fart it asks that it be read literally. Yet it is difficult, perhaps impossible, to interpret even a fart exclusively *ad litteram*. As Richard Leppert reminds us, "sounds produced or manipulated by humans result from conscious acts and hence carry a semantic and discursive charge."[33] The discursive charge of this fart is especially redolent because it is conceived within a literary register, that of the Christian pilgrimage, which is ideally fart-free. In an interview dwelling on the genre of the Western, Mel Brooks was asked about his movie *Blazing Saddles:* "What was the point of the vulgarity—the farting scene, for example?" Brooks answers, "The farts were the point of the farting scene":

> For 75 years these big, hairy brutes have been smashing their fists into each other's faces and blasting each other full of holes with six-guns, but in all that time, not one has had the courage to produce a fart. I think that's funny. I think the farting scene in *Blazing Saddles* is funny because farts in our world are funny. Farts are a repressed minority. The mouth gets to say all kinds of things, but the other place is supposed to keep quiet. But maybe our lower colons have something interesting to say. Maybe we should listen to them. Farts are human, more human than a lot of people I know. I think we should bring them out of the water closet and into the parlor, and that's what I did in *Blazing Saddles.*[34]

•••

By bringing his political fart to the lord's parlor and the scholars' critical wheel, Chaucer thus appears to be saying many things—or, more precisely, he is providing a complex sonic environment wherein many things may be said at once about this lower-order speech act. As in *The House of Fame,* where the sounds of history are glossed by secondary sounds whose admixtures then appear as the chronicled tidings of the *auctoritates,* so here a dozen viable glosses interchange with Thomas's authorial intent, which is itself a gloss, a fusion of *sonus* and *vox*. Resonating at such length in the tale (a total of 148 lines), Thomas's long-winded fart thus refuses any univocal significance—be it physiological, characterological, musicological, satiric, Marxian, folkloric, iconographic, parodistic, or historicist. In its resistance to monotonal analysis, it provokes the construction of a nuanced acoustics hypersensitive to a multitude of sounds intermeshed with a multitude of other sounds—linguistic and sub-linguistic, musical and cacophonous, classical and contemporary, social, political, artistic, religious and scholarly. Yet for all this dissonance, Chaucer, I maintain, is committed to positioning his readers so that they may not only hear the many individual and overlapping sounds compressed into this noise but also be ready to critique the counter-harmonic significance of disruptive social dissonance wherever it may be heard.

One of Mikhail Bakhtin's primary purposes in his extensive explorations of "heterglossia," a term with which he attempts to define a culture's discourse at any moment in its history, was to understand the political forces that are always at play in language:

> [A]t any given moment of its historical existence, language is heterglot from top to bottom: it represents the co-existence of socio-ideological contradictions between the present and the past, between differing epochs of the past, between different socio-ideological groups in the present, between tendencies, schools, circles and so forth, all given in bodily form.[35]

Given in bodily form, the fart in *The Summoner's Tale* is heterglot from top to bottom, a complex and contentious mixture of physical, political, social, clerical and intellectual sounds. Or, to be more precise, it is heterglot from bottom to top, for as Bakhtin is careful to emphasize, as it exists in *history* heteroglossia is rarely an egalitarian, horizontal continuum of contending speech forms, but rather a dialogic interaction among socially unequal registers in which prestige languages are persistently attempting to maintain and extend their control. In some forms of *literature*, however, and in certain social activities ranging from carnival celebration to political revolution, lower-order discourse at least momentarily contests the dominant forms of political hegemony and provides a rereading of reality from a perspective often proscribed from speaking.[36]

A rereading of contemporary political realities, I believe, is what Chaucer's literary fart allows. The fart is eloquent in part because it is a proscribed *sonus* whose nether-orifice origin parodies all the higher-orifice *voces* that normally control and determine meaning.[37] Equally important, the heterglot fart undercuts the power of any single discourse to dominate the significance of *any* historical event, and of *any* political rebellion, for this "speech act" is the site of so many "socio-ideological contradictions" that it may well be the contradictions themselves that Chaucer is most intent upon foregrounding.[38] Because Chaucer does not unwaveringly align himself with the ideologies of the rebels, Patterson comes close to charging him with political fecklessness for ultimately muting and containing "the voice of political protest": retreating into a bourgeois subjectivity, Chaucer is caught in a Foucauldian loop of class power which inevitably circulates his beliefs back to the top. I have already indicated how my own critical position differs from Patterson's: Chaucer I believe is much less committed to defining his personal politics than he is committed to providing his readers a circumambient arena of varied critical discourses that collectively bring interpretative pressure upon the percussions of history, both in the present and in the past. Rather than suppressing or retreating from the sounds of overt political protest, as Patterson suggests, Chaucer instead collides them against the sounds of other expressive systems so that readers might construct for themselves a more "dissonant" and sophisticated set of auditory and interpretative strategies to determine the tidings of these and other historical/literary events.

Chaucer's historical hermeneutics would thus appear to be measurably different from the historical consciousnesses of his contemporaries who commented directly on the Revolt. In "Interpretative Models for the Peasants' Revolt," Derek Pearsall has shown how all the fourteenth- and fifteenth-century poets and historians who wrote about the Uprising constructed their narratives to conform to an *a priori* set of time-honored generic models; by any positivist standards, these texts are all forms of propagandistic fiction rather than reliable "history."[39] Furthermore, even the so-called documentary records of the Revolt are transparently subjective and self-serving: they too "must be understood in terms of the assumptions, prejudices, beliefs, and ingrained habits of mind that color them."[40] What is distinctive about Chaucer's strategy of oblique historical representation is the degree to which he does *not* coerce his readers into any single model, *a priori* or otherwise, but rather provides them with a host of strategies whose collective turbulence is meant, I believe, to subvert "the assumptions, prejudices, beliefs, and ingrained habits of mind" by which medieval literary and political events are characteristically glossed and understood. Ideally, this interpretive dissonance is designed to create in each reader a heteroglossic hermeneutics that is sensitive and "material" yet at the same time theoretical and self-critical. It may also serve as a thirteenth way of listening to a fart, wherein the politics of explosive noise is heard as a promising herald for change. But then again, it may not. The safest position, as long as you are not in the direct line of fire, is to hear this noise for what it most materially and literally is: nothing more nor less than a very loud fart.

NOTES

1. Anicius Manlius Severinus Boethius, *Fundamentals of Music,* trans. and intr., Calvin M. Bower, ed. Claude V. Palisca (New Haven: Yale University Press, 1989), 16.

2. Jacques Attali, *Noise: The Political Economy of Music,* trans. Brian Massumi (Minneapolis: University of Minnesota Press, 1985), 5–6.

3. Richard Leppert, *The Sight of Sound: Music, Representation, and the History of the Body* (Berkeley: University of California Press, 1993), 15.

4. Ibid.

5. Citations to Chaucer's works refer to Larry Benson, general ed., *The Riverside Chaucer* (Boston: Houghton Mifflin, 1987), as follows: *Canterbury Tales, CT* fragment line; *House of Fame, HT* and line number; *Parliament of Fowls, PF* and line number; *Boece* by book and prose numbers.

6. Lee Patterson, *Chaucer and the Subject of History* (Madison: University of Wisconsin Press, 1991), 321.

7. Ibid.

8. Ibid., 246.

9. Steven Justice, *Writing and Rebellion: England in 1381* (Berkeley: University of California Press, 1994), 207.

10. *Martianus Capella and the Seven Liberal Arts,* trans. William Harris Stahl and Richard Johnson with E. L. Burge, vol. 2 (New York: Columbia University Press, 1977), 352.

11. Boethius, *Fundamentals of Music,* 21.

12. Dante Alighieri, *The Divine Comedy,* trans. and ed. Charles S. Singleton, vol. 3 (1975; rprt. Princeton: Princeton University Press, 1982). Further citations by canto and line number in the text.

13. Jeffrey Schnapp, *The Transfiguration of History in the Center of Dante's Paradise* (Princeton: Princeton University Press, 1986), 163.

14. David Chamberlain, "The Music of the Spheres and *The Parliament of Foules,*" *ChauR* 5 (1970): 32–56, at 39–40 (emphasis added).

15. See, especially, Clement Hawes, "'More Stars, God knows, than a Pair': Social Class and the Common Good in Chaucer's *Parliament of Fowls,*" *Publications of the Arkansas Philological Association* 15 (1989): 12–25, and David Aers, *Chaucer* (Atlantic Highlands, N.J.: Humanities Press International, 1986), 16.

16. Justice, *Writing and Rebellion,* 45.

17. Ibid., 125. There has been considerable mobility among recent scholarly studies in determining the proper name of this revolt/rebellion/uprising. See, especially, Justice's discussion here.

18. Anne Hudson, *The Premature Reformation: Wycliffite Texts and Lollard History* (Oxford: Clarendon Press, 1988), 374–75.

19. Quoted by Justice, *Writing and Rebellion,* 147.

20. Wendy Scase, *Piers Plowman and the New Anticlericalism* (Cambridge: Cambridge University Press, 1989), 47–54. The erudition with which the friars supported their position is satirized, Scase notes, in *Piers Plowman B* 20.273–76:

> Enuye herde þis and heet freres go to scole
> And lerne logyk and lawe and ek contemplacion,
> And preche men of Plato, and preue it by Seneca
> That alle þynges vnder heuene ouȝte to ben in commune.

21. Patterson, *Chaucer and the Subject of History*, 321.

22. See *Riverside Chaucer*, 878, note to 2126–28.

23. Linda Georgianna, "Lords, Churls, and Friars: The Return to Social Order in *The Summoner's Tale*," in Susanna Greer Fein, David Raybin, and Peter C. Braeger, eds., *Rebels and Rivals: The Contestive Spirit in The Canterbury Tales* (Kalamazoo, Mich.: Medieval Institute Publications, 1991), 149–73.

24. See Alan Levitan, "The Parody of Pentecost in Chaucer's *Summoner's Tale*," *University of Toronto Quarterly* 40 (1971): 236–46; Bernard S. Levy, "Biblical Parody in the *Summoner's Tale*," *Tennessee Studies of Literature* 2 (1966): 45–60; and Roy Peter Clark, "Wit and Whitsunday in Chaucer's *Summoner's Tale*," *Annuale Mediaevale* 17 (1976): 48–57.

25. Cited by Justice, *Writing and Rebelllion*, 108.

26. Sarah Beckwith, *Signifying God: Social Relation and Symbolic Act in the York Corpus Christi Plays* (Chicago: University of Chicago Press, 2001), 29–30.

27. Aron Gurevich, *Medieval Popular Culture: Problems of Belief and Perception*, trans. Janos M. Bak and Paul A. Hollingsworth (Cambridge: Cambridge University Press, 1988), 11. Cited by Justice, *Writing and Rebellion*, 135.

28. Quoted and translated by Richard Firth Green, "A Possible Source for Chaucer's *Summoner's Tale*," *ELN* 24 (1987): 24–27.

29. Ibid.

30. Boethius, *Fundamentals of Music*, 89–91.

31. Chaucer, *Boece* 2, pr. 5, 26–33. The original passage is: "Et uox quidem tota pariter multorum replet auditum, uestrae uero diuitiae nisi comminutae in plures transire non possunt; *Ancii Manlii Severini Boethii Philosophiae Consolatio* II, pr. 5, ed. Ludovicus Biel (Turnhout: Brepols, 1982), 26.

32. For this insight I am indebted to Stephen K. Wright, "Jankyn's Boethian Learning in *The Summoner's Tale*," *ELN* 26 (1988): 4–7.

33. Richard Leppert, *The Sight of f Sound*, 15.

34 Mel Brooks, "Mel Brooks: A Candid Conversation with the Emperor of Off-the-Wall Comedy," *Playboy* (February 1975): 64–65.

35. Mikhail Bakhtin, *The Dialogic Imagination*, ed. M. Holquist, trans. C. Emerson and M. Holquist (Austin: University of Texas Press, 1981), 291.

36. For these insights I am indebted to Allon White, "Bakhtin, Sociolinguistics, and Deconstruction," in *Carnival, Hysteria, and Writing: Collected Essays and Autobiography* (Oxford: Clarendon Press, 1993), 135–59.

37. This reading of the fart has also been explored by James M. Cox, in "Toward Vernacular Humor," *Virginia Quarterly Review* 46 (1970): 311–30, at 315.

38. The twelve-spoked critical cartwheel I have provided is of course not meant to represent the definitive interpretative circle—other interpretative circles are readily available; in this regard it is significant that the squire specifies that Thomas should give not only one, but "fartes thre" (*CT* 3.2284).

39 Derek Pearsall, "Interpretative Models for the Peasants' Revolt," *Hermeneutics and Medieval Culture*, ed. Patrick J. Gallacher and Helen Damico (Albany: SUNY Press, 1989), 63–70.

40. Ibid., 68.

WILLIAM F. WOODS

Symkyn's Place in the Reeve's Tale

W‌hen Aleyn and John, the Cambridge clerks, make their way back to miller Symkyn's house, they are weary and wet, having spent the day chasing their horse Bayard about the fen, and this is when he offers them his famous invitation:

> Myn hous is streit, but ye han lerned art;
> Ye konne by argumentes make a place
> A myle brood of twenty foot of space. (I 4122–24)[1]

The pithy sarcasm of these lines displays Symkyn's resentment of the clerks' education and their station in life, yet leads us to wonder whether, by "argumentes," he might be implying something in particular, some clerkly craft which would shed additional light on the action of the tale.[2] In a passage by Albert of Saxony, a fourteenth-century Aristotelian philosopher at that great center for learned clerks, the University of Paris, we hear a distinct echo of Symkyn's words. Referring to the infinite extent of the divine power, Albert says God "could place a body as large as the world inside a millet seed and he could achieve this in the same manner as Christ is lodged in the host, that is, without any condensation, rarefaction, or penetration of bodies. Within that millet seed, God could create a space of 100 leagues, or

The Chaucer Review Volume 39, Number One (2004): pp. 17–40. © 2004 Pennsylvania State University.

1,000, or however many are imaginable. A man inside that millet seed could traverse all those many leagues simply by walking from one extremity of the millet seed to the other."[3]

What sort of man was Albert, and what was he writing? Albert of Saxony, or Albert of Rickmersdorf (sometimes called Albertus Parvus, to distinguish him from Albert the Great), was born in Helmstedt, Germany, around 1316.[4] At the University of Paris he studied with Jean Buridan and others, becoming Master of Arts in 1351; in 1353, he was named rector of the university and taught in the arts faculty for another ten years. He also studied theology, but along with a few other prominent thinkers, notably Jean Buridan and John of Jandun, he did not finish the degree.[5] Yet in 1365 he became the first rector of the University of Vienna and in 1366 was named bishop of Halberstadt, remaining in that position until his death in 1390. Although he is no longer considered an original thinker—his work is derivative of the ideas of Buridan and Nicole Oresme[6]—Albert was a prolific author; his writings, especially those in logic and natural philosophy, helped to spread the ideas of Ockham, Buridan, Oresme, and Bradwardine in western Europe, and they had an influence upon subsequent scientific thought. The above passage, a thought experiment or imaginative exploration of contrary-to-fact conditions, occurs in *De Celo,* Albert's commentary on Aristotle's *On the Heavens* (Book 1, Question 9, 93v, col. 2).

It is probably impossible to know whether Chaucer looked at, or had even heard of Albert's *De Celo,* although it seems likely that a university library such as the one at Oxford's Merton College, or perhaps the even greater libraries at Dover, Canterbury, York, or Bury might have acquired a copy. As J. A. W. Bennett has said, we cannot know whether Chaucer entered any of these places or knew of their resources, yet such libraries did hold collections that were used, and they testify to a culture of educated readers like Strode and others who were Chaucer's acquaintances.[7] Furthermore, Chaucer's interest in cosmology, which we infer from his treatise on the astrolabe and the many astronomical references throughout his work, suggests that he was not unaware of the prevailing opinions and controversies on the subject. These are ideas that Chaucer could have encountered in sermons, popular anecdotes, or conversations with his university connections. Theories of medieval cosmology, and the matrix of Aristotelian philosophy that sustained them, were in fact common knowledge among academics, for astronomy was part of the Master of Arts curriculum required for both philosophers and theologians. In addition, these issues were broadcast throughout the university community by disputation, and, in a larger sense, the copying and circulation of manuscripts and the travel of masters between universities made Aristotelian thought a fairly homogeneous intellectual tradition in western Europe.[8]

The first object of this essay will be to develop a context for Albert's lines, and perhaps for Symkyn's, by describing the theological reaction to Aristotelian philosophy in the thirteenth and fourteenth centuries, and the changes in ideas—especially the idea of place—that resulted from this conflict. This general discussion of place will lead us to particular problems of containment that are implied by Albert's reference to the dimensions of inner space and the eucharistic doctrine of transubstantiation. In the final two sections, correspondingly, I will indicate some ways in which Symkyn's desire to extend himself is suggested by metaphors of place and space, and then—his ultimate pretension!—how Symkyn contrives to colonize inner space, as it were, by converting the substance of others into his own. In general, I attempt to evaluate the explanatory power and expressiveness of certain ideas drawn from cosmology and theology when they become metaphors for the crude ambitions of a "clerkly" mind like Symkyn's.

I

The first thing to be said about Aristotelian thought in the thirteenth century is that it was dominant. Aristotle's logic provided a powerful method for thinking about theology, and his science offered precepts that continued to be in general use throughout the Middle Ages. Aristotle's work on physics is a case in point. Lost to the West during the early medieval period, the *Physics* was preserved in Arabic translations and retranslated into Latin in the twelfth century by Gerard of Cremona. As such, it joined what has been called a "massive" translation of many texts written by Aristotle and Averroes, which led to Aristotle's books on logic and cosmology becoming "the heart of the arts curriculum at Oxford, and, by 1255, Paris."[9] This energetic revival of Aristotle was so successful that theologians in Paris began to feel threatened by the strength of Aristotle's thought, and by their colleagues, the Aristotelian philosophers of Paris. They wondered, that is, whether "the Aristotelian cosmology hamper[ed] God's powers unduly." For example, despite what Aristotle had argued,

> Is the extent of God's creative force limited to *this* admittedly finite world? Are not other worlds possible? Could not God jostle our world sideways in space, moving it into a new place and leaving an empty place behind?[10]

In 1277, these and other concerns led Etienne Tempier, bishop of Paris, having received a request from Pope John XXI, and after consulting with theologians of the Sorbonne, to issue a series of 219 condemnations of (mainly Aristotelian) doctrines that denied or limited the power of God.[11]

The Paris Condemnations were intended as constraints on the natural philosophers of Paris and elsewhere, in order to guard against the erosion of the authority of Christian doctrine, but their more pronounced and significant effect was to enable new ways of thinking about the natural world, and particularly the cosmos: the earth and heavens. Indeed, despite its flamboyant certitude, the claim of Pierre Duhem, the prominent early historian of science, that "[i]f we must assign a date for the birth of modern science, we would, without doubt, choose the year 1277,"[12] is worthy of serious consideration. One effect of the Condemnations was to call into question the Aristotelian concept of place and thus to make possible, even to stimulate, imaginative explorations of spatial infinity (like that of Albert of Saxony), for infinite space could be seen as a necessary corollary to God's immensity. Ultimately, according to the analysis of Edward S. Casey, these explorations "exceeded their theological origins; directly or indirectly they inspired the bold thought experiments of thinkers in the fourteenth and fifteenth centuries, engendering the conceptual ventures that laid down the foundations of modern physics, above all its commitment to the infinity of the physical universe."[13]

It is exhilarating to know that the Condemnations of 1277, and the discussions of place and space that they helped to initiate, look forward to the great work of Newton, Locke, and Leibnitz—in other words, the cosmology of the seventeenth century has its roots in medieval *theology*—but our interest here is with Aristotle's concept of place and the alternatives to it that were proposed in the thirteenth and fourteenth centuries. Aristotle's idea of place, to begin with, was not what medieval philosophers called the "vulgar" or "common" conception of place—which was like our own idea: location and extensiveness in three-dimensional space. His more precise description of place, as we find it in Book IV of the *Physics,* was "the limit of the containing body, by which the container makes contact with what it contains."[14] Or to put it a different way, "the immediate container of that of which it is the place."[15] Aristotle found it convenient, in other words, to define place as a two-dimensional containing surface that contacts the outer limits of a given body. Thus each body has its own place that is exactly its own size, and in addition each body "naturally moves up or down to its own proper place and stays there,"[16] for as a result of the rotation of the heavens, lighter things will move away ("up") from the still center, and heavier things will descend ("down") toward that center. Thus even the cosmos—the earth and the heavens—has its proper place because it has limits, and those limits define its place. And since, in Aristotle's opinion, there could not be anything outside the heavens, because there was no reason to assume that there should necessarily be other worlds than this one, it also made sense to say that there was no place beyond the place of the world. Finally, to follow this idea to its extremity, if no place existed outside this world, then one could not go outside the world, for there was literally no place to go.

The containing—or from a different point of view, the comforting—nature of Aristotle's concept of place may have had its primitive beginnings in finite models: the place that is a house, for instance, or a clearing in the woods, a field of battle, a town in the midst of fields. The parts of a place, as well as relations between places, could be thought of as analogous to the arrangement of the limbs of a body—everything in its proper place, in other words. But when applied to the world, such containment provoked curiosity. For if our world did have its limit, what would prevent us from reaching a hand, or perhaps a spear beyond that limit, into the nothing, or something, that was there? Such questions had been asked since before the time of Plato,[17] and were known throughout medieval times. There were also attempts to define the place of the world in ways that implied, although they did not specify, a larger cosmological context. Thomas Aquinas, for example, accepted Aristotle's account of the outer sphere of the heavens, but he thought that if the place of the world were to be more than simply a container, if we want to think of the world as being in a *particular* place, that emplacement is to be found "in a set of relations to the celestial spheres that surround earth itself."[18] Thus the earth could be thought of as emplaced in relation to the surrounding heavenly bodies, which were, as Casey argues, "an expanded domain that increasingly demands the term 'spatial' rather than 'placial.'"[19]

This one example from Aquinas may suggest that perspectives on cosmological place were changing and expanding, but it was the Condemnations of 1277, undergirded by the threat of excommunication, that most directly contradicted Aristotelian conclusions and encouraged theologians and philosophers to speculate about what infinite void spaces might open out if God willed them to be so. Two of the condemned articles or precepts are relevant here.

Article 34 states "That the first cause [i.e., God] could not make several worlds."[20] But Bishop Tempier and the Paris theologians reasoned that if God is truly omnipotent, there is no reason why He cannot make worlds other than *this* world. Evidently, however, several worlds that coexist with each other must share a space larger than the place taken up by any one of them. And if there are an infinite number of such worlds—for why would an omnipotent God make only a few other worlds?—then the space shared must be infinite in extent. Another movement of the imagination toward infinite space was enabled by article 49: "That God could not move the heavens [i.e., the cosmos] with rectilinear motion *(de moto rectu)*."[21] Rectilinear motion meant motion along a straight line, as opposed to rotation. Aristotle had said that such lateral motion can only be defined in relation to other bodies, other *places*. But if no other place existed beyond this place, then this place could not meaningfully be said to move at all. Bishop Tempier breaks this paradigm by allowing that God could move the world in and by itself without reference to anything else—in other words, "a sheer motion . . . in an absolute space"[22]—and that is a model of space that Isaac Newton would have found quite acceptable.

The thought experiments enabled by the Condemnations of 1277 accustomed medieval minds to think in terms of infinite space, even if they believed, as most of them did, that in the material, as opposed to the imagined world, things were as Aristotle had described them. What gave authority to that imagined world, what gave the imaginary infinite void space a necessary presence, because forever filled with God's presence, was the rigorous, dogmatic, and theologically conservative *De causa Dei contra Pelagium* of Thomas Bradwardine (1290–1349),[23] who taught at Oxford, and ended his career as archbishop of Canterbury and a confidant of Edward III. Bradwardine's nine-hundred-page polemic was begun as a course of lectures at Oxford. In his preface he writes that the origin of the work "lay in his revulsion against the emphasis upon free will and the disregard for God's grace which he had heard preached as a student in the schools."[24] Bradwardine probably continued to lecture from his developing manuscript until its completion (manuscript evidence indicates that this occurred in 1344, late in his career). By that time, Gordon Leff argues, "since he was a member of a medieval university, Bradwardine's ideas would have been known [through disputation] to his colleagues, opponents and pupils long before he published them."[25] The "Pelagians" in question were William of Ockham and his followers. Against their nominalist tendencies and their emphasis on the importance of the human will, Bradwardine opposed the authority of divine creation, divine will, and man's need to guide himself by God's will, to the limited degree that it was humanly knowable (hence Chaucer associates him with the problem of *necessitee* in the *Nun's Priest's Tale*). Bradwardine was a brilliant mathematician and physicist, and his long, unrelenting, yet closely reasoned and coherent argument reflects an intensely disciplined mind. On the other hand, taken as theology, his treatise is, in effect, a conservative holding action, allowing very little latitude for free will and offering what Leff calls an "inhumane" program for the faithful that has something in common with the later but equally rigorous theology of John Calvin.[26]

Positing God's omnipotence as "first cause," Bradwardine set forth his evidence in a series of corollaries, two of which are relevant here: "First, that essentially and in presence, God is necessarily everywhere in the world and all its parts"; and second, that God is "also beyond the real world in a place, or in an imaginary infinite void."[27] God's "presence . . . necessarily everywhere' converts the void from what had been a purely negative and imaginary entity for other thinkers into something at once positive and real . . . real insofar as it is filled with God's being (which is not only real but *most* real)." Furthermore, this void has *parts* (which can belong to things other than God); it has *places* (which are beyond the place of the world); and if it is beyond the world, then it is implied that God could move the world there—and if there, then anywhere—within that infinite space that is coextensive with God.[28] This was a way of thinking about infinite space followed by John of Ripa and Nicole Oresme in the fourteenth century, and by philosophers and theologians in succeeding generations.

There were, however, philosophers who did not share Bradwardine's grand conception of the cosmos, and here, finally, we return to the *Reeve's Tale*, for one of these conservative thinkers was Albert of Saxony. Albert held with Aristotle that, in fact, no void space existed outside the world: "Merely because God could create such entities did not mean that he had actually done so."[29] Nonetheless, like most scholastic philosophers after the condemnations, Albert appears to have taken a twofold approach: he followed Aristotle and "denied that a void space was *naturally* possible, but conceded that it was *supernaturally* possible."[30] Perhaps such concessions were difficult for him. In any case, in Book I of his commentary on Aristotle's *De caelo*,[31] he envisions four imaginary situations in which God creates concentric or eccentric worlds beyond our world or inside our world that are located in what is presumably a void space. Most of these thought experiments (we would probably call them hypotheses) illustrate the sometimes playful process of inquiry whereby new ideas were, and are, discovered.[32] Here are two examples, one describing exterior, the other interior space:

> Similarly, we can imagine several eccentric worlds: either (1) one lies wholly outside the other, and this could be [imagined] in the way several globes are placed in a sack, or [it might be imagined that they are inside but] do not touch; or (2) that one does not lie wholly outside the other, but that there is another world in some part of our world, as if, [for example,] another world were imagined in the moon, or in the sun, and in the other planets. (I, Question 11, fol. 95r, col. 1)[33]

One of the two remaining situations is the apparently whimsical sketch quoted at the beginning of this essay, about how "God could place a body as large as the world inside a millet seed." This certainly illustrated the power of God, and just as certainly it violated Aristotle's (perhaps anyone's) idea of place. Nonetheless, exasperated as he might have been with Bishop Tempier and the theologians of Paris, Albert was not alone in speculating about whether there could be void space within the world. Bradwardine himself was interested in this ancient question, and in Book I, Ch. 5 of his long polemic on God's will, concluded that "[i]ndeed, by means of his absolute power, God could make a void anywhere that he wishes, inside or outside of the world."[34]

And so we return to Symkyn's provocatively ungenerous offer: these clerks have "lerned art"—they can "by argumentes make a place / A myle brood of twenty foot of space." Had we known about the Condemnations of 1277, or about the kind of speculative thinking they inspired in sober clerks like Albert, Symkyn's insulting paradox might have seemed to carry a bit more weight. Or if we had heard Bradwardine lecture, had we read the first book of his treatise, or known anything at all about this famous and dogmatic clerk who had risen so high in the ranks of the Oxford (Merton College) philosophers, and in the politics of the church, we might have been more sensitive to the social import of these lines, with their sly anticlerical overtone, tempered with the pride of knowing what the clerks were up to, what was really being debated—even at Cambridge, where there were not and would never be first-rank thinkers like Bradwardine.[35] Surely we would also have heard the common man's scorn for philosophical notions that ran counter to his own myopic common sense—somewhat in the way that Albert of Saxony preferred the established thinking (which happened to be Aristotle's), conceding to the infinite power of God the imaginary possibilities of infinite void space, and indeed, interior void space, yet conducting these thought experiments sometimes with an ironic air,[36] sometimes with just a bit of wildness, for theology was not in fact his métier,[37] and these imaginary scenarios weren't really going to happen anyway, not in material reality.

II

Symkyn, of course, offers more than the possibility of a place within the place of his house; he grandly invites Aleyn and John to make an enormous, mile-broad place within those narrow walls, and this leads us to the part of Albert of Saxony's thought experiment where he imagines God creating a space of 100 leagues, no, 1,000—indeed, a potentially infinite space within a millet seed—and all this without altering its dimensions, without "rarefaction, condensation, or penetration of bodies." As we have seen, the possibility of infinite void space received official validation from the Condemnations of 1277 . . . for instance, number 49: "That God could not move the heavens [that is, the world] with rectilinear motion; and the reason is that a vacuum would remain."[38] The vacuum was an important objection because Aristotle had argued in various ways that nature abhors a vacuum, that in fact God could not make a vacuum, partly because it was contradictory, indeed it was absurd, to say that God could create nothing.[39] By condemning this assertion, it was allowed that God *could* move the world to a different place in space, and if to one place, then to infinite places, which would require the existence of infinite space. But the idea of introducing infinite space into a smaller, interior dimension, as both Symkyn and Albert propose, was a paradox that violated (Aristotelian) nature in a different way, and was validated by a different set of condemnations.

"What articles 34 and 49 did for the existence of extracosmic space," Edward Grant has observed, "articles 139, 140 and 141 did, somewhat less intelligibly perhaps, for possible dimensional spaces within the world."[40] These articles are somewhat redundant, and may be represented by the text of article 141: "That God cannot make an accident exist without a subject, nor make several dimensions exist simultaneously [in the same place]."[41] In the language of Aristotle's science, a subject refers to an underlying substance—not matter, but being, the fundamental identity of a body. Accidents, on the other hand, are the qualities of a body that inhere in it—its color, size, and weight, for instance. Accidents have their being in a subject, according to Aristotle, so that it would be nonsensical to imagine an accident without a subject—whiteness without anything being white, as Jean Buridan once said. Yet in condemning article 141, the theologians of Paris maintained that accidents *could* exist independently of a subject, and this was because Thomas Aquinas, among others, had used the philosophical language of substance and accident to describe the transubstantiation that takes place in the Eucharist when the bread and wine is changed into the body and blood of Christ. The sacrament of the Eucharist is a miracle, a supernatural event, which Aquinas accepted as an article of faith. His arguments, which I will take to be representative,[42] define the nature of the transubstantiation with the clarity of Aristotelian terminology, but the Aristotelian unity of subject and accident is violated in the interests of faith. The "physics of the Eucharist," as this complex of ideas came to be called, would be a topic of philosophical discussion until the time of Locke, and its effect on fourteenth-century scientific thought was significant. We will follow these arguments briefly, for it is here in particular that we find the clerkly "art" that Albert echoes and Symkyn parodies in his remarks to Aleyn and John.

In the Synoptic Gospels, Christ says during the Last Supper, "This is my body," and the meaning of the Eucharist depends upon the interpretation of these words. If understood symbolically, they would mean that the bread and wine of communion represent Christ's body, and the relationship draws the communicant toward heaven. But Aquinas understands "the body of Christ" as being *literally* inside the host: "We have under this sacrament—under the appearance of the bread—not only the flesh, but the whole body of Christ, that is, the bones and nerves and all the rest" (3a. 76, 1 ad 2 [95]).[43] This argument creates obvious difficulties. To begin with, if, at a certain point in the Mass, Christ's body is the Eucharist, what happened to the bread and wine? Aquinas is sometimes thought to be saying that the bread and wine are annihilated and the body of Christ begins to exist in their place,[44] but that would require Christ's body to move from heaven to the altar, and a ubiquitous deity cannot be said to move. Thus he argues for the change, or "transubstantiation," of bread and wine into the body of Christ.

On the other hand, it does not *seem* that the bread and wine have become the body of Christ, since their color, taste, dimension remain that of bread and wine. Only the *substance* of the bread and wine—that which underlies its sense appearances—has been changed into Christ; the accidental qualities of the bread and wine have been left behind, and the substance of the body of Christ is now contained beneath their appearances. The accidents left behind are no longer accidents of the bread and wine, for it has been changed into Christ; but they are not accidents of Christ, either, for he does not look or taste like bread and wine. "We are left to conclude," Aquinas says, "that the accidents in this sacrament do not inhere in any subject. God's power is able to bring this about" (3a. 77, 1 [129]). Instead, he continues, "the other accidents which remain in this sacrament have as their subject the dimensive quantity of the bread and wine which remains" (3a. 77, 2 [133]). For "its dimensive quantity is the very first accident which affects a material thing. . . . And because the material substance is the basic subject in which all the accidents are received, it follows that the other accidents cling to the substance through the medium of the quantity" (3a. 77, 2 [133]).

Aquinas does not mean that the body of Christ is coextensive with the bread and wine, or that when the bread is broken, Christ's body is similarly divided. As Richard Fishacre had argued around 1235, in his commentary on the *Sentences* of Peter Lombard, "God's infinite immensity always remains indivisible because he is wholly and indivisibly in every part of space," an interpretation that came to be called the "whole-in-every-part" doctrine.[45] Indeed, it makes no sense to say that the body of Christ can be divisible, because the *dimensions* of Christ's body are not in the bread and wine, except in the way that they are implied by the "complete specific nature" of his substance *(totalitas substantia)*. In fact, "the dimensions of the bread and wine are not changed into the dimensions of Christ's body; it is substance that is changed into substance" (3a. 76, 1 ad 3 [97]).

It becomes clear, then, that even though "the whole 'quantified' and individuated living body of Christ" is contained by the quantity of the bread,[46] it is there in a spiritual sense, as substance which contains the *idea* of dimensions, as it were, but no length and breadth. Consequently, it does not matter that the body of Christ is larger than the host. As Aquinas puts it,

> the whole specific nature of a substance is as truly contained by small as by large dimensions; for example, the complete specific nature of air is as truly found in a large as in a small amount, and

human nature in its specific wholeness is equally present in a large and in a small man. (3a. 76, 1 ad 3 [97])

Christ, contained whole and entire within the tiny host: this is a miracle of God's power, but it is also a stunning paradox, God's immensity in little, the universe within a grain of sand. It was at once an obstacle and a stimulant to philosophical investigation. As Albert of Saxony and Symkyn demonstrate, it had an imaginative impact both on scientific thinking and on the average person's habits of mind. In regard to science, given the sacramental truth of the Eucharist, it appears, *contra* Aristotle but in accord with article 141 of the Condemnations of 1277, "that God *[can]* make an accident exist without a subject, [and] make several dimensions exist simultaneously [in the same place]." Thus Walter Burley could argue that just as in the Eucharist, God made a quantity (i.e., the body of Christ) with no inhering qualities (such as dimension), so also could he, in violation of Aristotle's physics, make an extended vacuum (again, a quantity without qualities) through which light and heavy bodies could move.[47] Or one might consider the case of Jean Buridan, who found in article 141 a support for his conception of the true nature of motion. According to the established thinking, motion was a disposition, an accidental form inhering in a body. But if God were to destroy that body and the places it might occupy, then motion would remain as an independent entity, "a non-permanent, pure flow" *(res pure successiva)*—that is, it *could* remain as an independent quality (we would say "phenomenon"), because it was forbidden to say that "God cannot make an accident exist without a subject."[48] The ability to postulate qualities without subjects aided also in the development of inertial theory and the Merton College "mean speed theorem . . . which eventually served as the foundation of Galileo's new mechanics."[49]

In sum, the theological exceptions to Aristotelian science we have just examined were a significant influence on medieval scientific thinking, and on medieval thought in a broader sense as well. According to Grant,

> the Condemnation of 1277 . . . was taken seriously throughout the fourteenth century . . . it encouraged innumerable invocations of God's absolute power in a variety of hypothetical physical situations. . . . So widespread was the contemplation of such hypothetical possibilities in the late Middle Ages that it is no exaggeration to view them as an integral feature of late medieval thought.[50]

In the context of the thought experiments provoked by the Condemnations, we can see Albert of Saxony's passage as a somewhat typical imaginative exercise, in which he applies the "physics of the Eucharist" to a millet seed, emphasizing the paradoxical nature whereby dimensions are folded into one another, as it were, and the tiny is simultaneously immense, but demonstrating all this from the mundane point of view of a man "walking from one extremity of the millet seed to the other." Probably we are struck more forcibly by the paradox, the violation of commonsense physical laws, than we are by the underlying theology and its scientific implications. And that, I would suggest, is pretty much how Symkyn's words on place and space are supposed to strike the informed reader. One is aware of the possible references to certain aspects of the art of clerks, yet this is a miller speaking, after all, and we can only wonder what significance his paradoxical lines might have for his own artful scheming.

III

For in his cheating, his scheming, and his dreams of great estate, Symkyn is indeed an expansive character. His oppressive greed, betrayed by the clerkly jingle on *place* and *space,* gains its full expression through spatial relationships and metaphors that imply the tension between self and other, inner and outer, small and great.[51] In these ways, cosmology and theology themselves become part of a chain of associations, attenuating into the mundane events of a miller's life. The expansiveness of "a place / A myle brood" resonates with Albert's "space of 100 leagues, or 1,000 leagues," and indeed with Bradwardine's infinite void space; at the same time it looks in the other direction, toward Symkyn's "[g]reet sokene" (I 3987), and his ambition to enlarge it even further through blood alliances. But some narrative sequences directly reflect the sense of Symkyn's couplet, just as they imply Aquinas's "physics of the Eucharist"—in other words, the outer and greater may be assimilated to a smaller, inner space.[52] For if simple engrandization were desirable, how much better, and in fact more realistic, if by milling and marriage Symkyn could create wealth and power—a lordly presence—*within* the humble confines of his yeoman's estate? That is what he really means by the ironic paradox of the millet seed. And isn't that what Oswald himself has done, by cheating his lord in a hundred ways, to build himself a house "ful faire upon an heeth" (I 606), but out of the way, shadowed by green trees, a fair retreat only vaguely justified by his subordinate reeve's duties? For clarity, and because the metaphors of expansiveness and assimilation correspond, respectively, to ideas developed in parts I and II of this essay, I will devote a brief discussion to each complex, in parts III and IV.

We do not have to read far in the tale to gain a spatial sense of Symkyn's grasping nature. His very portrait might be said to express a kind of perimeter, establishing the conditions that other characters—wife, daughter, two clerks, and others—have to contend with, and giving us a thumbnail sketch of how the imagery of the tale will be configured. If we took the measure of

Robin the Miller by scrutinizing his nose, with all its gross vitality, our first sustained image of Miller Symkyn is an array of edged weapons:

> Ay by his belt he baar a long panade,
> And of a swerd ful trenchant was the blade.
> A joly poppere baar he in his pouche;
> Ther was no man, for peril, dorste hym touche.
> A Sheffeld thwitel baar he in his hose. (I 3929–33)

The general impression we take from these lines, surely, is that this is a resourceful, heavily defended, and dangerous man. The resourcefulness and the threat it projects is implicit in the layered defenses that at once protect and express him. It is obvious, for instance, that no one anywhere near Symkyn is safe, for the "long panade" extends his reach considerably (Chaucer notes that its edge is sharp as a sword, emphasizing the length of the cutlass by association). But even those allowed within that reach, for reasons of business, perhaps, carry out their transactions virtually at knife point, for the Sheffield knife waits conveniently inside the waistband of his hose, quite visible, no doubt, as an aid to bargaining. And in the off chance that someone might lose his temper or lay hold of him, there is still the inner threat, the "joly" little dagger hidden in his pocket for close work. We get the impression that he appears in this manner even on holy days (I 3952), accompanied by his wife:

> Was noon so hardy that wente by the weye
> That with hire dorste rage or ones pleye,
> But if he wolde be slayn of Symkyn
> With panade, or with knyf, or boidekyn. (I 3957–60)

Summing up the concentric, increasingly intimate boundaries of his person, these are all essentially phallic blades; their vaguely eroticized aggressiveness prepares us for Symkyn's appropriate punishment later in the tale; and their expanding zones of lethal potential prepare us for the rapacious greed that defines this haughty miller, his grand dreams so narrowly contained by his modest yeoman's estate.[53]

As the story begins, Symkyn's plans are already afoot, for within the tiny house are his wife and daughter—for his purposes, magic vessels of engrandization. Symkyn's wife, for instance, brings to the marriage her education by the nuns, and "many a pan of brass" (I 3944), her dowry from her simoniacal father the Parson. That was a good start, but what is really going to expand Symkyn's estate of yeomanry is the baby in crib. This was a late child (the daughter is already twenty years old), a determined attempt to foster a male heir. The narrator calls the child "a proper page" (I 3972), as if Symkyn were already imagining him in livery, working his way toward knighthood in a great house. The daughter, it is hoped, will bring off a similar conversion: "hooly chirches blood" (and, of course, its "good") will lure "som worthy blood of auncetrye" (I 3982–3984), some lucky young man from a good, or at least better, family that nevertheless has need of additional capital.

Passing from marriage to milling—from Symkyn's imagination to his practices—the practical reality that lends credibility to all his schemes is his "[g]reet sokene" to grind the wheat and malt for "al the land aboute" (I 3987–3988). These are grand terms, and they reflect the thinking of someone for whom "al the land aboute" is far too little. Similar language is used to describe "a greet collegge / Men clepen the Soler Halle at Cantebregge" (I 3989–3990), which is part of Symkyn's monopoly, but also a worthy adversary. Before, he stole from them "but curteisly" (I 3997; we would not suppose that Symkyn stole *courteously* from mere peasant farmers!). Now, however, the manciple is sick (bad teeth), and Symkyn's bite on the collegiate economy is increased "outrageously" (I 3998). Consequently, when Aleyn and John appear at Symkyn's mill, wearing their swords, they join the ongoing contest between university and country wits. Suffice it to say that "their preconceptions are no match for the wily, *ad hoc* stratagems of Symkyn," as Peter Brown observes.[54] Despite themselves, they are disarmed, forced to strip off their swords, just as Symkyn had stripped the bridle from their horse. They spend the remainder of the day chasing him about the mile-broad fens, while back in the mill Symkyn steals freely from their sack of meal. Symkyn's centralization of resources, as opposed to the clerks' marginalization, is a typical demonstration of the spatial logic of his guile.

The next episode takes place within Symkyn's small house and is again a reversal, but this time the clerks remain inside, while *his* social, economic and even intellectual pretentions are reduced, restricted, "contained," as Brown puts it. In effect, the boys run to Symkyn's girls, just as Bayard escaped into those glorious, extensive, wild-mare-haunted fens. In a way, they *do* make a place "a myle brood"—an erotic green meadow, as it were—within "twenty foot of space."[55] But the final and climactic way that "nature" reverses Symkyn's expansion is by the light of the moon, and here Symkyn is returned to his low estate, his mundane place in the world, by a configuration of cosmic relations that any fourteenth-century clerk would have recognized. After the wife finds a staff—she knows the house perfectly, as we suspected—she looks around and sees "a litel shymeryng of a light" (I 4297): the moon is shining in through a hole in the roof, and by its light she identifies and smites the "false clerke" (I 4291), her husband. Symkyn is illuminated, or more precisely, spotlighted by the radiance of that heavenly body, and thus a good target for his earnest, helpful wife.

This is not to suggest that the finger of God has pointed to Symkyn, or even that the strange concatenation of man's will and stellar fate has restored him to his proper socioeconomic niche—although both things are true in their way. I merely note that Symkyn's *place* in the house, indeed his unique place in the cosmos, is established in this moonlit moment by his observed relationship to the overarching heavenly bodies. For as Aquinas said, "[t]he true immobility [or "placement"—the property of being some*where*] that is required if a place is to be more than a sheer container [as it was for Aristotle]"—that immobility

> is not to be found in the centrated earth but in a set of relations to the celestial spheres that surround earth itself. Hence the place of something subcelestial is determined by these relations, or more exactly, by the "order and situation" (*ordo et situ*) they offer.[56]

Symkyn has not, in fact, risen to great estate, nor has he entered the infinite void space of his dreams in any way. He is precisely in *this* place, situated relative to the moon and, thus, to the other heavenly bodies, but also to the "order and situation" of his house, family, and occupation.[57] Quite possibly, it was the nature of this place that caused him to dream, but now it is his emplacement here—and here *exactly*—that has inevitably returned him to himself, with what Herman Melville, quite appropriately one would think, referred to as "the universal thump."[58]

IV

Thus comes the containment of Symkyn and the reduction of his vast pretensions. And yet the greater part of his guile has been the subtler art of creating a kind of internal space, hoping to make great his yeoman's estate from within by drawing into it the limitless resources of the nobility, the church, and "al the land aboute." Such a transformation cannot be achieved by extension. A yeoman's estate cannot expand into a duchy, not in social reality. Rather, the small estate must somehow be made to contain the great one. But how can there be "a place / A myle brood [in] twenty foot of space," or, for that matter, infinite leagues within a millet seed? What is needed is a change of substance, on the analogy of what happens to the bread and wine in the sacrament of the Eucharist. Symkyn's most ambitious craft is that of changing the substance of others into his own, as thieves try to do, and here it is helpful to remember the thieves in Dante's *Inferno*, damned to exchange substance with serpents, who become the thieves, only to lose their substance to other serpents *ad infinitum* (Canto XXV). Symkyn, of course, is not really able to transcend himself in such a way—substance is being, and being can only be altered by its creator—but the will is there, as the tale demonstrates in several ways.

When Symkyn encounters the clerks, he is already accustomed to stealing from their college. This time they try to police his activities, but the process goes very much as usual, its focus being the sack of grain they bring with them. Chaucer keeps the sack before us, noting when Aleyn loads it on their horse and when John lays it down at the mill. John says they have come to have their corn ground, and that he will watch it pour into the hopper, while Aleyn promises to see how the meal falls down into the trough. It is only when "hir corn was faire and weel ygrounde. / And whan the mele is sakked and ybounde" (I 4069–4070) that John finds the horse missing. They run off, and Symkyn steals half a bushel of the flour, giving it to his wife to knead and bake into a loaf of bread, *his* bread. While they chase Bayard, who is chasing the wild mares of the fens,[59]—while they are milling around, in other words—Symkyn is grinding up their substance and making (baking!) it into his own. The series of changes by which the grain is reduced to a heap of infinite parts, and then transformed, raised again to form a round, unified loaf, is a little mystery that suggests the greater art of Symkyn's self-enrichment, both of them reminiscent, at least, of that profound mystery, the Eucharistic transubstantiation.[60]

The bag of meal is a model for other conversions Symkyn is attempting. One must keep in mind that Symkyn's house, where he raises his family, is also a means of his advancement, a kind of surrogate mill. For if the mill itself (with its sexual overtones)[61] enables the transformation of grain into his own substance, his wife is a far greater source of wealth. By combining his life with hers, Symkyn received a substantial dowry. More important, he stands to benefit from his children being, in effect, heirs of the church. And here is the transformative magic. The parson is a man of the Church—in fact he is *part* of that great ecclesiastical body—and so he intends to pass on, through his loins, as V. A. Kolve has said,[62] the substance of that greater body:

> For hooly chirches good moot been despended
> On hooly chirches blood, that is descended.
> Therfore he wolde his hooly blood honoure,
> Though that he hooly chirche sholde devoure. (I 3983–3986)

This brilliant and famous chiastic passage contrasts with maximum effect the sublime and the base, charity and greed, the many and the one. The repetition of "hooly" in each line keeps in mind the Christian ideal, while the transition from "hooly chirches blood" to "his hooly blood" in the middle lines demonstrates the corruption of that ideal, and the final line, the grim consequences ("hooly [wholly] . . . devoure").[63] The flow of blood (and "good") from holy church, to the parson, to his heirs, illustrates how, through the mystery of mingled blood, the substance of the church passes into Symkyn's own dominion. When the daughter finally marries, perhaps into some great family, and when the little boy hoists Symkyn's wealth upon fresh shoulders, then will Symkyn himself be transformed into the father of a dynasty—noble blood indeed!

There is, however, a more intimate way in which Symkyn tries to assimilate the substance of others, and this is by becoming a sort of clerk himself. We have already heard what Symkyn thinks of clerks. His contempt for their "art" (I 4122) and "sleighte" (I 4050) combines professional and class resentment with a kind of envy: for is he not as clever as any clerk? Chaucer often indicates such feelings through apparently random echoes in the dialogue, and so here. The clerks, with their book learning and broad north-country accents are certainly "ill . . . millere[s]" (I 4045)—

> Aleyn answerede, "John, and wiltow swa?
> Thanne wil I be bynethe, by my croun,
> And se how that the mele falles doun
> Into the trough; that sal be my disport." (I 4040–4043)

—yet when they chase their horse into the fens, Symkyn begins to swear like any clerk ("by my croun," I 4099), and in fact is echoing Aleyn's words. Moreover, nearly all of what we hear in this tale about clerks and the art of clerks is contributed by Symkyn, in a series of passages culminating in his invitation to make his little house "rowm with speche, as is *youre* gise" (I 4126, my emphasis).

With Symkyn's envy and resentment in mind, we may recall what happens when the clerks' counterattack is discovered. When Aleyn finally creeps back to bed, he finds the cradle, stops, moves on, gets in bed with John, as he thinks, and immediately tells him about the "noble game" (I 4263) with Malyne. *Noble?* As we might expect, Symkyn loves/hates the word, and wakes with a roar: "'Ye, false harlot,' quod the millere, 'hast? / A, false traitour! False clerk!' quod he" (I 4268–4269). Then they fight, wallowing on the floor of the dark bedroom, as the personal pronouns mingle, become indistinguishable— "he smoot hym [who?] with his [whose?] fest" (I 4275)—until Symkyn falls down, falling on his wife, who calls out "Help, Symkyn, for the false clerkes fighte" (I 4291). This confusion of identities climaxes when the wife finds a staff and, seeing what she thinks is the "clerk's" white nightcap, brains that clerk—who turns out to be Symkyn, the moon gleaming off his "pyled skulle" (I 4306).

The wife's confused reasoning seems crucial for our understanding of Symkyn's hybrid identity at this point, and Susan Yager, quoting from Murray Wright Bundy, offers an analysis of exactly what the wife has perceived:

> If we use the terminology of faculty psychology, the wife's actions in sensing and judging the white thing are three-fold. These are, first, simply perceiving the white thing; then identifying it in what Bundy calls "a simple case of predication," or what faculty psychology theory explains as the function of the *cognitive;* and finally, reaching a specific judgment about the thing, or in Bundy's terms, attaching "further attributes" to it, the function of the *aestimativa*. . . . The wife slips into error at that point when, as Bundy puts it, through the "special power of the mind, one may attach to this white object further attributes of motion and magnitude, or reference to time."[64]

Seeing only "a whit thyng," in other words, the wife attributes other appearances, or accidental qualities to it in order to arrive at a judgment of what it is. "She *wende* the clerk hadde wered a volupeer / . . . / And *wende* han hit this Aleyn at the fulle" (I 4303, 4305, my emphasis), Chaucer is careful to say, focusing our attention on her reasoned choice. But what does Chaucer want us to understand about this honest mistake? Yager thinks it calls into question "whether opinions can be believed . . . whether knowledge, as distinct from belief, is possible,"[65] and certainly, the faultiness of opinion is demonstrated here. But the relevance of the wife's error to the tale is probably that Symkyn's identity as miller has been blurred by a recurrent series of slight misidentifications beginning with the milling episode, and hers is the crowning one, as it were. We really cannot know why the wife thinks a clerk (both clerks?) wore a nightcap, although she has been through a lot this night, and perhaps that has had an effect on her. The point is that she attributes clerkly (nightcapped) attributes to the person in the light, and when she hits that person, and it is Symkyn, he is being brained for his clerkliness—that is, his substance, or being, is concealed by the accidental qualities of a clerk. In a perverse way, it is like the transubstantiation of the Eucharist: beneath the accidents of a clerk (as she perceives them) lies the substance of a miller.[66] Thus, with the wife's ironically accurate blow, this hubristic, overbearing "false clerk" has been identified, and thereby reduced to his own modest yeoman's place.

We have reviewed Symkyn's efforts to extend his reach, to assimilate the substance of others to his own, and even to beat someone else at their own game, which means to adopt someone else's identity, to *become* that person in some way, and yet we do not finally believe that Symkyn wants to be a clerk.

He is simply a miller who wants to be more than what he is; he longs to transcend himself, to become something he knows he is not. That is no more than what the men in the *Miller's Tale* want from being in the little house in Oxford, or from Alysoun herself. Finally, each one overreaches himself and falls from grace, which is to say that none of them really belongs there. Symkyn's little house is also a desirable interior—in various social, sexual, and economic ways, a source of plenty—yet he belongs there only as a miller yeoman, not as a clerk or anything other than who, in fact, he is. The larger sense of this theme is that we are what we are: being can not be transcended, for only God, who created us, can change the substance of our being. Once again, we may turn to Aquinas on transubstantion, in a passage any clerk would recognize:

> Form cannot pass into form nor matter into matter by the power of a created agent. But the power of an infinite agent which bears on the whole being of a thing can bring about such a change. To the form of each thing and to the matter of each thing the nature *being* is common; and the author of being is able to change that which is *being* in the one into that which is *being* in the other, by taking away what kept this from being that. (3a. 75, 5 ad 3 [73])

This passage states the absolute limits of being[67] and, by extension, identity and even vocation. Not only clerks but millers, too, were aware of this cultural truism, whether they liked the idea or not. The *Reeve's Tale* is concerned with breaking the ranks of social hierarchy,[68] but more centrally with the inner emptiness, or lack, that creates the desire to transcend these ranks. The tale turns upon frustrated desire—that of the clerks, and also the women and poor (gelded?) Bayard—but the central emptiness must be that of Symkyn himself, driven to expand into outer or inner space, because he is unable to accept the nature of his own small place.

NOTES

1. All quotations from Chaucer's works are drawn from *The Riverside Chaucer*, ed. Larry D. Benson, 3rd edn. (Boston, 1987). A note on the terminology of place and space: initially, I will be discussing place and space as physical terms, but the "place" that is Symkyn's house, and Symkyn's "place" in his community, for example, are metaphors. As such they typify the lexical spread of these terms as they become a part of social life. Rather than deplore the loss of precision as exact terms adapt themselves to human affairs, we probably do well to celebrate what the philosopher, geographer, and social theorist Henri Lefebvre called the "polyvalence" of social space: "Is space a social relationship? Certainly—but one which is inherent in property relationships (especially the ownership of the earth, of land) and also closely bound up with the forces of production (which impose a form on that earth or land); here we see the polyvalence of social space, its 'reality' at once formal and material"

(*The Production of Space,* trans. Donald Nicholson-Smith [1974; repr. Oxford, 1991], 85). See also Edward Dimendberg, "Henri Lefebvre on Abstract Space," in *Philosophy and Geography II: The Production of Public Space,* ed. Andrew Light and Jonathan M. Smith (New York, 1998), 17–47.

2. J.A.W. Bennett refers to Richard Campsall's *Quaestiones* on Aristotle's *Prior Analytics*—a "convenient example of the topics argued in the Oxford schools"—and suggests that it is "this sort of fine-spun syllogistic argument the Miller of the *Reeve's Tale* seems to be sneering at" when he says they can make a small place broader by "argumentes" (*Chaucer at Oxford and Cambridge* [Oxford, 1974], 61).

3. Albert of Saxony, *Quaestiones et decisiones physicales insignium virorum: Alberti de Saxonia in octo libros Physicorum; tres libros De celo et mundo* . . . (Paris: vaenundantur in aedibus Iodici Badii Ascensii et Conradi Resch, 1518), *De celo,* bk. 1, qu. 9, 93v, col. 2. Quoted in Edward Grant, *Planets, Stars, and Orbs: The Medieval Cosmos,* 1200–1687 (Cambridge, England, 1994), 171n8.

4. The account of Albert's life is drawn from Joël Biard, *Routledge Encyclopedia of Philosophy,* ed. Edward Craig et al., 10 vols. (New York, 1998), 1:143–44; Joseph R. Strayer, *Dictionary of the Middle Ages,* ed. Joseph R. Strayer, 14 vols. (New York, 1982), 1:125–26, and Gordon Leff, *The Encyclopedia of Philosophy,* ed. Paul Edwards et al., 8 vols. (New York, 1967), 1:63–64. For a discussion of Albert's works, see Ernest A. Moody, *Dictionary of Scientific Biography,* ed. Charles Coulston Gillispie, 16 vols. (New York, 1970–1980), 1:93–95.

5. Grant, *Planets,* 747n7.

6. Gordon Leff, *Bradwardine and the Pelagians: A Study of His 'De Causa Dei' and Its Opponents* (Cambridge, England, 1957), 64.

7. Bennett, *Chaucer,* 69.

8. See Grant: "The best candidate for a 'social context' for scholastic natural philosophy between the thirteenth and seventeenth centuries is the company of Aristotelian natural philosophers (embracing both secular and theological masters) whose loci were the higher-educational institutions of Europe. What they shared by virtue of a common higher education was a bookish and learned tradition that flourished in the universities and colleges and was centered on the works of Aristotle set within a larger matrix of Greco-Arabic learning" (*Planets,* 56). See also David Luscombe: "One feature of the fourteenth century which fully deserves to be highlighted—it is the one which could also be illustrated during the thirteenth century, but not to such an extent—is the remarkable penetration of philosophy into cultural life in general. There were many ways in which this penetration occurred. One example comes from the numerous sermons preached at the time. . . . Rigorous logical argument, the marshalling of philosophical texts, citations from the works of recent or contemporary masters, explicit problem-solving and *quaestiones*—in other words, many forms of the staple activity of masters and students in universities were also deployed in other contexts" (*Medieval Thought* [Oxford, 1997], 136).

9. Grant, *Planets,* 20, 52.

10. Edward S. Casey, *The Fate of Place: A Philosophical History* (Berkeley, Calif., 1997), 107.

11. See Edward Grant, "The Condemnation of 1277, God's Power, and Physical Thought in the Late Middle Ages," *Viator* 10 (1979): 211–44; and John F. Wippel, "The Condemnations of 1270 and 1277 at Paris," *Journal of Medieval and Renaissance Studies* 7 (1977): 169–201.

12. Pierre Duhem, *Études sur Léonard de Vinci*, 3 vols. (Paris, 1906–13), 2:412 (trans. Casey, *Fate of Place*, 107n12). But see, too, David C. Lindberg, *The Beginnings of Western Science: The European Scientific Tradition in Philosophical, Religious, and Institutional Context, 600 B.C. to A.D. 1450* (Chicago, 1992), 238–40, for a more conservative view: "Thus, to put the event in its proper light, the condemnations represent a victory not for modern science but for conservative thirteenth-century theology. The condemnations were a ringing declaration for the subordination of philosophy to theology" (238).

13. Casey, *Fate of Place*, 107.

14. Aristotle, *Physics*, trans. Robin Waterfield (Oxford, 1996), 87–8 (IV, 4, 212a2).

15. Aristotle, *Physics*, trans. Waterfield, 85 (IV, 4, 210b32).

16. Aristotle, *Physics*, trans. Waterfield, 85 (IV, 4, 210b32).

17. According to Richard Sorabji, *Matter, Space and Motion: Theories in Antiquity and Their Sequel* (Ithaca, N.Y., 1988), "[t]he most compelling argument ever produced for the infinity of space was devised by Plato's friend, the Pythagorean Archytas" (125). Sorabji quotes Simplicius, a sixth-century Greek, in his commentary on Aristotle's *Physics* (Simplicius reports Archytas's experiment as described by Eudemus of Rhodes, Aristotle's pupil): "If I came to be at the edge, for example at the heaven of the fixed stars, could I stretch my hand or my stick outside, or not? That I should not stretch it out would be absurd *(atopon)*, but if I do stretch it out, what is outside will be either body or place. . . . If it is always something different into which the stick is stretched, it will clearly be something infinite" (125). See also David E. Hahm, *The Origins of Stoic Cosmology* (Columbus, Oh., 1977), 106–7.

18. In *Libros Physicorum Aristotelis*, IV, 6 (paraphrased in Casey, *Fate of Place*, 105).

19. Casey, *Fate of Place*, 105.

20. Edward Grant, ed., *A Source Book in Medieval Science* (Boston, 1974), 48.

21. Grant, *Source Book*, 48.

22. Casey, *Fate of Place*, 109.

23. Thomas Bradwardine, *De causa Dei contra Pelagium et de virtute causarum ad suos Mertonenses libri tres . . . opera et studio Dr. Henrici Savili Collegii Mertonensis in Academia Oxoniensis custodis, ex scriptis codicibus nunc, primum editi* (London: Ioannem Billium, 1618).

24. Leff, *Bradwardine*, 13, 14; see also Luscombe, *Medieval Thought*, 135.

25. Leff, *Bradwardine*, 266.

26. Leff, *Bradwardine*, 29–30. See also George Molland, *Mathematics and the Medieval Ancestry of Physics* (Brookfield, Vt., 1995): "In *[De causa Dei]* Bradwardine even gave hints of attempting to form a mathematical science of theology" (XIII, 572).

27. Grant, *Source Book*, 556–57.

28. Casey, *Fate of Place*, 112–13.

29. Grant, *Planets*, 170.

30. Grant, *Planets*, 170 (my emphasis). See also 160–61 on Albert's rejecting the natural (though not the supernatural) possibility that other worlds could exist.

31. See note 3 above.

32. Mary M. McLaughlin, *Intellectual Freedom and Its Limitations in the University of Paris in the Thirteenth and Fourteenth Centuries* (New York, 1977), in a discussion of Jean Buridan, refers to the "element of play that was strong in

contemporary speculation": "Although this spirit of intellectual play may seem at times love of paradox for its own sake, reflecting the sceptical mood of many four-teenth-century masters, it undeniably fostered a positive freedom of discussion and inquiry. What is most significant in Buridan's treatment of many problems, as in that of a number of his contemporaries, is the use of the method of hypothesis in the exploration of philosophical and scientific problems. Hypotheses, *imaginations* and 'probable explanations,' . . . were becoming the bases of scientific inquiry" (114).

33. Grant, *Source Book,* 548 (for Albert's edition, see note 3).

34. Grant, *Source Book,* 560.

35. Peter Brown observes that Symkyn "is like the self-educated father who feels he must keep abreast of his son's university education. The tone is proud and patronizing. . . . There is a strong sense of competitiveness, of challenge, underlying these lines" ("The Containment of Symkyn: The Function of Space in the *Reeve's Tale," Chaucer Review* 14 [1980]: 225–36, at 232).

36. Regarding the ironies called forth on the part of Aristotelian philosophers by the Condemnations of 1277, McLaughlin remarks: "Despite an occasional tinge of irony, there is in Buridan's approach to the problems of faith and theology none of the ring of insincerity that may seem at times to mark the easy protestations of his older contemporary, John of Jandun. That the condemnation of 1277 in no way hindered an extreme devotion to Aristotle and Averroes is manifest in the works of this master and others in the early fourteenth century" (*Intellectual Freedom,* 130).

37. In 1272, for substantially the same reasons that Bishop Tempier would issue the 219 Condemnations in 1277, the faculty of arts of the University of Paris, which possessed the authority to dictate what could and could not be included in university lectures, voted to "decree and ordain that no master or bachelor of our faculty should presume to determine or even to dispute any purely theological ques-tion." If a question were considered which concerned both philosophy and faith, it had to be resolved in favor of the faith. Moreover, "if any master or bachelor of our faculty reads or disputes any difficult passages or any questions which seem to undermine the faith, he shall refute the arguments or text as far as they are against the faith or concede that they are absolutely false and entirely erroneous, and he shall not presume to dispute or lecture further upon this sort of difficulties, either in the text or in authorities." See Lynn Thorndike, *University Records and Life in the Middle Ages* (New York, 1944), 64–65; see also Grant, *Planets,* 50.

38. Grant, *Source Book,* 48.

39. See Grant, "Condemnation of 1277," 227.

40. Grant, "Condemnation of 1277," 233.

41. Edward Grant, *The Foundations of Modern Science in the Middle Ages* (Cam-bridge, England, 1996), 78.

42. See Brian Davies, *The Thought of Thomas Aquinas* (Oxford, 1992): "[Aqui-nas] is often thought of as the eucharistic theologian *par excellence* of the Catholic Church" (361).

43. All quotations from the *Summa* will be drawn from vol. 58 of Thomas Aquinas, *Summa Theologiae,* ed. and trans. William Barden, O.P., 60 vols. (London, 1965). Page numbers in square brackets follow each citation.

44. Davies, *Thought,* 367.

45. Grant, *Foundations,* 124.

46. Aquinas, *Summa,* trans. Barden, 58:96c.

47. Grant, *Foundations,* 79.

48. Grant, "Condemnation of 1277," 234–35.

49. Grant, "Condemnation of 1277," 235. See also Marshall Claggett, *The Science of Mechanics in the Middle Ages* (Madison, Wisc., 1961), 255–418 (chapters 5 and 6).

50. Grant, "Condemnation of 1277," 239.

51. This section parallels some of Brown's important analysis of the spatial relationships in this tale. Brown argues that *Le meunier et les .II. clers*, the closest analogue to *RvT*, disregards those "descriptive elements which . . . help to foster the illusion of a three-dimensional locale" ("Containment," 227), while Chaucer's introduction does provide those elements. Brown then shows how the bedchamber scene is "conceived in three dimensions" (231), and concludes that "[m]etaphorically speaking [Symkyn's] space, his area of influence, is reduced, and . . . the act of achieving this is imaged in the manoeuvres and struggles that take place within the interior of the bedchamber" (234). My own essay treats some of the same "manoeuvres and struggles," and often I draw upon Brown's observations, but my attempt is to demonstrate how Symkyn's cryptic lines on place and space, and the ideas about cosmic space which they appear to echo, have their mundane reflection in his portrait, his language, his practices, and the appropriateness of his punishment.

52. I acknowledge here my indebtedness to Robert W. Frank Jr.'s invaluable essay, "The *Reeve's Tale* and the Comedy of Limitation," in *Directions in Literary Criticism*, ed. Stanley Weintraub and Philip Young (University Park, Pa., 1973), 53–69, which proposes several lines of inquiry regarding space in this tale. To begin, Frank seems to have been among the first to discuss relations in domestic space in this tale: "Space is undeniably the functional element in the *Reeve's Tale*. The whole plot hinges on it: the size of the room, the bedding of all parties in this one room, the shifting of the cradle" (63). But he also calls attention to clerkly ideas about place and space: "There were probably heated debates on the topic of space at Oxford and Cambridge in the late fourteenth century—an additional reason, perhaps, for the tale's odd anchoring in academia. As our knowledge, sadly inadequate, of fourteenth-century English philosophy becomes more detailed we may be able to point to a specific controversy. . . . [T]he attacks on Aristotelian physics, particularly Aristotelian doctrines about matter and space and about motion, and the sometimes extravagant working out of the logical implications of God's absolute power (*potentia absoluta*) led, among other conclusions, to some startling speculations about space" (63). And most helpful for the topic at hand: "Refinements of position on the doctrine of transubstantiation also led to comments on the nature of space" (63).

53. Symkyn's weapons have provoked a varied critical response. For Paul A. Olson, Symkyn's portrait exemplifies Chaucer's "naturalistic" style in this tale: "The sword that [Miller] Robin bears by his side is parodied grossly by the armory of knives and swords that Symkyn bears" ("The *Reeve's Tale*: Chaucer's *Measure for Measure*," *Studies in Philology* 59 [1962]: 1–17, at 16–17). John Block Friedman allegorizes the portrait: "With this array of ironwork, his short temper, his joy in violence, [Symkyn] seems to embody in every way the sin of wrath" ("A Reading of Chaucer's *Reeve's Tale*," *Chaucer Review* 2 [1967]: 8–19, at 17). Elizabeth Edwards, however, reads the portrait as a sign referring to gender economics: "Symkyn, bristling with weapons, guards his wife's and daughter's chastity as the lock boxes of the church's goods" ("The Economics of Justice in Chaucer's Miller's and Reeve's Tales," *Dalhousie Review* 82 [2002]: 91–112, at 103), while Jill Mann sees an example of "traditional gender roles" in Symkyn, "who goes armed to the teeth to impress his

ladylike wife with his manly courage" (*Geoffrey Chaucer* [Atlantic Highlands, N.J., 1991], 186). But Britton J. Harwood says that Symkyn's weapons imply his aristocratic pretensions: "The project that calls for the miller and his wife to parade like aristocrats calls for him to arm himself as well, for the fourteenth-century English aristocracy was of course a military one. Symkyn delivers to himself the *dagger* and *espee* that the 1388 parliament at Cambridge prohibited laborers from carrying" ("Psychoanalytic Politics: Chaucer and Two Peasants," *ELH* 68 [2001]: 1–27, at 11; he cites *Statutes of the Realm (1101–1713)*, ed. A. Luders, T. E. Tomlins, J. Raitby et al., 11 vols. [London, 1810–28], 2:57). And finally, T. A. Shippey calls what goes on in Symkyn's bedchamber "phallic aggression," which, not finding it in the dictionary, he defines as "a sexual act committed with the primary aim, not of physical pleasure, but of *either* causing pain or injury to the female victim *or* humiliating her male protector" ("Phallic, Ocular and Other Aggressions in Chaucer and His Analogues," unpublished essay, 3). But if Aleyn and John commit these sexual acts in direct response to Symkyn's armed insolence and cheating, his own paramilitary portrait-with-wife (they both wear red) would also, and pointedly, express a kind of "phallic aggression."

54. Brown, "Containment," 232.

55. Gerhard Joseph gives this passage a thematic reading which casts some light on the fabliaux, even though it does not address the particular significance of space in *RvT*: "For the 'ernest' pilgrim [i.e., the Knight] . . . human space is dreadfully narrow, a prison with which we must make do and which we can make bearable through carefully ordered rituals. But for the actor or observer who views the world as 'game,' a cramped 'twenty foot of space' easily widens out to become a room 'a myle brood,' world enough and time for the acting out of a lighthearted human drama" ("Chaucerian 'Game'— 'Earnest' and the 'Argument of Herbergage' in *The Canterbury Tales*," *Chaucer Review* 5 [1970]: 83–96, at 91).

56. Casey, *Fate of Place*, 105.

57. See Joseph E. Grennen: "the culminating incident in the tale [the wife's blow] is a crowning irony precisely because what is accidental from the point of view of the human participants is necessary in the sense that celestial motions are divinely ordained and that at the crucial moment Luna made its transit across the hole in the roof" ("The Calculating Reeve and His *Camera obscura*," *Journal of Medieval and Renaissance Studies* 14 [1984]: 245–59, at 255).

58. Herman Melville, *Moby-Dick, or The Whale* (New York, 1930), 6.

59. If Sandy Feinstein is right about Bayard being a gelding, the chase over the fens seems all the more barren ("*The Reeve's Tale*: About that Horse," *Chaucer Review* 26 [1991]: 99–106).

60. Cp. Frank: "We come very close to what may have agitated [Symkyn's] imagination in the statement from the *Centriloquium Theologicum* attributed to Ockham: 'In the whole universe there are no more parts than in one bean, because in a bean there is an infinite number of parts' [Conclusion 17, C, as quoted in A. C. Crombie, *Augustine to Galileo: The History of Science AD 400–1650* (Cambridge, Mass., 1953), 241]" ("Reeve's Tale," 64n51). Frank identifies in this passage terms and logic that resemble those in Symkyn's lines on place and space. While Ockham is not referring to the transubstantiation of the host, his equation of the parts of the universe with the parts of a bean does seem to suggest a paradoxical (if impossible) commensurability in size: somehow, the tiny and the infinitely great are made to

seem potentially convertible here, in somewhat the same way, perhaps, as the clerks' flour is related to Symkyn's bread.

61. More than one critic has remarked that the milling apparatus and milling in general are reminiscent of generation in this tale. Susanna Fein says that "the to-and-fro wagging of the hopper that passes the grain to the trough below . . . [is] a motional image that anticipates, in mechanistic terms, the copulative acts later to occur in the bedroom" ("'Lat the Children Pleye': The Game Betwixt the Ages in *The Reeve's Tale*," in *Rebels and Rivals: The Contestive Spirit in The Canterbury Tales*, ed. Susanna Greer Fein, David Raybin, and Peter C. Braeger [Kalamazoo, Mich., 1991], 73–104, at 82). According to Ian Lancashire, "[T]he double meanings that exist in Chaucer's language derive not simply from individual terms, but from the situation itself, the most immediately striking part of the *Reeve's Tale*, the plot line. Here Chaucer is tapping a vein of sexual humor as old as the machinery of the mill and the business of the miller, and as obvious. . . . The only prerequisite for understanding this traditional oral obscenity is membership in a society where the mill is a district's everyday landmark and business-place" ("Sexual Innuendo in *The Reeve's Tale*," *Chaucer Review* 63 [1972]: 159–70, at 160–61). Most recently, Mary Flowers Braswell, writing about the literary possibilities of legal language, states that "Documents such as milling ordinances, for example, contain a stock vocabulary that is straightforward and useful in its immediate context; but when it is removed from its particular setting, it is inevitably humorous and obscene. . . . '[G]rind' (denoting copulation) and 'stone' (meaning testicles) were medieval commonplaces" (*Chaucer's "Legal Fiction": Reading the Records* [Teaneck, N.J., 2001], 38–39).

62. See V. A. Kolve, *Chaucer and the Imagery of Narrative: The First Five Canterbury Tales* (Stanford, Calif., 1984), 234.

63. Again, Kolve: "The last line is mysterious and terrible, for Holy Church resides ultimately in the souls of the faithful. It is the faithful he is willing to devour" (*Chaucer*, 234).

64. Susan Yager, "'A Whit Thyng in Hir Ye': Perception and Error in the *Reeve's Tale*," *Chaucer Review* 28 (1994): 393–404, at 399; Murray Wright Bundy, *The Theory of Imagination in Classical and Medieval Thought* (Urbana, Ill., 1927), 69.

65. Yager, "Whit Thyng," 401.

66. John F. Plummer offers this comment on Malyne: "While we see the miller's pride and thievery and his wife's pride and scornfulness in their actions, we see Malyne's complicity in her family's knavery only in her physiology. She has all the physical signs of her breeding, but her act of restitution, returning rather than hoarding something stolen, sets her apart from her kin ("Hooly Chirches Blood: Simony and Patrimony in Chaucer's *Reeve's Tale*," *Chaucer Review* 18 [1983]: 49–60, at 57). As Plummer points out, Malyne's appearances (plainly, she is Symkyn's daughter) conceal an honest heart, while as we have seen, beneath Symkyn's accidental clerkliness lies the unredeemed miller.

67. Barden, editor of the *Summa Theologiae* (see note 43 above), quotes M.-T. Penido, *Le Rôle de l'analogie en théologie dogmatique* (Paris, 1931), 437, who thought that the words just quoted are "the most profound . . . ever said on the possibility and nature of the Eucharistic conversion" (73).

68. One of the most interesting treatments of this well-known theme is Britton Harwood's "Psychoanalytic Politics" (see note 53), where he rightly places Chaucer with those who aligned themselves with Richard II during the Peasants' Revolt: "[The] transgressive pretension [of Symkyn] and brutality [of his punishment] repeat,

in Chaucer's own fashion, the message that Walsingham attributed to Richard when the King met on 22 June with envoys from the Essex rebels, after the turning point of the rising of 1381: 'Rustici quidem fuistis et estis; in bondagio permanebitis' (Rustics indeed you were and are; you will remain in bondage). That is, you will continue to be serfs. Chaucer's class attributed the violence in 1381 peculiarly to serfs (nativi)" (12). And again: "Through Symkyn, Chaucer punishes 'laboreris' who take 'knyȝthod' upon themselves" (13).

Chronology

1340–43 Birth of the poet Geoffrey Chaucer, probably to John (a wine merchant) and Agnes Chaucer.

1347 Geoffrey, now about seven years of age, moves with his parents, his older brother John, and probably his younger sister Kate to the city of Southampton. By now, Chaucer has probably learned to read a little with the help of a clerical tutor back in London and is probably studying with the schoolmaster of his district, receiving lessons in manners, prayers, hymns, and the rudiments of reading and writing Latin. Truce between England and France. The Black Death reaches England. By October, it has reached London. In 1348, Parliament is cancelled and many schools closed down.

1349 The Chaucer family is back in their Thames Street house in London. Geoffrey begins school somewhere in the Vintry Ward area, probably the Almonry Cathedral School attached to St. Paul's. By mid-century, this school had an unusual schoolmaster, William Ravenstone, who possessed a large collection of books in Latin, including a large number of the classics. It is quite possible that the poet, who demonstrated an unusual knowledge of the classics from a young age, acquired this learning from Ravenstone's library. St. Paul's also inherited works of grammar, logic, natural history, medicine and law from William Tolleshunt in 1328, which the poet would have had the opportunity to use. However, the subjects Chaucer principally dealt with were the *trivium*—grammar, logic, and eloquence.

1357   At least sixteen years of age, Chaucer serves as a minor member of Elizabeth's household, the Countess of Ulster and wife of Prince Lionel (Edward III's second son).

1360   Chaucer is captured by French soldiers. King Edward III contributes funding to help pay Chaucer's ransom. Chaucer carries letters to England from Calais for Lionel, earl of Ulster.

1361   Chaucer likely receives legal education at the Inns of Chancery and may have attended Oxford. A terrible second wave of Black Plague strikes.

1361–67 Chaucer works on *Prior a Nostre Dame*, *The Romance of the Rose*, and early *Complaints*.

1365–66 Chaucer marries Philippa Pan, first daughter of Paon de Roet (in the household of Queen Philippa) and sister of Katherine (later mistress and third wife of John of Gaunt, Duke of Lancaster).

1366   February 22–May 24, Chaucer receives safe conduct to travel in Spain where he acquires at least one strong image for his poetry in *The House of Fame*—a mountain of ice with a building on top. Chaucer's father dies, and his mother remarries.

1367   Geoffrey Chaucer granted royal annuity of 20 marks as he enters the King's service as an esquire of the royal household.

1368–69 Probable date of Chaucer's *The Book of The Duchess*—an elegy to John of Gaunt's first wife, Blanche of Lancaster, and a tribute to Gaunt. Chaucer writes "Fragment A" of *The Romance of the Rose*.

1369   Chaucer serves with Gaunt in raid on Picardy. Death of Queen Philippa. Philippa Chaucer possibly enters Gaunt's household as a lady in waiting. Hostilities resume in the Hundred Years' War, marking the second major phase of military engagement.

1370   June 20–September 29, Chaucer possibly runs diplomatic errands in France for the King and may be with Gaunt in Aquitaine.

1373–77 "St. Cecelia"; The Monk's tragedies; and *Anelida*.

1372   On December 1, Chaucer is commissioned to establish an English seaport for Genoese trade. To this end for "other matters of the king's business," Chaucer leaves for Genoa, visits Florence. At this time, Boccaccio is in Florence, and Petrarch is in Padua. Chaucer remains in Italy until the summer of the next year.

1373   On May 23, Chaucer returns to London. Possible birth of Thomas Chaucer.

1374   On April 23, Chaucer receives a royal grant of a pitcher of wine daily. On May 10, Chaucer leases Aldgate house and sets up housekeeping. On June 8, Chaucer is made Comptroller of Wool Customs and Subsidy for the Port of London (a lucrative and powerful position). On June 13, Geoffrey and Philippa receive £10 annuity from Gaunt. Death of Petrarch.

1376   Chaucer begins early trips to France on diplomatic missions negotiating for peace.

1380   On May 1, Chaucer is released from suit for "raptus" of Cecily Champain. Birth of Lewis Chaucer (for whom Chaucer wrote the *Treatise on the Astrolabe* in 1391).

1380–82 Chaucer writes *The Parliament of Fowles.*

1382–86 Chaucer writes *Troilus and Criseyde, Legend of Good Women.* Langland is working on *Piers Plowman,* C Text.

1383   Chaucer obtains first loan against his annuity, possibly the first sign of financial troubles.

1385   October 12, Chaucer is appointed Justice of the Peace in Kent.

1386   In August, Chaucer is elected to parliament as Knight of the Shire for Kent. On December 4 Adam Yardley is appointed Comptroller of Customs. Chaucer is stripped of his position by King Richard II while Gaunt is on a military foray in Spain. Chaucer is not restored to an important post until his benefactor's return.

1386–87 *Canterbury Prologue;* early Tales (Knight, Part VII).

1387   Chaucer begins *The Canterbury Tales.*

1388   On May 1, Chaucer surrenders his royal annuities to John Scalby of Lincolnshire. The Lords Appellant and Parliament impeach several of King Richard II's favorite courtiers, including close supporters of the king such as Thomas Usk, one of Chaucer's "disciples" in literature.

1388–89 Chaucer's *fabliaux* (Miller and Reeve).

1389   Chaucer is appointed Clerk of the King's Works, and his pay rises to more than £30 a year. He is responsible for the construction at Westminster, the Tower of London, and several castles and manors.

1390–94 Probable dates of Chaucer's "Marriage Group" of tales: "Wife of Bath," "Friar," "Summoner," "Merchant," "Clerk," "Franklin," and the *Astrolabe* and *Equatorie of Planets.*

1390   Chaucer is commissioned to repair Saint George's chapel, Windsor; oversees repairs on the lower Thames sewers and conduits between Woolwich and Greenwich; instructed to build bleachers for jousts at Smithfield, etc. Chaucer is robbed of the king's money on the highway.

1391   On June 17, Chaucer resigns as Clerk of the King's Works, and another clerk is appointed. Chaucer is appointed Deputy Forester of the Royal Forest of North Petherton, Somerset.

1393   Chaucer is granted a gift of £10 from Richard II for services rendered.

1394   Chaucer is granted a new annuity of £20 for life.

1396–99 Probable dates of "The Nun's Priest's Tale," the final version of "The Canon Yeoman's Tale," and "The Parson's Tale"; probable dates of Balades to Scogan, Bukton (mentioned in "Wife of Bath").

1397   Chaucer is granted a tun of wine a year. Gaunt marries Katherine Swynford.

1398   Financial woes return, Chaucer borrows against his annuity; action for debt is taken against Chaucer. The king provides letters of protection from these debts. Richard II's final gift to Chaucer is a "tonel" (252 gallons) of wine a year for life.

1399   Richard II is overthrown. Henry Bolingbroke (Henry IV) lands in Yorkshire with 40 followers and soon has 60,000 supporters. He takes control of government and is promptly "elected" regent. On October 13, his coronation day, Henry IV confirms and doubles Chaucer's annuity (now 40 marks). On December 24, Chaucer signs a 53-year lease for tenement in the garden of the Lady Chapel, Westminster Abbey.

1400   September 29 is the last record of Chaucer. He signs a receipt for a tun of wine delivered to him.

1556   Chaucer's tomb is erected in Westminster Abbey, the first poet of "the Poets' Corner." The date on the tombstone is October 25, 1400.

1598   Thomas Speght prints a version of *Chaucer's Works* aimed at Protestant readers. His biography of Chaucer includes an account stating that Chaucer was fined for beating up a friar on Fleet Street.

Contributors

HAROLD BLOOM is Sterling Professor of the Humanities at Yale University. He is the author of 30 books, including *Shelley's Mythmaking* (1959), *The Visionary Company* (1961), *Blake's Apocalypse* (1963), *Yeats* (1970), *A Map of Misreading* (1975), *Kabbalah and Criticism* (1975), *Agon: Toward a Theory of Revisionism* (1982), *The American Religion* (1992), *The Western Canon* (1994), and *Omens of Millennium: The Gnosis of Angels, Dreams, and Resurrection* (1996). *The Anxiety of Influence* (1973) sets forth Professor Bloom's provocative theory of the literary relationships between the great writers and their predecessors. His most recent books include *Shakespeare: The Invention of the Human* (1998), a 1998 National Book Award finalist, *How to Read and Why* (2000), *Genius: A Mosaic of One Hundred Exemplary Creative Minds* (2002), *Hamlet: Poem Unlimited* (2003), *Where Shall Wisdom Be Found?* (2004), and *Jesus and Yahweh: The Names Divine* (2005). In 1999, Professor Bloom received the prestigious American Academy of Arts and Letters Gold Medal for Criticism. He has also received the International Prize of Catalonia, the Alfonso Reyes Prize of Mexico, and the Hans Christian Andersen Bicentennial Prize of Denmark.

FIONA SOMERSET is associate professor of English at Duke University. She is author of *Clerical Discourse and Lay Audience in Late Medieval England* (1998) and co-editor of *The Lollards and Their Influence in Late Medieval England* (2003) and *The Vulgar Tongue: Medieval and Post-Medieval Vernacularity* (2003).

COLIN WILCOCKSON is emeritus fellow at Pembroke College, Cambridge.

KATHERINE LITTLE is assistant professor of English at Fordham University. She wrote *Confession and Resistance: Defining the Self in Late Medieval England* (2006).

LEE PATTERSON is professor of English at Yale University. He is author, most recently, of *Fallible Authors: Chaucer's Pardoner and Wife of Bath* (2007), and co-editor with Ian Johnson of *The Cambridge History of Literary Criticism, vol. 2: The Middle Ages* (2005).

ELIZABETH ROBERTSON is professor of English at the University of Colorado. She is author of *Early English Devotional Prose and the Female Audience* (1990).

LOUISE M. BISHOP is associate professor of honors-college literature at the University of Oregon. She is author of *Words, Stones, and Herbs: The Healing Word in Medieval and Early Modern England* (2007).

RICHARD FIRTH GREEN is Humanities Distinguished Professor of English at Ohio State University. He is the author of *A Crisis of Truth: Literature and Law in Ricardian England* (1998) and *Poets and Princepleasers: Literature and the English Court in the Late Middle Ages* (1980).

LIANNA FARBER is associate professor of English at the University of Minnesota, Minneapolis.

PETER W. TRAVIS is Henry Winkley Professor of Anglo-Saxon and English Language and Literature at Dartmouth College. He is author of *Dramatic Design in the Chester Cycle* (1982).

WILLIAM F. WOODS is professor of English at Wichita State University. He is author of *Chaucerian Spaces: Spatial Poetics in Chaucer's Opening* Tales (2008).

Bibliography

Ackroyd, Peter. *Chaucer.* London: Chatto & Windus, 2004.

Allen, Mark, and John H. Fisher. *The Essential Chaucer: An Annotated Bibliography of Major Modern Studies.* Boston: G. K. Hall, 1987.

Allen, Judson Boyce, and Theresa Anne Moritz. *A Distinction of Stories: The Medieval Unity of Chaucer's Fair Chain of Narratives for Canterbury.* Columbus: Ohio State University Press, 1981.

Ames, Ruth M. *God's Plenty: Chaucer's Christian Humanism.* Chicago: Loyola University Press, 1984.

Andrew, Malcolm, ed. *Critical Essays on Chaucer's* Canterbury Tales. London: Open University Press; Toronto: University of Toronto Press, 1991.

Ashton, Gail, and Louise Sylvester. *Teaching Chaucer.* New York: Palgrave Macmillan, 2007.

Astell, Ann W. *Chaucer and the Universe of Learning.* Ithaca, N.Y.: Cornell University Press, 1996.

Beidler, Peter G., and Elizabeth M. Biebel, eds. *Chaucer's "Wife of Bath's Prologue and Tale": An Annotated Bibliography, 1900–1995.* Toronto and Buffalo: University of Toronto Press, in association with the University of Rochester, 1998.

Benson, Carl David. *Chaucer's Drama of Style: Poetic Variety and Contrast in* The Canterbury Tales. University of North Carolina Press, 1986.

Benson, Larry D. "The Order of the *Canterbury tales.*" *Studies in the Age of Chaucer* 3 (1981): pp. 77–120.

Besserman, Lawrence. *Chaucer and the Bible: An Introduction, Critical Reviews of Research, Indexes, and Bibliography.* New York: Garland, 1988

Bishop, Ian. *The Narrative Art of* The Canterbury Tales. London: Dent, 1987.

Bisson, Lillian M. *Chaucer and the Late Medieval World.* London: Macmillan, 1998.

Braswell, Mary Flowers. *The Medieval Sinner: Characterization and Confession in the Literature of the English Middle Ages.* New York: Associated University Presses, 1982.

Brewer, Derek. *Chaucer in His Time.* London: Thomas Nelson, 1963.

———. *A New Introduction to Chaucer.* 2nd ed. London. New York: Longman, 1998.

———. *Chaucer and Chaucerians: Critical Studies in Middle English Literature.* London: Thomas Nelson, 1966.

Burnley, David, and Matsuji Tajima. *The Language of Middle English Literature.* Woodbridge, Suffolk, and Rochester, N.Y.: Boydell & Brewer, 1994

Cooper, Helen. *The Canterbury Tales.* Oxford Guides to Chaucer. Oxford: Oxford University Press, 1989.

Correale, Robert M., and Mary Hamel, eds. *Sources and Analogues of* The Canterbury Tales *[I].* Chaucer Studies. Woodbridge, Suffolk: Boydell and Brewer, 2002.

Davenport, W A. *Chaucer and His English Contemporaries: Prologue and Tale in* The Canterbury Tales. New York: St. Martin's Press, 1998.

Davidson, Linda K. and Maryjane Dunn-Wood. Pilgrimage *in the Middle Ages: A Research Guide.* New York: Garland, 1992.

Davis, Norman, *et al.,* ed. *A Chaucer Glossary.* Oxford: Clarendon Press, 1979.

Dempster, Germaine. *Dramatic Irony in Chaucer.* New York: Humanities Press, 1959.

Donaldson, E. Talbot. *Speaking of Chaucer.* London: Athlone, 1970.

Edwards, Robert. *Chaucer and Boccaccio: Antiquity and Modernity.* Houndmills, Basingstoke, Hampshire, New York: Palgrave, 2002.

Ellis, Steve. *Chaucer. An Oxford Guide.* Oxford. New York: Oxford University Press, 2005.

Fisher, Sheila. *Chaucer's Poetic Alchemy: A Study of Value and Its Transformation in* The Canterbury Tales. New York: Garland, 1988.

Hallisy, Margaret. *Clean Maids, True Wives, Steadfast Widows: Chaucer's Women and Medieval Codes of Conduct.* Westport, Conn.: Greenwood, 1995.

Hines, John. *The Fabliau in English.* Harlow: Longman, 1993.

Hoffman, R. L. *Ovid and the* Canterbury Tales. Philadelphia: University of Pennsylvania Press, 1966.

Hornsby, Joseph A. *Chaucer and the Law.* Norman, Oklahoma: Pilgrim Books, 1988.

Howard, Donald R. *Chaucer: His Life, His World, His Works.* New York: Dutton, 1987.

Huppé, Bernard, and D. W. Robertson, Jr. *Fruyt and Chaf: Studies in Chaucer's Allegories.* Princeton: Princeton University Press, 1963.

Jost, Jean E., ed. *Chaucer's Humor: Critical Essays.* New York: Garland, 1994.

Kay, Sara. *The 'Romance of the Rose.'* London: Grant & Cutler, 1995.

Kean, Patricia Margaret. *Chaucer and the Making of English Poetry.* 2 vols. London, Boston: Routledge and Kegan Paul, 1972.

———. *Chaucer's Love Vision and Debate.* London: Kegan Paul, 1972.

Kelly, Henry Ansgar. *Love and Marriage in the Age of Chaucer.* Ithaca, N.Y.: Cornell University Press, 1975.

Koff, Leonard Michael. *Chaucer and the Art of Storytelling.* Berkeley: University of California Press, 1988.

Kolve, V A. *Chaucer and the Imagery of Narrative.* London: Edward Arnold, 1984.

Lerer, Seth. *Chaucer and His Readers: Imagining the Author in Late-Medieval England.* Princeton: Princeton University Press, 1993.

Lindahl, Carl. *Earnest Games: Folkloric Patters in* The Canterbury Tales. Bloomington: Indiana University Press, 1987.

McCall, John P. Chaucer *Among the Gods: The Poetics of Classical Myth.* University Park: Pennsylvania State University Press, 1979.

McGavin, John J. *Chaucer and Dissimilarity: Literary Comparisons in Chaucer and Other Late-Medieval Writing.* Madison, N.J.: Fairleigh Dickinson University Press; London: Associated University Presses, 2000.

Miller, Mark. *Philosophical Chaucer: Love, Sex, and Agency in* The Canterbury Tales. Cambridge: Cambridge University Press, 2004.

Minnis, A. J. (Alastair J.) *Chaucer and Pagan Antiquity.* Cambridge: D. S. Brewer; Totowa, N.J.: Rowman & Littlefield, 1982.

Miskimin, Alice. *The Renaissance Chaucer.* New Haven: Yale University Press, 1975.

Morris, Colin, and Peter Roberts, eds. *Pilgrimage: The English Experience from Becket to Bunyan.* Cambridge: Cambridge University Press, 2002.

Morrison, Susan Signe. *Women Pilgrims in Late Medieval England: Private Piety as Public Performance.* London and New York: Routledge, 2000

Myles, Robert. *Chaucerian Realism.* Cambridge: D. S. Brewer, 1994

Owen, Charles A., Jr. *Pilgrimage and Storytelling in* The Canterbury Tales. Norman, Oklahoma: University of Oklahoma Press, 1977.

Patterson, Lee. *Chaucer and the Subject of History.* London: Routledge, 1991.

Payne, E. Anne. *Chaucer and Menippean Satire.* Madison: University of Wisconsin Press, 1981.

Payne, Robert O. *The Key of Remembrance: A Study of Chaucer's Poetics.* New Haven: Yale University Press, 1963.

Pearsall, Derek. *The Canterbury Tales.* London: Allen & Unwin, 1985.

Percival, Florence. *Chaucer's Legendary Good Women.* Cambridge: Cambridge University Press, 1998.

Phillips, Helen. *An Introduction to* The Canterbury Tales: *Reading, Fiction, Context.* Basingstoke: Macmillan, 2000.

Richardson, Janette. *Blameth Not Me: A Study of Imagery in Chaucer's Fabliaux.* The Hague: Mouton, 1970.

Robertson, D. W, Jr. *A Preface to Chaucer: Studies in Medieval Perspectives.* Princeton: Princeton University Press, 1962.

Rudd, Gillian. *The Complete Critical Guide to Geoffrey Chaucer.* London and New York: Routledge, 2001.

Ruggiers, Paul. *The Art of* The Canterbury Tales. Madison: University of Wisconsin Press, 1987.

Scanlon, Larry. *Narrative, Authority, and Power: The Medieval Exemplum and the Chaucerian Tradition.* Cambridge: Cambridge University Press, 1994.

Smalley, Beryl. *English Friars and Antiquity in the Early Fourteenth Century.* Oxford: Blackwell, 1960.

Strohm, Paul. *Social Chaucer.* Cambridge, Mass.: Harvard University Press, 1989.

Szarmach, Paul E., M. Teresa Tavormina, and Joel T Rosenthal, eds. *Medieval England: An Encyclopedia.* New York: Garland, 1998.

Thompson, N. S. *Chaucer, Boccaccio and the Debate of Love: A Comparative Study of* The Decameron *and* The Canterbury Tales. Oxford: Oxford University Press, 1996.

Tuve, Rosemond. *Allegorical Imagery: Some Medieval Books and Their Posterity.* Princeton: Princeton University Press, 1966.

Volk-Birke, Sabine. *Chaucer and Medieval Preaching: Rhetoric for Listeners in Sermons and Poet.* Tübingen: G. Narr, 1991.

Weever, Jacqueline de. *A Chaucer Name Dictionary: A Dictionary of Astrological, Biblical, Historical, Literary, and Mythological Names.* New York: Garland, 1986.

Weisl, Angela. *Conquering the Reign of Femeny: Gender and Genre in Chaucer's Romance.* Cambridge: D. S. Brewer, 1995.

West, Richard. *Chaucer, 1340–1400: The Life and Times of the First English Poet.* New York: Carroll & Graf, 2000.

Wood, Chauncey. *Chaucer and the Country of the Stars: Poetic Uses of Astrological Imagery.* Princeton: Princeton University Press, 1970.

Yeager, R. E., ed. *Chaucer and Gower: Difference, Mutuality, Exchange.* Victoria, B.C.: University of Victoria, 1991.

Acknowledgments

Fiona Somerset, "As just as is a squyre': The Politics of 'Lewed Translacion' in Chaucer's *Summoner's Tale*"; *Studies in the Age of Chaucer* Volume 21 (1999): pp. 187–207. Reprinted by permission of The New Chaucer Society, One Brookings Drive, Washington University, Campus Box 1122, Saint Louis, MO 63130, chaucer@artsci.wustl.edu.

Colin Wilcockson, "The Opening of Chaucer's *General Prologue* to *The Canterbury Tales:* A Diptych"; *Review of English Studies: A Quarterly Journal of English Literature and the English Language,* Volume 50, Number 199 (August 1999), pp. 345–350. Reprinted by permission of Oxford University Press, http://res.oxfordjournals.org.pallas2.tcl.sc.edu/content/vol50/issue199/index.dtl.

Katherine Little, "Chaucer's Parson and the Specter of Wycliffism"; *Studies in the Age of Chaucer* Volume 23 (2001): pp. 225–253. Reprinted by permission of The New Chaucer Society, One Brookings Drive, Washington University, Campus Box 1122, Saint Louis, MO 63130, chaucer@artsci.wustl.edu.

Lee Patterson, "'The Living Witnesses of Our Redemption': Martyrdom and Imitation in Chaucer's *Prioress's Tale*"; *Journal of Medieval and Early Modern Studies,* Volume 31, Number 3 (2001): pp. 507–560. © 2001, Duke University Press. All rights reserved. Used by permission of the publisher.

Elizabeth Robertson, "The 'Elvyssh' Power of Constance: Christian Feminism in Geoffrey Chaucer's *The Man of Law's Tale*"; in *Studies in the Age of Chaucer* Volume 23 (2001): pp. 143–180. Reprinted by permission of The New Chaucer

Society, One Brookings Drive, Washington University, Campus Box 1122, Saint Louis, MO 63130, chaucer@artsci.wustl.edu.

Fiona Somerset, "'Mark him wel for he is on of þo': Training the 'Lewed' Gaze to Discern Hypocrisy"; *English Literary History* Volume 68 (2001): pp. 315–334. © The Johns Hopkins University Press. Reprinted with permission of The Johns Hopkins University Press.

Louise M. Bishop, "'Of Goddes pryvetee nor of his wyf': Confusion of Orifices in Chaucer's *Miller's Tale*"; *Texas Studies in Literature and Language,* Volume 44, Number 3 (Fall 2002): pp. 231–247. © 2002 University of Texas at Austin (University of Texas Press). Reprinted by permission of the publisher.

Richard Firth Green, "Changing Chaucer"; *Studies in the Age of Chaucer* Volume 25 (2003): pp. 27–52. Reprinted by permission of The New Chaucer Society, One Brookings Drive, Washington University, Campus Box 1122, Saint Louis, MO 63130, chaucer@artsci.wustl.edu.

Lianna Farber, "The Creation of Consent in the *Physician's Tale*"; *The Chaucer Review* Volume 39, Number 2 (2004): pp. 151–164. © 2004 The Pennsylvania State University. Reprinted by permission of the publisher.

Peter W. Travis, "Thirteen Ways of Listening to a Fart: Noise in Chaucer's *Summoner's Tale*"; *Exemplaria: A Journal of Theory in Medieval and Renaissance Studies* Volume 16 (2004): pp. 323–348. Reprinted by permission of the University of Florida, Department of English, P.O. Box 117310, Gainesville, FL 32611-7310, rashoaf@clas.ufl.edu / jshoaf@clas.ufl.edu.

William F. Woods, "Symkyn's Place in the *Reeve's Tale*"; *The Chaucer Review* Volume 39, Number 1 (2004): pp. 17–40. © 2004 The Pennsylvania State University. Reprinted by permission of the publisher.

Index